Skyhooks
for Leadership

SKYHOOKS
FOR LEADERSHIP

*A New Framework That Brings
Together Five Decades of Thought—
From Maslow to Senge*

John A. Shtogren, Editor

AMACOM

American Management Association
*New York • Boston • Chicago • Kansas City • San Francisco • Washington, D.C.,
Brussels • Mexico City • Tokyo • Toronto*

This publication is designed to provide accurate and authoritative information in regard to the subject matter covered. It is sold with the understanding that the publisher is not engaged in rendering legal, accounting, or other professional service. If legal advice or other expert assistance is required, the services of a competent professional person should be sought.

Library of Congress Cataloging-in-Publication Data

Skyhooks for leadership : a new framework that brings together five decades of thought : from Maslow to Senge / John A. Shtogren, editor.
  p.   cm.
  Includes index.
  ISBN 0-8144-0516-9
  1. Organizational change. 2. Leadership. 3. Organizational effectiveness.
I. Shtogren, John A.
HD58.8.S577 1999
658.4'092—dc21   99–20583
                                                                         CIP

Printing number

10 9 8 7 6 5 4 3 2 1

To the Shtogren men, all tried and true.
Those who have led—Grandfather Alexander,
Godfather Peter, Uncle Carl and John, my dad—
and those who will lead—sons Alex and Zack.

Contents

Preface

Skyhooks for Leadership is about how leaders create conditions for productive change in their organizations. That is what leaders do— they help make change happen. Given the ever-increasing rate of change, the enormous need we have for leadership today is less than it will be tomorrow.

The book covers the seven leadership factors I call "skyhooks." Calling them "operating principles" wouldn't really do them justice. Too mechanical. "Core values" comes closer because it reflects a transcendent and ethical dimension. Skyhooks are the anchor points for human interaction that hold fast even when everything else in organizational life is being tossed by change. Skyhooks keep the sky from falling and help people act bravely in the face of uncertainty.

BACKGROUND

This book has been in the works for much of my professional life. As I look back, it emerged from three distinct phases in my thirty years as a consultant:

Phase 1: By the late 1970s I began to see that my best and brightest clients had a lot in common, whether they were in business, in the military, or on campus. Beneath the pinstripes, khaki, or corduroy, the really good ones seemed to be a lot alike. I couldn't tell exactly what they had in common. In general, they were optimistic, enthusiastic and open. They genuinely liked what they were doing, whatever it was that they were doing. So did their coworkers.

Phase 2: During the 1980s I had the opportunity to work closely with more than 1,000 managers in ways that helped me to understand their strengths and weaknesses. They came from AT&T, IBM, Xerox and the like, all branches of the military service, even the CIA, and especially Coca-Cola and Ford. While there were clear differences among organizations and individuals, a pattern of behavior gradually took shape. At first the pattern seemed to have five elements, then twelve and finally the "magnificent seven."

Phase 3: The early 1990s were spent synthesizing the seven factors into a coherent leadership model, validating the process to make sure it really did represent effective leadership and developing a way to deliver the process to managers. The result was the Skyhooks Leadership Model and the Alpha Process Workshops. Since the mid-1990s, the workshops have been presented in the U.S., Europe and across the Pacific Rim. The leadership model has been universally accepted in all locations.

INTENDED AUDIENCE

Skyhooks has two audiences. Current managers are the primary audience, because leading change is rapidly becoming the major part of their role. The second audience is the manager's coworkers, those people who make up the rest of his or her team. When every team member is a leader, performance will be flat-out extraordinary.

CONTENT OVERVIEW

Two quotations may help introduce the content. One is a question, and the other is a statement. The question is asked repeatedly by managers looking for ways to improve their leadership— "What's new?" They hope someone somewhere has found the silver bullet, the sure-fire quick fix. But the question should really be "What's true?" What leadership characteristics have stood the test of time and are necessary today and will be necessary tomorrow?

The second quote is a statement made by Harvard's Rosabeth Moss Kanter. She, too, questions the constant search for "new and improved" ways to lead: "The problem before us is not to invent more tools, but to use the ones we have."

The introduction, chapters and addendums present the leadership tools we have. As you read, you will find out what they are and how well you are using them.

The introduction defines leadership in relation to management, and describes the Skyhooks Leadership Model, its seven components and their proper sequence.

Section 1 positions "vision" as the central focus of the leadership process. Vision provides a picture of an attractive future, a destination for leaders and coworkers.

Section 2 is about "trust," the glue that holds people together as they pursue their vision. Mutual trust is based on a strong belief in the ability and integrity of others.

Section 3 emphasizes the need for "open communication" in changing times. Candor and respect further trust and help people adapt.

Section 4 describes the need for "meaningful work" to bring out the best in people. The tasks we do have to make a real contribution.

Section 5 presents "empowerment" as a way of helping people act on their own. Change requires on-the-spot individual initiative.

Section 6 presents "teamwork" as a way of developing commitment and innovation. Change moves more quickly when everyone is involved.

Section 7 is about "transformational style" and a way of looking at change in a positive way. Change must be seen as an opportunity, the only path to growth, development and realizing the vision.

Within each section, two chapters are offered to illustrate the topic. One is a classic which first appeared between the early 1950s and mid-1970s. The other is more contemporary, written in the 1980s or 1990s. Together they show the topics' enduring importance for leadership and change.

The first appendix summarizes the Best Manager–Worst Manager characteristics identified by more than 2,000 managers in different organizations and in different countries. The similarities are extraordinary and match the Skyhooks Model. The second appendix presents research studies on the relationship between the Skyhooks components and individual and organizational success. The payoffs are clear. The third appendix contains "frequently asked questions" from managers who are trying to become better leaders. The suggested readings section lists twenty-one titles for further reading on leadership.

ACKNOWLEDGMENTS

The only safe way for me to give proper acknowledgment to those who contributed to *Skyhooks,* one way or another, would be to list just about every manager and colleague I've worked with over thirty years. Almost everyone taught me something about leadership. But I can mention only a few and apologize to the rest.

I had the privilege of learning from leaders in action, especially those at Ford, past and present—Harold "Red" Poling, Bobbie Gaunt, Ron Goldsberry, Keith Magee, Tom Mignanelli and Tom Wagner, to name a few. I also enjoyed the good counsel of other Ford folks like Jim Carey, Jim Simpson, and Ross Tudor.

All my colleagues made me smarter when I was smart enough to listen, three in particular. Two have been working on me for more than twenty years. Ronne Jacobs reviewed early drafts of *Skyhooks* and made valuable content suggestions. She also taught me that rationality has its limits for leaders and for others. Intuition is critical, and, besides, it's a lot more fun. Dick Johnson has been my alter ego since *Skyhooks* was just a glimmer. We've discussed and argued every aspect from start to finish. It's good to have a partner who won't give you an inch that you don't deserve but who can finish your sentences for you when you clutch. For ten years Ann Rudy has shown me that a computer is more the artist's brush and palette than a fancy adding machine. The elegance our work has displayed over the years has been her doing.

A special thanks is due a more recent colleague, Adrienne Hickey, my editor at AMACOM Books. She was quick to see *Skyhooks'* merit and proved, to my delight, you really can get good things done in less than a New York minute.

Finally, I must thank my family for enduring the consultant's life. Christine, my real partner, and my sons, Alex and Zack, have been more tolerant and supportive than I deserved. "Well, what exactly does John do?" "Oh, uh, well, he's a high planes drifter."

Richmond, Virginia   John A. Shtogren
May 1999

Prologue

In mining technology, skyhooks are bolts driven upward into the mine shaft's ceiling and locked into the hard strata to keep the ceiling from caving in.

In leadership, skyhooks work the same way. They are the governing ideas about the future and the way we relate to each other that hold rock-solid even when everything seems to be slipping and sliding away.

The essential act of leadership is to put up skyhooks so that people can reach for the dream, do what is right, and do it bravely.

About the Editor

John A. Shtogren is president of HELMS and cofounder of the Alpha Group. Both organizations focus on leadership and organizational development in the private and public sectors through research, training and consulting.

For more than thirty years he has been a consultant to clients such as Anheuser-Bush, AT&T, Coca-Cola, Ford, 3M, United Technologies, and the Army's Training and Doctrine Command. He has been deeply involved in Ford's renewal process since the early 1980s, primarily in leadership development and executive team building. He has practiced overseas in London, Paris, Sydney, and Tokyo.

In addition to his consulting work, Shtogren directed leadership development programs at the Medical College of Virginia at Virginia Commonwealth University and instructional design programs at the University of Michigan's Division of Management Education. He also taught at Albion College, Dartmouth College, and the University of Michigan, where he received his doctorate.

His other publications include *Models for Management, Administrative Development, Administrative Evaluation,* and *Quest,* a guide for learning how to learn. *Ten-Star Service,* a book on becoming customer-driven from the inside out, is at press.

Shtogren's research and experience underpin four of his primary workshops—*Alpha Process: Leadership Development for Managers, Customer First: Customer-Focused Team Building, Destiny: Executive Development and Team Building,* and *Diversity in Thinking Styles: Valuing Differences for Innovation.*

Introduction

When Ford Chairman Harold "Red" Poling stepped aside in the mid-1990s, he summed up what had made Ford successful in the past and what would make it successful in the next century:

> *A company like Ford attracts, grows, and develops good management . . . leadership, however, is another matter— more elusive yet absolutely vital to our future success.*[1]

At Ford, as at most other well-run companies, success came from good management. Tough-minded management got things under control when they were getting out of hand, important things like cost, quality, and customer service.

But good, or even great, management won't be enough to ensure future success at Ford, or any other enterprise, because management's core function, getting things under *control*, is only one part of the new equation. The other part, the big part, is dealing with *change*. That is where leadership, Mr. Poling's elusive factor, comes in. Leadership has little to do with control and everything to do with change.

Skyhooks' purpose is to make leadership less elusive for managers and their coworkers. It provides a better understanding of what leadership is all about and how to go about it. Simply put, it will help you do your new job.

The Introduction demystifies leadership, differentiates it from management and describes a seven-part model for leadership and change. The chapters that follow illustrate each part of the model. At the end, guidelines are offered to continue your leadership development process.

LEADERSHIP MYTHS

To start, we need to clear the smoke, to blow off some of the mystery that shrouds the leadership concept and where we fit in. In

Leaders, Warren Bennis identifies five common leadership myths and offers a counterpoint for each.

Myth 1   Leadership exists only at the top of an organization.
          We need leadership in every unit at every level.
Myth 2   Leadership is a rare skill.
          Everyone has leadership potential.
Myth 3   Leaders are born, not made.
          Leadership can be learned.
Myth 4   Leaders are charismatic.
          Some are (damned few); most aren't.
Myth 5   The leader controls, directs, prods, manipulates.
          Leadership is not so much the exercise of power itself as the empowerment of others.[2]

When Bennis says, "We need leadership in every unit at every level," he means it as a right-here, right-now, I-mean-you mandate. Defining the future, rallying coworkers, transforming people, processes, and products—that is what every manager's job is coming to be. Dealing with change is moving to the top of everyone's must-do list.

ROLE DEFINITIONS

Our management and leadership roles are different, but we need to do both very well. The roles can be defined along two lines, one dealing with complexity and one dealing with change.[3]

The function of management is to cope with complexity. Management is a twentieth-century phenomenon that grew out of the increased complexity of modern industrial organizations. A four-worker shop did not need management; a 400-worker factory does. Good management was developed to keep things under control, to make sure things did not get out of hand. To keep things under control, managerial skills were developed in planning, budgeting, organizing, and staffing. The test of good management is the achievement of results according to plan.

The function of leadership is to cope with change. Leadership did not have any real meaning in the marketplace until recently, when radical change became the norm. Good leadership needs to be developed to proactively change products, systems and people. To lead change, skills are needed for creating an attractive vision of the future and making it a real possibility. The test of good leadership is the achievement of intended change in systems and people.

Coping with complexity and coping with change—management and leadership—are both required. However, we need to rebalance the management–leadership mix with a clear shift to the leadership side. Just what the exact mix turns out to be will depend on the degree of change in the leader's area. The more things change, the greater the need for leadership.

Exhibit 1 fleshes out the functional definition of leadership with comments from current leaders.[4] Exhibit 2 shows how we behave differently when managing and when leading.[5]

LEADERSHIP, CHANGE AND SKYHOOKS

Downsizing, re-engineering, globalization and other euphemisms for all-bets-are-off don't do much for anybody's sense of well-being. Peter Drucker, the distinguished management professor, who is not given to overstatement, put it this way: "We are in one of those great historical periods that occur every 200 to 300 years when people don't understand the world anymore, and the past is not sufficient to explain the future."[6] If chaos on the job weren't bad enough, our basic values, social, political and religious institutions and family structures all seem to be in a state of flux, if not downright disintegration.

Normal people do not behave well when, as Drucker says, everything they've known is coming apart, when the center won't hold, when their best guess about the future is that it won't be as good as the past. When change is threatening, they withdraw and seek shelter. A stay-low-and-cover-your-assets strategy makes good sense. Initiative, risk-taking, cooperation—not likely when survival is the best you can hope for. Nothing ventured, nothing lost.

Leadership can help people act bravely in the face of uncertainty. Instead of taking cover, leadership helps us stand up, face the future and realize we can take charge of our own destiny, that change really can be an opportunity for growth, not loss. The leader's job is to put up "skyhooks," enduring anchor points, that provide a sense of heightened purpose, continuity, and stability. Skyhooks help us transcend the immediate sense of dislocation and deal creatively with change. In mine shafts, skyhooks keep the ceiling from caving in. In changing organizations, leadership skyhooks do the same job—keep the sky from falling when it feels like it just might.

Exhibit 1. Leaders on Leadership

There are definitely common denominators among successful leaders. The first is that all good leaders have vision.

—John C. Whitehead, Chairman of
United Nations Associations

The need for vision is timeless.

—Bruce K. MacLaury,
President of the Brookings Institution

A leader is asking for the trust of people. A leader has to have impeccable integrity. There has to be a sense that leaders are dealing straight, that they are leveling with people.

—Bernadine Healy, Director of NIH

An effective leader must provide an open and honest environment, in which debate is encouraged, where people can relax and enjoy themselves. . . . Leadership will especially require the ability to listen to people and to really hear their concerns, ideas, ambitions.

—Marshall Loeb, Managing Editor of *Fortune*

True leaders bring people along, no matter what their qualities are, and raise them to a higher standard. A very important part of leadership is lifting people up and making them realize they can be better than they are.

—J. Richard Munro, Chairman of the
Executive Committee of Time-Warner

Everyone's dignity is raised by having a say in where the enterprise is going. Empowerment is really about involvement. Empowerment starts with truly believing that everyone counts.

—Jack Welch, Chairman of General Electric

Everyone has the right and duty to influence decision making and to understand the results. Participative management guarantees that decisions will not be arbitrary, secret, or closed to questioning. Participative management is not democratic. Having a say is different from having a vote.

—Max De Pree, CEO of Herman Miller

What it takes to be a leader in the 1990s and beyond is really handling change.

—Robert Goizueta, Chairman of Coca-Cola

As business leaders we have to find out how to make change a satisfier rather than a dissatisfier.

—David T. Kearns, Former Chairman of Xerox

Exhibit 2. Management and Leadership Behaviors

When managing we:	When leading we:
• Deal with what needs to be done today.	• Envision what is possible tomorrow.
• Try to give the organization more of what it's got by keeping things going.	• Try to get things started and deliver something new.
• Rely on rules and procedures to ensure predictable, uniform practice—Do as I say.	• Lead by example to show our values in action. We walk the talk—Do as I do.
• Speak clearly so that others will understand and follow directions.	• Listen carefully so we will understand and convey respect.
• Provide need-to-know details to get the job done.	• Share the big picture to show how everyone fits in.
• Use quantitative skills to define methods and systems	• Provide broad guidelines and occasional checkpoints.
• Pay close attention to detail and micromanage where needed.	• Create a sense of continuity, a "We're in this together!" feeling.
• Use the chain of command to pass on directives.	• Empower people to do what they think is best.
• Compensate people for doing unpleasant tasks.	• Work with people to design tasks that are worth doing.
• Push people to do more.	• Inspire people to bring out the best in them.
• Rely on experts and delegate to our top performers.	• Build teams to take on complex issues.
• Reduce resistance with compelling logic and facts.	• Increase commitment by actively involving everyone.
• Minimize the fear of change.	• Maximize the excitement and challenge of change.
• Minimize risks and discourage mistakes—Go slow and be careful.	• Encourage experimentation and risk-taking—Play with it, run with it, try it out.
• Strive for simplicity, clarity, and continuity.	• Embrace complexity and welcome disorder.
• Emphasize accuracy and efficiency—Do it right!	• Emphasize honesty and integrity—Do what's right!

SKYHOOKS LEADERSHIP MODEL

Exhibit 3 shows the Skyhooks Leadership Model for dealing creatively with change. When all the seven components are in place, change can become a true adventure, an opportunity to push back boundaries and explore new frontiers.

Vision, the primary skyhook, is at the center of the model and is the indispensable first step in the leadership process. Vision provides a view of future possibilities and acts like a beacon that cuts through the fog and swirl of immediate change.

Surrounding vision are six other skyhooks, the enablers that make achieving the vision a real possibility. These six are the enduring values that govern the way we interact as we pursue new possibilities. We *will* work together this way. Trust starts the enabling process, which continues with Open Communication, Meaningful Work, Empowerment, Teamwork, and Transformational Style.

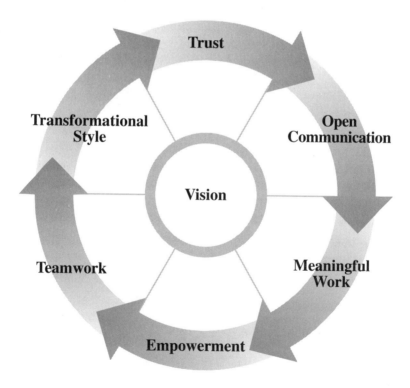

Exhibit 3.
Skyhooks Leadership Model

Each skyhook can be described in attainable, "What to do" leadership terms.

- **Skyhook 1 Vision—Develop and communicate a picture of an attractive future.** First of all, you cannot lead others to a better place without having that place clearly in mind—your mind and theirs. Leadership is about change and movement, not about the status quo. You need a dream, a destination, before you can start to lead.

- **Skyhook 2 Trust—Convey confidence and respect for your coworkers' abilities, values, and aspirations.** To trust is to believe in the ability and integrity of others. Mutual trust makes relationships work, and it starts with the leader. Show them that you really believe they are resilient and adaptive and can change themselves and shape their destiny. They won't disappoint you.

- **Skyhook 3 Open Communication—Share organizational and personal data widely.** The need to know increases during changing times. Hard information helps reduce uncertainty and bolsters confidence. Soft interpersonal information furthers trust between people and departments. Strong informal communication networks help people adapt to change.

- **Skyhook 4 Meaningful Work—Make work more than just a job by appealing to the heart.** People have always looked for meaning in what they do, to see that it is worthwhile in more than material terms. Now, with traditional sources of support and self-worth in jeopardy, the need to care about work is greater than ever. Causes, commitment, and a sense of personal contribution are the great human needs and the driving forces behind individual and organization change.

- **Skyhook 5 Empowerment and Self-determination—Strengthen individuals and teams through education, autonomy, and accountability.** Shaping the future is an all-hands effort. All people must be prepared to seize the initiative and act in their own ways in pursuit of a shared vision. Human resources are the best resources for change.

- **Skyhook 6 Teamwork and Involvement—Make people partners by giving them a significant role in core business activities.** Change can be paralyzing because people feel they have lost control. Things are being done to them, not with them. Involving people in meaningful decisions and acting in concert with others gives them a renewed sense of potency and fate control.

- **Skyhook 7 Transformational Style—Face change with optimism and a conviction that apparent differences can be** reconciled in mutually satisfying ways. Find win-win solutions to traditional conflicts between organization and individual needs, profit and community service, work and play. Old "either-or" thinking needs to shift to an integrative "and-also" mindset. Lead by example and help everyone develop a can-do attitude and a culture of transformation. Move forward with a sense of urgency and patience.

The enabling process supporting vision is sequential and cyclical. For example, an adequate level of mutual trust must exist before people will venture into open and honest communication; unless the work is meaningful, empowerment will have little appeal; until the first four components are adequately in place, teamwork and transformational style will be largely unproductive. However, once the full process has been completed and a significant step has been taken toward realizing the vision, the cycle is renewed at a higher plane.

PROMISES MADE, PROMISES KEPT

The selected chapters illustrate each of the seven skyhooks. The selections are both classic and contemporary to show the enduring issues of leadership, not just the media's flavors of the month. They span the second half of the century, from the 1950s through the 1990s. Classics are drawn from the "golden age" of behavioral science research beginning after World War II and continuing through the 1970s. Contemporary selections start in the 1980s and continue through the 1990s.

The classics represent "promises made"—theory and research that suggested that certain leadership principles would produce predictable outcomes in the workplace. The contemporary selections represent "promises kept"—current research and field reports that demonstrate that classic leadership theory stands up very well in contemporary practice. All too often we ask, "What's new?" We dream of quick fixes and look for newly minted silver bullets. However, the important question is not "What's new?" The important one is "What's true?" What stands up over time? Our mentors should be those who have done the hard research, and we should not be distracted by others who are more adept at marketing than behavioral science.

About Vision. The lead selection and title source for this collection is by O. A. Ohmann. His article "'Skyhooks': With Special Implications for Monday Through Friday" first appeared more than 40 years ago, in *Harvard Business Review* (1955). His description of changing times and the need to restore faith and confidence through common vision and values reads as if he were writing straight from the heart today.

Peter Senge's chapter "Shared Vision" comes from his book *The Fifth Discipline.* He echoes Ohmann's thesis on the need for something to believe in and describes why and how the visioning process works (1990).

About Trust, Confidence, and Respect. Douglas McGregor called for a management philosophy based on trust and optimism about people in "The Human Side of Enterprise" (1957). Most people, he claimed, are inherently trustworthy just because they are normal adults, willing and able to do what needs to be done.

Twenty-five years later, Thomas J. Peters and Robert H. Waterman found that such positive assumptions about people are the bedrock of leadership in the successful organizations they studied before writing about "Productivity Through People" in *In Search of Excellence* (1982). People respond very positively to being treated with dignity and respect, since as adults they know they deserve nothing less.

About Open Communication. Chris Argyris's chapter, "Interpersonal Competence and Organizational Effectiveness," is from his book by the same title (1962). In it he describes why interpersonal relations based on openness, honesty, and integrity are needed for risk-taking, experimentation, and dealing with change.

Thomas J. Peters and Nancy M. Austin reinforce the value of authenticity and open communication in "Doing MBWA," from *A Passion for Excellence* (1985). MBWA stands for "managing by wandering around." The best leaders they found are in constant face-to-face contact, listening, teaching, and removing roadblocks. They do not just talk about open communication and candor; they walk the talk and set a standard for honesty and integrity for others to follow.

About Meaningful Work. Abraham Maslow provided the cornerstone for much of our thinking about what people need from leaders in "A Theory of Human Motivation" (1943). He pointed out that people have powerful psychological needs that drive them to pursue activities and conditions that have little to do with money or comfort. Instead, they seek opportunities to increase their sense of self-worth, contribution, personal growth, and change.

Frederick Herzberg recast Maslow's concepts in the work setting in his classic "Motivation Versus Hygiene," from *The Motivation to Work* (1959). He, too, emphasized the individual's need for self-actualization, to fulfill his or her unique creative ability through doing work. Conditions that surround work can make work tolerable but not intrinsically rewarding or truly meaningful.

Robert H. Waterman focuses on the leadership role in making work meaningful in "Causes and Commitment," from *The Renewal Factor* (1987). Without leaders who, like Maslow, understand our need to find meaning in work, work may never be more than a four-letter word. Those who do understand the need for meaning help make work a glorious adventure.

About Empowerment and Self-Determination. David McClelland and David Burnham's article "Power Is the Great Motivator" provided a new way of thinking about power and influence. It first appeared in *Harvard Business Review* (1976). Power can be a constructive force without being coercive or manipulative. The wonderful irony is that leaders who share power end up being more powerful than those who hoard it. They can get things done that autocrats cannot.

James Kouzes and Barry Posner extend the idea of power as a positive force in their chapter, "Strengthen Others," from *The Leadership Challenge* (1987). Empowering people allows them to act responsibly and take on new challenges. The authors provide guiding principles for empowerment as well as practical suggestions for sharing information and increasing discretion.

About Teamwork and Involvement. Robert Tannenbaum and Fred Massarik's article, "Participation by Subordinates in the Managerial Decision-Making Process" (1950), describes the advantages and prerequisite conditions for involving people in decision areas that are usually reserved for management. They noted then that the benefits of participation were clear, but there was still a lot to learn about overcoming the pitfalls.

Rosabeth Moss Kanter points out in "Dilemmas of Participation," from *The Changemasters* (1983), that teamwork and involvement are still full of pitfalls but more desirable than ever. She identifies more than 20 ways the effort can go wrong. Nevertheless teamwork and involvement are absolute requirements for innovation and change. Mastering change is an all-hands effort.

About Transformational Style. Robert R. Blake and Jane S. Mouton first described the Managerial Grid in "The Developing Revolution in Management Practices" (1962). Their model underscores the importance of integrating divergent opinions and entities and fashioning new ways of doing business. For true leaders conflict is the first step toward creativity and change, not chaos, and a natural part of the change process.

James O'Toole puts a more human face on an affirming and integrating leadership style in "The Corporate Rushmoreans," from *Leading Change: The Argument for Values-Based Leadership* (1996). His study shows that leaders can create a climate for change where vision, respect, flexibility, and power sharing are the norm and where moral principles are never compromised.

REAL-WORLD EVIDENCE

The Skyhooks Leadership Model has been validated in numerous real-world settings. For example, when over 2,000 managers were asked to identify the characteristics of the best leaders they had ever known, they unanimously selected the six Skyhooks components surrounding vision out of a long list of worthy attributes.[7] Furthermore, survey feedback from 10,000 of their coworkers encouraged them to continue to emphasize each component in their leadership. Real-world support is not limited to a particular industry or location. Data from companies like Abbott Laboratories, Anheuser-Busch, Coca-Cola, and Ford show that the Skyhooks Leadership Model receives the same high level of support, whether in Atlanta or Detroit, Paris or Tokyo.

ALPHA PROCESS

The starting point for leadership development, the "alpha point," is individual understanding and personal stock-taking. Once you understand what leaders must do, you need to determine how you measure up in your eyes and in the eyes of others. Then take action where needed.

Key points are noted before each section to help you read and understand. At the end of each section, questions help you gauge what you are doing versus what you should be doing. Answer the questions yourself, and then ask your coworkers the same questions to compare your sense of reality with theirs. In the appendices you will find additional information to add to your leadership understanding and practice.

While *Skyhooks for Leadership* can contribute greatly to your development as a leader, much of it will remain a personal journey. Beyond these pages there is still something elusive, an x factor that has to do with realizing your best self before leading others.[8] "What truly is my dream? Do I really trust others? What am I willing to share? How much am I willing to change?" These are intensely personal questions you need to ask and answer for yourself. Before you can lead others, you have to find your own way.

NOTES

1. Mr. Poling's comments were made in October 1993 in his farewell address to management at Ford. He was largely responsible for bringing the company back from the edge of disaster in the 1980s to its lead position in the 1990s. He well knew that management skills can correct an organization's faults and set it back on track, but it takes leadership skills to change the focus from not losing to winning.

2. Bennis, Warren, and Nanus, Burt. *Leaders: The Strategies for Taking Charge.* New York: Harper Collins, 1985, pp. 221–26.

3. Kotter, John P. *A Force for Change: How Leadership Differs from Management.* New York: The Free Press, 1990, pp. 4–7.

4. McFarland, L. J., Senn, L. E., and Childress, J. R. *21st Century Leadership: Dialogues with 100 Top Leaders.* Los Angeles: The Leadership Press, 1993.

5. Exhibit 2 was developed from numerous sources, especially the works of Warren Bennis and John Kotter.

6. Drucker's quote is from *21st Century Leadership*, p. 27. He discusses the issue at length in his own works, such as *Managing in a Time of Great Change.* New York: Dutton, Truman, Talley Books, 1995.

7. See Appendix A for more information.

8. Warren Bennis has referred to an ineffable quality that he sees in true leaders. The *x* factor is far beyond leadership skills and behaviors. True leadership comes from the heart, not just the head. At its core, leadership has to do with being, not just doing.

Skyhook 1

VISION

There are definitely common denominators among successful leaders. The first is, all good leaders have vision.
—JOHN C. WHITEHEAD,
CHAIRMAN OF UNITED NATIONS ASSOCIATIONS

The need for vision is timeless.
—BRUCE K. MacLAURY,
PRESIDENT OF THE BROOKINGS INSTITUTION

Skyhook 1 Vision—Develop and communicate a picture of an attractive future. After all, you cannot lead others to a better place without having that place clearly in mind—in your mind and in theirs. Leadership is about change and movement first of all, not about the status quo. You need a dream, a destination, before you can start to lead.

As you read O. A. Ohmann's "'Skyhooks': With Special Implications for Monday Through Friday," you will get a clearer sense of why "the need for vision is timeless." The article appeared in *Harvard Business Review* in 1955, but without that footnote you would think he is describing an end-of-the-century malaise. Leaders then and now must counteract demoralization in the workplace by providing "skyhooks," something more than compensation and benefits, "something to believe in . . . something that will give meaning to their jobs."

In his article Ohmann covers key points like these:

- Even in an age of unparalleled abundance, people feel spiritually impoverished.

- A world without stable values is neurotic and schizoid and breeds insecurity, not character.

- Devaluing the individual in the workplace produces a disaffected and demoralized workforce.

- Capitalism and competition miss the mark because people are not motivated merely by self-interest.

- People hunger for "skyhooks" in the workplace to give it higher meaning and enduring spiritual values.

- People want a boss who believes in something and one whom they can believe in.

- The individual is paramount and should develop to his or her maximum potential and maturity.

- Real leaders integrate individual goals into a common vision coupled with enduring spiritual values.

- The skyhooks mystique that gives work "a sense of special significance" comes more from process and working relationships than from the end product.

Peter Senge updates the "skyhooks" notion in "Shared Vision," from *The Fifth Discipline,* which appeared in 1990. He proposed new ways of revitalizing organizations by using "systems thinking" to see the interrelations of actions and events. To start, a shared vision connects people with a common purpose. It is the innate desire for common aspirations and meaningful connections that drives people to build shared visions. Senge's discussion of shared vision includes points like these:

- Simply put, a shared vision answers the question "What do we want to create?"

- It is a force in people's hearts—few forces in human affairs are as powerful as shared vision.

- It connects people and gives coherence to their diverse activities.

- With shared vision come excitement, exhilaration, and enhanced creativity, if done right.

- Shared vision is rooted in each individual's personal vision and is not the product of a top-down strategic planning exercise.

- Visions take time to emerge and gain real commitment rather than mere compliance.

- Systems thinking can give people confidence that they can shape the future and achieve their vision.

- Vision, "what we want to be," needs to be anchored with a set of governing ideas, core values that answer the question, "How must we behave?"

While separated by almost four decades, the two authors share the same conviction that there must be a spiritual dimension to the work we do. Enterprise must be more than economics, or work will be nothing more than just a job, a place where you trade time for money. With shared vision and common values, work can be a place to pursue your dreams.

1

SKYHOOKS:

With Special Implications for Monday Through Friday

O. A. OHMANN

This "HBR Classic" was first published in the May–June 1955 issue of HBR. It won immediate acclaim in the business community and started off a new line of thinking about the nature of effective leadership. When Mr. Ohmann wrote the article, he was Assistant to the President of the Standard Oil Company of Ohio and worked on problems and programs for management development. Now retired from that company and living in Hendersonville, North Carolina, he continues to consult with organizations on questions of management development, and is Director of The Church Executive Development Board, Inc., in New York. Earlier in his career he was head of the Department of Psychology at Cleveland College of Western Reserve University.

During the last several years, while my principal job assignment has been management development, I have become increasingly impressed with the importance of intangibles in the art of administration. With the managerial revolution of the last generation and the transition from owner-manager to professional executive, there has appeared a growing literature on the science and art of administration. A shift in emphasis is noticeable in these writing over the past 30 years.

Following the early engineering approach typified by the work of Frederick Taylor and others, there next developed a search for the basic principles of organization, delegation, supervision, and control. More recently, as labor relations became more critical, the emphasis has shifted to ways of improving human relations. The approach to the problems of supervisory relationships was essentially a manipulative one. Textbooks on the techniques of personnel management mushroomed. Still later it became more and more apparent that the crux of the problem was the supervisor, and this resulted in a flood of "how to improve yourself" books. Meanwhile the complexities of the industrial community increased, and the discontents and tensions mounted.

It seems increasingly clear, at least to me, that while some administrative practices and personnel techniques may be better than others, their futility arises from the philosophical assumptions or value judgments on which this superstructure of manipulative procedure rests. We observe again and again that a manager with sound values and a stewardship conception of the role of boss can be a pretty effective leader even though the techniques used are unorthodox. I am convinced that workers have a fine sensitivity to spiritual qualities and want to work for a boss who believes in something and in whom they can believe.

This observation leads me to suspect that we may have defined the basic purposes and objectives of our industrial enterprise too narrowly, too selfishly, too materialistically. Bread alone will not satisfy workers. There are some indications that our people have lost faith in the basic values of our economic society, and that we need a spiritual rebirth in industrial leadership.

Certainly no people have ever had so much and enjoyed so little real satisfaction. Our economy has been abundantly productive, our standard of living is at an all-time peak, and yet we are a tense, frustrated, and insecure people full of hostilities and anxieties. Can it be that our *god of production* has feet of clay? Does industry need a new religion—or at least a better one than it has had?

I am convinced that the central problem is not the division of the spoils as organized labor would have us believe. Raising the price of prostitution does not make it the equivalent of love. Is our industrial discontent not in fact the expression of a hunger for a work life that has meaning in terms of higher and more enduring spiritual values? How can we preserve the wholeness of the personality if we are expected to worship God on Sundays and holidays and Mammon on Mondays through Fridays?

I do not imply that this search for real meaning in life is or should be limited to the hours on the job, but I do hold that the central values of our industrial society permeate our entire culture. I am sure we do not require a bill of particulars of the spiritual sickness of our time. The evidences of modern people's search for their souls are all about us. Save for the communist countries there has been a world-wide revival of interest in religion. The National Council of Churches reports that 59% of our total population (or 92 million) now claim church affiliation. The November 22, 1954 issue of *Barron's* devoted the entire front page to a review of a book by Barbara Ward, *Faith and Freedom.*[1]

Perhaps even more significant is the renaissance in the quality of religious thought and experience. Quite evidently our religion of materialism, science, and humanism is not considered adequate. People are searching for anchors outside themselves. They run wearily to the periphery of the spider web of their own reason and logic, and look for new "skyhooks"—for an abiding faith around which life's experiences can be integrated and given meaning.

WHY "SKYHOOKS"?

Perhaps we should assume that this need for "skyhooks" is part of people's natural equipment—possibly a function of their intelligence—or, if you prefer, God manifesting Himself in His creatures. It seems to me, however, that the recent intensification of this need (or perhaps the clearer recognition of it) stems in part from certain broad social, economic, political, and philosophical trends. I shall not attempt a comprehensive treatment of these, but shall allude to only a few.

Abundance Without Satisfaction

I have already indicated that on the economic front we have won the battle of production. We have moved from an economy of scarcity to one of abundance. We have become masters of the physical world and have learned how to convert its natural resources to the satisfaction of our material wants. We are no longer so dependent and so intimately bound to the world of nature. In a way we have lost our feeling of being part of nature and with it our humble reverence for God's creation.

While the industrialization of our economy resulted in ever-increasing production, it also made of individual man a production number—an impersonal, de-skilled, interchangeable production unit, measured in so many cents per hour. For most employees, work no longer promotes the growth of personal character by affording opportunities for personal decision, exercise of judgment, and individual responsibility. A recent issue of *Nation's Business* quotes the modern British philosopher Alexander Lindsay on this point as follows:

> Industrialism has introduced a new division into society. It is the division between those who manage and take responsibility and those who are managed and have responsibility taken from them. This is a division more important than the division between the rich and poor.[2]

Certainly modern industrial workers have improved their material standards of living at the cost of becoming more and more dependent on larger and larger groups. Not only their dignity but also their security has suffered. And so they reach out for new "skyhooks"—for something to believe in, for something that will give meaning to their jobs.

Disillusionment With Science

A second trend which seems to bear some relation to our urgent need for a faith grows out of our disillusionment with science. As a result of the rapid advance of science, the curtains of ignorance and superstition have been pulled wide on all fronts of human curiosity and knowledge. Many of the bonds of our intellectual enslavement have been broken. Reason and scientific method were called on to witness the truth, the whole truth, and nothing but the truth. We were freed from the past—its traditions, beliefs, philosophies, its mores, morals, and religion. Science became our religion, and reason replaced emotion.

However, even before the atom bomb there was a growing realization that science did not represent the whole truth, that with all its pretensions it could be dead wrong, and, finally and particularly, that without proper moral safeguards the truth did not necessarily make you free. Atomic fission intensified the fear and insecurity of every one of us who contemplated the possibility of the concentration of power in the hands of men without morals. We want science to be in the hands of men who not only recognize their responsibility to man-made ethical standards (which are easily perverted) but have dedicated themselves to the eternal and absolute standards of God. Thus, while the evidence of material science has been welcomed, our own personal experiences will not permit us to believe that life is merely a whirl of atoms without meaning, purpose, beauty, or destiny.

Trend Toward Bigness

A third factor contributing to our insecurity is the trend toward bigness and the resulting loss of individuality. This is the day of bigger and bigger business—in every aspect of life. The small is being swallowed by the big, and the big by the bigger. This applies to business, to unions, to churches, to education, to research and invention, to newspapers, to our practice of the professions, to government, and to nations. Everything is getting bigger except the individual, and the individual is getting smaller and more insignificant and more dependent on larger social units. Whether we like it or not, this is becoming an administrative society, a planned and controlled society, with ever-increasing concentration of power. This is the day of collectivism and public-opinion polls. It is the day when the individual must be *adjusted to the group*—when the individual must above all else be sensitive to the feelings and attitudes of others, must get an idea of how others expect the individual to act, and then react to this.

This is the insecure world which David Riesman has described so well in his book *The Lonely Crowd*.[3] He pictures man as being no longer "tradition directed" as was primitive man, nor as in Colonial days is he "inner directed" as if by the gyroscope of his own ideals, but today he is "outer directed" as if by radar. He must constantly keep his antenna tuned to the attitudes and reactions of others to him. The shift has been from morals to morale and from self-reliance to dependence on one's peer group. However, the members of one's peer group are each responding to each other. Obviously these shifting sands of public opinion offer no stable values around which life can be consistently integrated and made meaningful. The high-water mark of adjustment in such a society is that the individual be socially accepted and above all else that he appear to be *sincere*.

This is certainly not a favorable environment for the development of steadfast character. It is essentially a neurotic and schizophrenic environment which breeds insecurity.

This socially dependent society also offers an ideal market for the wares of the "huckster," the propagandist, and the demagogue. Lacking a religious interpretation of the divine nature of people, these merchants in mass reaction have sought the least common denominator in human nature and have beamed the movies and newspapers at the ten-year mental level. One wonders if this approach to people does not make them feel that they have been sold short and that they are capable of much better than is expected of them. Has this demoralizing exposure of the cheapness of our values not intensified our search for something better to believe in?

On top of all these disturbing socioeconomic trends came the war. This certainly was materialism, science, and humanism carried to the logical conclusion. The war made us question our values and our direction. It left us less cocksure that we were right, and more fearful of ourselves as well as of others. It made us fearful of the power which we had gained, and led us to search our soul to determine whether we had the moral strength to assume the leadership role that had been given to us. We have been humbled in our efforts to play god and are about ready to give the job back. Note, however, that this is not a characteristic reaction to war. Typically wars have been followed by a noticeable deterioration of moral standards, of traditional values, and of social institutions.

Perhaps none of these rationalizations for our return to religion is entirely valid. I suspect that the search for some kind of overarching integrative principle or idea is the expression of a normal human need. Certainly history would indicate that people's need for a god is eternal even though it may be more keenly sensed in times of adversity. A religion gives a point of philosophical orientation around which life's experiences can be organized and digested. Without the equivalent, a personality cannot be whole and healthy. Short-term goals which need to be shifted with the changing tide do not serve the same integrative function as do the "skyhooks" which are fastened to eternal values. I do not personally regard the current religious revival as a cultural hangover, nor as a regression. Being a mystic I prefer instead to view the need for such a faith as the spark of the Creator in us to drive us on to achieve His will and our own divine destiny.

WHY MONDAY THROUGH FRIDAY?

If we may grant for the moment that the modern person is searching for deeper meanings in life, we may then ask: What has this to do with industry? If people need "skyhooks," let them get them in church, or work out their own salvation. The business leaders of the past insisted that "business is business" and that it had little bearing on the individual's private life and philosophy.

There are several reasons why "skyhooks" must be a primary concern of the business administrator:

- For the individual the job is the center of life, and its values must be in harmony with the rest of life if the individual is to be a whole and healthy personality.

- This is an industrial society, and its values tend to become those of the entire culture.

- The public is insisting that business leaders are in fact responsible for the general social welfare—that the manager's responsibilities go far beyond those of running the business. They have delegated this responsibility to the business executive whether the executive wishes to play this role or not.

- Even if the administrator insists on a narrow definition of the administrative function as merely the production of goods and services as efficiently as possible, it is nevertheless essential that the administrator take these intangibles into account, since they are the real secrets of motivating an organization.

- Besides all this the administrator needs a better set of personal "skyhooks" if the administrator is to carry an ever-increasing load of responsibility without cracking up. The fact that so many administrators are taking time to rationalize, defend, and justify the private enterprise system is an outward indication of this need for more significant meanings.

ANYTHING WRONG WITH CAPITALISM?

We may ask, then: What specifically is wrong with our capitalistic system of private enterprise? What is wrong with production or with trying to improve our present standard of living? What is wrong with a profit, or with private ownership of capital, or with competition? Is this not the true American way of life?

Nothing is necessarily wrong with these values. There are certainly worse motives than the profit motive. A refugee from communism is reported to have observed: "What a delight to be in the United States, where things are produced and sold with such a nice clean motive as making a profit."

I am not an economist, and it is beyond the scope of this article to attempt a revision of our economic theory. I am tempted, however, to make a couple of observations about these traditional economic concepts:

1. That while the values represented by them are not necessarily wrong, they are certainly pretty thin and do not
   challenge the best in people.

2. That many of the classical economic assumptions are
   outmoded and are no longer adequate descriptions of
   the actual operation of our present-day economy.

For example, the concept of economic man as being motivated by
self-interest not only is outmoded by the best current facts of the
social sciences but also fails to appeal to the true nobility of spirit of
which we are capable.

The concept of the free and competitive market is a far cry
from the highly controlled and regulated economy in which business must operate today. General Motors does not appear to want
to put Chrysler out of business, and apparently the union also
decided to take the heat off Chrysler rather than to press its economic advantage to the logical conclusion. The assumption that
everyone is out to destroy competitors does not explain the sharing
of technology through trade associations and journals. No, we also
have tremendous capacity for cooperation when challenged by
larger visions. We are daily denying the Darwinian notion of the
"survival of the fittest"—which, incidentally, William Graham
Sumner, one of the nineteenth-century apologists for our economic
system, used for justifying unbridled self-interest and competition.

Certainly the traditional concept of private ownership of capital
does not quite correspond to the realities of today's control of large
blocks of capital by insurance companies and trusteed funds.

The notion of individual security through the accumulation of
savings has largely given way to the collectivist means of group
insurance, company annuities, and Social Security.

The concept that all profits belong to the stockholders is no
longer enthusiastically supported by either the government or the
unions, since both are claiming an increasing cut.

And so, while we may argue that the system of private enterprise is self-regulatory and therefore offers maximum individual
freedom, the simple, cold fact is that it is in ever-increasing degree a
managed or controlled economy—partly at the insistence of the
voters, but largely as the result of the inevitable economic pressures
and the trend toward bigness.[4]

Regardless of the rightness or wrongness of these changes in our
system of enterprise, the changes have been considerable, and I
doubt that classical economic theory can be used as an adequate

rationale of its virtues. I am therefore not particularly optimistic about the efficacy of the current campaign to have business executives "save the private enterprise system and the American way of life" by engaging in wholesale economic education, much of which is based on outmoded concepts.

Much as economic theory needs revision, I fear that this is not likely to cure our ills. Nor do I believe that profit-sharing or any other device for increasing the workers' cut (desirable as these efforts may be) will give us what we really want. It is, rather, another type of sharing that is needed, a sharing of more worthy objectives, a sharing of the management function, and a sharing of mutual respect and Christian working relationships.

Goals and Purposes

What is wrong is more a matter of goals and purposes—of our assumptions about what we are trying to do and how we can dignify and improve ourselves in the doing. There is nothing wrong with production, but we should ask ourselves: *Production for what?* Do we use people for production or production for people? How can production be justified if it destroys personality and human values both in the process of its manufacture and by its end use? Clarence B. Randall of Inland Steel, in his book, A *Creed for Free Enterprise,* says:

> We have come to worship production as an end in itself, which of course it is not. It is precisely there that the honest critic of our way of life makes his attack and finds us vulnerable. Surely there must be for each person some ultimate value, some purpose, some mode of self-expression that makes the experience we call life richer and deeper.[5]

So far, so good, Mr. Randall. But now notice how he visualizes industry making its contribution to this worthy objective:

> To produce more and more with less and less effort is merely treading water unless we *thereby release time and energy for the cultivation of the mind and the spirit* and for the achievement of those ends for which Providence placed us on this earth.[6]

Here is the same old dichotomy—work faster and more efficiently so that you can finish your day of drudgery and cultivate your soul on your own time. In fact he says: "A horse with a very evil disposition can nevertheless pull the farmer's plow." No, I am afraid the job is the life. *This* is what must be made meaningful. We cannot assume that the end of production justifies the means. What happens to people in the course of producing may be far more important than the end product. Materialism is not a satisfactory "skyhook." People are capable of better and want to do better. (Incidentally, I have the impression that Mr. Randall's practices line up very well with my own point of view even if his words do not.)

Perhaps we should ask: What is the really important difference between Russian communism and our system? Both worship production and are determined to produce more efficiently, and do. Both worship science. Both have tremendously improved the standard of living of their people. Both share the wealth. Both develop considerable loyalties for their system. (In a mere 40 years since Lenin started the communist revolution a third of the world's people have come to accept its allegiance.) True, in Russia capital is controlled by the state, while here it is theoretically controlled by individuals, although in actual practice, through absentee ownership, it is controlled to a considerable extent by central planning agencies and bureaus, both public and private.

No, the real difference is in the philosophy about people and how they may be used as means to ends. It is a difference in the assumptions made about the origin of rights—whether the individual is endowed with rights by the Creator and yields these only voluntarily to civil authority designated by the individual, or whether rights originate in force and in the will of the government. Is God a myth or the final and absolute judge to whom we are ultimately responsible? Are all standards of conduct merely human invention and relative, or absolute and eternal? Is humankind a meaningless happenstance of protoplasm or a divine creation with a purpose, with potential for improvement, and with a special destiny in the overall scheme of things? These are some of the differences— or at least I hope that they still are. And what a difference these intangible, perhaps mythical, "skyhooks" make. They are nevertheless the most real and worthwhile and enduring things in the world. The absence of these values permitted the Nazis to "process" people through the gas chambers in order to recover the gold in their teeth.

THE ADMINISTRATOR CONTRIBUTES

This, then, is part of our general cultural heritage and is passed on to us in many ways. However, it really comes to life in people— in their attitudes, aspirations, and behaviors. And in a managerial society this brings us back to the quality of the individual administrator. This manager interprets or crystallizes group values and objectives. This supervisor sets the climate within which these values either *do* or *do not* become working realities. This executive must define the goals and purposes of the group in larger and more meaningful perspective. This administrator integrates the smaller, selfish goals of individuals into larger, more social, and spiritual objectives for the group. This leader provides the vision without which the people perish. Conflicts are resolved by relating the immediate to the long range and more enduring values. In fact, we might say this *integrative function* is the core of the administrator's contribution.

The good ones have the mental equipment to understand the business and set sound long-term objectives, but the best ones have in addition the philosophical and character values which help them to relate the overall goals of the enterprise to eternal values. This is precisely the point at which deep-seated religious convictions can serve an integrative function, since they represent the most long-range of all possible goals.[7] Most really great leaders in all fields of human endeavor have been peculiarly sensitive to their historic role in human destiny. Their responsibility and loyalty are to some distant vision which gives calm perspective to the hot issues of the day.

This function of the administrator goes far beyond being a likable personality, or applying correct principles of organization, or being skillful in the so-called techniques of human relations. I am convinced that the difficulties which so many executives have with supervisory relationships cannot be remedied by cultivation of the so-called human relations skills. These difficulties spring, rather, from one's conception of the function or role of a boss, notions about the origin and nature of authority over others, the assumptions made about people and their worth, and a view of what administrator and staff are trying to accomplish together. To illustrate:

> If, for example, my personal goal is to get ahead in terms of money, position, and power; and if I assume that to achieve this I must best my competitors; that the way to do this is to establish a good production record; that my employees are means to this end; that they are replaceable production units which must be skillfully manipulated; that this can be done by appealing to the lowest form of immediate selfish interest; that the greatest threat to me is that my employees

may not fully recognize my authority or accept my leadership—if these are my values, then I am headed for trouble—
all supervisory techniques notwithstanding.

I wish I could be quite so positive in painting the picture of the right
values and approaches to management. I suspect there are many,
many different right answers. No doubt each company or enterprise
will have to define its own long-term purposes and develop its own
philosophy in terms of its history, traditions, and its real function in
our economy. I am also certain that no one philosophy would be
equally useful to all managers. The character of an organization is,
to a large extent, set by the top executive or the top group, and it is
inevitable that this be the reflection of the philosophy of these individuals. No one of us can operate with another's philosophy. I have
also observed that in most enterprises the basic faith or spirit of the
organization is a rather nebulous or undefined something which
nevertheless has very profound meaning to the employees.

A Successful Executive

While recognizing the futility of advocating any one pattern of
values, it occurs to me that it might, however, be suggestive or helpful if I told you something of the philosophy of one extremely
successful executive I have pumped a good deal on this subject (for
he is more inclined to live his values than to talk about them).

As near as I can piece it together, he believes that this world was
not an accident but was created by God and that His laws regulate
and control the universe and that we are ultimately *responsible to
Him*. Humans, as God's supreme creation, are in turn endowed
with creative ability. Each individual represents a unique combination of talents and potentials. In addition, humans are the only
animals endowed with freedom of choice and with a high capacity
for making value judgments. With these gifts (of heredity and
cultural environment) goes an obligation to give the best possible
accounting of one's stewardship in terms of maximum self-
development and useful service to one's fellows in the hope that one
may live a rich life and be a credit to the Creator.

This executive also assumes that each individual possesses
certain God-given rights of self-direction which only *the individual*
can voluntarily delegate to others in higher authority, and that this
is usually done in the interest of achieving some mutual cooperative
good. The executive therefore assumes that his own authority as
boss over others must be exercised with due regard for the atten-

dant obligations to his employees and to the stockholders who have temporarily and voluntarily yielded their rights in the interest of this common undertaking. (Notice that the executive does not view this authority as originating with or derived from an immediate superior.) This delegated authority must, of course, be used to advance the common good rather than primarily to achieve the selfish ambitions of the leader at the expense of the led.

He further assumes that the voluntary association of employees in industry is for the purpose of increasing the creativity and productivity of all members of the group and thus of bringing about increased benefits to all who may share in the ultimate use of these goods and services. What is equally important, however, is that in the course of this industrial operation each individual should have an opportunity to develop the maximum potential of skills and that the working relationships should not destroy the individual's ability to achieve greatest maturity and richness of experience. The supervisor must set the working conditions and atmosphere which will make it possible for employees to achieve this dual objective of increasing productivity and maximizing self-development.

These goals can best be achieved by giving employees maximum opportunity to exercise their capacity for decision making and judgment within their assigned area of responsibility. The supervisor is then primarily a coach who must instruct, discipline, and motivate all the members of the group, making it possible for each to exercise any special talent in order to maximize the total team contribution. Profits are regarded as a measure of the group's progress toward these goals, and a loss represents not only an improper but even an immoral use of the talents of the group.

There is nothing "soft" about this operation. He sets high quality standards and welcomes stiff competition as an additional challenge to the group. Complete cooperation and dedication are expected—and received—from everyone. Incidentally, he views the activity of working together in this manner with others as being one of life's most rewarding experiences. He holds that this way of life is something which we have not yet fully learned, but its achievement is part of our divine destiny. He is firmly convinced that such conscientious efforts *will* be rewarded with success. He manages with a light touch that releases creativity, yet with complete confidence in the outcome.

This is probably a poor attempt at verbalizing the basic philosophy which this man lives so easily and naturally. I hope, however, that it has revealed something of his conception of his role or function as an executive and his view of what he and his organization are trying to do together. With this account of his values I am sure that you would have no difficulty completing the description of his administrative practices and operating results. They flow naturally from his underlying faith, without benefit of intensive training in the principles and art of administration.

As you would suspect, people like to work for him—or with him. He attracts good talent (which is one of the real secrets of success). Those with shoddy values, selfish ambitions, or character defects do not survive—the organization is self-pruning. Those who remain develop rapidly because they learn to accept responsibility. He not only advocates but practices decentralization and delegation. His employees will admit that they have made mistakes, but usually add with a grin that they try not to make the same one twice. People respond to his leadership because he has faith in them and expects the best in them rather than the worst. He speaks well of the members of his organization, and they appear to be proud of each other and of their record of performance. He takes a keen interest in developing measurements of performance and in bettering previous records or competitive standards. He feels that no one has a right to "louse up a job"—a point on which he feels the stockholders and the Lord are in complete agreement.

While he does not talk much about "employee communications" or stress formal programs of this type, his practice is to spend a large proportion of his time in the field with his operating people rather than in his office. He is "people oriented," and he does a particularly good job of listening. The union committee members have confidence in his fairness, yet do a workmanlike job of bargaining. In administering salaries he seems to be concerned about helping the individual to contribute more so that a pay increase can be justified.

In his general behavior he moves without haste or hysteria. He is typically well organized, relaxed, and confident, even under trying circumstances. There is a high degree of consistency in his behavior and in the quality of his decisions because his basic values do not shift. Since he does not operate by expediency, others can depend on him; and this consistency makes for efficiency in the discharge of delegated responsibility. Those operating problems which do come to him for decision seem to move easily and quickly to a conclusion. His long-term values naturally express themselves in well-defined policies, and it is against this frame of reference that the decisions of the moment easily fall into proper perspective.

In policy-level discussions his contributions have a natural quality of objectivity because "self-concern" does not confuse. Others take him at face value because his motives are not suspect. When differences or conflicts do arise, his approach is not that of compromise; rather, he attempts to integrate the partisan views around mutually acceptable longer-range goals. The issues of the moment then seem to dissolve in a discussion of the best means to the achievement of the objective. I have no doubt that he also has some serious problems, but I have tried to give a faithful account of the impression which he creates. There is a *sense of special significance* about his operation which is shared by his associates.

THIS IS THE KEY

It is precisely this "sense of special significance" which is the key to leadership. We all know that there are many different ways of running a successful operation. I am certainly not recommending any particular set of administrative practices—although admittedly some are better than others. Nor am I suggesting that the set of values of the executive described in the preceding section should be adopted by others, or for that matter that they could be. What I am saying is that a person's real values have a subtle but inevitable way of being communicated, and they affect the significance of everything that is done.

These are the vague intangibles—the "skyhooks"—which are difficult to verbalize but easy to sense and tremendously potent in their influence. They provide a different, invisible, fundamental structure into which the experiences of every day are absorbed and given meaning. They are frequently unverbalized, and in many organizations they defy definition. Yet they are the most real things in the world.

The late Jacob D. Cox, Jr., former president of Cleveland Twist Drill Company, told a story that illustrates my point:

> Jimmy Green was a new union committee member who stopped in to see Mr. Cox after contract negotiations had been concluded. Jimmy said that in every other place he had worked, he had always gone home grouchy; he never wanted to play with the children or take his wife to the movies. And then he said, "But since I have been working here, all that has changed. Now when I come home, the children run to meet me and we have a grand romp together. It is a wonderful difference and I don't know why, but I thought you would like to know."[8]

As Mr. Cox observed, there must be a lot of Jimmy Greens in the world who want an opportunity to take part freely in a cooperative effort that has a moral purpose.

RETROSPECTIVE COMMENTARY

It's time I level with HBR readers about how "Skyhooks" came about. In a very real sense, I did not write it. It came as a stream of consciousness—but only after I had worked very hard for several weeks at putting my ideas together. I wrote the paper mainly to clear my own thinking, and to try it out for criticism on the Cleveland Philosophical Club. After much reading and thinking, I got absolutely nowhere. In desperation I was about to abandon the idea and write on a different subject. Deep inside my consciousness I said in effect to my silent partner within, "Look, if you want me to do this, you better help." About 1 a.m. that morning the ideas flowed in a continuous stream, and I put them down in shorthand notes as fast as I could.

The word "Skyhooks" for the title came in the heat of a discussion with a group of business executives attending the Institute of Humanistic Studies at Aspen, Colorado. As we debated the limits of the rational and scientific approach to life, it occurred to me that science appears rational on the surface, but at its very foundation typically lies a purely intuitive, nonrational assumption made by some scientist. He just hooked himself on a "piece of sky out there" and hung on. It was a complete leap of faith that led him.

In my studies of exceptional executives I had found a mystery not easily explainable by rational elements. These men, too, were hanging on skyhooks of their own—hidden and secret missions which went way beyond their corporate business objectives. Sometimes the mission was a "nutsy" one. Often it had long roots back in the executive's childhood and was emotional, intuitive, beyond rationality, selfless—but it stuck. For example, it might be like John F. Kennedy's determination to become President; reportedly he was doing it for his older brother, who had the ambition to be President but never made it because he was a war casualty.

Or perhaps the mission was like that of the president of one of our largest corporations. When he was 12 years old, his father died. He promised his mother he would help her work the farm in the hills so that his eight younger brothers could go through school. This is what he continued to do all of his life—helping other young men to make something of themselves. He was a great developer of managers.

I could fill a book with such examples. Many great executives I have known have something deep inside that supports them; something they trust when the going gets tough; something ultimate; something personal; something beyond reason—in short, a deep-rooted skyhook which brings them calm and confidence when they stand alone.

There is another interesting aspect to this question. In our rational, analytical, and highly successful Western culture, we have come to place great value on the material gains which represent the end results of our achievements. This is what our kids are complaining about: that we have gone overboard on material values and made a culture of things. But the *results* of our strivings are dead works; the life is in the *process* of achieving, in the leap of faith. David was great not when he slew Goliath, but when he decided to try.

So it seems to me that the skyhooks mystique is also characterized by a commitment to value the *process,* the working relationships with others, the spiritual bonds growing out of the faith in the God-potential deep within another person, and the basis of genuine community. The rest is the means, not the end.

In 1955, when my article was published, the generation gap had not been invented, and Marshall McLuhan had not alerted us to the fact that "the medium is the message." Yet a quick look backward reveals the considerable impact of youth and "McLuhanism" on our history and our future. The "McCarthy Kids" have ousted a President and his party, halted the military domination of our foreign policy, radically changed our educational and religious institutions, revised industry's approach to management recruiting, and made the Peace Corps type of job competitive with the "goodies" offered by business. Generalizing about the medium having greater impact than the message, they have pointed out that our values are dictated by our social systems—especially the technological, political, and managerial systems. More important than the things we create in industry, they say, is the way we create them—the kind of community we establish in our working together.

Without debating the merits of "pot" versus liquor, or anarchy versus order, I believe their emphasis on social process is introducing a new dimension into our corporate life and values.

"Skyhooks" was written for myself and not for publication. For a while I refused to give anybody a copy, but under pressure I duplicated a small number of copies for my friends, and they wanted copies for their friends. When the Editor of HBR got his copy and asked, "How about publishing it?" I answered, "Only if you take it as it is; I don't want to revise it." I see little need for revising it now—except perhaps the reference (in the beginning paragraphs of this article) to the increase in membership in the institutional church. The search for ultimate values and meanings is keener than in 1955, but it is apparently no longer satisfied merely by church affiliation.

NOTES

1. Barbara Ward, *Faith and Freedom* (New York, Norton, 1954).

2. John Kord Lagemann, "Job Enlargement Boosts Production." *Nation's Business.* December 1954, p. 36.

3. David Riesman, *The Lonely Crowd* (New Haven, Yale University Press, 1950).

4. See John Kenneth Galbraith, *American Capitalism* (Boston, Houghton Mifflin, 1952).

5. Clarence B. Randall, *A Creed for Free Enterprise* (Boston, Little, Brown, 1952), p. 16.

6. Ibid.

7. For further elaboration, see Gordon W. Allport, *The Individual and His Religion* (New York, Macmillan, 1953).

8. Jacob D. Cox, Jr., *Material Human Progress* (Cleveland, Cleveland Twist Drill Company, 1954), p. 104.

2

SHARED VISION

PETER M. SENGE

A COMMON CARING

You may remember the movie *Spartacus*, an adaptation of the story of a Roman gladiator/slave who led an army of slaves in an uprising in 71 B.C.[1] They defeated the Roman legions twice, but were finally conquered by the general Marcus Crassus after a long siege and battle. In the movie, Crassus tells the thousand survivors in Spartacus's army, "You have been slaves. You will be slaves again. But you will be spared your rightful punishment of crucifixion by the mercy of the Roman legions. All you need to do is turn over to me the slave Spartacus, because we do not know him by sight."

After a long pause, Spartacus (played by Kirk Douglas) stands up and says, "I am Spartacus." Then the man next to him stands up and says, "I am Spartacus." The next man stands up and also says, "No, I am Spartacus." Within a minute, everyone in the army is on his feet.

It does not matter whether this story is apocryphal or not; it demonstrates a deep truth. Each man, by standing up, chose death. But the loyalty of Spartacus's army was not to Spartacus the man. Their loyalty was to a shared vision which Spartacus had inspired— the idea that they could be free men. This vision was so compelling that no man could bear to give it up and return to slavery.

A shared vision is not an idea. It is not even an important idea such as freedom. It is, rather, a force in people's hearts, a force of impressive power. It may be inspired by an idea, but once it goes further—if it is compelling enough to acquire the support of more than one person—then it is no longer an abstraction. It is palpable. People begin to see it as if it exists. Few, if any, forces in human affairs are as powerful as shared vision.

At its simplest level, a shared vision is the answer to the question, "What do we want to create?" Just as personal visions are pictures or images people carry in their heads and hearts, so too are shared visions pictures that people throughout an organization carry. They create a sense of commonality that permeates the organization and gives coherence to diverse activities.

A vision is truly shared when you and I have a similar picture and are committed to one another having it, not just to each of us, individually, having it. When people truly share a vision they are connected, bound together by a common aspiration. Personal visions derive their power from an individual's deep caring for the vision. Shared visions derive their power from a common caring. In fact, we have to come to believe that one of the reasons people seek to build shared visions is their desire to be connected in an important undertaking.

Shared vision is vital for the learning organization because it provides the focus and energy for learning. While adaptive learning is possible without vision, generative learning occurs only when people are striving to accomplish something that matters deeply to them. In fact, the whole idea of generative learning—"expanding your ability to create"—will seem abstract and meaningless *until* people become excited about some vision they truly want to accomplish.

Today, "vision" is a familiar concept in corporate leadership. But when you look carefully you find that most "visions" are one person's (or one group's) vision imposed on an organization. Such visions, at best, command compliance—not commitment. A shared vision is a vision that many people are truly committed to, because it reflects their own personal vision.

WHY SHARED VISIONS MATTER

It is impossible to imagine the accomplishments of building AT&T, Ford, or Apple in the absence of shared vision. Theodore Vail had a vision of universal telephone service that would take fifty years to bring about. Henry Ford envisioned common people, not just the wealthy, owning their own automobiles. Steven Jobs, Steve Wozniak, and their Apple cofounders saw the power of the computer to empower people. It is equally impossible to imagine the rapid ascendancy of Japanese firms such as Komatsu (which grew from one third the size of Caterpillar to its equal in less than two decades), Canon (which went from nothing to matching Xerox's global market share in reprographics in the same time frame), or Honda had they not all been guided by visions of global success.[2] What is most important is that these individuals' visions became genuinely shared among people throughout all levels of their companies—focusing the energies of thousands and creating a common identity among enormously diverse people.

Many shared visions are extrinsic—that is, they focus on achieving something relative to an outsider, such as a competitor. Pepsi's vision is explicitly directed at beating Coca-Cola; Avis's vision at Hertz. Yet, a goal limited to defeating an opponent is transitory. Once the vision is achieved, it can easily migrate into a defensive posture of "protecting what we have, of not losing our number-one position." Such defensive goals rarely call forth the creativity and excitement of building something new. A master in the martial arts is probably not focused so much on "defeating all others" as on his own intrinsic inner standards of "excellence." This does not mean that visions must be either intrinsic *or* extrinsic. Both types of vision can coexist. But reliance on a vision that is solely predicated on defeating an adversary can weaken an organization long term.

Kazuo Inamori of Kyocera entreats employees "to look inward," to discover their own internal standards. He argues that, while striving to be number one in its field, a company can aim to be "better" than others or "best" in its field. But his vision is that Kyocera should always aim for "perfection" rather than just being "best." (Note Inamori's application of the principle of creative tension—"it's not what the vision is, but what it does . . .").[3]

A shared vision, especially one that is intrinsic, uplifts people's aspirations. Work becomes part of pursuing a larger purpose embodied in the organizations' products or services—accelerating learning through personal computers, bringing the world into communication through universal telephone service, or promoting freedom of movement through the personal automobile. The larger purpose can also be embodied in the style, climate, and spirit of the organization. Max de Pree, retired CEO of the Herman Miller furniture company said his vision for Herman Miller was "to be a gift to the human spirit"—by which he meant not only Herman Miller's products, but its people, its atmosphere, and its larger commitment to productive and aesthetic work environments.[4] Visions are exhilarating. They create the spark, the excitement that lifts an organization out of the mundane. "No matter how problematic the competition or our internal troubles," wrote John Sculley about Apple's renowned visionary product, "my spirit rebounded when I strolled into the Macintosh Building. We knew we would soon bear witness to an event of historical proportions."[5]

In a corporation, a shared vision changes people's relationship with the company. It is no longer "their company;" it becomes "our company." A shared vision is the first step in allowing people who mistrusted each other to begin to work together. It creates a common identity. In fact, an organization's shared sense of purpose, vision, and operating values establish the most basic level of commonality. Late in his career, the psychologist Abraham Maslow studied high-performing teams. One of their most striking characteristics was shared vision and purpose. Maslow observed that in exceptional teams

> the task was no longer separate from the self ... but rather he identified with this task so strongly that you couldn't define his real self without including that task.[6]

Shared visions compel courage so naturally that people don't even realize the extent of their courage. Courage is simply doing whatever is needed in pursuit of the vision. In 1961, John Kennedy articulated a vision that had been emerging for many years among leaders within America's space program: to have a man on the moon by the end of the decade.[7] This led to countless acts of courage and daring. A modern-day Spartacus story occurred in the mid-1960s at MIT's Draper Laboratories. The lab was the lead contractor with NASA for the inertial navigation and guidance system to guide the Apollo astronauts to the moon. Several years into the project, the lab directors became convinced that their original design specifications were wrong. This posed considerable potential embarrassment, since several million dollars had already been spent. Instead of trying to jerry-rig an expedient solution, they asked NASA to disband the project and start over again. They risked not just their contract but their reputation. But no other action was possible. Their entire reason for being was embodied in one simple vision—having a man on the moon by the end of the decade. They would do whatever it took to realize that vision.

Apple Computer during the mid-1980s, when the entire small computer industry rallied behind the IBM PC, persevered with its vision of a computer which people could understand intuitively, a computer which represented the freedom to think on one's own.

Along the way, Apple not only refused the "sure thing" opportunity to be a leading PC "clone" manufacturer, but its leaders gave up an innovation which they had pioneered: open architecture, where people could add their own components. This did not fit with a computer that was easy to use. Strategically, the change paid off in a company profile and reputation which even the foremost "clone" makers, such as Compaq, have never been able to equal. Apple's Macintosh was not only easy to use, it became a new industry standard and made having fun a priority in personal computing.

You cannot have a learning organization without shared vision. Without a pull toward some goal which people truly want to achieve, the forces in support of the status quo can be overwhelming. Vision establishes an overarching goal. The loftiness of the target compels new ways of thinking and acting. A shared vision also provides a rudder to keep the learning process on course when stresses develop. Learning can be difficult, even painful. With a shared vision, we are more likely to expose our ways of thinking, give up deeply held views, and recognize personal and organizational shortcomings. All that trouble seems trivial compared with the importance of what we are trying to create. As Robert Fritz puts it, "In the presence of greatness, pettiness disappears." In the absence of a great dream, pettiness prevails.

Shared vision fosters risk taking and experimentation. "When you are immersed in a vision," says Herman Miller's president Ed Simon, "you know what needs to be done. But you often don't know how to do it. You run an experiment because you think it's going to get you there. It doesn't work. New input. New data. You change direction and run another experiment. Everything is an experiment, but there is no ambiguity at all. It's perfectly clear why you are doing it. People aren't saying, 'Give me a guarantee that it will work.' Everybody knows that there is no guarantee. But the people are committed nonetheless."

Lastly, shared vision addresses one of the primary puzzles that has thwarted efforts to develop systems thinking in management: "How can a commitment to the long term be fostered?"

For years, systems thinkers have endeavored to persuade managers that, unless they maintained a long-term focus, they will be in big trouble. With great vigor we have proselytized the "better before worse" consequences of many interventions, and the "shifting the burden" dynamics that result from symptomatic fixes. Yet, I have witnessed few lasting shifts to longer term commitment and action. Personally, I have come to feel that our failure lies not in unpersuasiveness or lack of sufficiently compelling evidence. *It may simply not be possible to convince human beings to take a long-term view.* People do not focus on the long term because they *have* to, but because they *want* to.

In every instance where one finds a long-term view actually operating in human affairs, there is a long-term vision at work. The cathedral builders of the Middle Ages labored a lifetime with the fruits of their labors still a hundred years in the future. The Japanese believe building a great organization is like growing a tree; it takes twenty-five to fifty years. Parents of young children try to lay a foundation of values and attitude that will serve an adult twenty years hence. In all of these cases, people hold a vision that can be realized only over the long term.

Strategic planning, which should be a bastion of long-term thinking in corporations, is very often reactive and short-term. According to two of the most articulate critics of contemporary strategic planning, Gary Hamel of the London Business School and C. K. Prahalad of the University of Michigan:

> Although strategic planning is billed as a way of becoming more future oriented, most managers, when pressed, will admit that their strategic plans reveal more about today's problems than tomorrow's opportunities.[8]

With its emphasis on extensive analysis of competitors' strengths and weaknesses, of market niches and firm resources, typical strategic planning fails to achieve the one accomplishment that would foster longer range actions—in Hamel's and Prahalad's terms, setting "a goal that is worthy of commitment."

With all the attention given to this component of corporate learning, however, vision is still often regarded as a mysterious, uncontrollable force. Leaders with vision are cult heroes. While it is true that there are no formulas for "how to find your vision," there are principles and guidelines for building shared vision. There is a discipline of building vision that is emerging, and practical tools for working with shared visions. This discipline extends principles and insights from personal mastery into the world of collective aspiration and shared commitment.

THE DISCIPLINE OF BUILDING SHARED VISION
Encouraging Personal Vision

Shared visions emerge from personal visions. This is how they derive their energy and how they foster commitment. As Bill

O'Brien of Hanover Insurance observes, "My vision is not what's important to you. The only vision that motivates you is your vision." It is not that people care only about their personal self-interest—in fact, people's personal visions usually include dimensions that concern family, organization, community, and even the world. Rather, O'Brien is stressing that caring is *personal*. It is rooted in an individual's own set of values, concerns, and aspirations. This is why genuine caring about a shared vision is rooted in personal visions. This simple truth is lost on many leaders, who decide that their organization must develop a vision by tomorrow!

Organizations intent on building shared visions continually encourage members to develop their personal visions. If people don't have their own vision, all they can do is "sign up" for someone else's. The result is compliance, never commitment. On the other hand, people with a strong sense of personal direction can join together to create a powerful synergy toward what I/we truly want.

Personal mastery is the bedrock for developing shared visions. This means not only personal vision, but commitment to the truth and creative tension—the hallmarks of personal mastery. Shared vision can generate levels of creative tension that go far beyond individuals' "comfort levels." Those who will contribute the most toward realizing a lofty vision will be those who can "hold" this creative tension: remain clear on the vision and continue to inquire into current reality. They will be the ones who believe deeply in their ability to create their future, because that is what they experience personally.

In encouraging personal vision, organizations must be careful not to infringe on individual freedoms. . . . [N]o one can give another "his vision," nor even force him to develop a vision. However, there are positive actions that can be taken to create a climate that encourages personal vision. The most direct is for leaders who have a sense of vision to communicate that in such a way that others are encouraged to share their visions. This is the art of visionary leadership—how shared visions are built from personal visions.

From Personal Visions to Shared Visions

How do individual visions join to create shared visions? A useful metaphor is the hologram, the three-dimensional image created by interacting light sources.

If you cut a photograph in half, each part shows only part of the whole image. But if you divide a hologram, each part shows the whole image intact. Similarly, as you continue to divide up the hologram, no matter how small the divisions, each piece still shows the whole image. Likewise, when a group of people come to share a vision for an organization, each person sees his own picture of the organization at its best. Each shares responsibility for the whole, not just for his piece. But the component "pieces" of the hologram are not identical. Each represents the whole image from a different point of view. It's as if you were to look through holes poked in a window shade; each hole would offer a unique angle for viewing the whole image. So, too, is each individual's vision of the whole unique. We each have our own way of seeing the larger vision.

When you add up the pieces of a hologram, the image of the whole does not change fundamentally. After all, it was there in each piece. Rather the image becomes more intense, more lifelike. When more people come to share a common vision, the vision may not change fundamentally. But it becomes more alive, more real in the sense of a mental reality that people can truly imagine achieving. They now have partners, "cocreators"; the vision no longer rests on their shoulders alone. Early on, when they are nurturing an individual vision, people may say it is "my vision." But as the shared vision develops, it becomes both "my vision" and "our vision."

The first step in mastering the discipline of building shared visions is to give up traditional notions that visions are always announced from "on high" or come from an organization's institutionalized planning processes.

In the traditional hierarchical organization, no one questioned that the vision emanated from the top. Often, the big picture guiding the firm wasn't even shared—all people needed to know were their "marching orders," so that they could carry out their tasks in support of the larger vision. Ed Simon of Herman Miller says, "If I was the president of a traditional authoritarian organization and I had a new vision, the task would be much simpler than we face today. Most people in the organization wouldn't need to understand the vision. People would simply need to know what was expected of them."

That traditional "top-down" vision is not much different from a process that has become popular in recent years. Top management goes off to write its "vision statement," often with the help of consultants. This may be done to solve the problem of low morale or lack of strategic direction. Sometimes the process is primarily reflective. Sometimes it incorporates extensive analysis of a firm's competitors, market setting, and organizational strengths and weaknesses. Regardless, the results are often disappointing for several reasons.

First, such a vision is often a "one-shot" vision, a single effort at providing overarching direction and meaning to the firm's strategy. Once it's written, management assumes that they have now discharged their visionary duties. Recently one of my Innovation Associates colleagues was explaining to two managers how our group works with vision. Before he could get far, one of the managers interrupted. "We've done that," he said. "We've already written our vision statement." "That's very interesting," my colleague responded. "What did you come up with?" The one manager turned to the other and asked, "Joe, where is that vision statement anyhow?" Writing a vision statement can be a first step in building shared vision but, alone, it rarely makes a vision "come alive" within an organization.

The second problem with top management going off to write their vision statement is that the resulting vision does not build on people's personal visions. Often, personal visions are ignored altogether in the search for a "strategic vision." Or the "official vision" reflects only the personal vision of one or two people. There is little opportunity for inquiry and testing at every level so that people feel they understand and own the vision. As a result, the new official vision also fails to foster energy and commitment. It simply does not inspire people. In fact, sometimes, it even generates little passion among the top management team who created it.

Lastly, vision is not a "solution to a problem." If it is seen in that light, when the "problem" of low morale or unclear strategic direction goes away, the energy behind the vision will go away also. Building shared vision must be seen as a central element of the daily work of leaders. It is ongoing and never-ending. It is actually part of a larger leadership activity: designing and nurturing what Hanover's Bill O'Brien calls the "governing ideas" of the enterprise—not only its vision per se, but its purpose and core values as well. As O'Brien says, "The governing ideas are far more important and enduring than the reporting chart and the divisional structure that so often preoccupy CEOs."

Sometimes, managers expect shared visions to emerge from a firm's strategic planning process. But for all the same reasons that most "top-down" visioning processes fail, most strategic planning also fails to nurture genuine vision. According to Hamel and Prahalad:

Creative strategies seldom emerge from the annual planning ritual. The starting point for next year's strategy is almost always this year's strategy. Improvements are incremental. The company sticks to the segments and territories it knows, even though the real opportunities may be elsewhere. The impetus for Canon's pioneering entry into the personal copier business came from an overseas sales subsidiary—not from planners in Japan.[9]

This is not to say that visions cannot emanate from the top. Often, they do. But sometimes they emanate from personal visions of individuals who are not in positions of authority. Sometimes they just "bubble up" from people interacting at many levels. The origin of the vision is much less important than the process whereby it comes to be shared. It is not truly a "shared vision" until it connects with the personal visions of people throughout the organization.

For those in leadership positions, what is most important is to remember that their visions are still personal visions. Just because they occupy a position of leadership does not mean that their personal visions are *automatically* "the organization's vision." When I hear leaders say "our vision" and I know they are really describing "my vision," I recall Mark Twain's words that the official "we" should be reserved for "kings and people with tapeworm."

Ultimately, leaders intent on building shared visions must be willing to continually share their personal visions. They must also be prepared to ask, "Will you follow me?" This can be difficult. For a person who has been setting goals all through his career and simply announcing them, asking for support can make him feel very vulnerable.

John Kryster was the president of a large division of a leading home products company who had a vision that his division should be preeminent in its industry. This vision required not only excellent products but that the company supply the product to their "customer" (retail grocers), in a more efficient and effective manner than anyone else. He envisioned a unique worldwide distribution system that would get product to the customer in half the time and with a fraction of the cost in wastage and reshipments. He began to talk with other managers, with production workers, with distribution people, with grocers. Everyone seemed enthusiastic, but pointed up that many of his ideas could not be achieved because they contradicted so many traditional policies of the corporate parent.

In particular, Kryster needed the support of the head of product distribution, Harriet Sullivan, who—while technically Kryster's peer in the firm's matrix organization—had fifteen years more experience. Kryster prepared an elaborate presentation for Sullivan to show her the merits of his new distribution ideas. But for every piece of supporting data he offered, Sullivan had a countering criticism. Kryster left the meeting thinking that the doubters were probably right.

Then he conceived of a way to test the new system out in only one geographic market. The risk would be less, and he could gain the support of the local grocery chain which had been especially enthusiastic about the concept. But what should he do about Harriet Sullivan? His instincts were just not to tell her. After all, he had the authority to undertake the experiment himself, using his own distribution people. Yet, he also valued Sullivan's experience and judgment.

After a week of mulling it over, Kryster went back to ask for Sullivan's support. This time, though, he left his charts and data at home. He just told her why he believed in the idea, how it could forge a new partnership with customers, and how its merits could be tested with low risk. To his surprise, the crusty distribution chief started to offer help in designing the experiment. "When you came to me last week," she said, "you were trying to convince me. Now, you're willing to test your idea. I still think it's wrongheaded, but I can see you care a great deal. So, who knows, maybe we'll learn something."

That was five years ago. Today, John Kryster's innovative distribution system is used worldwide by almost all the corporation's divisions. It has significantly reduced costs and been part of broad strategic alliances the corporation is learning to forge with retail chains.

When visions start in the middle of an organization the process of sharing and listening is essentially the same as when they originate at the top. But it may take longer, especially if the vision has implications for the entire organization.

Bart Bolton was a middle manager in IS (Information Systems) at Digital Equipment Corporation when, back in 1981, he and a small group of colleagues began to form an idea of Digital as an interconnected organization. "A group of us had been together at a workshop, and when we came back we just started talking about how we were going to turn around IS. The fundamental problem as we all saw it was that there simply was no IS vision. Everyone ar-

gued about the 'how to's' but no one knew the 'what.' Yet, we felt
we could see an end result that was really worth going for. We
didn't know exactly what it would look like, but the idea of tying
the organization together electronically just felt 'right.' Given our
products and technology we could become one of the first, if not
the first large corporation that was totally and completely electronically interconnected." The idea was so exciting that he couldn't
sleep much for several days as he thought about the implications.

But in 1981, no one had any idea how this could be done. "It
was simply beyond the realm of what was possible at that time. We
could transfer files between computers, but we couldn't network.
There was some networking software under development but there
were lots of problems with it. Perhaps, if we worked really hard at it
we could interconnect ten or twenty machines, but no one even
dreamed of interconnecting a hundred machines, let alone thousands. Looking back, it was like they say about Kennedy when he
announced the 'Man on the Moon' vision—we knew about 15 percent of what we needed to know to get there. But we knew it was
right."

Bolton and his compatriots had no "authority" to pursue the
idea, but they couldn't stop thinking about it. In November 1981,
he wrote a short paper which he read to all the senior IS people at a
staff meeting. In it he said that the organization of the future would
involve new IS technologies, would see "data as a resource just like
the organization of the past saw capital and people as resources,"
and that "networks would tie together all the functions." "When I
finished, no one spoke. It was like being in church. I really thought
I'd blown it. My boss, Al Crawford, the head of IS, suggested a
ten-minute break. When people came back, all they wanted to
know was, 'How do we promote it? How can we make it happen?'
My only response was, 'This has got to be your vision not mine, or
it will never happen.' "

"I knew the guys at the top had to be 'enrolled,' and my job was
to help them lead. By enrolling others, they too would become
messengers." An IS group prepared a 35-mm slide show to be used
by Crawford throughout the organization. He came up with the
image of "wiring up the corporation." "It became incredibly exciting," says Bolton, "to watch the vision build, each person adding
something new, refining it and making it come alive. We literally
began talking about the 'copper wires running around the world.' "

Crawford presented the slide show to all Digital's major functional staffs in 1982. The idea, "the what," started to take hold.

Then the IS organization created five overlapping programs to tackle the "how to's": a network program, a data program, an office automation program, a facilities program, and an applications program. By 1985 the first network was in place. By 1987, over 10,000 computers were on line. Today, Digital has over 600 facilities in over 50 countries and they are all interconnected. There are over 43,000 computers interconnected. Digital is now seen by experts as one of the pioneer "networked organizations." Moreover, the "networked organization" is a dominant theme in Digital's marketing strategy and advertising.

Organizational consultant Charlie Kiefer says that, "Despite the excitement that a vision generates, the process of building shared vision is not always glamorous. Managers who are skilled at building shared visions talk about the process in ordinary terms. 'Talking about our vision' just gets woven into day-to-day life. Most artists don't get very excited about the *process of* creating art. They get excited about the results." Or, as Bill O'Brien puts it, "Being a visionary leader is not about giving speeches and inspiring the troops. How I spend my day is pretty much the same as how any executive spends his day. Being a visionary leader is about solving day-to-day problems with my vision in mind."

Visions that are truly shared take time to emerge. They grow as a by-product of interactions of individual visions. Experience suggests that visions that are genuinely shared require ongoing conversation where individuals not only feel free to express their dreams, but learn how to listen to each others' dreams. Out of this listening, new insights into what is possible gradually emerge.

Listening is often more difficult than talking, especially for strong-willed managers with definite ideas of what is needed. It requires extraordinary openness and willingness to entertain a diversity of ideas. This does not imply that we must sacrifice our vision "for the larger cause." Rather, we must allow multiple visions to coexist, listening for the right course of action that transcends and unifies all our individual visions. As one highly successful CEO expressed it: "My job, fundamentally, is listening to what the organization is trying to say, and them making sure that it is forcefully articulated."

Spreading Visions:
Enrollment, Commitment, and Compliance[10]

Few subjects are closer to the heart of contemporary managers than commitment. Prodded by studies showing that most

American workers acknowledge low levels of commitment[11] and by tales of foreign competitors' committed work forces, managers have turned to "management by commitment," "high commitment work systems," and other approaches. Yet, real commitment is still rare in today's organizations. It is our experience that, 90 percent of the time, what passes for commitment is compliance.

Today, it is common to hear managers talk of getting people to "buy into" the vision. For many, I fear, this suggests a sales process, where I sell and you buy. Yet, there is a world of difference between "selling" and "enrolling." "Selling" generally means getting someone to do something that he might not do if they were in full possession of all the facts. "Enrolling," by contrast, literally means "placing one's name on the roll." Enrollment implies free choice, while "being sold" often does not.

"Enrollment is the process," in Kiefer's words, "of becoming part of something by choice." "Committed" describes a state of being not only enrolled but feeling fully responsible for making the vision happen. I can be thoroughly enrolled in your vision. I can genuinely want it to occur. Yet, it is still your vision. I will take actions as need arises, but I do not spend my waking hours looking for what to do next.

For example, people are often enrolled in social causes out of genuine desire, for example, to see particular inequities righted. Once a year they might make a donation to help in a fund-raising campaign. But when they are committed, the "cause" can count on them. They will do whatever it takes to make the vision real. The vision is pulling them to action. Some use the term "being source" to describe the unique energy that committed people bring toward creating a vision.

In most contemporary organizations, there are relatively few people enrolled—and even fewer committed. The great majority of people are in a state of "compliance." "Compliant" followers go along with a vision. They do what is expected of them. They support the vision, to some degree. But, they are not truly enrolled or committed.

Compliance is often confused with enrollment and commitment. In part, this occurs because compliance has prevailed for so long in most organizations, we don't know how to recognize real commitment. It is also because there are several levels of compliance, some of which lead to behavior that looks a great deal like enrollment and commitment:

Possible Attitudes Toward a Vision

Commitment: Wants it. Will make it happen. Creates whatever "laws" (structures) are needed.

Enrollment: Wants it. Will do whatever can be done within the "spirit of the law."

Genuine compliance: Sees the benefits of the vision. Does everything expected and more. Follows the "letter of the law." "Good soldiers."

Formal compliance: On the whole, sees the benefits of the vision. Does what's expected and no more. "Pretty good soldier."

Grudging compliance: Does not see the benefits of the vision. But, also, does not want to lose job. Does enough of what's expected because he has to, but also lets it be known that he is not really on board.

Noncompliance: Does not see benefits of vision and will not do what's expected. "I won't do it; you can't make me."

Apathy: Neither for nor against vision. No interest. No energy. "Is it five o'clock yet?"

The speed limit is fifty-five in most states in the United States today. A person who was genuinely compliant would never drive more than fifty-five. A person formally compliant could drive sixty to sixty-five because in most states you will not get a ticket so long as you are below sixty-five. Someone grudgingly compliant would shy below sixty-five and complain continually about it. A noncompliant driver would "floor it" and do everything possible to evade troopers. On the other hand, a person who was genuinely committed to a fifty-five mph speed limit would drive that speed even if it were not the legal limit.

In most organizations, most people are in states of formal or genuine compliance with respect to the organization's goals and ground rules. They go along with "the program," sincerely trying to contribute. On the other hand, people in noncompliance or grudging compliance usually stand out. They are opposed to the goals or ground rules and let their opposition be known, either through inaction or (if they are grudgingly compliant) through "malicious obedience"—"I'll do it just to prove that it won't work." They may not speak out publicly against the organization's goals, but their views are known nonetheless. (They often reserve their truest sentiments for the rest room or the cocktail lounge.)

Differences between the varying states of compliance can be subtle. Most problematic is the state of genuine compliance, which is often mistaken for enrollment or commitment. The prototypical "good soldier" of genuine compliance will do whatever is expected of him, willingly. "I believe in the people behind the vision; I'll do whatever is needed, and more, to the fullest of my ability." In his own mind, the person operating in genuine compliance often thinks of himself as committed. He is, in fact, committed, but only to being "part of the team."

In fact, from his *behavior* on the job, it is often very difficult to distinguish someone who is genuinely compliant from someone who is enrolled or committed. An organization made up of genuinely compliant people would be light-years ahead of most organizations in productivity and cost effectiveness. People would not have to be told what to do more than once. They would be responsive. They would be upbeat and positive in their attitude and manner. They might also be a bit "drone-like," but not necessarily. If what was expected of high performers was to "take initiative" and be "proactive," they would exhibit those behaviors as well. In short, people in genuine compliance would do whatever they could to play by the "rules of the game," both the formal and subtle rules.

Yet, there is a world of difference between compliance and commitment. The committed person brings an energy, passion, and excitement that cannot be generated if you are only compliant, even genuinely compliant. The committed person doesn't play by the "rules of the game." He is responsible for the game. If the rules of the game stand in the way of achieving the vision, he will find ways to change the rules. A group of people truly committed to a common vision is an awesome force. They can accomplish the seemingly impossible.

Tracy Kidder, in his Pulitzer-prize-winning book *The Soul of a New Machine,* tells the story of a product development team at Data General, brought together by a talented team leader to create an ambitious new computer. Against a business atmosphere of urgency bordering on crisis, the team turned out a ground-breaking computer in remarkable time. Visiting with the team manager Tom West in the book, and team members several years later, I learned just how remarkable their feat was. They told me of a stage in their project where certain critical software was several months behind schedule. The three engineers responsible came into the office one evening and left the next morning. By all accounts they accomplished two to three months of work that evening—and no one could explain how. These are not the feats of compliance.

What then is the difference between being genuinely compliant and enrolled and committed? The answer is deceptively simple. People who are enrolled or committed truly *want* the vision. Genuinely compliant people accept the vision. They may want it in order to get something else—for example, to keep their job, or to make their boss happy, or to get a promotion. But they do not truly want the vision in and of itself. It is not their own vision (or, at least, they do not know that it is their own vision).

Highly desired, shared commitment to a vision can be an elusive goal. One executive VP at a consumer goods company deeply desired to turn the very traditional organization into a world-class competitor by developing shared commitment to a new business vision. But after a year's effort, people continued to follow orders and do what they were told.

At this point he began to see the depth of the problem. People in his organization had *never been asked to commit to anything in their careers.* All they had ever been asked to do was be compliant. That was all they knew how to do. That was their only mental model. No matter what he said about developing a real vision, about being truly committed, it didn't matter because they heard it within their mode of compliance.

Once he grasped this, he shifted tactics. He asked, "What might people be able to commit to?" He initiated a "wellness program," reasoning if there was anything to which people might become committed, it would be their own health. Over time, some did. They began to see that true commitment was possible in the workplace, and a near "ear" for the vision was opened.

Traditional organizations did not care about enrollment and commitment. The command and control hierarchy required only compliance. Still, today, many managers are justifiably wary of whether the energy released through commitment can be controlled and directed. So, we settle for compliance and content ourselves with moving people up the compliance ladder.

Guidelines for Enrollment and Commitment

Enrollment is a natural process that springs from your genuine enthusiasm for a vision and your willingness to let others come to their own choice.

- *Be enrolled yourself.* There is no point attempting to encourage another to be enrolled when you are not. That is
  "selling," not enrolling and will, at best, produce a form
  of superficial agreement and compliance. Worse, it will
  sow the seeds for future resentment.

- *Be on the level.* Don't inflate benefits or sweep problems
  under the rug. Describe the vision as simply and honestly
  as you can.

- *Let the other person choose.* You don't have to "convince"
  another of the benefits of a vision. In fact, efforts you
  might make to persuade him to "become enrolled" will
  be seen as manipulative and actually preclude enrollment.
  The more willing you are for him to make a free choice,
  the freer he will feel. This can be especially difficult with
  subordinates, who are often conditioned to feel as though
  they must go along. But you can still help by creating the
  time and safety for them to develop their own sense of
  vision.

There are many times when managers need compliance. They
may want enrollment or commitment, but cannot accept anything
below formal compliance. If that is the case, I recommend that you
be on the level about it: "I know you may not agree wholeheartedly
with the new direction, but at this juncture it is where the management team is committed to heading. I need your support to help it
happen." Being open about the need for compliance removes
hypocrisy. It also makes it easier for people to come to their choices,
which may, over time, include enrollment.

The hardest lesson for many managers to face is that, ultimately, *there is nothing you can do to get another person to enroll or
commit.* Enrollment and commitment require freedom of choice.
The guidelines above simply establish conditions most favorable to
enrollment, but they do not *cause* enrollment. Commitment
likewise is very personal; efforts to force it will, at best, foster
compliance.

Anchoring Vision in a Set of Governing Ideas

Building shared vision is actually only one piece of a larger activity: developing the "governing ideas" for the enterprise, its vision,
purpose or mission, and core values. A vision not consistent with
values that people live by day by day will not only fail to inspire
genuine enthusiasm, it will often foster outright cynicism.

These governing ideas answer three critical questions: "What?" "Why?" and "How?"

- Vision is the "What?"—the picture of the future we seek to create.

- Purpose (or "mission") is the "Why?"—the organization's answer to the question, "Why do we exist?" Great organizations have a larger sense of purpose that transcends providing for the needs of shareholders and employees. They seek to contribute to the world in some unique way, to add a distinctive source of value.

- Core values answer the question "How do we want to act, consistent with our mission, along the path toward achieving our vision?" A company's values might include integrity, openness, honesty, freedom, equal opportunity, leanness, merit, or loyalty. They describe how the company wants life to be on a day-to-day basis, while pursuing the vision.

Taken as a unit, all three governing ideas answer the question, "What do we believe in?" When Matsushita employees recite the company creed: "To recognize our responsibilities as industrialists, to foster progress, to promote the general welfare of society, and to devote ourselves to the further development of world culture," they're describing the company *purpose*. When they sing the company song, about "sending our goods to the people of the world, endlessly and continuously, like water gushing from a fountain," they're proclaiming the corporate *vision*. And when they go to in-house training programs that cover such topics as "fairness," "harmony and cooperation," "struggle for betterment," "courtesy and humility," and "gratitude," the employees are learning the company's deliberately constructed *values*. (Matsushita, in fact, calls them its "spiritual values.")[12]

At Hanover Insurance, articulating all three of these "governing ideas" made an enormous difference in the firm's revival from near bankruptcy to a leader in the property and liability industry. Hanover's experience also illustrates the interdependencies among vision, values, and purpose.

"Early on," says O'Brien, "we recognized that there is a burning need for people to feel part of an ennobling mission. If it is absent many will seek fulfillment only in outside interests instead of in their work.

"But we also discovered that stating a mission or purpose in words was not enough. It ends up sounding like 'apple pie and motherhood.' People need visions to make the purpose more concrete and tangible. We had to learn to 'paint pictures' of the type of organization we wanted to be. My simple vision for the company is 'unquestioned superiority.' This simple term has great meaning for me. It leads me to envision an organization that serves the customer in unique ways, maintains a reputation for quality and responsibility, and creates a unique environment for its employees.

"Core values are necessary to help people with day-to-day decision making. Purpose is very abstract. Vision is long term. People need 'guiding stars' to navigate and make decisions day to day. But core values are only helpful if they can be translated into concrete behaviors. For example, one of our core values is 'openness,' which we worked long and hard to understand—finally recognizing that it requires the skills of reflection and inquiry within an overall context of trusting and supporting one another."

Positive Versus Negative Vision

"What do we want?" is different from "What do we want to avoid?" This seems obvious, but in fact negative visions are probably more common than positive visions. Many organizations truly pull together only when their survival is threatened. They focus on avoiding what people don't want—being taken over, going bankrupt, losing jobs, not losing market share, having no downturns in earnings, or "not letting our competitors beat us to market with our next new product." Negative visions are, if anything, even more common in public leadership, where societies are continually bombarded with visions of "anti-drugs," "anti-smoking," "anti-war," or "anti-nuclear energy."

Negative visions are limiting for three reasons. First, energy that could build something new is diverted to "preventing" something we don't want to happen. Second, negative visions carry a subtle yet unmistakable message of powerlessness: our people really don't care. They can pull together only when there is sufficient threat. Lastly, negative visions are inevitably short term. The organization is motivated so long as the threat persists. Once it leaves, so does the organization's vision and energy.

There are two fundamental sources of energy that can motivate organizations: fear and aspiration. The power of fear underlies negative visions. The power of aspiration drives positive visions. Fear can produce extraordinary changes in short periods, but aspiration endures as a continuing source of learning and growth.

Creative Tension and Commitment to the Truth

. . . I [have] argued that personal vision, by itself, is not the key to more effective creativity. The key is "creative tension," the tension between vision and reality. The most effective people are those who can "hold" their vision while remaining committed to seeing current reality clearly.

This principle is no less true for organizations. The hallmark of a learning organization is not lovely visions floating in space, but a relentless willingness to examine "what is" in light of our vision.

IBM in the early 1960s, for example, carried out an extraordinary series of experiments in pursuit of a daring vision, a single family of computers that would make virtually all its previous machines obsolete. In the words of a *Fortune* writer, IBM staked "its treasure, its reputation, and its position of leadership in the computer field" on a radical new concept: a series of compatible machines serving the broadest possible range of applications, from the most sophisticated scientific applications to the relatively small business needs.[13]

Jay Forrester once remarked that the hallmark of a great organization is "how quickly bad news travels upward." IBM's capacity to recognize and learn from its mistakes proved pivotal during this period. One of the most discouraging was an early attempt at a high-end machine called "Stretch," introduced in 1960. IBM CEO Tom Watson, Jr., effectively killed the project in May 1961, after only a few had been sold. (Watson cut Stretch's hefty $13.5 million price tag almost in half, thereby making it uneconomical to produce.) To him, there was little choice: the machine did not satisfy its customers, never achieving more than 70 percent of its promised specifications. A few days later, Watson spoke candidly to an industry group. "Our greatest mistake in Stretch," he said, "is that we walked up to the plate and pointed at the center field stands. When we swung, it was not a homer but a hard line drive to the outfield. We're going to be a good deal more careful about what we promise in the future."

Indeed they were. Under the direction of many of the same men who had learned from Stretch, IBM introduced the System 360 three years later, which proved to be the platform for its extraordinary growth over the next ten years.

SHARED VISION AND THE FIFTH DISCIPLINE

Why Visions Die Prematurely

Many visions never take root and spread—despite having intrinsic merit. Several "limits to growth" structures can come into play to arrest the building of momentum behind a new vision. Understanding these structures can help considerably in sustaining the "visioning process."

Visions spread because of a reinforcing process of increasing clarity, enthusiasm, communication and commitment. As people talk, the vision grows clearer. As it gets clearer, enthusiasm for its benefits builds.

And soon, the vision starts to spread in a reinforcing spiral of communication and excitement. Enthusiasm can also be reinforced by early successes in pursuing the vision (another potential reinforcing process, not shown on this diagram).

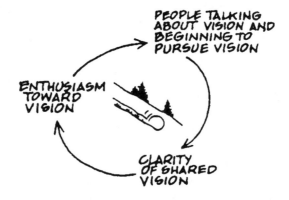

If the reinforcing process operated unfettered, it would lead to continuing growth in clarity and shared commitment toward the vision, among increasing numbers of people. But any of a variety of limiting factors can come into play to slow down this virtuous cycle.

The visioning process can wither if, as more people get involved, the diversity of views dissipates focus and generates unmanageable conflicts. People see different ideal futures. Must those who do not agree immediately with the emerging shared vision change their views? Do they conclude that the vision is "set in stone" and no longer influenceable? Do they feel that their own visions even matter? If the answer to any of these questions is "yes," the enrolling process can grind to a halt with a wave of increasing polarization.

This is a classic "limits to growth" structure, where the reinforcing process of growing enthusiasm for the vision interacts with a "balancing process" that limits the spread of the visions, due to increasing diversity and polarization:

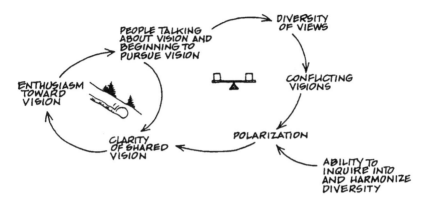

Reading clockwise around the balancing circle, from the top: As enthusiasm builds, more people are talking about the vision, the diversity of views increases, leading to people expressing potentially conflicting visions. If other people are unable to allow this diversity to be expressed, polarization increases, reducing the clarity of the shared visions, and limiting the growth of enthusiasm.

In limits to growth structures, leverage usually lies in understanding the "limiting factor," the implicit goal or norm that drives the balancing feedback process. In this case, that limiting factor is the ability (or inability) to inquire into diverse visions in such a way that deeper, common visions emerge. Diversity of visions will grow until it exceeds the organization's capacity to "harmonize" diversity.

The most important skills to circumvent this limit are the "reflection and inquiry" skills. . . . In effect, the visioning process is a special type of inquiry process. It is an inquiry into the future we truly seek to create. If it becomes a pure advocacy process, it will result in compliance, at best, not commitment.

Approaching the visioning as an inquiry process does not mean that I have to give up my view. On the contrary, visions need strong advocates. But advocates who can also inquire into others' visions open the possibility for the vision to evolve, to become "larger" than our individual visions. *That* is the principle of the hologram.

Visions can also die because people become discouraged by the apparent difficulty in bringing the vision into reality. As clarity about the nature of the vision increases so does awareness of the gap between the vision and current reality. People become disheartened, uncertain, or even cynical, leading to a decline in enthusiasm. The limits to growth structure for "organizational discouragement" looks like this:

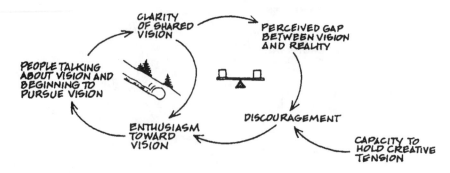

In this structure, the limiting factor is the capacity of people in the organization to "hold" creative tension, the central principle of personal mastery. This is why we say that personal mastery is the "bedrock" for developing shared vision—organizations that do not encourage personal mastery find it very difficult to foster sustained commitment to a lofty vision.

Emerging visions can also die because people get overwhelmed by the demands of current reality and lose their focus on the vision. The limiting factor becomes the time and energy to focus on a vision:

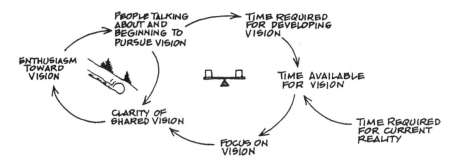

In this case, the leverage must lie either in finding ways to focus less time and effort on fighting crises and managing current reality, or to break off those pursuing the new vision from those responsible for handling "current reality." In many ways, this is the strategy of "skunk works," small groups that quietly pursue new ideas out of the organizational mainstream. While this approach is often necessary, it is difficult to avoid fostering two polar extreme "camps" that no longer can support one another. For example, the group that developed the Macintosh computer in the early 1980s broke off almost completely from the rest of Apple, most of whom were focused on the more mundane Apple II. While the separation resulted in a significant breakthrough product, it also created a significant organizational rift which took considerable time to heal and led John Sculley to reorganize Apple into a more conventionally functional hierarchy.[14]

Lastly, a vision can die if people forget their connection to one another. This is one of the reasons that approaching visioning as a joint inquiry is so important. Once people stop asking "What do we really want to create?" and begin proselytizing the "official vision," the quality of ongoing conversation, and the quality of relationships nourished through that conversation, erodes. One of the deepest desires underlying shared vision is the desire to be connected, to a larger purpose *and* to one another. The spirit of connection is fragile. It is undermined whenever we lose our respect for one another and for each other's views. We then split into insiders and outsiders—those who are "true believers" in the vision and those who are not. When this happens, the "visioning" conversations no longer build genuine enthusiasms toward the vision:

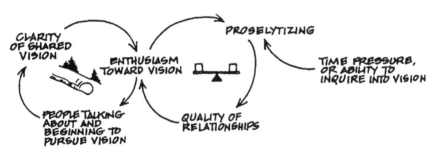

The limiting factor when people begin proselytizing and lose their sense of relationship can be time or skills. If there is great urgency to "sign up" for the new vision, people may just not perceive that there is time to really talk and listen to one another. This will be especially likely if people are also unskilled in how to have such a conversation, how to share their vision in such a way that they are not proselytizing, but are encouraging others to reflect on their own visions.

The Missing Synergy: Shared Vision and Systems Thinking

I believe that the discipline of building shared vision lacks a critical underpinning if practiced without systems thinking. Vision paints the picture of what we want to create. Systems thinking reveals how we have created what we currently have.

In recent years, many leaders have jumped on to the vision bandwagon. They've developed corporate vision and mission statements. They've worked to enroll everyone in the vision. Yet, the expected surges in productivity and competitiveness often fail to arrive. This has led many to become disaffected with vision and visioning. The fad cycle has run its course, and the "baby" is about to be "thrown out with the bath water."

The problem lies not in shared visions themselves, so long as they are developed carefully. The problem lies in our reactive orientation toward current reality. Vision becomes a living force only when people truly believe they can shape their future. The simple fact is that most managers do not *experience* that they are contributing to creating their current reality. So they don't see how they can contribute toward changing that reality. Their problems are created by somebody "out there" or by "the system."

This attitude can be elusive to pin down because in many organizations the belief "We cannot create our future" is so threatening that it can never be acknowledged. There is a strong "espoused view" that being a good manager and leader means being "proactive," being in charge of your own destiny. A person who questions publicly that the organization can achieve what it has set out to do is quickly labeled as "not on board" and seen as a problem.

Yet, this "can do" optimism is a thin veneer over a fundamentally reactive view, because most organizations are dominated by linear thinking, not systems thinking. The dominance of the "event mentality" tells people that the name of the game is reacting to change, not generating change. An event orientation will eventually drive out real vision, leaving only hollow "vision statements," good ideas that are never taken to heart.

But as people in an organization begin to learn *how* existing policies and actions are creating their current reality, a new, more fertile soil for vision develops. A new source of confidence develops, rooted in deeper understanding of the forces shaping current reality and where there is leverage for influencing those forces. I'll always remember a manager emerging from an extended "microworld" session at one of the companies in our research program. When asked what he had learned, he replied: "I discovered that the reality we have is only one of several possible realities."

NOTES

1. Some facts about the man Spartacus come from Arthur Koestler's postscript to his novel *The Gladiator,* translated by Edith Simon (New York: Macmillan), 1939.

2. These cases of corporate vision have been analyzed by G. Hamel and C. K. Prahalad in "Strategic Intent," *Harvard Business Review,* May-June, 1989.

3. Kazuo Inamori, "The Perfect Company: Goal for Productivity," speech given at Case Western Reserve University, Cleveland, Ohio, June 5, 1985.

4. Max de Pree, *Leadership is an Art* (New York: Doubleday/Currency), 1989.

5. John Sculley with John A. Byrne, *Odyssey: Pepsi to Apple* (New York: Harper and Row), 1987.

6. A. Maslow, *Eupsychian Management* (Homewood, Ill.: Richard Irwin and Dorsey Press), 1965.

7. William Manchester, *The Glory and the Dream* (Boston: Little, Brown and Company), 1974.

8. G. Hamel and C. K. Prahalad, "Strategic Intent."

9. Ibid.

10. The ideas expressed in this section come from many hours of discussion with my colleagues at Innovation Associates, notably Charles Kiefer, Alain Gauthier, Charlotte Roberts, Rick Ross, and Bryan Smith.

11. For example the Daniel Yankelovich and John Immerwahr study in 1983, which found that only 25 percent of U.S. workers said they were working as hard as they could be. "Are U.S. workers lazy?" by Joani Nelson-Horchler, *Industry Week,* June 10, 1985, 47.

12. M. Moskowitz, *The Global Marketplace* (New York: Macmillan Publishing Company), 1987.

13. "IBM's $5,000,000,000 Gamble," *Fortune,* September 1966, and "The Rocky Road to the Marketplace," *Fortune,* October 1966 (two-part article).

14. Sculley with Byrne, *Odyssey.*

VISION

Some men see things as they are and say, "Why?"
I dream of things that never were, and say, "Why not?"
—GEORGE BERNARD SHAW

Leadership starts with vision, or it doesn't start at all. Without vision there is nowhere to lead. Vision is a "dream" of an attractive future, but it can't be so fuzzy or quixotic that when we hear it we roll our eyes. It has to work in our hearts and in our heads, inspiring and energizing us while also making good business sense.

A simple self test will begin to help you see how well you are performing. Asking your coworkers, "How am I doing?" will complete the picture.

ASK YOURSELF

Test out your leadership vision by rating the accuracy of the following statements. Use a 1–5 scale ranging from "a little" to "a great extent."

- I communicate a clear vision to my
  coworkers of all that we can be.   1 2 3 4 5

- My day-to-day actions are consistent
  with the vision we hope to achieve.   1 2 3 4 5

- We discuss how our short-term goals
  line up with our long-term goals.   1 2 3 4 5

- I help each individual to see how
  his or her job contributes to our vision. 1 2 3 4 5

- I encourage my coworkers to challenge
  our vision to make sure it remains
  attractive and credible.   1 2 3 4 5

ASK YOUR COWORKERS

If you gave yourself a "4" or "5" rating on each statement, your leadership vision probably is in good shape. However, you can verify your self-assessment by having a two-part discussion with your coworkers. First, ask them to talk about the importance of vision so that you understand it in the same way. Second, ask them for feedback on your performance.

You'll know you're developing a common understanding about the importance of vision when you hear comments like these:

> - "Trading time for money is all you do without a vision, without something to work toward."
> - "Fitting into the big picture—we need to see how we personally contribute, no matter how small the contribution."
> - "All dreams are fragile, so you have to 'walk the talk' every day in every way. You can't say one thing and do another and keep the dream alive."
> - "Praising and rewarding actions that promote our vision shows that it's more than fancy words on a poster."
> - "The really hard part is making our vision real to the support people and helping them see how their efforts help us get where we're going."

After discussing the importance of vision, check out your coworkers' view of your performance by asking them to consider the five items in your self-assessment. You may find it more productive for them to answer the following questions than to give you numerical ratings on each item:

> - What am I doing right now that supports each statement?
> - What else can I do—either more or less—to show greater support for each statement?

As you listen, try to clarify your coworkers' answers and ideas. Express your appreciation for their feedback without becoming defensive. After you've listened, ask yourself, "What am I ready to do to improve my leadership vision?" Develop an action plan to build on your strengths and continue to improve.

Skyhook 2
TRUST

My belief is that vision, trust, and commitment are interdependent and that one without the others will not succeed.
—ARTHUR KNIGHT,
C.E.O. OF MORGAN PRODUCTS, LTD.

If you trust people, it's because you believe they have ongoing characteristics that permit you to trust them. All human relationships are built on trust, and the more trust that is there, the more productive the relationship can be.
—JAMES E. BURKE,
FORMER CHAIRMAN OF JOHNSON & JOHNSON

Skyhook 2 Trust—Convey confidence and respect for your coworkers' abilities, values and aspirations. To trust is to believe in the ability and integrity of others. Mutual trust makes relationships work, and it starts with the leader. Show them that you really believe they are resilient and adaptive and can change themselves and shape their destiny. Only when they believe they have your trust are they likely to reciprocate and be willing to follow.

Douglas McGregor was the first to advocate that people at work are inherently trustworthy. He describes two different sets of beliefs in "The Human Side of Enterprise." The article appeared in 1957, three years before his landmark book by the same title. As you read about Theory X and Theory Y, you can substitute the words "distrust" and "trust" to summarize each belief set. Only Theory Y proposes that people "have ongoing characteristics that permit you to trust them, that they are naturally graced with ability and integrity." McGregor notes:

- Social sciences are giving us a new view of human nature and a glimpse of untapped creative human energy.

- Conventional Theory X management emphasizes direction and control because it holds that most people are indolent, passive, and resistant to change by nature (i.e., untrustworthy).

- People who behave as if Theory X is correct are retaliating because they have been treated badly, not because of their nature.

- Motivation concepts indicate conventional management, whether "hard" or "soft," emphasizes issues which are largely irrelevant.

- Theory Y, a new theory in 1957, is based on more adequate assumptions about human nature and emphasizes individual development, personal responsibility, self-direction, and self-control (i.e., the average person is inherently trustworthy).

- In short, Theory X management treats people as children in need of control, while Theory Y management treats them as mature adults who can run their own lives.

- If managers truly hold Theory Y assumptions (that people are trustworthy), decentralization, delegation, job enlargement, participation, self-guided performance appraisal, and similar strategies will be effective in releasing human energy.

After McGregor's works appeared, there was no revolutionary shift to Theory Y–based management. Trust did not suddenly bloom in the workplace. It wasn't until 1982 that trust began to emerge as a key success factor in stellar companies, as reported by Tom Peters and Bob Waterman in *In Search of Excellence*. Their chapter, "Productivity Through People," reads as if they found organizations with managers who read McGregor carefully, took him to heart, and developed Theory Y trust-driven practices. The authors make points like:

- Excellent companies with a people orientation share one key—trust.

- People respond well when treated as grownups.

- Treating people as adults means treating them as partners with dignity and respect and as the primary source of productivity.

- Respect for the individual means giving people control over their destinies.

- A true people orientation requires intense top management support and does not allow lip service or tolerate gimmicks.

- Excellent companies have a "toughness related to high expectations for performance"—they expect people to live up to the trust and confidence given to them.

- Success stories come from diverse companies—manufacturing, electronics, retailing, transportation, fast foods. A people orientation doesn't guarantee success, but it does make it possible.

- Common themes cut across different companies: special language, family feeling, informality, celebration, training intensity, and widespread information sharing, which reinforces trust.

- Planned "smallness" makes sure the individual still counts and can stand out.

- In excellent companies, a shared and deeply held philosophy ensures that people can be trusted to do the right thing when left on their own.

Even after one has read and reflected on McGregor's and Peters and Waterman's arguments for initiating trust, questions will undoubtedly remain. "What if I trust you, and you let me down?" Trust certainly involves risk-taking, but since most people have the integrity and ability to do what needs to be done, the risk is minor. The real risk is in not trusting others. The consequences of distrust were clearly posted on an auto plant wall: "Without trust, any relationship will inevitably degenerate into conflict." The promise of having trust and confidence in others was written on the same wall: "With trust, anything is possible."

3

THE HUMAN SIDE OF ENTERPRISE

DOUGLAS McGREGOR

It has become trite to say that industry has the fundamental know-how to utilize physical science and technology for the material benefit of mankind, and that we must now learn how to utilize the social sciences to make our human organizations truly effective.

To a degree, the social sciences today are in a position like that of the physical sciences with respect to atomic energy in the thirties. We know that past conceptions of the nature of man are inadequate and, in many ways, incorrect. We are becoming quite certain that, under proper conditions, unimagined resources of creative human energy could become available within the organizational setting.

We cannot tell industrial management how to apply this new knowledge in simple, economic ways. We know it will require years of exploration, much costly development research, and a substantial amount of creative imagination on the part of management to discover how to apply this growing knowledge to the organization of human effort in industry.

MANAGEMENT'S TASK: THE CONVENTIONAL VIEW

The conventional conception of management's task in harnessing human energy to organizational requirements can be stated broadly in terms of three propositions. In order to avoid the complications introduced by a label, let us call this set of propositions "Theory X":

Reprinted from *Management Review*, November 1957. Copyright© 1957 American Management Association International. Reprinted by permission of American Management Association International, New York, NY. All rights reserved. http://www.amanet.org.

1. Management is responsible for organizing the elements of productive enterprise—money, materials, equipment, people—in the interest of economic ends.

2. With respect to people, this is a process of directing their efforts, motivating them, controlling their actions, modifying their behavior to fit the needs of the organization.

3. Without this active intervention by management, people would be passive—even resistant—to organizational needs. They must therefore be persuaded, rewarded, punished, controlled—their activities must be directed. This is management's task. We often sum it up by saying that management consists of getting things done through other people.

Behind this conventional theory there are several additional beliefs—less explicit, but widespread:

4. The average man is by nature indolent—he works as little as possible.

5. He lacks ambition, dislikes responsibility, prefers to be led.

6. He is inherently self-centered, indifferent to organizational needs.

7. He is by nature resistant to change.

8. He is gullible, not very bright, the ready dupe of the charlatan and the demagogue.

The human side of economic enterprise today is fashioned from propositions and beliefs such as these. Conventional organization structures and managerial policies, practices, and programs reflect these assumptions.

In accomplishing its task—with these assumptions as guides—management has conceived of a range of possibilities.

At one extreme, management can be "hard" or "strong." The methods for directing behavior involve coercion and threat (usually disguised), close supervision, tight controls over behavior. At the other extreme, management can be "soft" or "weak." The methods for directing behavior involve being permissive, satisfying people's demands, achieving harmony. Then they will be tractable, accept direction.

This range has been fairly completely explored during the past half century, and management has learned some things from the exploration. There are difficulties in the "hard" approach. Force breeds counterforces: restriction of output, antagonism, militant unionism, subtle but effective sabotage of management objectives. This "hard" approach is especially difficult during times of full employment.

There are also difficulties in the "soft" approach. It leads frequently to the abdication of management—to harmony, perhaps, but to indifferent performance. People take advantage of the soft approach. They continually expect more, but they give less and less.

Currently, the popular theme is "firm but fair." This is an attempt to gain the advantages of both the hard and soft approaches. It is reminiscent of Teddy Roosevelt's "speak softly and carry a big stick."

IS THE CONVENTIONAL VIEW CORRECT?

The findings which are beginning to emerge from the social sciences challenge this whole set of beliefs about man and human nature and about the task of management. The evidence is far from conclusive, certainly, but it is suggestive. It comes from the laboratory, the clinic, the schoolroom, the home, and even to a limited extent from industry itself.

The social scientist does not deny that human behavior in industrial organization today is approximately what management perceives it to be. He has, in fact, observed it and studied it fairly extensively. But he is pretty sure that this behavior is *not* a consequence of man's inherent nature. It is a consequence rather of the nature of industrial organizations, of management philosophy, policy, and practice. The conventional approach of Theory X is based on mistaken notions of what is cause and what is effect.

Perhaps the best way to indicate why the conventional approach of management is inadequate is to consider the subject of motivation.

PHYSIOLOGICAL NEEDS

Man is a wanting animal—as soon as one of his needs is satisfied, another appears in its place. This process is unending. It continues from birth to death.

Man's needs are organized in a series of levels—a hierarchy of importance. At the lowest level, but pre-eminent in importance when they are thwarted, are his *physiological* needs. Man lives for bread alone, when there is no bread. Unless the circumstances are unusual, his needs for love, for status, for recognition are inoperative when his stomach has been empty for a while. But when he eats regularly and adequately, hunger ceases to be an important motivation. The same is true of the other physiological needs of man—for rest, exercise, shelter, protection from the elements.

A satisfied need is not a motivator of behavior! This is a fact of profound significance that is regularly ignored in the conventional approach to the management of people. Consider your own need for air: Except as you are deprived of it, it has no appreciable motivating effect upon your behavior.

SAFETY NEEDS

When the physiological needs are reasonably satisfied, needs at the next higher level begin to dominate man's behavior—to motivate him. These are called *safety needs*. They are needs for protection against danger, threat, deprivation. Some people mistakenly refer to these as needs for security. However, unless man is in a dependent relationship where he fears arbitrary deprivation, he does not demand security. The need is for the "fairest possible break." When he is confident of this, he is more than willing to take risks. But when he feels threatened or dependent, his greatest need is for guarantee, for protection, for security.

The fact needs little emphasis that, since every industrial employee is in a dependent relationship, safety needs may assume considerable importance. Arbitrary management actions, behavior which arouses uncertainty with respect to continued employment or which reflects favoritism or discrimination, unpredictable administration of policy—these can be powerful motivators of the safety needs in the employment relationship *at every level*, from worker to vice president.

SOCIAL NEEDS

When man's physiological needs are satisfied and he is no longer fearful about his physical welfare, his *social needs* become important motivators of his behavior—needs for belonging, for association, for acceptance by his fellows, for giving and receiving friendship and love.

Management knows today of the existence of these needs, but it often assumes quite wrongly that they represent a threat to the organization. Many studies have demonstrated that the tightly knit, cohesive work group may, under proper conditions, be far more effective than an equal number of separate individuals in achieving organizational goals.

Yet management, fearing group hostility to its own objectives, often goes to considerable lengths to control and direct human efforts in ways that are inimical to the natural "groupiness" of human beings. When man's social needs—and perhaps his safety needs, too—are thus thwarted, he behaves in ways which tend to defeat organizational objectives. He becomes resistant, antagonistic, uncooperative. But this behavior is a consequence, not a cause.

EGO NEEDS

Above the social needs—in the sense that they do not become motivators until lower needs are reasonably satisfied—are the needs of greatest significance to management and to man himself. They are the *egoistic needs*, and they are of two kinds:

1. Those needs that relate to one's self-esteem—needs for self-confidence, for independence, for achievement, for competence, for knowledge.

2. Those needs that relate to one's reputation—needs for status, for recognition, for appreciation, for the deserved respect of one's fellows.

Unlike the lower needs, these are rarely satisfied; man seeks indefinitely for more satisfaction of these needs once they have become important to him. But they do not appear in any significant way until physiological, safety, and social needs are all reasonably satisfied.

The typical industrial organization offers few opportunities for the satisfaction of these egoistic needs to people at lower levels in the hierarchy. The conventional methods of organizing work, particularly in mass-production industries, give little heed to these aspects of human motivation. If the practices of scientific management were deliberately calculated to thwart these needs, they could hardly accomplish this purpose better than they do.

SELF-FULLFILLMENT NEEDS

Finally—a capstone, as it were, on the hierarchy of man's needs—there are what we may call the *needs for self-fulfillment*. These are the needs for realizing one's own potentialities, for continued self-development, for being creative in the broadest sense of that term.

It is clear that the conditions of modern life give only limited opportunity for these relatively weak needs to obtain expression. The deprivation most people experience with respect to other lower-level needs diverts their energies into the struggle to satisfy *those* needs, and the needs for self-fulfillment remain dormant.

MANAGEMENT AND MOTIVATION

We recognize readily enough that a man suffering from a severe dietary deficiency is sick. The deprivation of physiological needs has behavioral consequences. The same is true—although less well recognized—of deprivation of higher-level needs. The man whose needs for safety, association, independence, or status are thwarted is sick just as surely as the man who has rickets. And his sickness will have behavioral consequences. We will be mistaken if we attribute his resultant passivity, his hostility, his refusal to accept responsibility to his inherent "human nature." These forms of behavior are *symptoms* of illness—of deprivation of his social and egoistic needs.

The man whose lower-level needs are satisfied is not motivated to satisfy those needs any longer. For practical purposes they exist no longer. Management often asks, "Why aren't people more productive? We pay good wages, provide good working conditions, have excellent fringe benefits and steady employment. Yet people do not seem to be willing to put forth more than minimum effort."

The fact that management has provided for these physiological and safety needs has shifted the motivational emphasis to the social and perhaps to the egoistic needs. Unless there are opportunities *at work* to satisfy these higher-level needs, people will be deprived, and their behavior will reflect this deprivation. Under such conditions, if management continues to focus its attention on physiological needs, its efforts are bound to be ineffective.

People *will* make insistent demands for more money under these conditions. It becomes more important than ever to buy the material goods and services which can provide limited satisfaction of the thwarted needs. Although money has only limited value in satisfying many higher-level needs, it can become the focus of interest if it is the *only* means available.

THE CARROT-AND-STICK APPROACH

The carrot-and-stick theory of motivation (like Newtonian physical theory) works reasonably well under certain circumstances. The *means* for satisfying man's physiological and (within limits) his safety needs can be provided or withheld by management. Employment itself is such a means, and so are wages, working conditions, and benefits. By these means the individual can be controlled so long as he is struggling for subsistence.

But the carrot-and-stick theory does not work at all once man has reached an adequate subsistence level and is motivated primarily by higher needs. Management cannot provide a man with self-respect, or with the respect of his fellows, or with the satisfaction of needs for self-fulfillment. It can create such conditions that he is encouraged and enabled to seek such satisfaction for *himself*, or it can thwart him by failing to create those conditions.

But this creation of conditions is not "control." It is not a good device for directing behavior. And so management finds itself in an odd position. The high standard of living created by our modern technological know-how provides quite adequately for the satisfaction of physiological and safety needs. The only significant exception is where management practices have not created confidence in a "fair break"—and thus where safety needs are thwarted. But by making possible the satisfaction of low-level needs, management has deprived itself of the ability to use as motivators the devices on which conventional theory has taught it to rely—rewards, promises, incentives, or threats and other coercive devices.

The philosophy of management by direction and control—*regardless of whether it is hard or soft*—is inadequate to motivate because the human needs on which this approach relies are today unimportant motivators of behavior. Direction and control are essentially useless in motivating people whose important needs are social and egoistic. Both the hard and the soft approach fail today because they are simply irrelevant to the situation.

People, deprived of opportunities to satisfy at work the needs which are now important to them, behave exactly as we might predict—with indolence, passivity, resistance to change, lack of responsibility, willingness to follow the demagogue, unreasonable demands for economic benefits. It would seem that we are caught in a web of our own weaving.

A NEW THEORY OF MANAGEMENT

For these and many other reasons, we require a different theory of the task of managing people based on more adequate assumptions about human nature and human motivation. I am going to be so bold as to suggest the broad dimensions of such a theory. Call it "Theory Y" if you will.

1. Management is responsible for organizing the elements of productive enterprise—money, materials, equipment, people—in the interest of economic ends.

Performance Appraisal

Even a cursory examination of conventional programs of performance appraisal within the ranks of management will reveal how completely consistent they are with Theory X. In fact, most such programs tend to treat the individual as though he were a product under inspection on the assembly line.

A few companies—among them General Mills, Ansul Chemical, and General Electric—have been experimenting with approaches which involve the individual in setting "targets" or objectives *for himself* and in a *self*-evaluation of performance semiannually or annually. Of course, the superior plays an important leadership role in this process—one, in fact, which demands substantially more competence than the conventional approach. The role is, however, considerably more congenial to many managers than the role of "judge" or "inspector" which is usually forced upon them. Above all, the individual is encouraged to take a greater responsibility for planning and appraising his own contribution to organizational objectives; and the accompanying effects on egoistic and self-fulfillment needs are substantial.

APPLYING THE IDEAS

The not infrequent failure of such ideas as these to work as well as expected is often attributable to the fact that a management has "bought the idea" but applied it within the framework of Theory X and its assumption.

Delegation is not an effective way of exercising management by control. Participation becomes a farce when it is applied as a sales gimmick or a device for kidding people into thinking they are important. Only the management that has confidence in human capacities and is itself directed toward organizational objectives rather than toward the preservation of personal power can grasp the implications of this emerging theory. Such management will find and apply successfully other innovative ideas as we move slowly toward the full implementation of a theory like Y.

THE HUMAN SIDE OF ENTERPRISE

It is quite possible for us to realize substantial improvements in the effectiveness of industrial organizations during the next decade or two. The social sciences can contribute much to such developments; we are only beginning to grasp the implications of the growing body of knowledge in these fields. But if this conviction is to become a reality instead of a pious hope, we will need to view the process much as we view the process of releasing the energy of the atom for constructive human ends—as a slow, costly, sometimes discouraging approach toward a goal which would seem to many to be quite unrealistic.

The ingenuity and the perseverance of industrial management in the pursuit of economic ends have changed many scientific and technological dreams into commonplace realities. It is now becoming clear that the application of these same talents to the human side of enterprise will not only enhance substantially these materialistic achievements, but will bring us one step closer to "the good society."

4

PRODUCTIVITY THROUGH PEOPLE

THOMAS J. PETERS and ROBERT H. WATERMAN, JR.

The Navy, said ex-Chief of Naval Operations Elmo (Bud) Zumwalt, assumes "that everyone below the rank of commander is immature." A friend who runs several plants for General Motors passed on a poem from the auto workers' underground. Its message is poignantly similar:

> Are these men and women
> Workers of the world?
> or is it an overgrown nursery
> with children—goosing, slapping, boys giggling, snotty girls?
> What is it about that entrance way,
> those gates to the plant? Is it the
> guards, the showing of your badge—the smell?
> is there some invisible eye
> that pierces you through and
> transforms your being? Some aura
> or ether, that brain and spirit washes you
> and commands, "For eight hours
> you shall be different."
> What is it that instantaneously makes
> a child out of a man?
> Moments before he was a father, a husband,

Chapter 8 "Productivity Through People" from *In Search of Excellence: Lessons from America's Best-Run Companies* by Thomas J. Peters and Robert H. Waterman, Jr. Copyright © 1982 by Thomas J. Peters and Robert H. Waterman, Jr. Reprinted by permission of HarperCollins Publishers, Inc.

an owner of property,
a voter, a lover, an adult.
When he spoke at least some listened.
Salesmen courted his favor.
Insurance men appealed to his family responsibility
and by chance the church sought his help. . . .

But that was before he shuffled past the guard,
climbed the steps,
hung up his coat and
took his place along the line.

The man who gave us this said there was but one key to a people
orientation: trust. Some will abuse it. "Three to eight percent," he
says, with a smile at the precision of his estimate. Nonbelievers will
give you "an infinite number of reasons why workers can't be
trusted. Most organizations are governed by rules that assume the
average worker is an incompetent ne'er-do-well, just itching to screw
up." He gives a symbolic illustration: "Ever go to parks? Most are
peppered with signs that say, 'Stay off the grass,' 'No parking here,'
'No this,' 'No that.' A few say, 'Campers welcome,' or, 'Picnic
tables for your convenience.' One tells you that you *shouldn't*. The
other says that you *should*, urges you to join in, take advantage of
the facilities." Such a difference in assumptions is monumental in its
impact on people, he argues persuasively.

Zumwalt revolutionized the Navy's practices in just a few short
years at the helm. It all stemmed from his simple belief that people
will respond well to being treated as grownups. He traces his beliefs
back to an early command assignment:

> What I tried hardest to do was ensure that every officer and
> man on the ship not only knew what we were about, not
> only why we were doing each tactical evolution, however
> onerous, but also managed to understand enough about how
> it all fitted together that he could begin to experience some
> of the fun and challenge that those of us in the top slots
> were having. Our techniques were not unusual. We made
> frequent announcements over the loudspeaker about the
> specific event that was going on. At the beginning and the
> end of the day, I discussed with the officers who, in turn,
> discussed with their men what was about to happen and
> what had just happened, what the competition was doing
> and what we should do to meet it. We published written

notes in the plan of the day that would give the crew some of the color or human interest of what the ship was doing. I had bull sessions in the chief petty officers' quarters, where I often stopped for a cup of coffee. More important than any of these details, of course, was the basic effort to communicate a sense of excitement, fun and zest in all that we were doing.

Zumwalt adds that, within a short eighteen months, practices like this vaulted his ship from being last to first in efficiency within his squadron. "I knew from experience," he said, "the impact of treating sailors like the grown men they were." Tandem's chairman James Treybig sings the same tune: "We assume people are adults." Our Tokyo colleague Ken Ohmae asserts: "Japanese management keeps telling the workers that those at the frontier [first line] know the business best, and that innovation and improvement *must* come from the *genba* (where the action is)." Peter Smith, a recent Wharton MBA grad who eschewed the analyst route and became a General Signal factory manager, agrees: "People will flood you with ideas if you let them."

A work experience related by an MBA student underscores these points (including the typically unhappy ending):

I was operations manager for a major trucking company's San Francisco facility. This terminal was not the leader within the district in any category except unprofitability. I expressed my concerns to some of the Teamsters. They responded by saying that they loved being truckers and felt competent in their roles, but no supervisor had *ever* asked them to help solve the terminal's routing problems or had made them feel as though they were crucial to the operation. My first move with the drivers was to ensure that when they arrived for work in the morning, their tractors were fueled, warmed up, and washed up—ready to go. I hoped the action would impart a sense of urgency to their job. Second, I gave each of them some company caps and brochures to distribute among the customers as they saw fit. (This was strictly forbidden; only salesmen could do this. I had to steal the caps from a salesman's car one morning.)

Most important, supervisors had traditionally routed all the local freight (usually unsuccessfully); I instructed them to leave every third or fourth freight bill unrouted, so that when they were asked for routing instructions by the dockman, they could gracefully ask for suggestions. I kept most of these ideas secret from my bosses and the union hierarchy. To my surprise, the operation became profitable. I posted the financial figures on the *union* bulletin board (again, strictly against the rules) and never received a complaint. It even got to the point where the salesmen realized that the drivers were soliciting more new customers than they were, so several decided to ride with the drivers to learn their "secrets."

The profitability lasted for several periods, until my boss saw what was happening and became nervous of the leeway given the Teamsters. About that time, the company instituted a control system that required each Teamster to account for every fifteen minutes of his work day. Profitability disappeared and customer complaints increased. I left for school.

Treat people as adults. Treat them as partners; treat them with dignity; treat them with respect. Treat *them*—not capital spending and automation—as the primary source of productivity gains. These are fundamental lessons from the excellent companies research. In other words, if you want productivity and the financial reward that goes with it, you must treat your workers as your most important asset. In *A Business and Its Beliefs*, Thomas J. Watson, Jr., puts it well: "IBM's philosophy is largely contained in three simple beliefs. I want to begin with what I think is the most important: *our respect for the individual*. This is a simple concept, but in IBM it occupies a major portion of management time. We devote more effort to it than anything else. This belief was bone-deep in my father."

There was hardly a more pervasive theme in the excellent companies than *respect for the individual*. That basic belief and assumption were omnipresent. But like so much else we have talked about, it's not any one thing—one assumption, belief, statement, goal, value, system, or program—that makes the theme come to life. What makes it live at these companies is a plethora of structural devices, systems, styles, and values, all reinforcing one another so that the companies are truly unusual in their ability to achieve extraordinary results through ordinary people. . . . These companies give people control over their destinies; they make meaning for people. They turn the average Joe and the average Jane into winners.

They let, even insist that, people stick out. They accentuate the positive.

Let us make clear one final prefatory point. We are not talking about mollycoddling. We are talking about tough-minded respect for the individual and the willingness to train him, to set reasonable and clear expectations for him, and to grant him practical autonomy to step out and contribute directly to his job.

Genuine people orientation is in marked contrast to the two major alternatives all too often seen in companies: the lip service disaster and the gimmicks disaster.

The lip service disaster is arguably the worse of the two. Almost every management we've been around says that people are important—vital, in fact. But having said that, they then don't pay much attention to their people. In fact, they probably don't even realize their omissions. "People issues take up all my time," is the typical rejoinder. What they often really mean is, "This business would be so easy if it weren't for people."

Only when we look at the excellent companies do we see the contrast. The orientation toward people in these companies often started decades ago—full employment policies in times of recession, extraordinary amounts of training when no training was the norm, everybody on a first-name basis in times much more formal than ours, and so on. Caring runs in the veins of the managers of these institutions. People are why those managers are there, and they know it and live it.

The orientation is bone-deep and embedded in the language itself. At Delta, it's the "Family Feeling." At Hewlett-Packard, it's "the HP Way," and "Management by Wandering Around." At Dana, it's simply the constant use of the word "people"—in annual reports, in top executive speeches, in statements of policy. (Rene McPherson, ex-chairman, is vehement about it. In a casual conversation he brings up a new Ford blockbuster ad campaign. "Damn it," he says. "They talk about 'workers.' Why not 'people'?") Employees are called "crew members" rather than personnel at McDonald's, "hosts" at Disney Productions, and "associates" at J.C. Penney.

Although it may be corny, it's unabashed hoopla and people respond to it. When we first looked at the phenomenon, we thought large doses of hoopla and celebration might be limited to companies like Tupperware, where the president and his senior managers are said to participate for thirty days a year in Jubilees, aimed at feting the success of their top *15,000* salespersons and

managers. But we found hoopla going on in the high tech companies as well (e.g., HP's song, "Grab a Grizzly," in celebration of its
3000 series computer). And at Caterpillar we were told of an event
to introduce new equipment where huge pieces of earth-moving
machinery were dressed in costume.

Perhaps surprisingly, the people orientation also has a *tough* side.
The excellent companies are measurement-happy and performance-
oriented, but this toughness is borne of mutually high expectations
and peer review rather than emanating from table-pounding managers and complicated control systems. The tough side is, in fact,
probably tougher than that found in the less excellent and typically
more formal systems-driven companies, for nothing is more entic-
ing than the feeling of being needed, which is the magic that
produces high expectations. What's more, if it's your peers that
have those high expectations of you, then there's all the more
incentive to perform well. People like to compare themselves to
others, as we noted earlier, and they also like to perform against
standards—if the standard is achievable, and especially if it is one
they played a role in setting.

The point, then, is the *completeness* of the people orientation in
the excellent companies. In lip service institutions, no matter what
they say, almost all of what we have just described is missing.
Layoffs are certainly not taken lightly, but we find few stories that
parallel IBM's, Delta's, Levi's, or HP's truly unusual efforts to avoid
the ups and downs of employment. And the language *is* different.
The war stories in the less well performing institutions do not refer
nearly so much to the care, handling, and feeding of employees as
they do at a Dana, a Digital, or an IBM. The word "manager" in lip
service institutions often has come to mean not someone who rolls
up his or her sleeves to get the job done right alongside the worker,
but someone who hires assistants to do it. These companies never
mention peer review. They are secretive and purposely hide information from employees. The message here is clear: the employees
supposedly aren't grown up enough to handle the truth. And the
hoopla, razzle-dazzle, and constantly changing menu of prizes,
awards, and other incentives? Missing as well. Sure, sometimes a
new program like MBO, or quality circles, or Scanlon Plan is tried
when it becomes faddish. But each is soon rejected or bureaucra-
tized. The failing is often attributed to "the unions," or "lack of
employee goodwill." Seldom is it attributed to lack of persistence
and true caring on the part of management.

That leads directly to the second problem: the gimmicks trap. The current gimmick is the quality circle. There is absolutely nothing wrong with the idea, as the Japanese have so forcefully reminded us. But quality circles are only the latest in a long line of tools that can either be very helpful, or can simply serve as a smoke-screen while management continues to get away with not doing its job of real people involvement. Ten years ago, it was job enlargement. Before that it was the seemingly ubiquitous organization development movement, replete with team building, T-groups, conflict resolution, and managerial grids. The bones of these programs are scattered on America's low-productivity desert. Very little has changed. Consultants and other practitioners sold their programs to lower levels of management, like the training officers, and top management let them go ahead with it, as much to avoid getting their own hands messy as anything else. But these supposed panaceas could not successfully be applied in a wholly bottom-up way—that is to say, applied without intense top management interest. It simply won't work. The implicit changes required are nothing short of earth-shaking. There is no way that such programs will ever take hold without the unstinting support of the whole top management team.

As there is no way that just a few programs will take hold and bring about fundamental change, so also there is no reason to expect any particular technique to have an effective life of more than a few years. Most of the excellent companies *do* have MBO systems, and they *do* have quality circles, and they probably *have* tried team building, and maybe they still use all of these. But they have lots more. We were astounded, as we did our research, by the sheer number of people programs we encountered and the frequency with which they are replenished or refurbished. And these programs are neither lip service nor gimmicky. We found rich systems of monetary incentives; but we expected that. We also discovered an incredible array of nonmonetary incentives and an amazing variety of experimental or newly introduced programs. No one device—even in the best institutions—is likely to be effective indefinitely. The point is to treat the problem as one would the new-product challenge. The pipeline must always be filled with the next score of candidate programs, most of which will turn out to be duds, just as do new-product ideas. If job enrichment doesn't work at the Milwaukee plant, try seven other programs that are working in other plants, or that have worked in other companies.

SUCCESS STORIES

Although most top managements assert that their companies care for their people, the excellent companies are distinguished by the intensity and pervasiveness of this concern. The only way to describe it adequately is through example.

RMI

RMI is a good one to start with. A subsidiary of U.S. Steel and National Distillers, it is an integrated producer of titanium products. For years its performance was substandard. Poor productivity, poor profits. But in the last five years RMI has had a remarkable success, owing almost entirely to its adoption of an intensely people-oriented productivity program.

The program started when "Big Jim" Daniell, a former professional football player, ex-captain of the Cleveland Browns, was made chief executive. The program he installed was described by *The Wall Street Journal* as "pure corn—a mixture of schmaltzy sloganeering, communication, and a smile at every turn." His plants are peppered with notices that say: "If you see a man without a smile, give him one of yours," or: "People rarely succeed at anything unless they enjoy it." All are signed "Big Jim."

The story doesn't get much more complicated than that. The company's logo is a smile-face, which is on the stationery, on the front of the factory, on signs in the factory, and on the workers' hardhats. RMI's headquarters is in Niles, Ohio, which everyone now calls "Smiles, Ohio." Big Jim spends much of his time riding around the factory in a golf cart, waving and joking with his workers, listening to them, and calling them all by their first name—all 2,000 of them. Moreover, he spends a lot of time with his union. The local union president paid him the following compliment: "He calls us into his meetings and lets us know what's going on, which is unheard of in other industries."

What's the result of it all? Well, in the last three years, with hardly a penny of investment spending, he's managed an almost 80 percent productivity gain. And at last report, his average backlog of union grievances had declined from about 300 to about 20. Big Jim, say those of his customers that we've come across (e.g., at Northrop), simply exudes care about his customers and his people.

Hewlett-Packard

In one study, eighteen out of twenty HP executives interviewed spontaneously claimed that the success of their company depends on the company's people-oriented philosophy. It's called "the HP Way." Here's how founder Bill Hewlett describes it:

> I feel that in general terms it is the policies and actions that flow from the belief that men and women want to do a good job, a creative job, and that if they are provided with the proper environment they will do so. It is the tradition of treating every individual with consideration and respect and recognizing personal achievements. This sounds almost trite, but Dave [co-founder Packard] and I honestly believe in this philosophy. . . . The dignity and worth of the individual is a very important part, then, of the HP Way. With this in mind, many years ago we did away with time clocks, and more recently we introduced the flexible work hours program. Again, this is meant to be an expression of trust and confidence in people as well as providing them with an opportunity to adjust their work schedules to their personal lives. . . . Many new HP people as well as visitors often note and comment to us about another HP way—that is, our informality, and our being on a first name basis. I could cite other examples, but the problem is that none by themselves really catches the essence of what the HP Way is all about. You can't describe it in numbers and statistics. In the last analysis it is a spirit, a point of view. There is a feeling that everyone is part of a team, and that team is HP. As I said at the beginning, it is an idea that is based on the individual. It exists because people have seen that it works, and they believe that this feeling makes HP what it is.

The people orientation at HP started early. In the 1940s Hewlett and Packard decided "not to be a hire and fire company." That was a courageous decision in those times, when the electronics business was almost entirely government-supported. Later, HP's collective mettle was to be tested when business was severely down during the 1970 recession. Rather than lay people off, Hewlett, Packard, and everyone else in the organization took a 10 percent cut in pay. Everyone worked 10 percent fewer hours. And HP successfully weathered the recession without having to sacrifice full employment.

The people philosophy at HP not only began early on but is also self-renewing. The corporate objectives were just rewritten and republished for all the employees, including a restatement of corporate philosophy. The very first sentence reads: "The achievements of an organization are the result of the combined efforts of each individual. . . ." And a few sentences later HP reinforces its commitment to innovative people, a philosophy that has been a driving force in the organization's success. "FIRST, there should be highly capable, innovative people throughout the organization . . . SECOND, the organization should have objectives and leadership which generate enthusiasm at all levels. People in important management positions should not only be enthusiastic themselves, they should be selected for their ability to engender enthusiasm among their associates." The introduction to the revised corporate objective statement concludes: "Hewlett-Packard [should not] have a tight, military-type organization, but rather . . . give people the freedom to work toward [overall objectives] in ways they determine best for their own areas of responsibility."

The faith that HP has in its people is conspicuously in evidence in the corporate "open lab stock" policy that a few of our students encountered in the Santa Rosa division. The lab stock area is where the electrical and mechanical components are kept. The open lab stock policy means that not only do the engineers have free access to this equipment, but they are actually encouraged to *take it home for their personal use!* The idea is that whether or not what the engineers are doing with the equipment is directly related to the project they are working on, by fooling around with the equipment at work or at home, they will learn—and so reinforce the company's commitment to innovation. Legend has it that Bill [Hewlett]* visited a plant on a Saturday and found the lab stock area locked. He immediately went down to maintenance, grabbed a bolt cutter, and proceeded to cut the padlock off the lab stock door. He left a note that was found on Monday morning: "Don't ever lock this door again. Thanks, Bill."

The same language pervaded a conversation with a twenty-four-year-old engineer, on the scene for barely more than a year. Commenting on some problems with a new personnel procedure, he said: "I'm not sure Bill and Dave would have done it that way." It's truly remarkable to find the value set stamped in so quickly, and with such clarity. The young man went on to describe HP's dedication to "getting on with it," the need to be involved with successful new product introductions in order to get ahead, the litany of succeeding by a record of hard accomplishments rather

---

* All Hewlett or Packard stories, regardless of the teller's age, refer to "Bill" or "Dave."

than paper-pushing skills, the ability to talk to anyone, anywhere. He talks of his division's general manager and senior officers as though they were close friends and he were their only employee. He rambles on about MBWA. The discussion drifts to such publicly touted communications devices as the "coffee klatch," where informal problem solving (all hands attending) takes place weekly. The PR hype turns out to be justified.

In short, the most extraordinary trait at HP is uniformity of commitment, the consistency of approach and attitude. Wherever you go in the HP empire, you find people talking product quality, feeling proud of their division's achievements in that area. HP people at all levels show boundless energy and enthusiasm, so much so that many of our colleagues, after a chance encounter with an HP executive, engineer, or line worker, ask: "Is this guy for real?" And then they meet more, and invariably their skepticism, no matter how hard they try to keep it, begins to fade. We ourselves tried to remain sober, not to become fans. But it proved impossible.

Wal-Mart

Wal-Mart, with over 26,000 employees, is now the number four retailer in the United States. During the 1970s, growth took the company from $45 million in sales to $1.6 billion, from 18 stores to 330. Sam Walton, or "Mr. Sam," as he is called in the company, is the driving force behind this success, and Walton, quite simply, cares about his employees. In fact, almost all his managers, at his insistence, wear buttons that say, "We Care About Our People."

Walton learned the people business at J.C. Penney. Like Penney's, his people are referred to as "associates," not employees. And he listens to them. "The key is to get out into the store and listen to what the associates have to say," he says. "It's terribly important for everyone to get involved. Our best ideas come from clerks and stockboys." Walton stories have become legends. According to *The Wall Street Journal*: "Mr. Walton couldn't sleep a few weeks back. He got up and bought four dozen donuts at an all night bakery. At 2:30 a.m., he took them to a distribution center and chatted for a while with workers from the shipping docks. As a result he discovered that two more shower stalls were needed at that location." Again, the astonishing point is not the story per se: any small business person could relate a host of similar tales. The surprising news is that a top executive still exhibits such a bone-deep form of concern for his people in a *$2 billion* enterprise.

The message that down-the-line people count is mirrored in every activity. The executive offices are virtually empty. Headquarters resemble a warehouse. The reason is that Walton's managers spend most of their time out in the field in Wal-Mart's eleven state service areas. And what are they doing? "Leading local cheerleading squads at new store openings, scouting out competing K-mart stores, and conducting soul-searching sessions with the employees." Walton himself visits every store every year (330 now, remember) as he has done since 1962.

Everyone at Wal-Mart feels like a winner. The regular management meetings start at 7:30 a.m. on Saturday. The buyer of the month receives a plaque. There are "honor roll" stores, every *week*. And every week the "SWAT" team that swoops down to remodel stores testifies to jobs well done. Mr. Sam stands up and yells, "Who's number one?" And everyone, of course, yells back "Wal-Mart!"

So, it's intense rah-rah, and, yes, it's hocum, and—like so many other situations we see—it's fun. As *The Wall Street Journal* reports: "Mr. Walton seems to have the most fun. Not long ago he flew his aircraft to Mt. Pleasant, Texas, and parked the plane with instructions to the co-pilot to meet him 100 or so miles down the road. He then flagged a Wal-Mart truck and rode the rest of the way to 'Chat with the driver—it seemed like so much fun.' "

The theme of fun in business runs through a great deal of the excellent companies research. The leaders and managers like what they do and they get enthusiastic about it. Or, as Howard Head said in a recent speech, "It seems to me you have to be personally associated with what you do. I just love design. If it weren't fun, I wouldn't do it."

Dana

One of the most impressive success stories in people and productivity is that of the Dana Corporation under the leadership of Rene McPherson. Dana is a $3 billion corporation, making unexotic products like brass propeller blades and gearboxes, primarily supporting the unexciting secondary market in the automobile and trucking industry. If you had looked at Dana as a proposition in strategic management, you would undoubtedly have labeled it a loser. Yet in the 1970s, this old-fashioned midwestern business became the number two *Fortune* 500 company in total return to investors. In the early 1970s, the sales per employee at Dana were the same as the all-industry average. By the late 1970s, and without massive capital spending, Dana's sales per employee had tripled while the all-industry average had not even doubled, (in Dana's industry segment, productivity had barely increased), a phenomenal productivity record for a huge business in an otherwise uninteresting industry. Furthermore, Dana is largely unionized, with the United Auto Workers (UAW) in most of its plants. But during the same decade, its grievance rate fell to a tiny fraction of the overall UAW average.

The key ingredient is productivity through people, pure and simple. . . . [W]hen McPherson took over in 1973, one of his first acts was to destroy 22½ inches of policy manuals and substitute a simple one-page statement of philosophy. It reads in the main:

- Nothing more effectively involves people, sustains creditability or generates enthusiasm than face to face communication. It is critical to provide and discuss all organization performance figures with all of our people.

- We have an obligation to provide training and the opportunity for development to our productive people who want to improve their skills, expand their career opportunities or simply further their general education.

- It is essential to provide job security for our people.

- Create incentive programs that rely on ideas and suggestions, as well as on hard work, to establish a reward pool.

Says McPherson: "The philosophy comes first. Almost every executive agrees that people are the most important asset. Yet almost none really lives it."

McPherson quickly reduced his corporate staff of 500 to 100 and the number of layers in his organization from eleven to five. His plant managers—about ninety of them—all became "store managers." In a litany repeated at Delta and at Disney, they were made responsible for learning *all* the jobs in the plants. And they were given the autonomy to get the overall job done. Their success led McPherson to say, in a statement that could get someone else kicked out of most board rooms in America, "I am opposed to the idea that less government, fewer regulations, capital formation incentives, and renewed research in development activity are what we need most to improve productivity. My suggestion: let our people get the job done."

At Dana, philosophy does come first; but then it's largely a matter of a voluntary diffusion of ideas. Everyone is responsible for ensuring that productivity increases take place. McPherson suggests the appropriate starting point: "Personal productivity of the top managers is a vital symbol." But nobody is told how to do it. If there is a how, it is a simple belief in the inherent will toward efficiency of the man down at the bottom of the organization. As McPherson points out:

> Until we believe that the expert in any particular job is most often the person performing it, we shall forever limit the potential of that person, in terms of both his own contributions to the organization and his own personal development. Consider a manufacturing setting: within their 25-square-foot area, nobody knows more about how to operate a machine, maximize its output, improve its quality, optimize the material flow and keep it operating efficiently than do the machine operators, material handlers, and maintenance people responsible for it. Nobody.

He adds:

> We didn't waste time with foolishness. We didn't have procedures, we didn't have lots of staff people. We let everybody do their job on the basis of what they need, what they say they'll do, and what their results are. And we gave them enough time to do it. . . . We had better start admitting that the most important people in an organization are those who actually provide a service or make and add value to products, not those who administer the activity. . . . That is, when I am in your 25 square feet of space, I'd better listen to you!

McPherson's focus is always the same. In casual conversation or formal presentation, he never wavers from his emphasis on people. As one of his former associates at Dana said to us, "I never heard him make a statement that didn't say something about people." McPherson says, "Look at the pictures in the annual reports. Don't worry about the chairman; he always gets his name under the picture—and it's spelled right, too. Look for pictures of people [down-the-line workers]. How many of them are identified by name?"

Like HP, Dana did away with time clocks, "Everybody complained," McPherson says. "'What do we do without time clocks?' I said, 'How do you manage any ten people? If you see them come in late regularly, you talk to them. Why do you need time clocks to know if the people who work for you are coming in late?'" He also reinforces the focus on starting from positive assumptions about people's behavior as he elaborates on the story: "My staff said, 'You can't get rid of the time clocks. The government requires a record of every person's attendance and time worked.' I said. 'Fine. As of now, everyone comes to work on time and leaves on time. That's what the record will say. Where there are big individual exceptions, we will deal with them on a case-by-case basis.'"

McPherson is a bug on face-to-face communication and on discussing *all* the results with *all* of the people. He required that there be a monthly face-to-face meeting between division management and *every* member of the division to discuss directly and specifically all of the detailed corporate individual results. (We see that time and again in the excellent companies. They are obsessed about widely sharing information and preventing secrecy. They willingly trade any marginal loss of competitive information for the added commitment.) McPherson even stressed face-to-face contact in institutional advertisements. He ran ads that, as he says, "made my middle managers *very* nervous at first." One said: "Talk Back to the Boss," another: "Ask Dumb Questions." McPherson deplores management's unwillingness to listen: "I wanted a picture, for a slide presentation, of a worker talking to his foreman. We had fourteen thousand photos in the file, but not one of a supervisor *listening* to a worker."

McPherson spent 40 to 50 percent of his time on the stump, carrying the message directly to his people. He insisted on what he called "Town Meetings," with everybody in attendance. He recalls an experience in Reading, Pennsylvania: "I wanted to talk to all the people. The boss said there is no place to do it. It went on that way for three years. Finally, I said, 'Clean out the shipping department.' Sixteen hundred people showed up. In all my years of travel, I never got one cheap shot question from an employee. Yet my plant manager and division manager, when I insisted they go with me, never wanted to go. . . . Look at these pictures," he adds, pushing the stack over to us. "They are from the meetings. Always machine operators, never managers asking questions. You know why? Managers won't ask questions. They're scared."

Another McPherson obsession is training, continuous self-improvement. McPherson's pride and joy is Dana University. Several thousand Dana employees trooped through Dana U. last year. Classes are practical, but at the same time they reinforce the people philosophy. Many classes are taught by seniors—corporate vice presidents (we found a similar phenomenon at Disney U. and McDonald's Hamburger U.). According to McPherson, there is no more prestigious position for any member of the management than an appointment as a regent of Dana University. The Board of Regents is usually composed of nine division general managers.

Nothing is forced at Dana. The Scanlon Profit Plan, for which Dana has gotten a lot of publicity, is a good example. Much to our surprise, it turns out that the Scanlon Plan is only in seven of the forty Dana divisions. McPherson says: "They go where they work. That's all. No division manager is under pressure to accept one."

The major pressure at Dana—and it's a very real one, as in most of our other excellent companies—is peer pressure. Dana's effort to foster it is capped by Hell Week. Twice a year about a hundred managers get together for five days to swap results and productivity improvement stories. McPherson encouraged the process, because he believes that peer pressure is what makes it all go. He says, "You can always fool the boss. I did. But you can't hide from your peers. They know what's really going on." And, of course, there is free and open communication, bordering on a free for all, during Hell Week. He ran ads that supported this one, too: "We put them through hell."

McPherson's philosophy on job security has been tested severely during the recent hard times in the American auto industry. Much as the company would have liked to avoid it, it had to lay people off. On the other hand, even those actions were accompanied by continued intense communications. Everyone was told what was going on—as it happened. Says McPherson of the practical results, "We had an eighty percent participation in the stock plan in 1979. Then there were nine thousand layoffs. What's our participation rate now, including those laid off? Still eighty percent." Moreover, the 1981 bounce back in results by Dana, going strongly against the tide, is truly phenomenal.

The McPherson philosophy comes down to the value of everyone's contributing ideas, not just keeping up the pace on the line. "The way you stay fresh," stresses McPherson, "is you never stop traveling, you never stop listening. You never stop asking people what they think." Contrast that with the following comment from a General Motors worker, recently laid off after sixteen years in the Pontiac division: "I guess I got laid off because I make poor-quality cars. But in sixteen years, not once was I ever asked for a suggestion as to how to do my job better. Not once."

Delta Airlines

Delta Airlines is one of the handful to go through deregulation in the airline industry with few scars on its unblemished record of strong financial performance. Delta's last strike was in 1942. The last union vote was in 1955. Francis O'Connell of the Transport Workers of America says of Delta: "[They have] a relationship with their employees that is most difficult to break into."

Delta is a people company. It advertises "the Delta Family Feeling," and lives that philosophy. The company promotes from within, pays better than most airlines, and goes to any length to avoid laying workers off in a traditionally cyclic industry.

As many of the excellent companies do to ensure a fit with the culture, Delta begins with a careful and lengthy screening process for all job applicants. *The Wall Street Journal* notes, "Stewardesses, for instance, are culled from thousands of applicants, interviewed twice and then sent to Delta psychologist, Dr. Sidney Janus. 'I try to determine their sense of cooperativeness or sense of team work. At Delta, you don't just join a company, you join an objective.'"

Success at Delta stems from a collection of lots of little things. The open door policy sets the tone. Ex-president Tom Beebe explains: "My rug has to be cleaned once a month. Mechanics, pilots, flight attendants—they all come in to see me. If they really want to tell us something—we'll give them the time. They don't have to go through somebody. The chairman, president, vice president—none of us has a single 'administrative assistant' to screen people out, no intermediaries." Of course, what makes it work is that something *happens* when the open door is used. Delta spends a lot of time and money (entirely inconceivable to those who don't practice such things) checking out the employee's side of the story. Often, the result is a substantial policy change—surrounding, say, pay or accounting procedures. It's all "brought about by the time-honored willingness of employees to use the open door and the time-honored willingness of top management to keep the door open," says one analyst.

Here is one very typical example of the policy at work, as reported by *The Wall Street Journal:*

> In February 1979, James Burnett's paycheck came up $38 short. Delta Airlines hadn't paid him enough overtime for the day he came in at 2:00 a.m. to repair an L-1011 engine. When his supervisor wouldn't help, the 41-year-old mechanic wrote Delta's President, David C. Garrett, Jr. He

complained that "the pay problem we have experienced is bad and it has caused a lot of good men to go sour on the company." Three days later, Mr. Burnett got his money and an apology from top management. Delta even changed the pay policy, increasing overtime pay for mechanics called in outside normal working hours.

One of the more interesting notions at Delta is that of inter-changeability of management parts. The chairman insists, for example, that all his senior vice presidents be trained to step into any job in the company (though not, presumably, flying the planes). Even the senior vice presidents are supposed to know one another's areas well enough to substitute for any other if need be. And, inci-dentally, it is a tradition for top management to pitch in and help baggage handlers at Christmas time.

Like Dana, Delta management spends an extraordinary amount of time just plain talking to its people. Senior management meets with all employees at least once a year in "open forum," where direct communications take place between the highest and lowest levels of the organization. The amount of management time required for all these communications is staggering and, again, dif-ficult to imagine for those who don't work in this kind of environ-ment. For example, very senior management holds four full days of meetings a year just to talk to flight attendants based in Atlanta. Senior vice presidents typically spend more than a hundred days a year on the road; they are not easy days, but include time down at the flight line at 1:00 or 2:00 a.m., checking out the graveyard shift. Intense communications start at the top. There is a ritual Monday morning staff meeting where all the company's programs, problems, finances are thoroughly reviewed. Afterward, senior vice presidents take their department heads to a late lunch to bring them up to date. And so the news is quickly and regularly passed through the company.

Listening to employees is taken seriously. For instance, a com-mittee of flight attendants chooses uniforms for Delta's 6,000 stew-ardesses and stewards. "That's important, you have to live in them," said one flight attendant. Mechanics even choose their immediate supervisor.

McDonald's

It seems appropriate that Fred Turner, McDonald's current chairman, started out as a shoe salesman. In such ways the leaders in many people-intensive organizations learned what it was to get the basics right—to meet customers, provide real-time service, and take pride in and responsibility for a mundane job. McDonald's is, above all, better at the basics. Says Turner: "History shows that [the competitors'] management involvement doesn't last. They just don't have the depth of attention to detail."

McDonald's believes that senior managers should be out in the field, paying attention to employees, training, and execution. Says the founder, Ray Kroc, "I believe that *less is more* in the case of corporate management; for its size, McDonald's today is the most unstructured corporation I know, and I don't think you could find a happier, more secure, harder working group of executives anywhere."

McDonald's talks endlessly about the individual's contribution. Kroc argues, "A well-run restaurant is like a winning baseball team, it makes the most of every crew member's talent and takes advantage of every split-second opportunity to speed up service." Kroc focuses on the little things: "I emphasize the importance of details. You must perfect every fundamental of your business if you expect it to perform well." Getting the details right, McDonald's way, requires an astonishing amount of learning and intensity. Says a former employee, "When I first started, they put a little white hat on me that said 'trainee.' They started me right off in the easiest of the jobs—cooking french fries. Then I moved to fries and shakes. So it went, on up to handling the buns and cooking the burgers. We only had one small room where we could take breaks. There was a TV and cassette going on all the time, stressing some aspect or another of the way McDonald's does things. How to cook a better burger, how to keep the fries crisp, the whole bit."

"The book" at McDonald's spells out procedures and details. For instance, "Cooks must turn, never flip, hamburgers." Or, "If they haven't been purchased, Big Macs must be discarded in ten minutes after being cooked and french fries in seven minutes. Cashiers must make eye contact with and smile at every customer." And on it goes.

Despite the rigidity of procedure surrounding many such areas, store managers are encouraged to exercise autonomy and keep things lively. *Fortune* reports that "Debbie Thompson, who started out at McDonald's as a cashier eight years ago, and now, at 24, manages the company-owned store at Elk Grove Village, sometimes livens up the lunchtime rush hour by offering $5 bonuses to the cashiers for taking in the most dollars and handling the most

customers. She gives a plaque to the crew member of the month."*
Another employee adds: "We always got paid a dollar for making a
record amount of sales for an hour. Also, if you had a three
hundred dollar hour [in food sales] you got a dollar. Everyone
working in that period got a dollar. On the record days you got
two dollars. We were all shooting for the extra bucks. It meant
something."

A vital part of the system is Hamburger U. *The New York
Times* reports:

> The American flag and the McDonald's flag fly high over
> the expressway running through the backyard of
> Hamburger University in a suburban Chicago town. Inside,
> McDonald's franchisers and company managers learn skills
> to reinforce what the golden arches of 614,000 similar brick
> buildings in mostly suburban and rural communities have
> come to symbolize: predictability in atmosphere and taste,
> or, as McDonald's founder Ray Kroc put it, "the gospel of
> Quality, Service, Cleanliness and Value." A high school
> dropout, Mr. Kroc has donated millions to charity and
> urges employees to become active in community charities to
> further McDonald's image, but he refuses to support higher
> education. In his book [*Grinding It Out*] he writes, "One
> thing I flatly refused to give money to is the support of any
> college. I have been wooed by some of the finest institutions
> in the land but I tell them they will not get a cent from me
> unless they put in a trade school." . . . Two thousand stu-
> dents "graduated" from the school [Hamburger U.] last
> year. . . . One lucky student in each course receives a golden
> chef's hat for making the largest contribution to class
> discussion. . . . Another walks away with a ceramic abstract
> model of a hamburger for highest academic honors. . . .
> McDonald's points to the fact that the American Council
> on Education recommends college credit of up to six
> semester hours for Hamburger U. courses taken by those
> pursuing a degree in two or four year colleges . . . [there are]

---

* Some consider such rewards trivial. However, a Stanford MBA student remembers winning a similar reward at Jack In The Box. "It may sound silly, but I have
carried it around with me for seven years." We have a friend, a salesman, who won
a barbecue as part of a sales contest. His barbecue at home was much better than
the model he won. Nonetheless, he ripped out the previous one and replaced it
with the new one, his prize.

18 courses from one or two day seminars to week long sessions on "market evaluation," "management skills," and "area supervision.". . . McDonald's success is based on fast food and friendly service at a low price. Courses deal with McDonald's style and emphasize motivation. . . .

McDonald's also turns to hoopla and razzle-dazzle. As one employee recalls:

> One of the guys in our store was an "All-American Hamburger Maker." He was the best hamburger cooker in McDonald's chains across the country. The competition begins in the spring. They have an All-American contest to see who is the best, literally the best hamburger cooker in the country. It means the quickest, but also the most nearly perfect, the top quality, cooking them exactly the way they are supposed to be cooked. To do it really right you get a little thermometer and you stick it on top of the grill. The grill would be shining, absolutely spotless. Then you lay out the burgers just so, six in a row, perfectly in line. You sear them all with the back of a spatula, you salt them at the right moment, put the onions on at the right moment. Then you take them off properly, lay them on the buns. . . . First, you have the in-store competition to find the best hamburger cooker in the store. The guy who won that then goes on to the regional championships. Then they go to the next level. Finally, they go to the All-American contest—I think it was in Chicago. There was a big trophy involved, and I think there was money involved, but I don't know how much. The important thing was that you got to wear an All-American patch on your shirt.

IBM

From McDonald's we circle all the way to IBM, perhaps one of the biggest and oldest American companies practicing an intense people orientation. The only issue with IBM is how to start describing it. With the seventy-year-old open door policy? The senior Mr. Watson's $1-a-year country club, established for all employees in the 1920s? The philosophy that starts with "respect for the individual"? Lifetime employment? Insistence upon promotion from within? IBM day-care centers, IBM hotels, IBM running tracks and tennis courts? *Monthly* opinion surveys by the personnel department? A very high success rate among salesmen? The intense training? IBM's total history is one of intense people orientation. And as at McDonald's, it's reflected in the tiniest details. Walk into IBM's New York financial branch. The first thing that greets you is a massive floor-to-ceiling bulletin board with glossy photographs of *every* person in the branch hung under the banner: NEW YORK FINANCIAL . . . THE DIFFERENCE IS PEOPLE.

Watson started an open door policy early and it is still maintained today. Some of his managers used to complain because he so regularly favored the employees. One former colleague of the senior Mr. Watson says, in fact, he can hardly ever remember the senior Watson taking the manager's side. That's the kind of thing that makes such policies work. They are credible. Managers *do* go to the trouble of thoroughly checking things out, as in similar open door situations at Levi, HP, Tandem, and Delta Airlines. It's used. Things happen.

Thomas Watson, Jr., describes how his father started, foreshadowing many continuing IBM policy cornerstones: "T. J. Watson didn't move in and shake up the organization. Instead, he set out to buff and polish the people who were already there and to make a success of what he had. That decision in 1914 led to the IBM policy on job security, which has meant a great deal to our employees." Watson notes that his father even adhered to the policy in the thick of the Great Depression. "IBM produced parts for inventory and stored them. From it has come our policy to build from within. We go to great lengths to develop our people, to retrain them when job requirements change, and to give them another chance if we find them experiencing difficulties in the job they are in." The senior Watson developed his enlightened views under the tutelage of the fabled John Patterson, the founder of NCR. According to Watson, Jr., when others were fighting the union, Patterson was breaking ground by "providing showers on company premises and company time, dining rooms serving hot meals at cost, entertainment, schools, clubs, libraries, and parks. Other businessmen were shocked at Patterson's notions. But he said that they were investments that would pay off, and they did."

Watson followed Patterson's footsteps in many other ways. In his own words, "Almost every kind of fanfare was tried to create enthusiasm. . . . Our early emphasis on human relations was not motivated by altruism but by the simple belief that if we respected our people and helped them to respect themselves, the company would make the most profit."

Detail after detail reinforces the people theme at IBM. A 1940 article in *Fortune* about IBM, then a $35 million company, talks about wholly immaculate factories, the $1-a-year country club for all employees, the IBM song book ("We know and we love you, and we know you have our welfare in your heart"—the "you" in the song being, of course, the senior Watson).

Of the senior Mr. Watson, *Fortune* says he was a "born homilist who began early to confect the altruistic rules of thumb that have since guided his life and policies. He journeys half the time, working 16 hours a day, spending almost every evening at the functions and celebrations at his innumerable employee clubs. . . . He relishes talking to employees, not as a curious supervisor, but as an old friend."

There is not much to add to the early Watson stories, except for the remarkable fact that IBM has stayed about the same. The open door policies, the clubs, the simplicity, the homilies, the hoopla, and the training are as intense in relation to the styles of today as they were fifty or sixty years ago. An IBM executive put it succinctly: "You can foul up on most anything and you'll get another chance. But if you screw up, even a little bit, on people management, you're gone. That's it, top performer or not."

Finally, to complete the story on people at IBM, as at other companies, the policies probably would not work if the people way down the organization were not proud of what that organization does. Buck Rodgers, the senior marketing man at IBM, says: "Above all, we seek a reputation for doing the little things well." What IBM stands for, the quality that a Hewlett-Packard or a McDonald's delivers, the ownership of productivity ideas at Dana—in every case the simple pride in what the company does is the keystone for an overarching orientation toward people.

COMMON THEMES

As we step back from the analysis of people and productivity, we find a number of strikingly similar themes running through the excellent companies data. First is language. *The language in people-oriented institutions has a common flavor.* In many respects, form precedes substance. We have seen it happen with some of our clients. Once they start talking the philosophy, they may start living it, even if, initially, the words have no meaning. For example, we doubt that "the HP Way" meant very much to anyone in Hewlett-Packard when the language was first introduced. As time went by, we suspect that the phrase took on deeper and richer meanings in ways that no one would have suspected—not even Hewlett or Packard.

In fact, we doubt that a true people orientation can exist unless there is a special language to go with it. Words and phrases like Family Feeling, open door, Rally, Jubilee, Management By Wandering Around, on stage, and so on—all of these special terms show people in the institutions that the orientation is bone-deep. The Eskimos, unlike the British or the Americans, have many words for various kinds of snow; accurate description of snow conditions is vital to their day-to-day lives, survival, and culture. If an institution is really to be people-oriented, it needs plenty of words to describe the way people ought to treat one another.

Most impressive of all the language characteristics in the excellent companies are the phrases that upgrade the status of the individual employee. Again, we know it sounds corny, but words like Associate (Wal-Mart), Crew Member (McDonald's) and Cast Member (Disney) describe the very special importance of individuals in the excellent companies.

Many of the best companies really do view themselves as an extended family. We found prevalent use of the specific terms "family," "extended family," or "family feeling" at Wal-Mart, Tandem, HP, Disney, Dana, Tupperware, McDonald's, Delta, IBM, TI, Levi Strauss, Blue Bell, Kodak, and P&G. 3M's chairman, Lew Lehr, states the case best:

> If you look at the entrepreneurship of American industry it's wonderful. On the other hand, if you look at the paternalism and discipline of the Japanese companies, it's wonderful, too. There are certain companies that have evolved into a blend of those industries, and 3M is one of them. . . . Companies like 3M have become sort of a community center for employees, as opposed to just a place to work. We have employee clubs, intramural sports, travel clubs, and a choral group. This has happened because the community in which people live has become so mobile it is no longer an outlet for the individual. The schools are no longer a social center for the family. The churches have lost their drawing power as social-family centers. With the breakdown of these traditional structures, certain companies have filled the void. They have become sort of mother institutions, but have maintained their spirit of entrepreneurship at the same time.

And, as Lehr suggests, the family means more than the collection of 3M employees. It includes employees' entire families. One of our colleagues was in the brand-management program at P&G for three months as a summer hire. He recalls that his family still received Thanksgiving turkeys from P&G five years later.

Another of the more striking characteristics of the excellent companies is the *apparent absence of a rigidly followed chain of command*. Of course, the chain of command does exist for big decisions, but it is not used much for day-to-day communication. For information exchange, informality is the norm. People really do wander around, top management is in regular contact with employees at the lowest levels (and with customers), everyone *is* typically on a first-name basis. At the extreme, at wildly successful Activision, a $50 million video games maker growing at 100 percent per year, the phone book is alphabetized by first name!

In trying to explain the phenomenon, a GM manager contrasted one key aspect of the striking difference in performance between two giant plants: "I know this sounds like caricature, but I guess that is how life is. At the poorly performing plant, the plant manager probably ventured out on the floor once a week, always in a suit. His comments were distant and perfunctory. At South Gate, the better plant, the plant manager was on the floor all the time. He wore a baseball cap and a UAW jacket. By the way, whose plant do you think was spotless? Whose looked like a junk yard?"

Wandering around, we suppose, is not for everyone. For many managers, this activity does not come naturally; if they were uncomfortable in such an informal role, their meandering might be viewed as condescending or checking up, and if they used their visits to make on-the-spot decisions, they would be undercutting the chain of command, not simply using the practice as a way of exchanging information. Wandering around and informality, then, probably are not for everybody. On the other hand, without a peripatetic management style, we wonder how vital an institution can really be.

We see important evidences of informality in many other traits. For example, at the excellent companies the physical configuration of facilities is different. Informality is usually delineated by spartan settings, open doors, fewer walls, and fewer offices. It is hard to imagine a free-flowing exchange of information taking place in the palatial, formal, expensively decorated suites that mark so many corporate or even divisional offices.

Hoopla, Celebration, and Verve

Consider this interchange:

General Motors finance staffer: Look, I've been in a foundry, there's no way those guys are going to sing songs like the Japanese or the Tupperware ladies.

Second person (from the Midwest): Caterpillar makes top-drawer equipment. Those people are UAW workers. They don't fool around with hoopla.

Third person (also from the Midwest): I was transferred to Peoria. I didn't work for Cat. But every year they put on a "machine day." All the Cat people and their families go out to the proving grounds and get free beer and sandwiches. Last year's theme was "Cowboys and Indians." All the machines were dressed up in costumes and given names. Then the machines engaged in contests, devouring hills and stuff like that. Everybody lapped it up.

Second GMer: You should see South Gate. The plant manager really enjoys whooping it up. The place became a smorgasbord of signs: "Beat Japan," and the like. Why, they even enticed some Hell's Angels types into singing "God Bless America" at a recent rally.

So Americans don't go in for hoopla? Want more evidence? When Bud Zumwalt was on the navy destroyer where he learned a people orientation, he spent an inordinate amount of time on one element of seeming trivia—changing his ship's voice call sign. He stated the case in a missive to his superiors:

Since recently assuming command of *ISBELL*, this commanding officer has been concerned over the anemic connotation of the present voice radio call. When in company with such stalwarts as *"FIREBALL," "VIPER,"* and others, it is somewhat embarrassing and completely out of keeping with the quality of the sailormen aboard to be identified by the relatively ignominious title *"SAPWORTH."*

Six months later, after much pulling and tugging, a call sign change was approved, with drastic subsequent effect. Zumwalt concludes: "The voice call *'Hellcat'* proved immensely popular. Arnold J. Isbell's officers and men proudly wore sleeve patches and baseball cap patches showing a black cat with a forked tail stepping out of the flames of hell and breaking a submarine with its paws. The impact on morale was remarkable."

Kyocera has 2,000 employees in and around San Diego. It's a subsidiary of Kyoto Ceramic, recently named the "foremost company in Japan." Every day at the six U.S. plants, all 2,000 employees assemble first thing in the morning to listen to a management talk about the state of the company. They engage in brisk calisthenics. Management's point of view is "that by doing one thing together each day, it reinforces the unity of the company. It's also fun. It gets the blood up." Top management takes turns making the presentations. Many of the speeches "are very personal and emotional, not approved beforehand or screened by anybody."

At our second meeting with the people at Hewlett-Packard, as we were waiting in the lobby, chief executive Young's voice came over a loudspeaker announcing that quarter's results to everyone in the organization. Young is a soft-spoken individual, but if there is such a thing as quiet cheerleading, that is exactly what Young was doing.

Peter Vaill is a student of "high performing systems"—businesses, orchestras, football teams. Such systems behave, according to Vaill, as self-fulfilling prophecies—something works, for discernible reasons. Then Vaill notes the inevitable emergence of a "private language and set of symbols": people feel "up" because something has worked, and, if allowed, they start to act in a new way. As they act in the new way, more good things happen. "Peak experiences . . . lead members to enthuse, bubble, and commu nicate joy and exultation. . . . People eat, sleep, and breathe the activity. . . . A Hall of Fame phenomenon arises . . . members acquire an aesthetic motivation." And finally an air of invincibility leads to the same reality.

We haven't the systematic data, so we can't conclude with finality that our excellent companies are far above the norm in the amount of time they spend on training activities. On the other hand, there are enough signs of *training intensity* to suggest that that might be the case. The most visible evidence is the universities— Disney U., Dana U., and Hamburger U., for example. As we saw earlier, IBM invests heavily in training. Caterpillar, similarly, takes its people through extensive training; for instance, all sales engineers spend months at proving grounds learning how the equipment works. Heavy doses of early on-the-job training also mark HP, P&G, and Schlumberger.

An element of Bechtel's on-the-job training may be the most unusual. This company, the builder of $5 billion cities in the Arabian desert, intentionally takes on small, uneconomical projects. "The sole purpose is to provide practical opportunities for fast-track young project managers to cut their teeth on a whole job early," notes a senior executive. (This, by the way, is exactly in the tradition of Alfred Sloan at GM. He almost always put his fast-trackers in the tiny divisions, so they could get an early feel for the full operation and not get lost in the catacombs of a Chevrolet.)

Another striking aspect of the orientation of the excellent companies is the way they *socialize incoming managers*. The first element, of course, is recruiting. The screening is intense. Many of the companies we talked to are known for bringing potential recruits back seven or eight times for interviews. They want to be sure of the people they hire, and they are also saying to would-be recruits, "Get to know our company. Decide for yourself whether or not you can be a good fit with our culture."

Next comes the entry job. This may be the most important element. These companies like to start their aspiring managers in "hands-dirty" positions that are in the mainstream of the business. At HP, according to chief executive Young, "The young MBAs and MSEEs must get immediate experience in new-product introduction. It's a typical starting job. It reinforces the whole concept of bringing new products to market, which is such an important business value to us." Likewise, *Business Week* notes that "Caterpillar has always started its potential managers near the bottom, usually right on the production line. There are no overnight stars in the organization."

The notion of socializing managers by starting them in hands-dirty jobs is strikingly different from what we see in many other large companies. MBAs or other would-be managers, because they are expensive, start in staff jobs and spend years there, never coming to know the reality of the business.

The important result is the realism. Those who start in the company's mainline jobs, the making or selling parts of the business, are unlikely to be subsequently fooled by the abstractions of planning, market research, or management systems as they are promoted. Moreover, their instincts for the business develop. They learn to manage not only by the numbers but also, and perhaps more important, by a real feel for the business. They have been there. Their instincts are good. Bechtel's guiding motto, "A fine feel for the doable," says it well.

The next part in the crucial socialization process is learning through role models the heroes and the myths. The new recruit learns how to do the job from war stories. At IBM the war stories surround customer service. At 3M the stories are about sometimes failing, but always persisting in pursuit of innovation. At P&G the tales are about quality. HP takes the direct approach by filling its basic indoctrination book, *The HP Way*, with vignettes about those who started at the bottom and made it to the top. HP even systematically collects "HP Way stories" via the suggestion box to add to and revitalize the stock.

Information Availability and Comparison

We are struck by the importance of available information as the basis for peer comparison. Surprisingly, this is the basic control mechanism in the excellent companies. It is not the military model at all. It is not a chain of command wherein nothing happens until the boss tells somebody to do something. General objectives and values are set forward and information is shared so widely that people know quickly whether or not the job is getting done and who's doing it well or poorly.

Some really do believe in the business of sharing information. A striking example comes from Crompton Corduroy. *Fortune* notes that in one old plant, with the push of a few buttons on a console, machine operators can check on their output and compare it with that of their peers. They do check up on themselves, with no coercion, often cutting a lunch break short to stop at the terminal for a readout. *Fortune* likewise reports on GM's recent decision to disseminate information widely:

> Bringing financial information down to the shop floor is a major step in bridging the gap between management and labor; *more than any other single act, it makes the goals explicit and the nature of the partnership concrete* [italics ours]. At the Gear [a huge old Chevrolet plant], managers tell workers the plant's direct labor costs, scrap costs and profit (or loss) and how these measure up against goals. Not even the foremen would have been privy to such information at GM in the past. The benefits, to GM's way of thinking, outweigh any harm that might come from revealing competitive information.

When Ed Carlson was president of United Airlines, he said: "Nothing is worse for morale than a lack of information down in the ranks. I call it NETMA—Nobody Ever Tells Me Anything—and I have tried hard to minimize that problem." Analyst Richard Pascale observes that Carlson "shared with the field staff confidential daily operating statistics that were previously regarded as too sensitive for the field to handle."

Blue Bell is similarly generous with its comparative productivity information. Individual, team, and unit results are available to everybody. (We have already observed the wealth of information available at companies like Dana.)

Perhaps the prime ingredient in the information-sharing process, a conclusion supported by extensive psychological research, is the nonevaluative nature of the process. There is a fine line here, we will agree. However, what we mean is nonevaluative in a definite sense. Management doesn't browbeat people with numbers. "Superiors" are not telling "subordinates" what to do. On the other hand, the information is evaluative in that it brings to bear a most potent force—namely, peer pressure. For instance, we saw that Dana shoves nothing down the division manager's throat; it just brings that person in for ten days a year, to a pair of five-day Hell Weeks, to swap results on productivity improvement. Intel revealed that its managers swap MBO results—with one another and *weekly*.

A long time ago, the organization theorist Mason Haire said, "What gets measured gets done." He argued that the simple act of putting a measure on something is tantamount to getting it done. It focuses management attention on that area. Information is simply made available and people respond to it. Our favorite story of simple systems, peer pressure, and easy measurement was related to a persistent and pernicious absenteeism problem at one of AT&T's Western Electric plants. Management tried everything; the level of absenteeism wouldn't go down. Finally they put up a huge, visible board with everybody's name on it and posted a gold star next to each name when people came to work. Absenteeism dropped dramatically—almost overnight. Another friend tells of a foreman who started writing production results, after a shift, in chalk on the floor in the machine area. Competition between shifts surfaced and quickly turned intense. Productivity leaped.

All of us, we suspect, are like those Crompton Corduroy machine operators. We sneak by the performance indicator board to find out how we are doing. We respond—more than we likely know or realize—to comparative performance information. The surprise to the unschooled is that we respond better and more strongly if the information is not blatantly evaluative, beating us over the head. Passing the information quietly seems to spur us on to greater effort. Sadly, the excellent companies' policy of making information available stands in vivid contrast to typical management practice, in which so many fear that "they" will abuse the information, and that only competitors will benefit. It's one more big cost of not treating people as adults—or indeed, as winners.

"A man wouldn't sell his life to you, but he will give it to you for a piece of colored ribbon," William Manchester asserts, in describing his World War II experiences as a foot soldier. He echoes a theme that goes back at least to Napoleon, who was a master ribbon-granter. If you want proof of the effect, go back and look through closets and drawers as we recently did. We still have Boy Scout merit badges, trophies gathering dust, and a medal or two from some insignificant ski races held decades ago.

As we did this research, we were struck by the wealth of non-monetary incentives used by the excellent companies. Nothing is more powerful than positive reinforcement. Everybody uses it. But top performers, almost alone, use it extensively. The volume of contrived opportunities for showering pins, buttons, badges, and medals on people is staggering at McDonald's, Tupperware, IBM, or many of the other top performers. They actively seek out and pursue endless excuses to give out rewards.

At Mars, Inc., the extremely successful consumer goods company, every employee, including the president, gets a weekly 10 percent bonus if he comes to work on time each day that week. That's an especially nice example of creating a setting in which virtually everybody wins regularly. . . . [P]eople like to think of themselves as winners. Even though IBM has a "gold circle" for the top 10 percent of its salesmen, in our minds it is arguably more important that they engage in lots of hoopla surrounding the One Hundred Percent Club, which covers over two thirds of the sales force. When the number of awards is high, it makes the perceived possibility of winning something high as well. And then the average man will stretch to achieve. Many companies do believe in special awards but use them exclusively to honor the top few (who already are so highly motivated they would probably have done their thing anyway). More vital are the ribbons for a good show by the common man. As McPherson states, the real key to success is helping the middle 60 percent a few steps up the ladder.

Our colleague Ken Ohmae described the low state of formal structure in Japan for *Chief Executive*: "Most Japanese corporations lack even an approximation of an organization chart. Managing

directors who enjoy great influence on operations seldom appear in
the company organization chart. . . . Many deputies have line
responsibilities, but are also absent from these charts. Honda, for
instance . . . is not clear how it is organized, except that it uses project teams quite frequently." Ohmae also makes the point that in
Japan it is unusual to talk about "organization" in any structural
sense, or as something different from the total entity itself.

We found *less obvious structuring* and *certainly less layering* at
most of the excellent companies. Remember Delta, Dana, and
Disney, where interchangeability of people and jobs is a bedrock
principle. And Rene McPherson challenges a class at Stanford
Business School as he says, "How many layers do you think it takes
to run the Catholic Church?" The students think about it and the
most they are able to think of is five—the laity, the priest, the
bishop, the cardinal, and the Pope. The point is that even in a huge
organization like the Church, very few layers are needed to make it
work. Excessive layering may be the biggest problem of the slow-
moving, rigid bureaucracy. It is done primarily, it sometimes seems,
to make place for more managers in an organization. But the excellent companies evidence challenges the need for all those layers. If
such layers exist, a kind of Parkinson's law of management structure
sets in: extra levels of management mainly create distracting work
for others to justify their own existence. Everyone appears busy; but
in reality it is simple management featherbedding.

Beyond relatively less structuring and less layering, there is one
more vital structural trait that characterizes the excellent companies.
We have mentioned it in passing before, but in our minds it is so
important in the context of people and productivity that it needs
pointed recognition here. The characteristic is: small is productive.

Smallness

A seminal conference on "the creative organization" took place
at the University of Chicago over a decade ago. In the midst of the
proceedings the following interchange occurred:

> *Peter Peterson* [then president of Bell & Howell]: In indus-
> try we are tending to develop a kind of sterile professional
> manager who has no emotional feelings about the product,
> who does not "love" the product. He doesn't create any-
> thing, but he kind of manages something in a rather
> artificial way. I heard Ted Bensinger talk about bowling and
> what he has done for bowling—he has a feeling for this

thing, as Ogilvy has a feeling for advertising. I was just wondering whether we have put enough emphasis on our emotional commitment to great cooking, or great advertising, or great something.

David Ogilvy [founder of Ogilvy and Mather]: It's the opposite of detachment.

Gary Steiner [University of Chicago and conference chairman]: The conception that the greatest chef would be the most effective leader in the kitchen is creatively sound, but isn't it restricted to businesses or organizations which would have one clear-cut professional skill? What would you say about General Motors or the University of Chicago, where there is no one, clear-cut professional skill; there is no one dimension?

Ogilvy: It is a bad institution, because it has excessive diversification.

Steiner: How do you make such an institution creative, short of saying: "Let's divide it up?"

Ogilvy: Divide it up.

Peterson: Break up the companies.

The banking industry is undergoing a revolution caused by deregulation. One outcome is the need to offer tailored services such as corporate cash management. These operations have typically been performed in an undifferentiated fashion in the so-called back office, with unskilled, sweatshop connotations. Barry Sullivan, chairman of First Chicago, in a recent address to the American Banking Association, offered a solution: "What I am really talking about is breaking up the back office factory into separate businesses." Tom Vanderslice, who recently left GE and took over as chairman of GTE, describes a principal objective of his at the new company: "I'm a big advocate of breaking this business—as best we can—into a series of manageable enterprises." A commentator recently said of one of the key ingredients of 3M's continuing success: "As divisions reach a certain size they somehow split, amoeba-like, into smaller, more manageable divisions." And another 3Mer reiterated: "There is only one point. Break it up. Competitive dynamics and efficiencies be damned. It will only stay vital if it's small."

The point of smallness is that it induces manageability and, above all, commitment. A manager really can understand something that is small and in which one central discipline prevails. More important, even in institutions that employ hundreds of thousands of people, if the divisions are small enough, or if there are other ways of simulating autonomy, the individual still counts and can stand out. We asserted earlier that the need to stick out, to count as an individual, is vital. We simply know no other way individuals can stick out unless the size of units—divisions, plants, and teams—is of human scale. Smallness works. Small *is* beautiful. The economic theorists may disagree, but the excellent companies evidence is crystal clear.

Emerson Electric and Dana are cost-driven companies, and their strategies work. But, at the same time, both hold their division size to well under $100 million. HP and 3M, as we have already noted, strictly limit division size, even though it means overlap and duplication. TI has ninety Product Customer Centers, on average between $40 and $50 million in size.

Johnson & Johnson uses the same magic, even in consumer goods, where large scale is seen as essential by most. With $5 billion in total revenues, J & J, remember, has around 150 divisions—about $30 to $40 million per division on average. Digital employs much the same strategy. "Essentially, we act like a group of smaller companies," says Ted Johnson, vice president for sales and service. At Digital, that means constant reorganization, product-line proliferation and overlap, salesmen out creating "one customer niche after another." People at Digital, and at many of the other excellent companies, regularly lament short production runs, inventory confusion, and sometimes dual coverage of customers. They lament, we'd add, all the way to the bank.

The process of keeping it small can start early. ROLM is a highly successful $200 million telecommunications equipment producer. It does well against giants like Western Electric. The primary reason is that it tailors its problem solving to modest-sized customer segments. In the words of one of its founders, the key to its winning formula is "we continuously divisionalize, and even set up new small buildings for the new units"—and the company grows and grows.

A rule of thumb starts to emerge. We find that the lion's share of the top performers keep their division size between $50 and $100 million, with a maximum of 1,000 or so employees each. Moreover, they grant their divisions extraordinary independence and give them the functions and resources to exploit it.

For us, the story on plant size was nothing short of astonishing. Repeatedly, we found that the better performers had determined that their small plants, not their big ones, were most efficient. Emerson is the best example. When named as one of the *Dun's Review* "best managed companies," a simple success ingredient was highlighted: "Emerson eschews giant factories favored by such competitors as General Electric. Few Emerson plants employ more than 600 workers, a size at which [Chairman Charles] Knight feels that management can maintain personal contact with individual employees. 'We don't need a 5,000 person plant to get our cost down,' he says, 'and this gives us great flexibility.' Emerson puts heavy stress on those personal contacts with employees."

Blue Bell is number two behind Levi Strauss in the apparel industry. This $1.5 billion giant has managed to stay competitive and profitable, principally on the basis of superb operating skills and low-cost production. In the Blue Bell scheme of things, smallness plays a commanding role. Its chairman, Kimsey Mann, keeps his manufacturing units down to 300 people. This is what he says he gets in return: "A management that is quickly responsive to problems . . . a staff that serves workers." He adds, "We get increased face-to-face contact. Our supervisors have got to know the families, the concerns, of every one of their people." He believes that from the smallness stems creativity and variety. "Who knows the job better than those close to it?" he asks, adding, "In big units, by the time something gets approved, the person who submitted the idea either doesn't remember it or doesn't recognize it as his." In summary, Mann says, "We want a series of plants where a man feels that 'my wife and daughter can work here.' We want every individual to be responsible for the company's image." Mann believes that these traits can exist only if small plant size is maintained.

At Motorola the story is similar. President John Mitchell said simply, "When a plant starts to edge toward fifteen hundred people, somehow, like magic, things start to go wrong." Dana, with its extraordinary record of productivity, tries determinedly to keep its plants down to fewer than 500 employees. Westinghouse is now undertaking a remarkable priority productivity drive; a principal element of the program is a series of thirty to forty small plants. A part of GM's new productivity efforts similarly involves keeping new facility size well under 1,000.

The negative argument appears equally persuasive. A former president of Consolidated Edison said: "In the last decade, the industry [electric utilities] has been euchred into buying individual generating units that are larger than the existing state of construction and operating technology can handle reliably." These words were echoed at one of our briefings by the chief executive of Georgia Power. "Big plants are great," he said, *when they work.*" Everyone laughed. He went on to point out that his big plants were shut down much too often, and consequently missed their theoretical potential by a wide margin.

Harvard's Wick Skinner, dean of academic thinkers about production processes, recounts a typical tale, quoted in *Fortune*, revealing what goes on underneath the surface when smallness pays off:

> Skinner cites an episode that took place at Honeywell, where he worked for ten years before joining the Harvard faculty. One Honeywell plant was devoted to making gyroscopes for highly specialized scientific and technical use, and fuel gauges for airplanes. The two production lines were intermingled on the factory floor and eventually trouble developed. "Gyroscopes were ten times harder to make," Skinner recalls, "but the Honeywell people were having trouble competitively with the fuel gauges. They did everything to try to figure out why the costs couldn't be kept down. They made accounting analyses, hired an MBA to come on board. Nothing worked, so they decided to get out of the business. Then one of the managers whispered a suggestion to the plant boss, who asked top management for $20,000. . . . They bought plywood and some two-by-fours and walled off a corner of the factory . . . and segregated the workers. Within six months the problem was licked."

The theoretical case is stated succinctly by the British researcher John Child, who reviewed hundreds of studies of the economics of scale: "The economic benefits of large-scale industry have on the whole been considerably exaggerated, especially during the merger and rationalization fever which gripped Europe in the 1960s. The general conclusion which can be drawn from studies of scale in industrial production is that, while there may be important economic thresholds for the small organization seeking to become medium sized, these are not much in evidence for larger units." He goes on to list some reasons. "There is a high correlation between the size of plants and the intensity of industrial unrest, levels of labor turnover, and other costly manifestations of dissatisfaction."

The conclusion we draw from all of this can be defined as a rough guideline. Regardless of industry, it seems that more than 500 or so people under one roof causes substantial and unanticipated problems. More significant, even for the cost-oriented companies, small is not only more innovative but also more productive.

The most significant evidence of small is beautiful is at an even lower level—that of the team, or section, or quality circle. In most of the companies not on our list, the strategic business unit or some other rather large aggregation of human beings is considered the basic building block of the organization. Among our winners the team is the critical factor, regardless of the issue—service, innovation, or productivity. The explanation from an executive at the Bank of America (he heads a large part of the operations organization) is typical:

It's always the same, it seems. We always try to get it exactly right. We always try to optimize. We look for the perfect giant system. I remember when I was in London. I was finally far enough away from the center of things that I could experiment. A long-term problem [endemic to the industry] is getting the operations, the systems, and the credit [lending] people together. We took a small service area. I thought it was a terrific opportunity to experiment with a minicomputer. We could put together a small team to work on the problem. We did, and the results were fabulous. You just can't count the number of ways in which hurdles were overcome. Once that group of ten or twelve people got working together, they were readily able to see each other's contributions. The operations guy had been a shy, bureaucratic sort. But pretty soon it became obvious to his colleagues in systems and credit that he really knew what the hell he was doing. He became the de facto leader of the bunch—even though his grade was substantially lower than that of several of his associates. In a period of only three to four months, they put together a remarkably effective system. It served a discrete bunch of customers. It made money. The morale of the group was sky-high. We ended up using that technique with a great deal of success throughout the London office. It's just amazing how you really can break things up into smallish bits—and get people motivated—if you'll only try.

We've already noted that a disproportionate share of innovation successes in business seems to come from "skunk works," tiny groups that tend to outperform the much larger labs that often have casts of hundreds. We have, now, several score examples of effective skunk works. At Bloomingdale's, 3M, HP, Digital, the entire institution is designed as a wholesale collection of ten-person skunk works. The team is the mainstay of productivity improvement per se. TI insists that virtually every one of its people be on a People Involvement Program team at least once a year. A PIP (or productivity team) is a way of life, arguably *the* way of life at TI.

What are the characteristics of a typical TI team? It is usually limited to eight to ten members, consisting of shop floor people as well as an outside engineer or two, who are typically called in on a voluntary basis by the team. It takes on a limited set of objectives; the point is to come up with something concrete that can pay off in the foreseeable future. The duration is limited to between three and six months. More important, the objectives are always set by the team. Mark Shepherd, chairman of TI, says: "Teams set their own improvement goals and measure their own progress toward these goals. Time after time, team members set what they feel are challenging but realistic goals for themselves, and once the program gets rolling, they find that they are not only meeting but exceeding their goals. This is something that rarely happens if goals are set *for* the team, rather than *by* the team. When we talk about 'improving people effectiveness,' then, we mean giving people these kinds of opportunities to tap their own creative resources." Finally, opportunity after opportunity is used to celebrate team achievements; reviews at all levels are frequent, including a couple of groups quite regularly telling their stories directly to the board of directors.

At TI, each of the 9,000 teams sets its own objectives. At 3M, each of the new product development teams is manned by volunteers, full-timers, headed by a champion. It's the same story for the Dana "store manager" or United Airlines' "station manager." Small size is *the* prime generator of commitment. The analytic model will have no part of such a soft argument, but the empirical evidence is crystal clear. In the words of E. F. Schumacher, "People can be themselves only in small, comprehensible groups."

Philosophy

The excellent companies have a deeply ingrained philosophy that says in effect, "respect the individual," "make people winners," "let them stand out," "treat people as adults."

As Anthony Jay observes, that lesson (treating people as adults) may have been in front of our eyes for a long time:

> One reason why the Roman Empire grew so large and survived so long—a prodigious feat of management—is that there was no railway, car, airplane, radio, paper, or telephone. Above all, no telephone. And therefore you could not maintain any illusion of direct control over a general or provincial governor, you could not feel at the back of your mind that you could ring him up, or he could ring you, if a situation cropped up which was too much for him, or that you could fly over and sort things out if they started to get into a mess. You appointed him, you watched his chariot and baggage train disappear over the hill in a cloud of dust and that was that. . . . There was, therefore, no question of appointing a man who was not fully trained, or not quite up to the job: you knew that everything depended on his being the best man for the job before he set off. And so you took great care in selecting him; but more than that you made sure that he knew all about Rome and Roman government and the Roman army before he went out.

Living by the Anthony Jay principle is the only way a company like Schlumberger can hope to function. The sole way that company can work is to place its faith in its 2,000 well-trained, perfectly socialized young engineers, who are sent to the ends of the earth for months—like the Roman general—and left on their own with only the Schlumberger philosophy and this extensive training to guide them. Dee Hock at Visa summed up the problem when he said, "Substituting rules for judgment starts a self-defeating cycle, since judgment can only be developed by using it."

NOTES

Page

81   The Navy . . . assumes: Elmo R. Zumwalt, Jr., *On Watch: A Memoir* (New York: Times Books, 1976), p. 183.

81   "Are these men and women": Given to authors by Gary D. Bello, Stanford Sloan Program, March 1982.

82   "What I tried hardest to do": Zumwalt, p. 186.

83   "I knew from experience": Ibid., p. 185.

83   "Japanese management keeps telling": Kenichi Ohmae, "The Myth and Reality of the Japanese Corporation," p. 29.

83   "People will flood you": Robert Lubar, "Rediscovering the Factory," *Fortune,* July 13, 1981, p. 60.

83   "I was operations manager": Sam T. Harper, personal communication (Graduate School of Business, Stanford University, January 1982).

84   "IBM's philosophy": Watson, *A Business and Its Beliefs,* p. 13.

88   RMI: Page 88 is based, in part, upon Cindy Ris, "Big Jim Is Watching at RMI Co., and Its Workers Like It Just Fine," *Wall Street Journal,* Aug. 4, 1980, p. 15.

89   "I feel that in general terms": Hewlett and Packard, *The HP Way,* p. 3.

91   Wal-Mart: Pages 91–92 rely heavily upon Lynda Schuster, "Wal-Mart Chief's Enthusiastic Approach Infects Employees, Keeps Retailer Growing," *Wall Street Journal,* Apr. 20, 1982, p. 21.

94   "Until we believe": Rene C. McPherson, "The People Principle," *Leaders,* January-March 1980, p. 52.

94   "We didn't waste time": "Rene McPherson: GSB Deanship Is His Way to Reinvest in the System," *Stanford GSB,* fall 1980–81, p. 15.

96   "The way you stay fresh": Ibid.

96   "I guess I got laid off": George H. Labovitz, Speech to the Opening Assembly, Western Hospital Association, Anaheim, Calif., Apr. 27, 1981.

97   Delta Airlines: Pages 97–98 are based, in part, upon Margaret R. Keefe Umanzio, "Delta Is Ready," unpublished manuscript (San Francisco: McKinsey & Co., July 1981).

97   "Stewardesses, for instance": Janet Guyon, " 'Family Feeling' at Delta Creates Loyal Workers, Enmity of Unions," *Wall Street Journal,* July 7, 1980, p. 13.

97   "My rug has to be cleaned": "W. T. Beebe: The Gold Winner," *Financial World,* Mar. 15, 1978, p. 21.

97   "In February 1979": Guyon, p. 13.

98   "That's important": Ibid.

99   "History shows": "The Five Best-Managed Companies," *Dun's Review,* December 1977, p. 50.

99   "I believe that *less is more*": Kroc, *Grinding It Out,* p. 143.

99   "A well-run restaurant": Ibid., p. 99.

99   "I emphasize the importance": Ibid., p. 101.

99   "The book" at McDonald's: Jeremy Main, "Toward Service Without a Snarl," *Fortune,* Mar. 23, 1981, p. 66.

99   "Debbie Thompson": Ibid.

100 "The American flag": Susan Saiter Anderson, "Hamburger U. Offers a Break," *Survey of Continuing Education (New York Times),* Aug. 30, 1981, pp. 27–28.

102 Walk into IBM's: Allan J. Mayer and Michael Ruby, "One Firm's Family," *Newsweek,* Nov. 21, 1977, p. 84.

102 "T. J. Watson didn't move in": Watson, *A Business and Its Beliefs,* p. 15.

102 "IBM produced parts": Ibid., pp. 15–16.

102 "providing showers on company premises": Ibid., p. 17.

102 "Almost every kind of fanfare": Ibid., p. 18.

103 "born homilist": Gil Burck, "International Business Machines," *Fortune,* January 1940, p. 41.

103 "Above all, we seek": Shook, *Ten Greatest Salespersons,* p. 73.

104 "If you look at the entrepreneurship": Thomas L. Friedman, "Talking Business," *New York Times,* June 9, 1981, p. D2.

106 "Since recently assuming command": Zumwalt, p. 187.

106 "The voice call *'Hellcat' ":* Ibid., p. 189.

107 Kyocera has 2,000 employees: Lad Kuzela, "Putting Japanese-Style Management to Work," *Industry Week,* Sept. 1, 1980, p. 61.

107 Peter Vaill is a student: Peter B. Vaill, "Toward a Behavioral Description of High-Performing Systems," in *Leadership: Where Else Can We Go?,* ed. Morgan W. McCall, Jr., and Michael M. Lombardo (Durham, N.C.: Duke University Press, 1978), pp. 109–11.

108 "Caterpillar has always started": "Caterpillar: Sticking to Basics to Stay Competitive," *Business Week,* May 4, 1981, p. 76.

109 in one old plant: Edward Meadows, "How Three Companies Increased Their Productivity," *Fortune,* Mar. 10, 1980, p. 97.

109 "Bringing financial information": Charles G. Burck, "What Happens When Workers Manage Themselves," *Fortune,* July 27, 1981, p. 68.

109 "Nothing is worse for morale": Richard T. Pascale, "The Role of the Chief Executive in the Implementation of Corporate Policy: A Conceptual Framework," Research Paper no. 357 (Graduate School of Business, Stanford University, February 1977), p. 39.

111 "A man wouldn't sell": Manchester, *Good-bye, Darkness,* p. 200.

111 At Mars, Inc.: Robert Levy, "Legends of Business," *Dun's Review,* June 1980, p. 92.

111 "Most Japanese corporations": Ohmae, p. 27.

112 *"Peter Peterson":* Ogilvy, "The Creative Chef," p. 209.

113 "What I am really talking about": Barry F. Sullivan, "International Service Products: The Opportunity of the 80s" (speech to the American Bankers

Association, International Banking Symposium, Washington, D.C., Mar. 29, 1981), p. 13.

113   "I'm a big advocate": John S. McClenahen, "Moving GTE Off Hold," *Industry Week,* Jan. 12, 1981, p. 67.

113   "As divisions reach a certain size": Barron, "British 3M's Multiple Management," p. 54.

114   "Essentially, we act": Bro Uttal, "The Gentlemen and the Upstarts," p. 100.

115   "We don't need a 5,000-person plant": *Dun's Review,* December 1977, pp. 54-55.

116   "In the last decade": Roger L. Cason, "The Right Size: An Organizational Dilemma," *Management Review,* April 1978, p. 27.

116   "Skinner cites an episode": Lubar, p. 55.

116   The theoretical case is stated: John Child, *Organization: A Guide to Problems and Practice* (New York: Harper & Row, 1977), pp. 222–23.

118   "Teams set their own": Shepherd, "Innovation at Texas Instruments," p. 84.

118   "People can be themselves": E. F. Schumacher, *Small Is Beautiful: Economics as If People Mattered* (New York: Harper & Row, 1973), p. 75.

119   "One reason why the Roman Empire": Anthony Jay, *Management and Machiavelli: An Inquiry into the Politics of Corporate Life* (New York: Holt, Rinehart and Winston, 1967), pp. 63–64.

119   "Substituting rules for judgment": "The Iconoclast Who Made Visa No. 1." *Business Week,* Dec. 22, 1980, p. 44.

Testing Skyhook 2

TRUST

Leaders who trust their coworkers are, in turn,
trusted by them. . . . Leadership without mutual trust
is a contradiction in terms.

—WARREN BENNIS,
ON BECOMING A LEADER

Showing your coworkers that you trust them, that you believe in their ability and integrity, is the first step in pursuit of vision. Treat them in ways that demonstrate your confidence in their capacity to create a better future. If they do not believe that you believe in them, they will not follow. Without followers you're not leading, you're just taking a walk.

A simple self test will begin to help you see how well you are performing. Asking your coworkers "How am I doing?" will complete the picture.

ASK YOURSELF

Test out your trust level by rating the accuracy of the following statements. Use a 1–5 scale ranging from "a little" to "a great extent."

• I believe my coworkers know more about their jobs than anyone else.	1 2 3 4 5
• I believe my coworkers are strong and resilient individuals.	1 2 3 4 5
• I believe my coworkers want to hold themselves accountable for their performance.	1 2 3 4 5
• I believe my coworkers can excel at creative problem solving.	1 2 3 4 5
• I believe my coworkers want to learn new skills and test their potential.	1 2 3 4 5

ASK YOUR COWORKERS

If you gave yourself a "4" or "5" rating on each statement, you probably show trust and respect for your coworkers. However, you can verify your self-assessment by having a two-part discussion with your coworkers. First, ask them to talk about the importance of trust so that you understand it in the same way. Second, ask them for feedback on your performance.

You'll know you're developing a common understanding about the importance of trust when you hear comments like these:

> - "Getting to know each person as a unique individual builds trust. Trust starts one-on-one."
> - "Letting go of the purse strings really shows you trust us, that we'll use the budget wisely."
> - "Backing us up in public when we're catching a lot of flak shows others that you trust our judgment."
> - "Telling us the bad news as well as the good news, the whole truth, shows us you think we're adults who can handle it."
> - "Being careful with the way you ask questions shows trust and respect. If you asked question after question, it could sound like an interrogation."

After discussing the importance of trust, check out your coworkers' view of your performance by asking them to consider the five items in your self-assessment. You may find it more productive for them to answer the following questions than to give you numerical ratings on each item:

> - What am I doing right now that supports each statement?
> - What else can I do—either more or less—to show greater support for each statement?

As you listen, try to clarify your coworkers' answers and ideas. Express your appreciation for their feedback without becoming defensive. After you've listened, ask yourself, "What am I ready to do to raise our trust level?" Develop an action plan to build on your strengths and continue to improve.

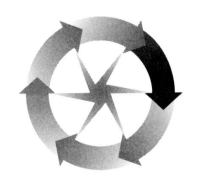

Skyhook 3

OPEN COMMUNICATION

*I believe **everyone** in an organization has an obligation to lead. . . .
They must be equipped with the tools of communicating
and listening and convinced that their personal needs and those
of their team members fit together.*
—RAYMOND W. SMITH,
CHAIRMAN AND CEO OF BELL ATLANTIC

*An effective leader must provide an open and honest
environment, in which debate is encouraged, where people can
relax and enjoy themselves. . . . Leadership will especially
require the ability to listen to people and to really hear their
concerns, ideas, ambitions.*
—MARSHALL E. LOEB,
MANAGING EDITOR OF *FORTUNE*

Skyhook 3 Open Communication—Share organization and personal data widely. The need to know increases during changing times. Hard information helps reduce uncertainty and bolsters confidence. Soft interpersonal information furthers trust between people and departments. Strong informal communication networks help people adapt to change.

Chris Argyris provides a useful framework for understanding the importance of open communication in "Interpersonal Competence and Organization Effectiveness," from his book by the same title (1962). His message is that the quality of face-to-face relationships will determine an organization's ability to function. Unfortunately, many organizations try to submerge the human element and operate on a Spock-like purely rational basis. Argyris makes a case for openness, honesty, and integrity in the pursuit of initiative, risk-taking, and dealing with change. Without interpersonal competence, an organization will be characterized by mistrust, defensiveness, and conformity, a deadly combination in a rapidly changing environment.

As Argyris makes his case he points out:

- Behavior in organizations is driven by values, so you need to understand what they are to understand what people do.

- Most formal organizations favor rational values for getting the job done and use coercion, rewards, and penalties.

- An emphasis on rational processes suppresses emotions and feelings—people learn to hide their feelings, especially about each other.

- Eventually people withhold their intellectual as well as emotional views—openness, experimentation, and risk-taking decrease, which lowers organizational vitality.

- Without interpersonal competence, people become confused and frustrated with their relationships and begin to mistrust their coworkers' motives.

- Without interpersonal competence people learn to "play it safe" and "say only the right thing"—conformity becomes the norm and diversity is unwelcome.

- Without interpersonal competence, decision making becomes flawed, and change efforts are thwarted because people refuse to point out deficiencies or express their misgivings.

- Increasing interpersonal competence can be achieved by "seeding" the system with individual role models who exemplify a more humanistic set of values.

- For increased interpersonal competence to be sustained, corresponding changes need to be made in policies, practices, and procedures so that individual and organizational behavior are aligned.

Tom Peters and Nancy Austin offer an antidote for the malaise that can overtake an organization as Argyris described. In "Doing MBWA," the letters stand for "Managing by Wandering Around."

It is their core concept in *A Passion for Excellence* (1985). They acknowledge that it is really leadership, not management, they are talking about and that face-to-face interpersonal competence is the essence of this very "hands-on art." Leaders not only rely on open communication and candor in their own working relationships; they set the tone for the rest of the organization.

Peters and Austin's ideas and suggestions include:

- MBWA provides leaders with a face-to-face opportunity to listen, teach, and facilitate by removing obstacles.

- Values must be transmitted face-to-face.

- MBWA is not about "gee-whiz socializing" or about giving orders or taking over.

- It should leave the employee with "more freedom to try more things—within the parameters of vision."

- It has to be done regularly for people to feel comfortable enough to speak their minds and give honest feedback—"state visits" don't work.

- MBWA has to demonstrate to the rank and file that they are important—listen to the people first before management, don't bring a retinue of note-takers, and dress casually so people feel comfortable enough to talk.

- Use the chain of command to act on what was heard—bottom-up listening becomes top-down problem solving.

- MBWA works only when the leader has absolute integrity—sources must be protected so that honest feedback has no repercussions.

- MBWA should not be attempted lightly because it exposes you—your vision, your honesty and integrity, your consistency, and your ability to listen (or the lack of any of these) are there for everyone to see.

Open communication, a decidedly human activity, has always been critical in healthy relationships. But it is becoming more difficult despite stunning technology. Communication is about more than exchanging information quickly and accurately: It is about trust and integrity, compassion and creativity, sharing a vision, and affirming common values. E-mail offers little here. As hard as it is to do with virtual offices in a global marketplace, leaders must go about the change process face-to-face.

INTERPERSONAL COMPETENCE AND ORGANIZATIONAL EFFECTIVENESS

CHRIS ARGYRIS

In the previous chapter [not included in this volume] we concluded that organizations are developed from, and conceived according to the image of a particular strategy. Implicit in the strategy were certain assumptions about how individuals will behave effectively in an organization. These assumptions were found to be questionable in light of what is known about the nature of human beings.

The next step is to become more specific so hypotheses can be stated regarding the impact of these assumptions on the individuals and the organization.

Recently there has developed an increasing awareness of the relevance of values to understanding human behavior[1,2] and decision making in organization.[3] Let us define values as commands or directives to which individuals are committed.[4] We may then ask what are the commands or directives (or imperatives) implicit in the formal strategy used to create organizations. If we can discover these organizational commands or directives, we can hypothesize that to the extent the participants follow them, their behavior can be understood, predicted, and influenced by knowing these values.

As Margenau suggests, a command may define a value, but it requires a dedication to command if the value is to affect human behavior.[5] The major factor to be evaluated, therefore, is the degree of commitment or dedication to these values. The stronger the dedication, the greater the probability that the behavior can be understood independently of the particular personality of each participant. To test this hypothesis one must not only learn the organizational values, but one must ascertain "the extent to which participants follow" are dedicated to these values as determiners of their behavior. (Indeed, we may find that it is easier for certain personality patterns to be dedicated to these values.[6] Important as this hypothesis is for our theory, we are not going to attempt to test it at this time.) In this study, we are going to ascertain the impact of a specific set of organizational values upon the behavior of the participants on the organization.

We begin to develop a model by asking what would happen if participants followed the organizational values. Once the consequences are spelled out, we can go to the empirical world to see if the predicted consequences do exist when the participants adhere to or are dedicated to the values.

THE VALUES IMPLICIT IN FORMAL ORGANIZATIONS

The basic values . . . about effective human relationships inherent in the formal organizational strategy can be summarized as follows:

1. The important human relationships are those that are related to achieving the organization's objective. (Getting the job done.)

2. Effectiveness in human relationships increases as behavior is rational, logical, and clearly communicated. Effectiveness decreases as emotionality increases.

3. Human relationships are most effectively influenced through direction, coercion, and control as well as a set of rewards and penalties that serve to emphasize the rational behavior and getting the job done.[7]

We may ask:

a) What would tend to happen to interpersonal competence and to interpersonal human relationships if these values are followed?

b) How do (the resulting) interpersonal relationships feed back to influence such rational activities as decision making, problem exploration, information transmission?

c) How do (the resulting) interpersonal relationships feed back to influence the norms of the organization toward or against such phenomena as dependence, conformity, interexecutive trust, and internal commitment?

d) How are such factors as organizational rigidity, flexibility, and climate influenced by all the factors above?

THE IMPACT OF THE FORMAL VALUES ON INTERPERSONAL COMPETENCE

To the extent that individuals dedicate themselves to the value of rationality and "getting the job done," they will tend to be aware of and emphasize the rational, intellective aspects of the interactions that exist in an organization and suppress the interpersonal and emotional aspects, especially those that do not seem to be relevant to achieving the task. For example, one frequently hears in organizations, "Let's keep feelings out of the discussion," or "Look here, our task today is to achieve objective x and not to get emotional."

As the interpersonal and emotional aspects of behavior become suppressed, we may hypothesize that an organizational norm will tend to arise that coerces individuals to hide their feelings. Their interpersonal difficulties will either be suppressed, or disguised and brought up as rational, technical, intellectual problems. In short, receiving or giving feedback about interpersonal relationships will tend to be suppressed.

Under these conditions we may hypothesize that the individuals will find it very difficult to develop competence in dealing with feelings and interpersonal relationships. In a world where the expression of feelings is not permitted, one may hypothesize the individuals will build personal and organizational defenses to help them suppress their own feelings or inhibit others in their attempts to express their feelings.[8] If feelings are suppressed, the tendency will be for the individual not to permit himself or others to *own* their feeling. For example, the individual may say about himself, "No, I didn't mean that," or "Let me start over again. I'm confusing the facts." Equally possible is for one individual to say to another, "No, you shouldn't feel that way," or "That's not effective executive behavior," or "Let's act like mature people and keep feelings out of this."

Another way to prevent individuals from violating the organizational values of rationality and from embarrassing one another, is to block out, refuse to consider (consciously or unconsciously) ideas and values which, if explored, could expose suppressed feelings.

Such a defensive reaction in the organization may eventually lead to a barrier of intellectual ideas as well as values. The participants will tend to limit themselves to those ideas and values that are not threatening, and so not violate organizational norms. The individuals in the organization will tend to decrease its capacity to be open to new ideas and values. As the degree of openness decreases, the capacity to experiment will tend to decrease, and the fear to take risks will tend to increase. As the fear to take risks increases, the probability of experimentation is decreased and the range or scope of openness is decreased, which decreases risks. We have a closed circuit that could be an important cause of the loss of vitality in an organization.[9]

To summarize, the extent that participants are dedicated to the values implicit in the formal organization, they will tend to create a social system where the following will tend to *decrease* (see Figure 1):

1. Receiving and giving nonevaluative feedback.
2. Owning and permitting others to own their ideas, feelings, and values.
3. Openness to new ideas, feelings, and values.
4. Experimentation and risk taking with new ideas and values.

As any one of these decreases, it acts to decrease all the others and to increase the opposite states of affairs. In terms of our model (Figure 1) inputs (values) feed into a "black box" composed of highly interrelated variables, where an increase or decrease in any one can set off a chain of reactions that influence all the others.

As the above states of affairs continue, we may hypothesize the following "outputs":

1. Members of this system of relationships will *not* tend to be aware of their interpersonal impact upon others (they may be aware of their rational, intellectual impact).
2. The members of this system of relationships will not tend to solve interpersonal problems in such a way that they (or similar problems) will not tend to occur.

We may conclude that the organizational values, if followed, will tend to create a social system in which the members' interpersonal competence will tend to decrease (see Figure 1). (Up to this point we are not hypothesizing the impact upon rational, intellective competence which presumably should not be so affected by these values.)

FIGURE 1

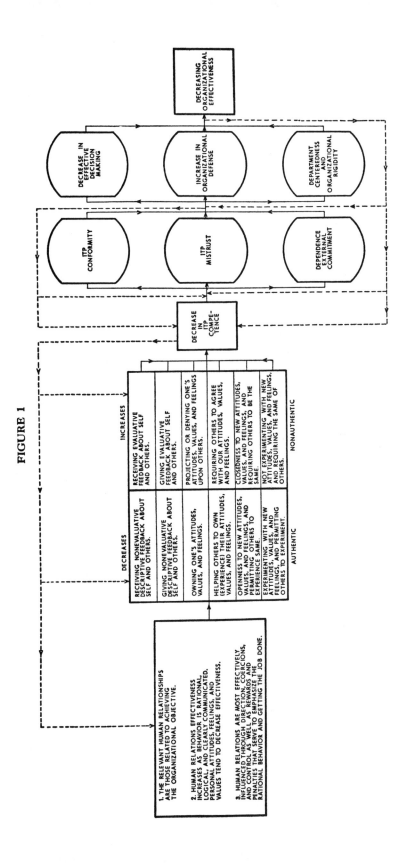

THE IMPACT UPON THE ORGANIZATION OF
DECREASING INTERPERSONAL COMPETENCE

Let us continue our theoretical analysis with the following question: What may we hypothesize are some of the implications upon the organization of decreasing interpersonal competence?

If individuals are in social systems where they are unable to predict accurately their interpersonal impact upon others, and others' impact upon themselves, they may begin to feel confused. "Why are people behaving that way toward me?" "Why do they interpret me incorrectly?" Since such questions are not sanctioned in a rationally dominated system, much less answered, the confusion will tend to turn to frustration and feelings of failure regarding interpersonal relations. In an attempt to maintain their sense of esteem, the members may react by questioning the honesty, and genuineness of the interpersonal behavior of their fellow workers. Simultaneously, they may place an even greater emphasis upon the rational, technical interactions, in which they are probably experiencing a greater degree of success. The increased emphasis upon rationality will act to suppress the feelings even more, which in turn will decrease the probability that the questions of confusion and the mistrust (of self and others) will be explored.

As interpersonal mistrust increases, and as the capacity (individual and organizational) to cope with this mistrust decreases, then the members may tend to adapt by "playing it safe." The predisposition will be to say those things that cannot be misunderstood and to discuss those issues for which there exist clear organizational values and sanctions. The desire "to say the right thing" should be especially strong toward one's superiors, toward one's peers with whom one is competing, and toward one's subordinates, who may be known to bypass their superiors. The result is that conformity begins to develop within an organization. Along with conformity, the interpersonal relationships will tend to be characterized by "conditional acceptance" (to use a Rogerian concept) where the members will tend to feel accepted if they behave in accordance with certain organizational specifications.

Another possible important force acting toward conformity is the predisposition of individuals to bring around them people whose self-concepts are congruent. There is a tendency to hire or upgrade individuals who manifest the accepted image of the system.[10] For example, Ward found that executives prefer subordinates who do not make trouble, are not argumentative, somewhat retiring, meek, and even bashful to the more argumentative, impatient, rebellious types. This would be understandable in terms of our model, since the latter qualities would violate the norms of the executive systems and consequently require a degree of interpersonal competence that may not exist. In the same study Ward showed that another preferred pattern was for the subordinate to be systematic, orderly, precise, and accurate. These qualities are consonant with the "inputs of rationality."[11] Evidence consonant with Ward's findings was published by Freeman and Taylor. They found that while 100 top executives said that they looked for aggressive, energetic applicants, they personally wanted "tactful subordinates." The executives tended to attribute their own success to "brain and character," but they preferred "emotionally controlled and balanced" subordinates rather than overly bright or highly ethical ones.[12]

Basic to the formal strategy is power over and control of the subordinates by the superior. The power is especially related to the capacity to direct, reward, and penalize. If we now add the existence of mistrust and conformity to dependence, we may hypothesize that the members' commitment to the organization will tend to be external as far as interpersonal activities are concerned. By "external commitment," I mean that the source of commitment to work for any given individual lies in the power, rewards, and penalties that some other individual may use to influence the first individual. Internal commitment exists when the motive for a particular behavior resides from within (for example, self-realization). A certain amount of internal commitment restricted to rational activities may be possible in this system, if the rational, intellective aspects of the job are consonant with the individual's abilities and expressed needs.

External commitment will tend to reinforce the conformity with, conditional acceptance of, and especially the dependence upon the leader. The subordinates will tend to look for cues from the leader and will be willing to be influenced and guided by him. In fact, they may develop great skill in inducing the leader to define the problems, the range of alternatives, and so on. The subordinates will tend to operate within limits that they know to be safe. As the dependence increases, the need for the subordinates to know where they "stand" will also tend to increase.[13]

Thus, interpersonal mistrust, conformity, conditional acceptance, external commitment, and dependence tend to be "outputs" of decreasing interpersonal competence. Each of these feeds back to reinforce itself. All, in turn, feed back upon interpersonal competence to decrease it further or to reinforce it at its existing level.

At some point (to be empirically determined) the consequences above will tend to feed back to influence the rational intellective competence of the executives. For example, in some of the situations to be discussed later we learned that executives (with mathematical and engineering background) dealing with highly technical issues developed strong emotional attachments to these issues. During discussions held to resolve technical rational issues, the emotional involvements tended to block understanding. Since the men did not tend to deal with emotions, their inhibiting effects were never explored. On the contrary, they were covered up by technical, rational arguments. Since these arguments were attempts by people to defend their self or attack others', there was a tendency for the rationality of the arguments to be weak. This in turn troubled the receiver of the argument, who tended to attack obvious rational flaws immediately. The attack tended to increase the degree of threat experienced by the first person, and he became even more defensive. Similar impacts upon rational decision making were also discovered in areas such as investment decisions, purchasing policies, quality control standards, product design, and marketing planning.

Similar problems tended to occur with decisions that involved human factors in an organization. They were not explored thoroughly, especially when the values and ideas to be explored were not tolerated by the system. Demotions, promotions, reprimands, discipline, and evaluation of ineffectiveness are but a few examples of such decisions. Finally, there were cases on record in which the organization never explored a new product or a new manufacturing process because the "powers that be wouldn't hear of it."

Another crucial area of decision making that could be influenced by interpersonal incompetence would be the area of organizational change. For example, let us consider an organization that desires to go from a highly centralized to a decentralized structure. One may predict that executives operating under the conditions above will not tend to explore or take adequate account of the feelings that subordinates under decentralization would have regarding decentralization. The executives will tend to "sell" decentralization by using rational reasons, largely missing such subordinates' feelings as dependence, conformity, and fear of authority. The subordinates in turn will tend to suppress such feelings (assuming they are even aware of them) and communicate to their superiors that they understand the meaning of decentralization and that they agree with it. However, one would predict that if the superiors actually did decentralize and give the subordinates authority and responsibility, the latter will tend to seek ways to induce their superiors to make the decisions. The superiors, in turn, will tend to feel perplexed if not irritated. However, since the expression of such feelings is not sanctioned, they will tend to find indirect ways to express their disappointment and/or hold new meetings loaded with new rational reasons "selling" the importance of decentralization.

When executives perceive that their present leadership is not as effective as they wish it to be, one finds that they tend to take two courses of action. The first is to emphasize even more the values of the formal organizational structure. This means that they tend to place greater emphasis on the use of rationality, direction, control, rewards, and penalties. In practice this tends to mean that they begin to check on other people's work not only to see if it is done but also how it was accomplished. Another activity is to manage through detailed questioning about issues and problems that may exist at levels lower than the man being questioned but for which he is responsible. For example, asking a personnel vice-president the capacity of a parking lot in a plant away from the home office.

The result of such action on the part of the superior is to create a defensiveness in the subordinate. The subordinate now finds himself constantly checking on all details so he will not be "caught" by the superior. However, the activity of the organization is not carried forward with such behavior. The result is simply one of making the subordinates (and usually his subordinates) more defensive. Their response is to build up organizational defenses to protect themselves. For example, in one case where executives were managing by detail, the subordinates created the "JIC" file, which stands for "just in case" some superior asks. This file was kept up to date by several lower-level managers who were full time and countless other people working part time. The JIC file is an organizational defense against threat experienced by individuals at various levels.

In short, one may hypothesize that organizational defenses may be developed in an organization to protect various individuals and groups.

These organizational defenses can be used to "needle" people. This tends to occur when the rational methods seem to fail. But since the use of feelings is deviant behavior and since the superior or subordinates do not have much experience in their use, the tendency may be to have feelings "overdetermined." By "overdetermined," I mean that feelings tend to be much stronger than the situation warrants. Their overdeterminedness is compounded by the fact that subordinates do not tend to be accustomed to dealing with feelings.

Executives may speak of "needling the boys," "once in a while, 'raising hell' to keep them on their toes," and so on. If these conditions continue, it is not long before the "hot" decisions of the organization are administered by using emotions. This is commonly known in industry as "management by crisis."

As management by crisis increases, the subordinate's defensive reaction to these crises will tend to increase. One way to protect himself is to make certain that his area of responsibility is administered competently and that no other peer executive "throws a dead cat into his yard." The subordinate's predisposition will tend to be centered toward the interests of his department. As the department centeredness increases, the interdepartmental rivalries will tend to increase. All these decrease the organization's flexibility for change as well as the co-operation among departments. This decrease, in turn, will tend to be adapted to by the top management by increasing their directives, which in turn begins to recentralize the organization.

The external commitment, conformity, interpersonal mistrust, ineffective decision making, management by crisis, and organizational rigidity will tend to feed back to reinforce each other and to decrease interpersonal competence (see Figure 1). Moreover, each will feed upon all the others to reinforce itself. We would conclude that under these conditions the tendency will be to increase the energy required to produce the same input, or some day it may even decrease the output, although the input remains constant. When this state of affairs occurs, the organization may be said to have begun to be ineffective.

This analysis may help us to understand some of the findings of Guetzkow and Cyr and March and his associates. Guetzkow and Cyr[14] found that groups in industry tend to postpone (withdraw from) complex problems. They prefer to play it safe and deal with the easier problems. In an interesting paper March concludes that rationality in an organization is qualified and constrained. Consequently, organizational decision-making behavior is primarily adaptive rather than rational. March mentions four critical activities that can constrain rationality, three of which would be predicted by our model. They are: (1) conflict among parties within the firm (intergroup competition in our terms), (2) avoidance of uncertainty,

(3) searching "in the neighborhood" of the problem symptom current alternative, and (4) organizational learning.[15]

We have suggested that intergroup conflict is inherent in the pyramidal structure, managerial controls, directive leadership.[16] In this study we suggest that it is also inherent in the emphasis upon rationality and suppression of emotionality. If the above is valid, in a world where interpersonal mistrust, dependence, conformity, management by crisis, thorough detail, and fear are prevalent, then playing it safe and not getting hurt would be predictable. Under these conditions avoiding uncertainty, searching for solutions close to the problem, and looking primarily at the available alternatives would be adaptive. In other words, the conditions March accepts as independent variables or "givens," we view as dependent and changeable. It is hoped that this study (plus the already mentioned work by Blake and Shepard) will suggest that changes can be made in organizations so that at least the first three conditions can be modified. If we learn to modify them to a considerable degree, we may even be able to change the degree to which, as well as the activities through which, an organization learns.

SOME FORCES INHIBITING ORGANIZATIONAL INEFFECTIVENESS

The reader may wonder if we mean to imply that when interpersonal competence is low, the organization is automatically doomed to failure. The answer is obviously, "No."

First, in any organization a large proportion of the decision making is related to "getting the widgets out." There are many technical, professional decisions that must be made if an organization is to achieve its objective. The more the organization requires intellective rational competence, and the more it has such competence, the *less* the probability up to a point (to be empirically determined) that a low interpersonal competence will tend to have negative impact of great significance. However, as we shall show, there is a point at which interpersonal competence becomes so crucial that it can significantly affect the rational (as well as the interpersonal) activities of the organization. Competing organizations are able to obtain the finest minds and the best equipment that they need then. In a competitive world, the one that is able to support these resources with effective human relationships may well increase its opportunity for survival.

Another important consideration is that the above state of affairs is consonant with the formal organizational values about effective human relationships. Thus, although the consequences (decreasing interpersonal trust, competence; increasing management by crisis, and so on) may be unintended, and even not desired, they flow naturally from the kind of organizational world in which men are placed. The unintended consequences are, therefore, functional. They are necessary if the executives are to survive in a world of organizational stress. In other words the values about effective human relationships held by the executives, and implicit in the formal organizational structure and managerial controls, lead to a stressful world where a subordinate is dependent upon a superior. To adapt to and operate within this dependence and stress, the subordinates adhere to the same values. The values will probably be maintained as long as their "maintenance cost" does not exceed the cost of their negative impact upon the executive system, the decision making, and the relationship throughout the entire organization.

A third moderating influence is the degree with which interpersonal feelings are openly discussed. One might hypothesize that in an organization feelings are never completely blocked. Our analysis above has been a theoretical one. We have purposely not considered the possibility that feelings may be discussed at times, even if they violate the organizational values. There are examples on record where executives describe a meeting as one in which "the lid blew off " or an interview situation where "we had it out." In studying a specific organization, the degree to which these meetings occur will be determined. If they occur frequently, we should find that (1) they are perceived as violating the organizational values and/or (2) the organization had, in addition to the values listed above, another set that sanctioned such behavior.

A fourth possibility is that after many years in such a system the members will tend to decrease their expectation that feelings are important and relevant in their everyday activities. Given such expectations, the "emotional apathy and noninvolvement" and the frustration of suppressed feelings will not tend to be as great. However, the organizational consequences of conformity, and so on, will still tend to arise.

Finally, although I know of no existing data, it may be that there are "threshold" points which prevent a system from increasing its interpersonal ineffectiveness indefinitely. Similarly there may exist threshold points which will tend to make it increasingly difficult to increase effectiveness indefinitely. One may also hypothesize that at some point and under certain conditions (at the moment unknown) the degree of effectiveness or ineffectiveness will not tend to increase or decrease but tend to remain constant. Any activity continuing in the direction of the dominant state of affairs (effectiveness or ineffectiveness) will only tend to reinforce these state of affairs.

A NOTE ON THE NATURE OF OUR PREDICTIONS

If one examines the model that we have presented, one will find that it contains certain assumptions about the behavior that it purports to understand. They are:

1. Some human behavior in organization can be understood as caused by individuals adhering or dedicating themselves to organizational values. The greater the commitment to the values, the less one needs to include personality factors to explain the behavior. For example, people with psychologically different personalities (as measured by a test of one's choosing) would still tend to behave in the direction and manner specified by the model. Thus, our focus is on the study of *systems of behavior* which, once in operation, are independent of the particular individuals that composed them.

   This does not mean that personality factors are completely irrelevant. The individuals must be capable of perceiving the values and becoming dedicated to them. The system would never be able to influence the behavior of the members, if the members were simply unable to recognize or have the values communicated to them. Nor could the system operate if one attempted to populate it with personality types who simply could not dedicate themselves to these values. One reason why the second condition tends to occur rarely in our society is that our schools, churches, recreational groups, and even some aspects of family life are also based upon formal organizational values. Thus, in our culture, individuals are prepared to live more or less in accordance with formal organization values.

2. The second assumption is that the system, with its inputs, outputs, and feedback processes will tend to remain relatively stable. The stability occurs as the individuals act within the values of the system, thereby keeping out disturbing influences.

Change may be induced in this system through external pressures (that is, environment) or through the "seeding" of the system with enough individuals who are capable of, indeed need to behave in accordance with, other values and have the necessary power to do so.

3. Any change attempted in the outputs (for example, through new policies) designed to be superimposed upon the individuals, will tend to be resisted. Changes that do not or are not permitted to influence the inputs (values) will tend to fail. One can make, for example, changes in organization structure policies that require a decrease in interdepartmental conflicts, and so on. None of these changes will have lasting effects unless the inputs are appropriately influenced. The appropriate influence is in the direction of increasing interpersonal competence.

Although increasing interpersonal competence is a necessary first step, *it is not enough*. We may recall that the structure of the organization, its technology, job design, controls, incentive systems, and so on, are all based on the same set of values. Consequently these factors must eventually be modified or else one can negate the changes that may occur through an increase in interpersonal competence. To summarize, the basic changes will require a modification or addition to the present values. To effect changes, organizational, technological, and interpersonal factors will require alteration. The interpersonal factors, however, should come first, closely followed by the others.[17]

NOTES

1. Donald W. Taylor, "Toward an Information Processing Theory of Motivation," Marshall R. Jones (ed.), *Nebraska Symposium on Motivation* (Lincoln, Neb.: University of Nebraska Press, 1960), pp. 51–79.

2. A. H. Maslow (ed.), *New Knowledge in Human Values* (New York: Harper & Bros., 1959).

3. Herbert Simon, *Administrative Behavior* (New York: The Macmillan Co., 1957).

4. Henry Margenau, "The Scientific Basis of Value Theory," *New Knowledge in Human Values*, pp. 42–43.

5. *Ibid.*, p. 45.

6. This is a hypothesis of men like Fromm, May, and men who worked on several of the research projects stemming from the California studies on the authoritarian personality.

7. For other studies consonant with these conclusions see Douglas McGregor, *The Human Side of Enterprise* (New York: McGraw-Hill Book Co., Inc., 1960); Robert L. Katz, "Toward a More Effective Enterprise," *Harvard Business Review,* Vol. 38, No. 5 (September-October, 1960), pp. 80-120; James March, and Herbert Simon, *Organizations* (New York: John Wiley & Sons, Inc., 1959).

8. This is a common phenomenon in the opening sessions of T-groups. To tell the "truth" is usually interpreted to mean "Let's clobber one another," "tell each other our faults," "to put me on the table and open me up," and so on.

9. For a recent student who emphasizes the importance of vitality see Marshall E. Dimock, *A Philosophy of Administration* (New York: Harper & Bros., 1957).

10. E. J. McCormick and R. W. Middaugh, "The Development of a Tailor-Made Scoring for the How-Supervise? Test," *Personnel Psychology,* Vol. IX (1956), pp. 27–37.

11. Lewis B. Ward, "Do You Want a Weak Subordinate?" *Harvard Business Review,* September-October, 1961, pp. 6–26.

12. G. L. Freeman and E. K. Taylor, *How to Pick Leaders* (New York: Funk & Wagnalls Co., 1950).

13. I am perplexed as to how many writers "prove" the importance of "merit ratings" or "evaluation" programs by citing peoples' needs to know. These data may simply show how dependent the subordinates are and how well the programs are institutionalizing the dependence.

14. H. Guetzkow and J. Cyr "An Analysis of Conflict in Decision-Making Groups," *Human Relations,* Vol. VII (1954), pp. 367–82.

15. James March, "Some Models of Organizational Decision Making," symposium at American Psychological Association, Sept. 5, 1961 (mimeographed, Carnegie Institute of Technology).

16. Chris Argyris, *Personality and Organization* (New York: Harper & Row Publishers, Inc., 1957).

17. This assertion has implications for planning laboratories. For example, one would not tend to focus on intergroup problems until interpersonal competence will not tend to be enough, if the organization is characterized by built-in "win-lose" battles among departments.

6

DOING MBWA

TOM PETERS and NANCY AUSTIN

We began with the technology of the obvious—MBWA; we explored MBWA with customers, suppliers, MBWA and innovation, MBWA and listening (to customers, as an unparalleled source of innovation), MBWA and leadership. That was introduction. Now we come full circle—to the process of *doing* MBWA. Leading (more so than managing) is a hands-on art. Coaching is the essence of leading—developing those with whom we work. Coaching *is* MBWA (or vice versa, we're not sure which, or whether it matters): This apparently obvious (we said it ourselves) trait/skill/process deserves a closer look.

First, it seems fair, honest, appropriate—and obvious to the many wounded among readers—to begin by saying that MBWA ain't as easy as it may sound! Doing it well is an art. However, it is an art that can probably be learned—and it is clearly unrelated to having an "outgoing" personality. In fact, arguably the best wanderers are the introverts who start with the ability to listen, because listening, and not tap dancing or pronouncing, is at the heart of effective MBWA.

There is a certain inappropriateness, frankly, to our use of the term "MBWA." In a way it makes the physical act of the wandering, per se, seem the most significant point. That is vital—but MBWA as we see it is much more. It is, as we have said, really a

NOTE: MBWA means Managing by Wandering Around.

code word for all the aspects of leadership we have stressed. That's why it turns out to be so tough.

To begin with, as the effective leader wanders/coaches/develops/engenders small wins, a lot is going on—at least three major activities, usually all at once. They are (1) listening, (2) teaching and (3) facilitating. Listening is the "being in touch" part, getting it firsthand and undistorted—from suppliers, customers and your own people. . . . The very act of listening suggests a form of caring. MBWA is also a "teaching" (and "coaching") act. Values simply must be transmitted face-to-face. The questioning routines, order of visits and a host of other variables add up willy-nilly to the teaching of values. Finally, the wanderer can also be of direct help! The role of the leader as servant, facilitator, protector from bureaucracy (and bureaucrats) is the third prime MBWA objective. That is, often as not, you'll find a project or team stalled for want of 250 square feet of space in which to build a prototype, or an extra $15,000 travel budget to invite ten would-be customers for a weekend-long evaluation of a projected service. You can relieve the bottleneck on the spot, but only if you're there. As we said, the three roles are usually being performed simultaneously, even in a twenty-minute drop-in visit to a team, accounting group, or what have you.

SPACE: REDUCED OR ENHANCED

Let's talk about MBWA as leadership, talk about the art, and talk about the difficulty. For starters, MBWA is all tied up with *delegation*, which we still find to be, by a country mile, the toughest issue in management. Let's consider two people, one of whom (the good guy) we'll mention by name. Both are connected with high tech companies. Both are wanderers. So far so good. But one wanders, and the result is the enhancement of the performance of those with whom he comes in contact. The other is a bull in a china shop; he seems to do about as much harm as he does good.

The "good guy" is a fellow by the name of Barney Oliver, former head of Research and Development at Hewlett-Packard. First, Barney is a brilliant scientist. Second, he's tough as nails, and intellectually demanding. And yet he was the personification of effective MBWA in HP Labs, the heart of its "next bench syndrome," which in turn is the heart of open and participative (albeit tough-minded) communication.

Barney would wander, we are told, with extraordinary regularity. And he'd stop and chat. And, indeed, you had darn well better have something worthwhile to chat about! He'd look at what you were working on and ask the toughest questions imaginable. He didn't shy away from anything. (MBWA *doesn't* mean, then, that most subjects are *verboten*.) He spoke his mind. But the consensus, among twenty-seven-year-olds and fifty-seven-year-olds alike, was that when Barney had finished with you, (1) you'd learned a heck of a lot, of both lasting and short-term significance, and (2) *the project you were working on was still yours*—Barney had not taken away the space, had not in any sense told you what to do or what the next steps should be.

Mr. Bad Guy also wanders in technical spaces. He also knows what he is talking about, and isn't afraid to speak his mind. But when he departs, invariably the consensus is that little is left in his wake. You get the tough-minded dialogue, but the conclusion is his *telling* you, directly or indirectly, almost exactly what you ought to do next (and had better do—given his authority). One blitzed survivor commented, "In six minutes he essentially took away a project that I'd been working on for four months. When he left, it was suddenly his project, not mine."

The important point in the above is the combination of tough-mindedness and space left enhanced (or diminished). Both wanderers are tough. MBWA is *not* about *not* speaking your mind. Good wanderers don't ramble around saying only things like "Howya doin'," "How're the kids?" "Looks like you're doing OK." It's fine to ask about the kids and the spouse if you know there are kids and a spouse (and you should, in fact, find out before you go down and do your wandering). But "gee-whiz socializing," per se, is decidedly not the prime objective of MBWA. It's to find out what's going on, to find out what's bugging people, and, indeed, to guide and direct by a questioning routine that conveys your value set—the sorts of things that "are important around here."

But there's a fine line between instilling your value set (via tough-minded, focused questions) and "managing" a project, and it's a line not easy to establish or maintain, because whether you are a first-line supervisor or CEO, your innocent question is so readily turned into a command—a stone tablet delivered from the mountaintop. Superior wanderers set parameters and draw mental pictures of what a good outcome would look like ("dramatizing the vision," as Bill Moore of Recognition Equipment puts it) instead of "suggesting" that "these three courses of action ought to be followed." Superior wanderers leave the "victim" enlarged, not diminished. They give him or her more freedom to try more things—within the parameters of the vision.*

Domino's Pizza Distribution Company president Don Vlcek demonstrated that fine line in the following story. He was on one of his regular field trips, and a supervisor was complaining that in the process of delivering dough to one particular shop, delivery people had repeatedly broken an exposed basement window. Vlcek whipped a $20 bill out of his pocket and said, "Buy some plywood and cover it—permanently." Afterwards, he talked to the supervisor about the episode: "We don't have any rules that prevented you from doing that. I expect you, within reasonable limits, to do what needs to be done." Let's look at what Vlcek did. He "taught" the young supervisor (by "a picture"—i.e., whipping out the $20 bill on the spot) what he ought to be up to—direct problem solving on his own. Yet he left the young man bigger, not smaller: "You do what's necessary and right, and let no Mickey Mouse get in your way." This was hardly a carte blanche to go out and buy Mercedes delivery trucks, but it was *guidance:* space-enhancing advice.†

"Space": Some Questions—and Things to Do Now

- This will not be easy! If you're up to it, select four or five down-the-line people with whom you've had more or less regular contact. Sit down individually with them and talk about your style, as a space eater or enhancer. (You might have an outside consultant do this for you. It is one of the rare cases when a clinically trained outsider may be helpful.) As a second best, gather a group of two or three trusted peers and spend a half-day talking about how all of you come out on this dimension. (You might try doing the data collection by talking to a trusted colleague's

---

* Tough-minded Tom West, hero of Tracy Kidder's *The Soul of a New Machine,* was a master. He set three or four crystal-clear guiding parameters for his team of youngsters developing a computer at Data General. Then he stayed out of the way, devoting the lion's share of his time to protecting them from corporate interventions. His ultimate genius was in not intruding, in the face of awesome outside pressures, during the critical debugging phase (all the more impressive given that debugging was his area of expertise). He left the space for his lads and the subsequent exhibition of the power of ownership to produce results was awe-inspiring.

† This story brings to mind a typical rejoinder we hear: "Show him he can spend $20 on window glass, and tomorrow he'll spend $100 on his girlfriend, if there's no explicit rule book." We believe it's the worst sort of straw man and reveals our interlocutors' complete lack of trust in their people.

people and getting some feedback on him or her—though it won't be easy.) Alternatively, start your data collection for the future (i.e., now). Have a trusted colleague go with you on your wanderings and give you feedback (or have your secretary do so by, say, sitting in on meetings; any setting is fair game).

• Repeat the process for you and your colleagues as a management team. The tone set by the team is at least as important as that set by an individual.

• Suppose you and your team come up as space eaters par excellence, then what? There are some gimmicky aids (gimmicky, but not silly), such as (a) talking last, not first; (b) consciously using "What do you think?" and avoiding "Why don't you try X, Y, Z?"; (c) pushing your "pupils" to give you a detailed narrative, so that they expose their reasoning to *themselves*, with you continually interjecting "And then what did you try?" rather than "Why didn't you do thus and such at that point?"; (d) not forcing them to blame others, via questions such as "Did purchasing get you the parts on time?"; (e) leading them to generate the next steps with indirect (at most) guidance, with queries such as "And what should that fact lead us toward in the way of tests?"; and (f) asking them to stop by and tell you what was tried, or to give you a call, if it would be helpful, when the next step is taken, thus instilling urgency but not forcing a next step or specific milestone. It boils down to thinking ahead some, and trying to replay (ahead of time) what a typical question from you sounds like. (Is it truly a question, merely aimed at stimulating thought? Or is it a piece of rigid "advice"?) Just "thinking about it" is a very useful first step. Few of us do so, regularly or systematically (and even if we do, we readily forget to what degree our innocent *question*—not direction—sounds like a direct order to those ten years or two rungs more junior).

FREQUENCY

The simplest point to make about MBWA—and the toughest to get most of us to act on—is one that has to do with frequency: If you are not a regular wanderer, the onset of wandering will be, in a word, *terrifying*. Terrifying for you *and* terrifying for those with whom you come in contact (this is true whether you are a first-line supervisor, a small business person or chairman of a Fortune 500 company). Nonwanderers' infrequent forays usually amount to "state visits," prepared for by the "subjects" months in advance,

with the result that what one beholds bears no relationship whatso-
ever to reality. MBWA is decidedly *not* about "state visits." It is a
method for keeping in touch, getting real impressions, reinforcing
strategic themes. The fact is that the most vital function of MBWA,
listening, is not accomplished effectively in the "state visit" or
"Select the good customer to visit" mode.

Both sides contribute to the problem. Suppose the sales vice
president or regional sales manager is going to descend upon a local
branch. He tells the top people there five weeks ahead of time. They
set up some calls for him, because he thinks he ought to go out on
calls. They pick patsy customers, who love the company. He learns
nothing. Then he leaves. Two weeks later, routinely, the branch
bitches to headquarters about not getting more support. Yet the
sales manager's "MBWA experience" has told him that everything is
rosy, so what's this about needing an extra $150 worth of tools for
each person's kit? All the customers *he* saw were happy as clams.

The best (only?) way to beat the state visit rap is by wandering
often, regularly, every day of the year. Barney Oliver was at first a
terrifying figure to young and innocent engineers, but the fact that
Barney was wandering around a good part of every day meant that
eventually they got used to having him around. (It was never easy to
have him around, but you did get used to it.) Given the size of HP
Labs, and the company's geographic spread, he could hardly be an
every-day visitor to every work space. But the real power of the
regular wanderer was demonstrated by an amazing comment from
a twenty-four-year-old HP engineer: "I know that Dave and Bill
and Barney [Packard, Hewlett, Oliver] have been out of active
management for quite a while now. But let me tell you, each of the
[many thousands of] engineers on HP's payroll still believes today
[this was 1983] that any one of the three is liable to stop by in the
next five minutes." That's what frequency is all about: expectation,
not mere statistical probabilities.

And, yes, it *will* be awkward at first. One president of a small
company said, "Well, look, if I make the effort to go down on the
shop floor, they [the people down there] have got to make the
reciprocal effort and give me honest feedback." Why? Why in the
hell should your people be committed to giving you "honest feedback" if your last three visits were to lay people off? So you read *In
Search of Excellence* and suddenly you think wandering is a great
idea—so what? You can't expect your people to give you a birthday
cake the first time out. (Or even the twenty-first.) You *earn* honest
feedback. And the main way you earn it is by the frequency of your

wandering (*and* by what you do after you return home—more on that in a bit).

By frequency we mean exactly that. In order to visit each of the over seven hundred Wal-Mart stores at least once a year, Sam Walton takes a minimum of three full days a week; much of the rest of his time is spent visiting distribution centers, riding with Wal-Mart drivers, and visiting suppliers. Robert O. Anderson, Arco's chairman, averaged about five hundred miles a day during his fifteen years as CEO of that company. *Quite frankly, we believe that any supervisor—accounting, first line in the factory, engineering, merchandising, information systems or Fortune 500 CEO—probably ought to be out of the office 75 percent of the time and in the field (if he or she has multiple, dispersed geographical sites) at least 50 percent of the time.*

And note: Doing away with the state visit doesn't mean that you should be afraid to *advertise* the fact that you are out wandering. The best way to have people think that you might come by is to let them know you are out and about—*listening*—most of the time.

"Frequency": Some Questions—and Things to Do Now

- How often are you out of your office? Be specific. Look at your calendar for the last sixty to ninety days. Break it down into meetings, visits and other. Take the meeting component and break it down into formal and informal, making note of the location of each meeting. Go over each in-office/in-headquarters event and ask yourself if it could have taken place as readily on the other person's turf: e.g., why not have the R&D review in the labs, rather than in your office?

  Could visits have been used more productively? Look at each. Could one or two (or five or six) brief "walk-throughs" of another field facility or another department have been added?

- Now look ahead sixty days. First, look at booked, must-do events: Can some be held at "their place" rather than "your place"? Look at your currently unprogrammed time; can you put "Don't book" in 25 percent of it, and save the time for spontaneous "wandering"?

- Think about putting a checklist or two in a reachable desk drawer (or even in your wallet). On it (them) note, for instance, your top twenty-five customers, your top twenty-five vendors, twenty-five upcoming milestones for project teams, twenty-five facilities or departments. Systematically plan to "do" two from each list each week (two customer calls, two departmental "drop-ins"). You might even use a desk-top personal computer for this. Have your secretary, if you have one, bug you about the lists (she or he should have duplicates), or even give you weekly gold stars if you get all of your "MBWA 'to dos'" completed.

- Repeat all the above as a team: analysis, meeting location shifts and checklists. Make your *team* MBWA Scorecard a regular (first?) agenda item when you get together for staff meetings. Force group feedback at least weekly.

TRAPPINGS OF MBWA

Trappings are vital. Anderson's (Arco) routine is highly instructive. Above all, he didn't travel with a retinue. There weren't seven hovering note-takers from staff in attendance, shaking their heads and clucking as they thought he would at forms not filled out appropriately.

The order or sequence of wandering is vital. Mr. Anderson's habit was to arrive at a district field office and immediately head for an ongoing, routine meeting of junior geologists and geophysicists discussing a minor property. He didn't begin with an hour-and-a-half, behind-closed-doors visit and strategic review with the district supervisor. He hopped in, virtually unannounced, and looked in on whatever was happening at the time. Andy Pearson followed about the same routine at PepsiCo. When he arrived, he'd drop in on a junior assistant brand manager, ask him, "What's up? What's going on?" or stop in on a meeting far down the line that was pretty routine. The bosses came later. A fellow who runs a mid-sized construction company has a similar ritual. One of his vice presidents remarks: "Whenever he arrives at a construction site, it's automatic. He makes a beeline for the crane operators or the welders. The site boss is last on his list." Senior people *will* get their time. They always do. *Starting* at the "lower" levels shows those people the importance you attach to them—that they are not, in fact, "lower" at all, but are vital to the organization.

Bank Wanderer

A manager of several branches of the retail part of Chase Manhattan decided to manage less by form and more by wandering. She didn't tell people when she was going to arrive, not in the state-visit sense, but she did give them a little warning.

> She'd stop at a phone booth before hitting a site and say, "See you in half an hour." When she arrived she'd go up to somebody in the operations area, look at what he or she was doing, and spend a little time chatting about it. The tail end of the visit would be the branch manager.

There are some other, smaller points to be made in connection with the trappings of MBWA. One president of a small business asked us, "What do you wear when you do MBWA?" Our answer? "Whatever feels comfortable." What we mean is that if you're a three-piece-suit wearer, and the vest is always buttoned and the cuffs of your shirts are monogrammed, wandering around in overalls is apt to make you look a bit of a fool. On the other hand, if you *can* pull it off—i.e., comfortably—we're all for overalls if you're in a plant. We heard a story about a well-run GM plant where the manager was a wanderer supreme. His relationships with his people were terrific. His costume for wandering was almost always the same (what it was, in fact, when he was sitting at his desk—unless the brass from Detroit were about to show up). It was a satin baseball warm-up jacket with the insignia of the UAW local on it; he wore that and a baseball hat pushed back on his head as he ceaselessly trooped around.

It is a little easier to be informal—and to listen—if you can wear informal clothes and not look strange in the process. But there are a lot of jerks who wander around in baseball jackets, so that doesn't mean everything, to put it mildly. And if you are one of the true buttoned-down types, and you are always seen in pictures in the company newspaper wearing a three-piece suit (even on the softball diamond), then don't suddenly head out to the field with a T-shirt on; if you do, people will probably think, "Ah, he's practicing wandering. Been to one of Peters' seminars." And that decidedly is not the point.

"Trappings": Some Questions—and Things to Do Now

- Think about the trappings when various people visit you. Analyze two or three recent visits in detail. Do the trappings make a difference? How? What are the smart-aleck remarks you make after visits of higher-ups? Could the visitors have avoided the faux pas that led to your snide assessments? How? Now, turn your attention to yourself (and yourself and your colleagues as a group). To what extent do you manage/think through the "trappings" issue—e.g., order of visits, formality of note taking, clothes? Do you consider this a useful exercise, or low priority, or silly? If you don't take it seriously, ask yourself why. The greatest world leaders have unfailingly been fanatics about trappings.

MAINTAINING THE CHAIN OF COMMAND

Except for the matter of leaving space (or, better yet, enhancing it) the toughest issue in MBWA has to do with abrogation (or not) of the chain of command. A score of points could be made. Quite simply, the best of the MBWAers do not abrogate the chain of command. But wait: Of course they *do,* in a way. Let's not kid ourselves. Wandering down, skipping two or five or six, or, heaven help us, ten layers *is* violating the chain of command. Regardless of your purpose. You're there to hear it firsthand, and you're there to do some teaching firsthand. No bones about it. But there *are* degrees.

Consider former Chairman Ed Carlson of United Airlines. Soon after taking over the ailing airline, he hit the field, asking very direct questions—in detail, for his objective was to clean up the bureaucratic mess he had inherited. He took endless notes, usually on scraps of paper, and stuffed them into his pocket. He never told people down the line what to do or change, he never fixed what he disliked (unless it was a matter of safety) on the spot. But what he did do—and this is vital—was *promise* that he would get back to people in a very short time (five working days at most). And he promised he would get back with *action*, not the announcement of the appointment of a six-month task force or study group. When he returned to home base, he played it straight: he let the chain of command know what he had found and that he wanted action taken, immediately. Then he initiated correspondence with the down-the-line people he had chatted with on his wanderings, letting them know that something was up, and had his staff check religiously to make sure that action was taken, and taken within the promised time.

Of course an abrogation of the chain of command was involved here. Carlson's unabashed objective was to skip steps, get on directly and rapidly with debureaucratizing, using himself in a highly visible fashion to make his point. (He called it "visible management.") But the implementation was done in a relatively traditional if uncommonly rapid fashion. In sum, to make MBWA credible one must promise fast action and then make damn sure that it occurs within the proposed time frame; but to do so does not mean (or should not mean) impetuously issuing the order to the first-line person on the spot.

Again, frequency is a key issue. The screams about violating the chain of command will be particularly loud at first. Your presence (even if you're a second-line supervisor) is initially awkward. People overlisten to you and overinterpret the subtle inflections in your voice. Many a million-dollar program has been started, or stopped, because of a frown by a division general manager at the wrong second (and because, it turns out, he had a fly land on his nose). And that *will* happen. But it will happen less—this is a simple law of nature—the more you are around. People will figure out what sort of person you are when they've had a chance to be exposed to you. Your managers will come to accept the fact that you're not going to destroy the chain of command only when you repeatedly demonstrate that you won't.

An Adventure in Excellence

An experienced wanderer recalls the first time he ventured out from the safety of his office to begin what was for him an utterly unfamiliar experience: "I was out of touch. I wanted to see with my own eyes what was going on in my division, but I never had the time. People came to me, but they never seemed to be very comfortable. Finally I decided to go to them. I came out of my office, turned the corner, headed for the coffee urn. It was break time, and everybody crowded around it, talking about the new product we'd just introduced. A supervisor in manufacturing thought the production time could be cut by 20 percent if two changes were made; one of the design engineers agreed. Another engineer joined the discussion—now a debate—and as I reached them, the whole group was involved in how the production cycle could be improved. Then they noticed me. The conversation thudded to a stop. Just like that. I could see the surprise on their faces: 'What's *he* doing here?' I didn't know what to do with my hands, so I shoved them in my pockets. It was awkward as hell. Our place is informal, but I had a meeting that afternoon, so I was wearing a tie—everyone else wore open collars or T-shirts. For a minute I seriously considered going back to my desk. But I didn't see how I could back up. Someone handed me a cup of coffee. I yanked my hands out of my pockets to reach for the cup—and loose change, car keys, a little tin of aspirin and a button fell to the floor. They all stared, didn't know what to do. I reached down for the keys and collided halfway with a supervisor, who was reaching for them at the same time. He grinned as he handed them to me. I had to smile. Two or three of the others collected the change. My boss's secretary retrieved the aspirin tin and remarked, 'Here, you'll probably need these in a few minutes.' I took a deep breath, gulped my coffee, loosened my tie, tried to look casual. I decided this wandering-around stuff was for the birds, it couldn't work. I was there to listen, and they didn't tell me anything. I'd be better off preparing for my meeting, getting all my charts ready. But I came back the next day, just to give it one more shot. How could it be worse than yesterday? People didn't open up and tell me about what they were concerned about that time, either, but I kept at it. I was determined, I'll tell you. I went around to see people at their desks. I was learning a lot. I was having fun! I realized that these people knew a hell of a lot more about what our company stands for, where we're heading, how our products could be improved, than I gave them credit for. They knew much more than how to do a given job. I didn't even know what half of them actually did. Now it's a regular thing with me—wandering around. A couple of my peers used to criticize me for not being at my desk enough. 'Why aren't you managing?' they'd ask! Well, now *they're* out more, too. It's amazing what we've learned from just simple listening."

A vital subpoint, in connection with this issue, is the necessity of assuring and accomplishing the absolute protection of those who talk with you. The objective is to find out what is going on, to listen especially to the clerks, the MIS gang, the assistant branch manager, the junior buyers and the people on the loading dock. There is a tendency among "real people" (those on the loading dock and in the PBX room) to be frank, interestingly enough. And it is vitally important, especially in a tradition-bound organization, to make sure that the provider of frank feedback isn't shot or exiled to Siberia after your visit. A lot of first-line supervisors don't take too kindly to an hourly person mouthing off to a vice president (or even a third-level supervisor) about the rotten state of the housekeeping ("The toilets stink"). A lot of second-line supervisors don't take kindly to first-line supervisors doing the same thing. So the all-pro wanderers are crystal clear on this point. If they find even the slightest hint that something negative has happened as a result of someone speaking out (and they actively listen to the grapevine to check), the person responsible is fired or demoted or sent to Siberia. The MBWA process rests, foursquare, on absolute integrity. If the integrity is not there, it all becomes a very bad joke. And, once again, the frequency of visits is involved. At first it will be tough enough for people to open up. But once they hear that you wander regularly (50 percent of the time), that you do get back to people quickly, and that you do watch out for the people who have spoken up, then gradually, the process will begin to work.*

Bourns' Bert Snider summarizes nicely: "There's always a chance that a foreman, for example, will think the CEO is screwing things up by getting involved. But I think there's a danger only if the foreman is singing a different song from the CEO. If they're all singing the same song, the CEO is only reinforcing that song in people's minds. If it's a song they've never heard before, then, yes, they'll be confused."

"Chain": Some Questions—and Things to Do Now

- Do you have an exact routine for getting back to everyone who talks to you? Does it include a harsh (for you) deadline for action—e.g., forty-eight to seventy-two hours? Do you meet your deadline? How do you handle the standard chain of command in asking for follow-up? Do you ensure that they conform to your promised deadline? How do you (if you do) ensure that subtle negative action is not taken against those who speak out (e.g., that snide remarks about "George airing our dirty linen with the boss" don't follow in the wake of a frank exchange about quality with a foreman)? Most important: do you pay slavish attention to and "manage" these issues?

Listening, Teaching, Facilitating: Some (More) Suggestions

Listening is best done on somebody else's turf. That is why we urge wandering. There are, however, many ways to do it, even on the other person's turf. One is to gather people together in formal question-and-answer sessions. That's not bad. Ren McPherson, the former Dana head, used to do a lot of this, sometimes gathering

---

* This is an extraordinarily thorny issue. We talked with one Fortune 500 president. He wears his integrity on his sleeve, in a company where it's sadly uncommon. People—junior clerks in the Austin, Texas, operation—*do* open up with him regularly. He is continually astonished at the havoc he creates when he inadvertently lets a clerk's name slip in subsequent conversations with his peers.

fifteen hundred people together in the same room and taking questions with all present. It's useful, because the group as a whole takes
the measure of the "boss" in this kind of a setting. Is he or she trying to pull the wool over our eyes? Is he or she being straight with
us? What is he or she hiding? Why? Small, impromptu get-
togethers with cross sections of five or ten people are also helpful.
Again, the trick is in the word "impromptu"—the people attending
should be picked at the last minute, on the spot. A carefully crafted
and preselected group merely sets you up to hear what some
supervisor thinks you want to hear. Also vital are wandering the line
and going out on calls with sales and service people.

Some other listening rituals: Our colleague Jack Zenger reports
that the president of the Syntex Corporation makes a habit of eat-
ing breakfast at the same table in the company cafeteria about twice
a week. It's well known that he will be there, and that anybody is
welcome to come up and sit with him. Note also, however, that nobody came and sat with him at first. Then, probably out of sympa-
thy, a few brave souls ventured to do so. And it's only now—after
twenty years—that it has become comfortable. That's MBWA for
you!

Bill Moore's turnaround at Recognition Equipment also involved breakfast—a ritual that became known as Biscuits with Billy.
Four or five mornings a week he was there in the company cafeteria,
to chat with all comers. What did they chat about? Anything,
everything, and nothing. His mere presence implied that he wanted
to listen and keep in touch. He shared heretofore sensitive data
about small gains and small losses, making it clear that everybody
was part of the team effort. His self-confidence and frankness con-
veyed a badly needed "Someone's in charge here" sense to the
whole organization. Above all, Moore is neither a time waster nor a
"How ya doin'" type. Times were tough and he was taking tough-
minded action. So the breakfast vehicle became a vital, frank, and
practical daily "state of the corporation . . . and you and me
[Moore]" interchange.

Listening is the number one objective of MBWA. Teaching is
almost as important, however, and it emphatically does *not* mean
telling people what to do (that delicate point again). It does mean
telling people in a direct, no-nonsense fashion what it is you think is
important about the world—their world and yours. It can as readily
be accomplished by the regular pattern of your questioning routine
as by a formal speech, but it is a big part of the MBWA process.

Wandering activity is, in this regard (and above all), a golden opportunity. The pattern of your questioning—and variations therein—*will* be noticed and interpreted, have no doubt about it. Everything about what you are up to—your dress, the order in which you talk to people, the things you focus on in your questions, the things you *fail* to focus on—will be, even if you *are* a regular wanderer, the subject of endless speculation. You have just two choices in the matter: to go about it in an erratic fashion or to go about it systematically. We would highly recommend the latter because it would mean that you will in fact be teaching what you want to teach and not something else.

By systematic we don't mean planning every second of your visit. We do mean making sure that your two or three simple messages are the focus of everything you do: the questioning pattern, the visiting pattern while on the site, etc. Tom followed Frank Perdue around for a day in Salisbury, Maryland, in the summer of 1983. In the course of that day he gave half-a-dozen impromptu talks, always on the same subject—product quality. It is what he's been jawing about for forty years, but he still takes every opportunity, no matter who's the target, to reinforce his point of view.*

On the other hand, we have followed many managers around who squander their opportunities. One colleague was involved in a life-and-death quality program: Get it better or lose a $100 million contract renewal. Several solid successes had been chalked up, and more were coming in every day. Yet in the course of a four-department visit, he missed opportunity after opportunity. In one of the four instances he said nothing about quality. In two others it was an afterthought. Only in one was quality an up-front topic. In no instance did he attempt to build momentum by giving accounts of the successes in other parts of the organization. Instead he became involved in putting out a series of routine brushfires on a variety of issues. It is not that he wasted time, but that he failed to use the time to hammer home his overarching priority.

. . . Coaching, teaching and transmitting values, more than any other responsibility of leadership, demand dramatic skills. However, it is vital that the show you put on not be fraudulent in any way, that you do not merely act a part. Your people will judge your integrity. And they will get it right! The smallest inconsistencies or hypocritical acts will be noted. The story is not a wholly negative one, of course. If you do act with total integrity, the

---

* And if you knew Frank, you'd know it surely wasn't for Tom's benefit!

MBWA process is the best and, in a sense, the only way in which to truly demonstrate it. That is, your people will judge your integrity by the cast of your eye (Napoleon said, "If you wish to lead people, speak to their eyes"), the firmness of your grip, and a multitude of other little things. You cannot fake it. Nor can you *convey* it except in person. A videotape helps, but it is no substitute for all the millions (literally) of bits of data that we process when we observe a person face-to-face.

There is an important point about communication behind all this. We have had many people, particularly in connection with such MBWAing as a daylong ride-around with a single salesman, say, "Look, it's such low leverage. I have got seven hundred fifty (or seventy-five hundred) people in my company. To spend one day with *one* salesman is too darned expensive." We think such a view is wrongheaded. The worldwide rumor mill will be grinding away *seconds* after that day comes to an end (if not before). Every item of your conversation will be known four thousand miles away about half an hour after it occurs—at the most. As one wise soul said about such visits: "The sound of the old man's voice travels at the speed of light around here." It travels at the speed of light *everywhere*. So the teaching that takes place on that day will not be lost—that is, unless it is lost through your squandering the opportunity.

MBWA's big three are listening, teaching and facilitating; we've talked of the first two and, peripherally, the third. Facilitating is Ed Carlson promising action within about five days after a visit. But even that's somewhat indirect. So what's direct facilitation? A successful senior manager at Bell Labs has it right: "My job? Run the Xerox machine for a team at three a.m. the morning their project is due for review. I spend half my time just asking dumb questions: 'What's bugging you?' 'What's getting in the way?' It turns out it's seldom big stuff. It's usually petty annoyances. A small group needed a personal computer, and was being dragged through an almost full-blown capital budget review to get one. I got them one in forty-eight hours. And so on. Running interference and kicking down small hurdles. And, you know, you can only do it if you're out there. Nobody will come to you with this stuff. They think it's 'too trivial' to bother you with! They think they ought to be able to do it themselves. So they'll tie themselves up in knots for a week on some little nit."

The only addendum we have to that is to point out that it's the small stuff that is almost always—because of its cumulative effect—

at the heart of major problems. As an IBM systems manager said, "How does a project come to be delayed by a year? One day at a time."

MBWA is not easy, and it shouldn't be easy. Estimating conservatively, we'd bet a thousand variables are at play! We have described only a handful. MBWA exposes you. Your ability to listen is exposed. Your honesty and integrity (or lack of it) are exposed. Your consistency is exposed to the scrutiny of the toughest watchers of all—hourly people. You can bullshit a vice president with ease. But it's almost impossible to BS somebody on the loading dock. They have been there and back. Your vision (or lack of it) is exposed. Your statements have coherence (or not) relative to the basics of that vision. Jan Carlzon's hammering home his vision of SAS's transformation from a "broker of assets" to a "service company" was and is the theme of a thousand impromptu chats.

Putting major effort and energy into learning MBWA and practicing it is worth the candle, but it won't be easy. In fact, it will be hard. If you haven't done much of it, we can guarantee that the first few days, weeks, months, and perhaps years, will be just plain awful. Few will trust you: "What's he up to?" "How long will it take for this 'wander phase' to pass?"

And ah, yes, how *do* you find the time? You are already busy. You already have forty-seven more legitimate priorities than you can deal with. Maybe you can play a game with yourself. A friend wanted to free 20 percent of his time for wandering. Together we did an analysis of his calendar for the week after next. He had some twenty-nine scheduled meetings; moreover, the phone log revealed that another fourteen people had requested meetings that he'd not been able to squeeze into his docket. The solution was simple: "Dave, cut your meetings to seventeen." His obvious (and reasonable) rejoinder: "Why seventeen?" The rebuttal: "Well, look, you could have had forty-three [the twenty-nine he was going to have plus the fourteen he hadn't been able to schedule], but you only had twenty-nine. Neither the forty-three nor the twenty-nine makes any sense at all as a number. So the seventeen can't make any less sense than the twenty-nine! Right? And it has a nice ring to it, seventeen, doesn't it? It sounds precise, sounds like you've given it a lot of thought."

Who among us can say that our calendar—in any way, shape or form—really makes sense? Perhaps it does reflect, directionally, our strategic priorities. But the set of a week's meetings can hardly be called "optimal." It's mostly random and reactive. And the only way to change it, unfortunately, is to change it. Not through immutable logic, there's none available. But just by doing it. And, perhaps, like our friend Dave, you can at least take some comfort in the fact that the new schedule makes no less sense than the previous one. That we can guarantee you. So what are you waiting for? . . . "Uh, Mr. Arnold, sorry to interrupt your reading, but your ten-forty-five is here."

Testing Skyhook 3

OPEN COMMUNICATION

If I had to name a single all-purpose instrument of leadership it would be communication. . . . Effective two-way communication is essential to proper functioning of the leader-follower relationship.

—JOHN W. GARDNER,
ON LEADERSHIP

Open, honest two-way communication helps clarify vision and enhances trust. Future possibilities become clearer through dialogue, discussion, and debate. Unknowns that "go bump in the dark" become fewer and our willingness to take risks edges upward. As we get to know our co-workers as "real people" with hopes and fears like our own, our confidence grows because we know we don't have to go it alone.

A simple self test will begin to help you see how well you are performing. Asking your coworkers "How am I doing?" will complete the picture.

ASK YOURSELF

Test out how well you set the standard for open communication by rating the accuracy of the following statements. Use a 1–5 scale ranging from "a little" to "a great extent."

• I am candid when sharing my ideas and opinions with everyone.	1 2 3 4 5
• I listen carefully to people no matter what their jobs or titles.	1 2 3 4 5
• I let my coworkers know about off-the-job matters if they affect the way we work together.	1 2 3 4 5
• I accept everyone's ideas as legitimate points of view even when I disagree.	1 2 3 4 5
• I welcome feedback on my performance from everyone.	1 2 3 4 5

ASK YOUR COWORKERS

If you gave yourself a "4" or "5" rating on each statement, you probably communicate with your coworkers. However, you can verify your self-assessment by having a two-part discussion with your coworkers. First, ask them to talk about the importance of open communication so that you understand it in the same way. Second, ask them for feedback on your performance.

You'll know you're developing a common understanding about the importance of open communication when you hear comments like these:

> • "Being available before, during, and after working hours is a must for open communication."
>
> • "Telling it like it is without filtering or sugar coating pays off. People feel respected when you put it all out on the table and will be just as candid in return."
>
> • "Listening completely without jumping to conclusions or quick fixes is important. Often, there is more to hear than you think at first."
>
> • "Meeting one-on-one regularly with each person ensures your lines are really open."
>
> • "Having off-hour get-togethers breaks down barriers between coworkers. After kicking back together it's easier to talk openly about work issues."

After discussing the importance of open communication, check out your coworkers' view of your performance by asking them to consider the five items in your self-assessment. You may find it more productive for them to answer the following questions than to give you numerical ratings on each item:

> • What am I doing right now that supports each statement?
>
> • What else can I do—either more or less—to show greater support for each statement?

As you listen, try to clarify your coworkers' answers and ideas. Express your appreciation for their feedback without becoming defensive. After you've listened, ask yourself, "What am I ready to do to open up our communication?" Develop an action plan to build on your strengths and continue to improve.

Skyhook 4

MEANINGFUL WORK AND MOTIVATION

True leaders bring people along, no matter what their qualities are, and raise them to a higher standard. A very important part of leadership is lifting people up and making them realize they can be better than they are.
—J. RICHARD MUNRO, CHAIRMAN OF THE
EXECUTIVE COMMITTEE OF TIME WARNER

It's through everyone's efforts that the vision is realized. And that springs into the next leadership capabilities of understanding people, being sensitive to human needs, and providing an environment in which a person can develop professionally and personally. I have an absolute burning desire to continue to improve myself and everyone around me.
—CHRISTEL DE HANN, PRESIDENT AND CEO OF
RESORT CONDOMINIUMS INTERNATIONAL

Skyhook 4 Meaningful Work—Make work more than just a job by appealing to the heart. People have always looked for meaning in what they do, to see that it is worthwhile in more than material terms. Now, with traditional sources of support and self-worth in jeopardy, the need to care about work is greater then ever. Causes, commitment, and a sense of personal contribution are the great human needs and the driving forces behind individual and organization change.

Two selections are included in the classics section, one by Abraham Maslow and the other by Frederick Herzberg. Together they show that the need for meaningful work has always been the foundation for effective motivation and leadership. Our jobs must be more than just a place where we trade time for money.

Since it was first published in 1943, Abraham Maslow's "A Theory of Human Motivation" has continued to provide a clear framework for understanding why people behave the way they do. He greatly influenced Douglas McGregor and other noted theorists and practitioners for over five decades. Leaders need to understand how successful change and transformation must appeal to our psychological needs for belonging, self-esteem, meaning, and growth.

Maslow's theoretical framework includes concepts like these:

- Our needs are arranged in a five-level hierarchy that calls for lower-level needs to be satisfied before higher-level needs become relevant.

- Needs range from fairly primitive physiological concerns to more sophisticated psychological concerns—most people are most concerned about higher-order needs that affect their feelings of self-worth.

- We can lose sight of "higher" needs if we focus too long on how people behave in atypical situations where they are deprived of the basics.

- We can expect the greatest creative effort from those who have met their lower-level needs and are self-actualizing, trying to fulfill their potential.

- At the apex of self-actualization is the desire to know, understand, and find meanings.

Frederick Herzberg builds on Maslow's motivation concepts while focusing on the workplace in "Motivation versus Hygiene" from *The Motivation to Work* (1959). He ties high levels of job satisfaction to work that is intrinsically rewarding. For example:

- Job satisfaction is greatest when people are self-actualizing, when they experience success, and when they see the possibility of professional growth.

- Conditions surrounding work, hygiene factors such as supervision, working conditions, and company policies can only demotivate people. They cannot motivate people and bring out the best in them.

- Factors related to performing the job, motivator factors such as interesting and worthwhile work, responsibility, challenge, and independence, can give a person's occupation far more meaning than merely a way to make a living.

Echoing the classics, Robert H. Waterman tells how leaders can meet our higher-level needs in "Causes and Commitment" from *The Renewal Factor* (1987). Individual and organizational renewal are symbiotic. Leaders must recognize the interdependency and connect the organization's needs with the individual's highest aspirations.

Waterman begins by emphasizing a fundamental truth—"Man seeks meaning in organizations"—and goes on to say:

- Only the best leaders turn organization causes into individual commitments—others find it too hard and lose their chance to change and renew.

- Focus on a few simple must-deal-with issues, but be prepared to modify the agenda as circumstances change.

- Transform issues that appear as dreary problems into inspiring causes—move the mind-set from "I'm breaking rocks" to "I'm helping build cathedrals."

- It is difficult to rally people around sterile issues like cost reduction or market share, even though they are vital.

- "Quality products, service, and the customer" can be meaningful causes because they relate equally to people and the organization.

- Making work meaningful also relates to the leader's ability to put adventure in work.

- Adventure calls for risk taking, which works only in a supportive environment.

- Commitment to a cause happens person by person as individuals choose whether or not to pledge support and take responsibility.

- A leader's honest, consistent communication and open dialogue help forge the link between causes and commitment.

- Commitment has a down side—it can trap you into giving more support than you intended or sticking with a cause long after it is lost.

When work is meaningful, motivation becomes a process that "pulls" rather than "pushes" people. Leaders do not coax, cajole, or manipulate people into doing something they would otherwise avoid. When a leader presents a business issue in such a way that its inherent worthiness and nobility are apparent, people enroll in the cause because they want to. It is win-win at its best. The organization ends up a stronger enterprise with problems solved and goals achieved; people end their day with the satisfaction that they have done much more than just trade time for money.

7

CLASSIC MOTIVATION THEORIES
A Theory of Human Motivation

ABRAHAM MASLOW

Obviously a good way to obscure the "higher" motivations, and to get a lopsided view of human capacities and human nature, is to make the organism extremely and chronically hungry or thirsty. Anyone who attempts to make an emergency picture into a typical one, and who will measure all of man's goals and desires by his behavior during extreme physiological deprivation is certainly being blind to many things. It is quite true that man lives by bread alone—when there is no bread. But what happens to man's desires when there is plenty of bread and when his belly is chronically filled?

At once other (and "higher") needs emerge and these, rather than physiological hungers, dominate the organism. And when these in turn are satisfied, again new (and still "higher") needs emerge and so on. This is what we mean by saying that the basic human needs are organized into a hierarchy of relative prepotency. . . .

The love needs. If both the physiological and the safety needs are fairly well gratified, then there will emerge the love and affection and belongingness needs, and the whole cycle already described will repeat itself with this new center. Now the person will feel keenly, as never before, the absence of friends, or a sweetheart, or a wife, or children. He will hunger for affectionate relations with people in general, namely, for a place in his group, and he will strive with great intensity to achieve this goal. He will want to attain such

Excerpts from *Psychological Review*, vol. 50, pp. 370–396, 1943. Copyright © 1943 by the American Psychological Association. Reprinted by permission.

a place more than anything else in the world and may even forget that once, when he was hungry, he sneered at love.

In our society the thwarting of these needs is the most commonly found core in cases of maladjustment and more severe psychopathology. Love and affection, as well as their possible expression in sexuality, are generally looked upon with ambivalence and are customarily hedged about with many restrictions and inhibitions. Practically all theorists of psychopathology have stressed thwarting of the love needs as basic in the picture of maladjustment. Many clinical studies have therefore been made of this need and we know more about it perhaps than any of the other needs except the physiological ones.

One thing that must be stressed at this point is that love is not synonymous with sex. Sex may be studied as a purely physiological need. Ordinarily sexual behavior is multi-determined, that is to say, determined not only by sexual but also by other needs, chief among which are the love and affection needs. Also not to be overlooked is the fact that the love needs involve both giving *and* receiving love.

The esteem needs. All people in our society (with a few pathological exceptions) have a need or desire for a stable, firmly based, (usually) high evaluation of themselves, for self-respect, or self-esteem, and for the esteem of others. By firmly based self-esteem, we mean that which is soundly based upon real capacity, achievement and respect from others. These needs may be classified into two subsidiary sets. These are, first, the desire for strength, for achievement, for adequacy, for confidence in the face of the world, and for independence and freedom. Secondly, we have what we may call the desire for reputation or prestige (defining it as respect or esteem from other people), recognition, attention, importance or appreciation. These needs have been relatively stressed by Alfred Adler and his followers, and have been relatively neglected by Freud and the psychoanalysts. More and more today however there is appearing widespread appreciation of their central importance.

Satisfaction of the self-esteem need leads to feelings of self-confidence, worth, strength, capability and adequacy of being useful and necessary in the world. But thwarting of these needs produces feelings of inferiority, of weakness and of helplessness. These feelings in turn give rise to either basic discouragement or else compensatory or neurotic trends. An appreciation of the necessity of basic self-confidence and an understanding of how helpless people are without it, can be easily gained from a study of severe traumatic neurosis.

The need for self-actualization. Even if all these needs are satisfied, we may still often (if not always) expect that a new discontent and restlessness will soon develop, unless the individual is doing what he is fitted for. A musician must make music, an artist must paint, a poet must write, if he is to be ultimately happy. What a man *can* be, he *must* be. This need we may call self-actualization.

This term, first coined by Kurt Goldstein, is being used in this paper in a much more specific and limited fashion. It refers to the desire for self-fulfillment, namely, to the tendency for him to become actualized in what he is potentially. This tendency might be phrased as the desire to become more and more what one is, to become everything that one is capable of becoming.

The specific form that these needs will take will of course vary greatly from person to person. In one individual it may take the form of the desire to be an ideal mother, in another it may be expressed athletically, and in still another it may be expressed in painting pictures or in inventions. It is not necessarily a creative urge although in people who have any capacities for creation it will take this form.

The clear emergence of these needs rests upon prior satisfaction of the physiological, safety, love and esteem needs. We shall call people who are satisfied in these needs, basically satisfied people, and it is from these that we may expect the fullest (and healthiest) creativeness.

Motivation Versus Hygiene

FREDERICK HERZBERG
BERNARD MAUSNER
BARBARA BLOCH SNYDERMAN

Let us summarize briefly our answer to the question, "What do people want from their jobs?" When our respondents reported feeling happy with their jobs, they most frequently described factors related to their tasks, to events that indicated to them that they were successful in the performance of their work, and to the possibility of professional growth. Conversely, when feelings of unhappiness were reported, they were not associated with the job itself

From *The Motivation to Work*, John Wiley & Sons, Inc., New York. Copyright © 1959. Chapter 12, pp. 113–115. Reprinted by permission of the author.

but with conditions that *surround* the doing of the job. These events suggest to the individual that the context in which he performs his work is unfair or disorganized and as such represents to him an unhealthy psychological work environment. Factors involved in these situations we call factors of hygiene, for they act in a manner analogous to the principles of medical hygiene. Hygiene operates to remove health hazards from the environment of man. It is not a curative; it is, rather, a preventive. Modern garbage disposal, water purification, and air pollution control do not cure diseases, but without them we should have many more diseases. Similarly, when there are deleterious factors in the context of the job, they serve to bring about poor job attitudes. Improvement in these factors of hygiene will serve to remove the impediments to positive job attitudes. Among the factors of hygiene we have included supervision, interpersonal relations, physical working conditions, salary, company policies and administrative practices, benefits, and job security. When these factors deteriorate to a level below that which the employee considers acceptable, then job dissatisfaction ensues. However, the reverse does not hold true. When the job context can be characterized as optimal, we will not get dissatisfaction, but neither will we get much in the way of positive attitudes.

The factors that lead to positive job attitudes do so because they satisfy the individual's need for self-actualization in his work. The concept of self-actualization, or self-realization, as a man's ultimate goal has been focal to the thought of many personality theorists. For such men as Jung, Adler, Sullivan, Rogers, and Goldstein the supreme goal of man is to fulfill himself as a creative, unique individual according to his own innate potentialities and within the limits of reality. When he is deflected from this goal he becomes, as Jung says, "a crippled animal."

Man tends to actualize himself in every area of his life, and his job is one of the most important areas. The conditions that surround the doing of the job cannot give him this basic satisfaction; they do not have this potentiality. It is only from the performance of a task that the individual can get the rewards that will reinforce his aspirations. It is clear that although the factors relating to the doing of the job and the factors defining the job context serve as goals for the employee, the nature of the motivating qualities of the two kinds of factors is essentially different. Factors in the job context meet the needs of the individual for avoiding unpleasant situations. In contrast to this motivation by meeting avoidance needs, the job factors reward the needs of the individual to reach his aspirations. These effects on the individual can be conceptualized as an actuating approach rather than avoidance behavior. Since it is in the approach sense that the term motivation is most commonly used, we designate the job factors as the "motivators," as opposed to the extra-job factors, which we have labeled the factors of hygiene. It should be understood that both kinds of factors meet the needs of the employee; but it is primarily the "motivators" that serve to bring about the kind of job satisfaction and . . . the kind of improvement in performance that industry is seeking from its work force.

We can now say something systematic about what people want from their jobs. For the kind of population that we sampled, and probably for many other populations as well, the wants of employees divide into two groups. One group revolves around the need to develop in one's occupation as a source of personal growth. The second group operates as an essential base to the first and is associated with fair treatment in compensation, supervision, working conditions, and administrative practices. The fulfillment of the needs of the second group does not motivate the individual to high levels of job satisfaction and . . . to extra performance on the job. All we can expect from satisfying the needs for hygiene is the prevention of dissatisfaction and poor job performance.

In the light of this distinction, we can account for much of the lack of success that industry has had in its attempts to motivate employees. Let us examine two of the more ubiquitous avenues through which industry has hoped to gain highly motivated employees: human-relations training for supervisors and wage-incentive systems.

As part of this era of human relations, supervisory training directed toward improving the interpersonal relationships between superior and subordinate has been widely incorporated into industrial-relations programs. These programs have been initiated with expectations of bringing about positive job attitudes and, hopefully, increased performance on the job. When we examine the results of our study, we find interpersonal relationships appearing in an exceedingly small number of the high sequences; in only 15 percent of the low sequences are poor interpersonal relationships with the superior reported. The negligible role which interpersonal relationships play in our data tallies poorly with the assumption basic to most human-relations training programs that the way in which a supervisor gets along with his people is the single most important determinant of morale. Supervisory training in human relations is probably essential to the maintenance of good hygiene at work. This is particularly true for the many jobs, both at rank-and-file and managerial levels, in which modern industry offers little chance for the operation of the motivators. These jobs are atomized, cut and dried, monotonous. They offer little chance for responsibility and achievement and thus little opportunity for self-actualization. It is here that hygiene is exceptionally important. The fewer the opportunities for the "motivators" to appear, the greater must be the hygiene offered in order to make the work tolerable. A man who finds his job challenging, exciting, and satisfying will perhaps tolerate a difficult supervisor. But to expect such programs to pay dividends beyond the effects that hygiene provides is going contrary to the nature of job motivation. In terms of the approach-avoidance concept, the advocates of human relations have suggested that by rewarding the avoidance needs of the individual you will achieve the desired approach behavior. But a more creative design will not emerge from an engineer as a result of fair supervisory treatment. To achieve the more creative design, one or more of the motivators must be present, a task that is interesting to the engineer, a task in which he can exercise responsibility and independence, a task that allows for some concrete achievement. The motivators fit the need for creativity, the hygiene factors satisfy the need for fair treatment, and it is thus that the appropriate incentive must be present to achieve the desired job attitude and job performance.

8

CAUSES AND COMMITMENT

ROBERT H. WATERMAN, JR.

> *To venture causes anxiety, but not to venture is to*
> *lose one's self. . . . And to venture in the highest sense*
> *is precisely to become conscious of one's self.*
> —SØREN KIERKEGAARD

> *When great causes are on the move in the world . . .*
> *we learn that we are spirits, not animals.*
> —WINSTON CHURCHILL

Man seeks meaning in organizations. Theorists Michael Cohen and James March argue that an organization is "a collection of choices looking for problems . . . solutions looking for issues . . . and decision makers looking for work." Sound familiar? Karl Weick suggests that people in organizations make meanings by engaging in "retrospective sense-making"; they identify the "decision" they've made *after* they act—not before.

Meaning contributes fundamentally to survival, just as food and water do. Viktor Frankl makes this point most powerfully in his book *Man's Search for Meaning*. Frankl, a survivor of Auschwitz and Dachau, was profoundly influenced by what he observed during his agonizing years at the death camps. If ever there was an event in history that challenged meaning, it was the Holocaust. The message that many took from that event, from the two World Wars, from the bomb, is that life is *not* meaningful. But Frankl saw the reverse.

The concentration camp survivors, in his view, were not necessarily the strongest physically. They were the ones who could cling to a shard of hope in a hopeless situation—those who could hang on to meaning under conditions that defied all meaning.

The need for meaning runs so deep in people that organizations must supply it if they are to renew. Many don't. The best they can come up with is "more profit, continued growth." Serve the shareholder, and the rest will take care of itself. That is a dangerous perspective. For most of us, "the shareholder" is an abstraction—that fickle and faceless money manager who buys shares on rumors of good news and sells on hints of adversity.* If this view gives meaning, it does so for only a few. Pursuit of profit is hardly a cause that inspires loyalty or makes life meaningful for most people, unless company survival is at issue, and even then it may not be enough. Meaning should be bound up in the work we do. If we cannot find meaning in work, we spend our eight hours every weekday in quiet desperation. If we can find meaning in work, we can keep ourselves recharged, and the organizations we work for stand a chance of staying renewed themselves.

Leaders who are successful seem to understand the importance of making work meaningful for themselves and the people who work for them. The pattern that emerges is one of a constantly shifting set of issues that surface as the organization sails into uncharted waters. Some managers avoid the issues or put them in the "too hard" basket; their organizations don't renew. Others not only welcome the issues but take some pains to dig them out and turn them into causes. Their organizations have a chance. A few leaders are able to find adventure and nobility in the causes. Their companies will probably stay fresh. Some are able to turn organizational causes into individual commitment. Their organizations will almost certainly regenerate.

---

* Making the employee a shareholder through an employee stock ownership plan (the ESOP) helps a little but doesn't solve the problem. ESOPs are just a nonsalary or nonwage way of distributing wealth to the employees. But money is not necessarily a prime motivator. Research shows that when people aren't paid fairly they lose motivation; but given fair compensation, money is far down on the list of what motivates most people. ESOPs have other problems. They used to have a tax advantage; with the new tax law, that is gone. ESOPs signal ownership, which is good, but the fraction of employee ownership is so small that no participation in company affairs is implied. What's more, ESOPs put the burden of market risk on the employee.

MOVEABLE ISSUES

Andy Pearson says that when he was president of PepsiCo, one of his most valuable management tools was a handwritten list that he kept and updated three or four times a year. On the list were the short- and long-term problems and opportunities for each division he managed. He says, "You'd be amazed how helpful that is to keep things in focus."

Pearson's management tool might be called a "moveable issues list." For different companies it takes different forms. It is not always as explicit as Pearson's list. Or it might be more formal than his handwritten notes. The concept behind it is simple. At any point a company is faced with a set of problems and opportunities. A good brainstorming session will bring most of these out. A little more attention and they can be stated as issues to be addressed. A touch more work and they can be summarized into a few top-priority, must-deal-with items.

In some situations the issues are obvious. When Manufacturing VP Dick Burke joined the Schipke team at GE, he says, "I was sitting in a meeting when I first arrived here and someone was reporting that we had an SCR of sixty-five for one of our products. I asked what that was, and he said that sixty-five percent of the appliances needed a service call during the warranty period. I was appalled. He asked, 'What's wrong with that? It used to be a hundred and thirty-five percent.' " That's more than one service call per appliance while it was under warranty. Burke had come from GE's turbine division, where even a minor glitch in quality could knock out a city's electric power. Quality went straight to the top of his issue list.

Priorities are not always obvious; the important thing is to pick one that is directionally right and let it stand for the rest. In 1980, when John Egan took the helm of the Jaguar automobile company, the whole company was on strike. We/they fences were everywhere, especially in the form of job boundaries dictated by the trade unions. The company was losing money. Jaguar wasn't even a complete company; only engineering and manufacturing were on-site. Sales, marketing, and other activities had vanished into the functional structure that had resulted from the nationalization of Jaguar's predecessor, British Leyland. Everything was a problem, an issue, and a potential cause.

Egan says he decided that the place to start was with quality. "Companies in crisis cannot tackle too many things at the same time," he says. He reasons that in times of crisis there will always seem to be a crushing list of conflicting problems and priorities. But Egan knows that you have to make it simple; he picked quality as the top issue and cause.

His choice showed a good understanding of the market situation. Jaguar has always had a strong following in the luxury car market, but in the late 1970s and early 1980s the standing joke was that you had to own two—one to drive and the other to have at the shop, being fixed. Quality as cause gave focus to the company's energies. They looked at their internal inspection system, which demerited the cars with faults. They looked at the warranty numbers and the problems those numbers reflected. Then they got a quick fix on how their own numbers stacked up by phoning a sample of one hundred Jaguar customers, one hundred Mercedes Benz owners, one hundred BMW owners, and so on, to ask about their experience in using each car over a twelve-month period. "We mobilized the whole company to solve these problems [the ones they pinpointed from their own analysis and market feedback]," Egan says. There were about two hundred of them: paint work, steering gear that leaked, gear boxes that failed, and so on. That information provided a way to target their "quality" push.

Morgan Bank recognizes the importance of articulating the issues and of keeping the issues list in motion as times change. Says one executive: "We haven't done a detailed five-year plan in quite some time. We realized that we can't do them anyway, so we're better off taking strategic issues and dealing with them. Our strategic planning meetings for the last two or three years have been highly issue-oriented. First the staff puts together a long paper on the issue; then it's discussed extensively."

At IBM a very similar process is at work. Bernard Puckett describes it: "One of the parts of the planning system is something we call strategic planning conferences. Twice a year Akers takes his top twenty executives and goes off for two and a half days. What we do is try to focus on some area. In my former job I'd go in to [Akers] and say, 'John, I think we ought to look at. . . .' I'd pick a specific issue, try to sell it, and if he bought it, he'd select people to work on it. Then we'd sit in a room for two and a half days with people from all over the world. That's really where we set the rudder [IBM's major directions], as far as I'm concerned."

To explain the value of focusing on a few issues, Puckett elaborates: "You never notice any red cars when you're driving around; now you'll see twice as many because I mentioned it." At the time of our talk, IBM had just announced a major thrust in systems integration. Puckett commented that only two years before, that concept had been viewed negatively around IBM. People felt getting into systems integration would require IBM to take on much more responsibility for the total package than the company had been used to assuming. Then, many believed, IBM would run the risk of not living up to customer expectations. "In a *relatively* short period of time—less than twelve months—the attitude switched from 'I'm not interested in doing that at all' to Akers's saying, 'That's a major thrust for the IBM company.' The change resulted from spending time at these conferences discussing the issue. You put something on the table there, and then guys like Rizzo, or Akers, or Phyphers [all very senior IBM executives] who have their own close contacts with customers, ask, 'How are you buying things now?' The customers tell them something like: 'I've got seven vendors; the equipment never all works together; I don't know how to install it myself; I need somebody to come take that problem off my hands.' "

According to Puckett, it was a similar set of meetings that led IBM to conclude that, despite their sales prowess, they were never as market-oriented as legend made them out to be. This issue, combined with the need for systems integration and their determination to keep costs down while keeping their no-layoff policy, has led to a massive shift of people within IBM. They are moving away from factory, staff, and office positions and into the field, where the customers are.

My own certitude about the value of a moveable-issues list comes from my days with the Long Range Planning Committee for the San Francisco Symphony. One of the committee's first actions was to frame a very complete list of issues. To do that, we interviewed everyone who was influential and knowledgeable about the Symphony, to find out what bothered them.

In the first year, there were two priority issues. First, what could be done about the deficit? Second, did everyone truly buy into the Symphony's stated aspiration to become a great symphony, one recognized as world class?

As the years went by, the committee, and the rest of the Symphony in turn, kept updating the issues list and setting new priorities. By the end of the second year the deficit had been erased, but if the Symphony was going to be world class, it needed more world-class musicians. It also needed to tour more and find a way to attract more top-flight guest conductors. Those became priority issues.

A few years later, the deficit that had been so nicely erased several years back wouldn't stay erased. By that time, the financials on a "what-if" computer model were completed, but no matter how the budget was cut, the Symphony would probably be bathing in red ink five years out. Building the size of the endowment and thinking of new ways to do that were problems that got moved to the top of the issues list.

One of the recent issues has been to knock down some we/they barriers between board members, staff, and musicians. During one meeting, a musician who had been quiet for most of the session said, "I'll tell you what the biggest we/they barrier is: us and the hall." The new Davies Symphony Hall was giving the musicians fits—it's built with adjustable curtains and reflectors so that it can be "tuned." Every time it gets tuned right for the audience, or for recording, the musicians have difficulty hearing one another. There are some dead spots on stage, and one section of the orchestra might hear an echo from another section rather than the direct sound. The strings can't be sure they are precisely with the horns— and so on. Acoustics in the hall moved right to the top of the issues list.

What makes the issues list work is that it was conceived as an "issue broker," not an "issue resolver." The concern was with implementation. To get anything done, the committee had to enlist the people who could resolve the issue. Who were those people? It depended on the issue. Sometimes it was another board committee member, sometimes a person on the Symphony staff, sometimes the president, the executive director, or the conductor, sometimes a task force involving musicians.

Another part of the process that made it practical was that although we were called the Long Range Planning Committee, there was never a long-range plan. There was plenty of documentation. But it was flexibility that made the planning process a force for renewal.

The *moveable* part of the moveable-issues concept reminds us that the world keeps changing, that it does so in hard-to-predict ways, and that renewal is a constant challenge, something you live with—not solve. H. Ross Perot has a sign in his office that captures this spirit: EVERY GOOD AND EXCELLENT THING STANDS MOMENT BY MOMENT ON THE RAZOR'S EDGE OF DANGER AND MUST BE FOUGHT FOR. In a lighter vein, John Gardner remarks that Sisyphus just misses being a good metaphor for renewal. For those of you who don't remember, he's the fellow from Greek mythology who is eternally condemned to push a rock up a hill, only to have it roll back down as he nears the top. "But," Gardner says, deadpan, "Sisyphus had a very flat learning curve."

REFRESHING THE CAUSE

"We run on causes around here," declared many of the executives we interviewed. Their way of keeping their companies fresh was to keep their causes fresh—and inspiring. A moveable-issues list can be the source of the cause that refreshes and renews organizations. The flip side of any top-priority issue is a top-priority cause. As the Symphony example suggests, it's not that hard for most organizations to list and to rank issues. The challenge for leadership is adding the magic—transforming the issue from just another dreary problem to a cause that inspires people.

Porsche's CEO, Peter Schutz, brings the point to life with this story: "Three people were at work on a construction site. All were doing the same job, but when each was asked what his job was, the answers varied. 'Breaking rocks,' the first replied. 'Earning my living,' said the second. 'Helping to build a cathedral,' said the third." In his classic book *Working*, Studs Terkel found that some of the happiest manual laborers were stonemasons. They could look back on what they'd built and take pride in it.

Few of us can build cathedrals or work as stonemasons. But to the extent we can see the cathedral in whatever cause we are following, the job seems more worthwhile. Good leaders help us find those cathedrals in what otherwise could be dismal issues and empty causes. The point seems obvious, but failure to pay it any heed was one of the main problems CEO John Egan inherited at Jaguar. Executives there report that in 1975 an effort was made to subjugate Jaguar under the umbrella of Leyland Cars. The Jaguar signs at the entry to the factory were torn down. Only Leyland flags could be flown on the premises. Switchboard operators were threatened with disciplinary action if they answered, "Good morning, Jaguar Cars." Instead they were supposed to say: "Good morning, Leyland Cars—large car assembly plant number one."

The assortment of causes among the renewing organizations was as varied and individual as the organizations themselves. At Children's Television Workshop the original cause was to use the television medium to teach economically disadvantaged preschoolers. As time passed the cause was broadened to include all preschoolers and then children worldwide. Today's cause, and the basis for their new program, *3-2-1 Contact,* is to use television to help rectify America's decline in math scores.

One cause that most of the renewing companies seem to have moved away from is growth for its own sake. The volume-oriented, shove-it-out-the-door mentality, which went unchallenged for too long, put many organizations on the brink of disaster. Many of the leading banks, for example, were preoccupied with growth. When the American market for big lending dried up, the banks went after foreign credits, which turned out to be much riskier than the banks had ever imagined.

The volume cause was what got GE, Ford, and other manufacturers into so much trouble in the late 1970s and early 1980s. It was also one culprit behind Jaguar's troubles. Jaguar executives say that those were the days of the dual ethic; "big is beautiful" and "economies of scale" were everything.

The situation at GE typified what happened when volume stood as the premier, unchallenged cause. An assembly worker said, "Back then, if you said that you had a bad part, and if they felt they had to get the job done, they'd tell you to run it anyway. They didn't want to hear any more about it. We had to supply John Q. Customer, and if he got a bad [product], why we'd just go out later and fix it."

GE managers, along with many others in the Western world, were transfixed with volume, quite possibly trapped by groupthink, and could not make the necessary common-sense decisions. Faulty product was pushed out the factory door despite the fact that GE knew it cost them $3.50 to fix a defect in the factory and $60 to fix it in the home. Several people told us that bad parts received from suppliers would often be rejected, but not discarded. In a production bind, people would fish out the bad parts and build them into the appliances to meet the targeted volume. Another trick for meeting production targets was to produce the appliance short an unavailable part or two, send it to the warehouse to get production credit, then try to find and fix it later in the warehouse.

As long as quality was sacrificed in the name of volume, worker unrest had to follow. Their work lost its meaning; people had no source of pride in what they were doing. Folks were treated as if they were stupid. GE's Dick Burke says, "The biggest problem in U.S. industry today is the arrogance of management. We had nineteen thousand people here—a tremendous resource—but our management team hadn't communicated anything to them [except, implicitly, the importance of volume]." According to Burke, the attitude of past management was "Hourly people aren't very bright; why should we take the trouble to instruct them or ask them for help?" Contrast his depiction with what we heard from one of the hourly employees who had lived through the old era: "Just like all these child psychologists say, 'If your child has an inquiring mind, teach him.' My mind's not stagnant. Teach me." The simple act of informing people down the line and asking for their help goes a long way toward making their jobs meaningful.

At Appliance Park the situation had gotten so bad that work had lost meaning even for the middle managers. An executive told us: "For eight to ten years management had been saying, 'We don't want any strikes,' and tried to buy their way out with sweetheart deals. We had double-digit absenteeism. Time clocks were broken. Restrooms were a mess. There were no employee cafeterias. Management was accustomed to not being backed." In one outrageous incident, an employee threw a cup of coffee in his supervisor's face, the supervisor tried to take disciplinary action, there was a strike, and the *supervisor* was fired. Burke says, "In 1982 only a tiny percent of the middle managers trusted upper management. The middle managers looked, acted, and smelled like losers—they had to be the most beat group I've ever seen."

For Roger Schipke, finding a renewing cause was easy. He says, "*I got mad!* I saw all the fumbling and waste here. The Japanese were beating us. American manufacturing was going down. People were saying our factory workers weren't as good as they used to be, and certainly not as good as the Japanese." With so much wrong, there was no lack of causes. But, as people who survived the worst of it recall, the problems seemed insurmountable. Focus was desperately needed. When Schipke got mad, he was heading up dishwasher manufacturing in Building C within Appliance Park. His initial cause was not to take on the problems of a Don Quixote–like joust with all the issues at Appliance Park. It was to make something called "Project C" work—automating the dishwasher line in Building C.

Better quality and better treatment of people are the causes most frequently heard about. Each of these comes inherently packaged with themes that motivate. Each has a kind of Golden Rule quality to it. Do a better job on quality or on treating your employees well, and you display an attitude that says "We care." The quality and employee-involvement themes, newly instituted at Jaguar, Ford, GE—and historically in place at Maytag, IBM, HP—are natural sources of pride.

The push for quality at Jaguar has done the seemingly impossible: It's turned a near-failing British company into one that is competitive on a world scale. J.D. Powers is a company that ranks automobile manufacturers in terms of customer satisfaction. Egan told us: "In 1980 we were so bad we weren't even on the [Powers] list; last year we were fifth."

In recent years Jaguar has been gaining a share in the U.S. luxury car market segment—the only company other than BMW to do so. Even more recently, Jaguar picked up a small share of the market in that bastion of quality luxury cars, West Germany.

As a cause, better service has precisely the same attributes to recommend it that better quality has. But, despite the fact that a large number of the companies we interviewed are in the service business, and that 85 percent of the new jobs being created these days are in the service sector, we didn't hear "better service" put forward as a cause nearly as often as "better quality" was. There are some notable exceptions, but the fact remains: We heard more about quality products than about quality service. The reason could easily be that because of poor quality, American manufacturing has recently suffered mightily at the hands of foreign competition and is just now getting its act back together. Poor service, however, can be harder to detect; it rarely even makes its way *onto* the issues list, let alone to the top of it.

Dartmouth professor James Brian Quinn concludes that the same inattention to quality that spelled near-disaster for American manufacturing is pervasive in the service industries today. It could have similar disastrous results for service companies that don't get with it. If Quinn's conclusion is right, the tragedy is due to the myopia of American leadership. Service companies have been under pressure from deregulation and heavy competition from the discounters. A natural reaction is to cut costs, which is to say cut service payroll, training, and the caliber of employees.

But service is like quality. There's every indication that it's a moneymaker. The most convincing evidence comes from The Strategic Planning Institute in Cambridge, Massachusetts, which tracks the fortunes of more than 2,500 business units worldwide. Using sophisticated statistical measures, they compare businesses producing high quality, or high service, with competitors in the same business who offer lower quality or lower service. The high-quality, high-service firms return, on average, twice as much on invested capital as do their typical low-end counterparts. The secret to success in the service business is simple: Offer service.

A frequent, and motivating, cause we heard was "be a winner." That cause appeals to our need to feel special, the positive side of Martin Luther King, Jr.'s "drum major instinct." When Peter Schutz left Cummins Engine to take over the helm of Porsche in Stuttgart, Porsche was on the verge of losing money for the first time in its history. The strategy Schutz inherited was to shrink the business, in hopes that, at some smaller size, Porsche could hang on to a profitable niche. Schutz believed that this cause would do nothing but breed losers. One day when he was talking with Professor Porsche, the visionary behind most of the Porsche line and the man who designed the Volkswagen Beetle, Schutz asked him: "What is the all-time best car? What is your personal favorite? Which car are you most proud of?" Porsche answered, "We haven't built it yet." It was then that Schutz began to believe he could restore the old spirit.

The winning cause began to infuse the Porsche team when Schutz asked a group of his managers to name the most important race of the year. They unanimously nominated the twenty-four-hour Le Mans Grand Prix. As usual, the company was planning to enter their 924 turbo in that race. When Schutz asked what their chances were of winning with that model, he was told they might be able to win within their class, but there was no chance of winning overall. At that point, he adjourned the meeting, saying, "As long as I'm in charge of the company, we won't talk about not winning."

Twenty-four hours later he called for another meeting, this time to talk about how they could win. According to Schutz, the interesting thing was how excited people got. In the past they had all been muttering under their breath about how they could win if someone in the company would only let them try. Now they had the chance. What they did not have was much time. There were two 936s in inventory. They figured they could take the transmission out of a 917, "kludge" together some other parts, and put together something that might win. This was just sixty-two days before the race. Two days later Schutz got a call from a fellow who had retired a couple of years previously as a race driver. He had heard via the grapevine what Porsche was doing, and he wanted to volunteer to drive whatever they came up with. They did win that race and were on the way to restoring both a winning spirit and profitability.

Cost reduction is another common issue for the renewing companies. No cause may be more crucial to top management than lowering costs or increasing productivity. But it's a more difficult one to make meaningful than quality or service. It usually means lost jobs. Too often managers avoid the problem of trying to explain it, or they explain it in a way that relates only to the needs of the organization and not to the needs of the people who work there. One boss decided that a sense of discipline might instill pride in his employees. The discipline he used was to clock the employees' arrival time. Anyone getting to work later than 8:00 a.m. would get a demerit. Three demerits and you work on Saturday. This company is on the ropes. It desperately needs renewal. Getting to work at 8:00 is not a cause that will help turn it around.

Other companies have been able to define the cost issue in terms of a cause that has some nobility, integrity, and urgency by letting everyone know what will happen to the enterprise—and jobs in the long run—if the issue is not met head-on. We found managers who had taken workers and union leadership to Japan or Korea so they could see firsthand what they were up against. At Ford, Brunswick, Nucor, and Wells Fargo, we found people up and down the line who were highly motivated to control costs. Management had spent countless hours explaining to them the importance of productivity to the viability of the company.

Another common theme for renewal, which can become a cause, is technology. By definition it's important in the high-tech companies—HP, Digital, Olivetti, IBM. But technology was a theme for renewal in steelmaking at Nucor, in truck-parts manufacture at Dana, in printing at Quad/Graphics, in papermaking at both James River and Potlatch, and in banking at Citicorp. There, CEO John Reed made his mark by automating the so-called "back-office" operations. Information technology has become a cornerstone of much of the change happening at Morgan, where executives told us that one of every six people there is in programming, systems design, or related technical fields.

Cost control, productivity, technology, and certain other causes that pop out of the issues list can be meaningful for a while. However, the most motivating causes focus on *quality products, service, and the customer*—making the work people do seem worth the effort—and *people quality*—making people believe in their individual worth. These causes are motivating because they relate equally to people and the organization. In all the other issues and causes, the organization comes first and the individual is secondary. An important leadership challenge is to find ways of articulating causes so that they make meaning for people. Causes that speak only to the needs of the organization—or to individual needs—are not the stuff of permanent renewal. A cause, put forward with some inspiration, can be what turns the dreary issue into a catalyst for renewal.

ADVENTURE CAPITAL

Erich Fromm comments: "Man is not free to choose between having or not having 'ideals,' but he is free to choose between different kinds of ideals, between being devoted to the worship of power and destruction and being devoted to reason and love." In a very similar way, it is not just the existence of a cause that engenders renewal in a company; the nature of the cause counts for a great deal. If the history of nations, governments, or companies has done nothing else, it has taught us that wrongly intentioned leaders can rally people to loathsome causes as well as to noble ones. Dictatorial regimes can change organizations quickly, but often for the worse, and certainly without the ability to renew.

But companies can find worthwhile causes to engage. That's the way manufacturing czar Jack Kuehler describes his company. "One unique feature of IBM is our ability to articulate causes and let them become the next mountain to climb." In the early 1980s, IBM recognized that the company no longer stood for quality in the way IBMers felt it should. Back then, regardless of the accuracy of public perceptions, many believed that the Japanese made a better-quality computer than IBM's. Kuehler says, "We decided to do everything we could to improve both the reality and perception of IBM's quality." As Hewlett-Packard did with the TQC program, the whole company recommitted to quality and to a new set of quality objectives—in development, in manufacturing, in accounting, and even in the handling of paperwork and documentation.

When there is a choice, part of the magic a leader can lend to the cause is to find adventure in it. We see a little of this in the GE story. For all their problems, there is a sense of adventure at Appliance Park. Demolishing the matrix organization. Convincing Welch that Project C could work. Roger Schipke recalls: "I argued that nothing better had been offered to him, so he might as well let me try it. He answered, 'It's going to fail. You guys in Louisville can't walk and chew gum at the same time. What's different about this?'" Making it work: "Project C was like changing a fan belt on a running engine. We built six hundred thousand dishwashers while we were modernizing the factory." It *was* an adventure, and behind it lies Schipke's willingness to risk a little.

Even in less dire circumstances, making work meaningful is closely related to the ability to find and articulate *adventure* in work. Often you will meet someone you haven't seen in years. Sometimes you take up right where you left off; the bond is still there. Other times, the person is a stranger, someone you knew once but don't know anymore. One difference seems to be whether you've had some kind of adventure together. Have you tried something, risked a little bit, done something you weren't sure you could do? The *size* of the adventure doesn't seem to matter much. A pickup game of touch football might do it. So might making a joint investment in a small project. The *content* of the adventure does matter; it has to be something positive, something that seems worthwhile, noble in its own small way.

Adventure and risk go together. One man's risk is another's terror, and if the risk is too high, adventure becomes disaster. We don't learn, and we don't renew. Behind the ability to risk has to be a basis for security. Friendly facts. Healthy people policies. Tolerance for mistakes. Safety nets.

At Porsche, Peter Schutz subscribes to the adventure theory in an interesting way. First, he says that one of the things you look for in the people you hire is courage. You can't teach them that. Second, he declares that money alone won't keep good people. You may attract them that way, but you hold them by giving them interesting work. One of the specific things that keeps the Porsche engineering staff tuned up, in touch, and turned on is doing contract engineering work for others. When I talked to Schutz his engineers had just helped design the airbus, they were working with the Russians on designing small automobiles, and they were developing a fuel-injection motor for a car to be manufactured in Spain. They were also developing a Formula 1 racing car.

One of the bigger adventure-filled causes we ran into was across town from Appliance Park in Louisville. Tired of taking the kind of flak that says for-profit hospitals don't serve the community, Humana decided to assume the management of Louisville's General Hospital. At the time, the hospital was providing indigent care and serving as a teaching facility for the University of Louisville's medical school. Facing a projected 1981 deficit of $3.6 million, the hospital eliminated jobs, reduced services, and began turning away the indigents it was supposed to serve. Despite these cost-saving measures, the situation grew worse. A year later, upon completion of a new facility to replace an old one that was actually crumbling, the hospital was projecting a $10 million loss.

Conditions were awful. Ann Powell, director of surgery, remembers all too clearly: "The old facility had added no new capital equipment in ten years. Daily we ran out of essential supplies. The hospital couldn't pay its bills without additional money from somewhere, so suppliers refused to send us anything more. Between 1980 and 1983 we had three layoffs. That left us with five people to cover twenty-four hours a day, seven days a week—and that wasn't just for the recovery room; we were also used for intensive care. We called the ICU 'pre-mortem'—it was that bad. I can't imagine more horrible environmental conditions. Needless to say, we couldn't recruit or retain quality staff." Mary Bennett, head RN for the trauma center, chimes in: "During the summer at the old hospital some of the wards reached a hundred and five degrees. Patients were perspiring so much we had to use a lot more IV fluid than normal. It was medicine from another era."

Humana approached the University of Louisville. David Jones and Wendell Cherry offered to lease the new hospital complex, purchase equipment, support medical education, and underwrite indigent-care deficits. The university would receive 20 percent of the hospital's pretax profits. In return Humana got a new 404-bed facility and the "opportunity" to make a profit if it could survive the challenge of this unusual public-private partnership.

Jones and Cherry might have appeared foolhardy hanging the General Hospital albatross around their necks. But in truth, they were relatively certain Humana's expertise in hospital administration could turn the place around. By taking on this particular cause, Humana could reaffirm its public commitment to improving the existing health-care delivery system and prove that public/private partnerships can work. Furthermore, Jones and Cherry would be able to show that for-profit businessmen aren't the heartless ogres the medical establishment has portrayed them to be.

The speed of the turnaround surprised everyone, even Humana. By fiscal year 1985 the hospital realized a $3.7 million profit, despite an 11.6 percent increase in indigent use that cost Humana over $6 million. Gary Sherlock, who runs the facility, is modest about what he did. He admits it sounds a little too simple to be true, but there were really only four factors. First, he brought in business practices that had worked for Humana elsewhere, and they yielded the same results they had produced elsewhere—more service, lower cost. The second factor was treating people—both staff and patients—with dignity. Third, he encouraged open and honest communication with lots of feedback. Fourth was his continuing belief that people want to think well of themselves, and thus are motivated more by the vision of what could be than the need to make immediate profit.

The numbers depict the magnitude of the change, but to get a real sense of it you have to be there, to talk to some of the people who had seen it before and after. Dr. Donald Thomas, chairman of the department of emergency medicine, says, "Now we're both more efficient and more oriented to patient care. We no longer have to turn patients away. Instead of being in wards with thirty to forty others, patients are in double rooms. Nursing is on flexible hours now. Managers are more accessible, and they are willing to act if you convince them something should be done." Ann Powell declares that Humana's presence hasn't just improved the hospital; it has turned around her life. "We've got a happy bunch of people around here—productive people with creative ideas. Our education budget is twice that of other Humana hospitals, because people here are so interested in furthering their education. We do unique things here because of our equipment, personnel competence, and the aura of the place."

There is no magic in the way Humana turned the place around. It was work, but they simply did the thing they do well. For Humana the magic is in the adventure of taking a risk that nobody on the outside thinks possible, turning it into a cause, making it work, and enabling the whole organization to feel proud of itself for doing so well. The issue: the poor public image of for-profit hospitals. The cause: Louisville General Hospital. The adventure: Could anyone turn it around, let alone make a profit, given its abysmal situation? The continuing challenge: finding more ways to improve service to patients, support medical education and research, and cut costs.

COMMITMENT

Causes and commitment are the core of renewal—both individual and institutional. Stating an organization-wide cause is one thing, but the words mean nothing unless people get committed. The rub is that you can't legislate commitment, and at some level you can't quite manage it, either. Commitment is an individual state of mind, something that falls into place person-by-person.

It isn't all that easy. Our society is very outspoken on the need for individual rights and freedom. But we have trouble thinking and talking clearly about how to balance individual freedom on the one hand and organizational commitment on the other. We are suspicious of causes; they dilute autonomy and sometimes compromise individual freedom for broader purposes that are questionable. We think it's better to keep our options open than to make a commitment we may regret later.

The below-the-surface conflict between rugged individualism and social commitment that many Americans experience is the subject of the recent book *Habits of the Heart*. Interviewing hundreds of people throughout the United States, the authors (five sociologists) uncovered a "classic case of ambivalence" between our need for both freedom and commitment. We feel the need for freedom so deeply, we have trouble making commitments. We all can recognize a part of ourselves reflected in the mirror *Habits of the Heart* holds up. The authors observe:

> We found all the classic polarities of American individualism still operating: the deep desire for autonomy and self-reliance combined with an equally deep conviction that life has no meaning unless shared with others in the context of community; a commitment to the equal right to dignity of every individual combined with an effort to justify inequality of reward, which, when extreme, may deprive people of dignity; an insistence that life requires practical effectiveness and "realism" combined with the feeling that compromise is ethically fatal. . . . We deeply feel the emptiness of a life without sustaining social commitments. Yet we are hesitant to articulate our sense that we need one another as much as we need to stand alone, for fear that if we did we would lose our independence altogether. The tensions of our lives would be even greater if we did not, in fact, engage in practices that constantly limit the effects of an isolating individualism, even though we cannot articulate those practices nearly as well as we can the quest for autonomy.

Today, in the context of many organizations, this polarity becomes even more confusing. People relinquish a great deal of autonomy in order to hold down a job. They earn a paycheck in return. In contrast to previous generations, they feel that a salary alone is small compensation if they have no sense that their work isn't contributing to the greater good. Even worse, many believe that their work is accomplishing the reverse. As metaphor for the conflict, the authors of *Habits of the Heart* pick the modern American hero: the hard-boiled detective. Whether the detective is Sam Spade, Travis McGee, Columbo, or Serpico, "When [he] begins his quest, it [the crime] appears to be an isolated incident. But as it develops, the case turns out to be linked to the powerful and privileged of the community. Society, particularly 'high society,' is corrupt to the core."

All of us make commitments. They may erode our freedom to act autonomously, but in return they provide some meaning in our lives and on the job. What we need are causes that we can identify with—ones we believe are worth supporting. James Brian Quinn notes which goals work best: "To forge a common bond among individuals with widely diverse personal values, expectations and capacities . . . goals must . . . satisfy people's more basic psychological needs: to produce something worthwhile, to help others, to obtain recognition, to be free or innovative, to achieve security, to beat an opponent, or to earn community respect."

Besides defining causes in a relevant, exciting way, it's necessary to give people a choice about whether or not they will commit. Nothing engenders resentment—or limp submission—more quickly than ordering someone to be committed. When people have no choice in the matter, they're not likely to make a genuine commitment. Organizational theorist Gerald Salancik argues that "Volition . . . is the cement that binds the action to the person and that motivates him to accept the implications of his acts. . . . Without volition, a behavior is not necessarily committing, for the person can always assert that he really did not cause the behavior himself." In other words, if someone cannot choose *not* to commit, he probably won't take responsibility for his actions. The natural fallback position in this case is: "I was forced to do it."

The turnaround at Zebco,* Brunswick Corporation's fishing reel manufacturing division in Tulsa, Oklahoma, can be attributed to the choice every employee made to commit to improving quality and productivity. Faced with near-annihilation by offshore competitors, Zebco's management decided to take the matter to the people. They understood that gains were impossible if employees on the line weren't aware of the situation and what each of them individually could do about it.

Zebco had enjoyed twenty-five years of solid success after its beginnings in 1949. But the oil crisis of 1974 changed all that.

---

* Originally the Zero Hour Bomb Company. They made bombs for fracturing oil wells. One day a man who invented the fishing reel they now make showed up and asked the company if they wanted to manufacture it. A man in the toolroom took it out to the parking lot and tried it for ten minutes. He opined that it looked good. That was the strategy that launched Zebco.

People quit buying additional fishing reels, and the bottom fell out of the market. To make matters worse, the foreign manufacturers Zebco was competing with didn't turn off the switch. Between 1982 and 1985 an excess of 8 million rods poured into the U.S. market. The wholesale price of fishing reels was $9.50, and they retailed for $9.99.

By 1980, Zebco division manager John Charvat was convinced that the company couldn't survive if it didn't reduce costs. Zebco was driven initially by a survival-based cause; foreign competition was making Zebco's prices noncompetitive. But it was redefined into something positive and more meaningful to everyone: increase quality and productivity. The hope was that it would cut costs.

Charvat knew that *communication* was the crucial link between this cause and individual commitment to it. Every employee needed to understand that Zebco's foreign competitors were here to stay, but that there still was plenty of room for improvement on their own home court. The situation was bad, but the game wasn't lost yet.

Jim Dawson, vice-president of manufacturing, offered to get this message across to everyone. He didn't do it by scheduling one big "something's gotta give" session. Instead, he started having two-hour meetings with people in groups of four, explaining to them that the only way they could stay in business was to improve quality while they increased productivity and kept the costs down. Charvat comments: "We took the time to visit with the people and let them know what we were doing and why. We taught them that quality starts within and that they should try to work smarter, not harder." It took two years for Dawson to meet with all of the employees.

Those get-togethers were supplemented by plant meetings. Charvat explains: "We asked everyone what they needed to be able to do their job better. They told us: 'Give us better parts and tools, and have them here when we need them.' We discovered that 85 percent of the problems were rooted in bad parts from suppliers." Zebco began working with suppliers and developed a vendor certification program. That corrected much of the difficulty, but lots of other measures were needed. For example, now employees can stop the line themselves if they see there's a problem with quality control.

There are three notable aspects to this story. For one, Charvat's management approach reflects his belief that "everyone wants to contribute and be recognized." So the obvious place to begin was in helping each employee understand the gravity of the situation *and* the degree to which he or she could help turn it around. Charvat was convinced that employee attitudes were the key to the quality and productivity improvements he was looking for. And those attitudes couldn't be legislated; they had to be nurtured. This is very similar to Gary Sherlock's approach at Humana Hospital University.

Second, the link between an overriding cause and individual commitment to it doesn't appear automatically. It has to be forged over time by honest, consistent communication. Charvat and Dawson went about persuading the staff to make a commitment to their cause by talking straight to them, face-to-face and in small-group meetings that were long enough to be both informative and convincing. They didn't threaten, cajole, or use any "motivational" techniques. Dialogue continues all the time at Zebco—not just during scheduled meetings. As Charvat comments: "The people on the line are quick to tell us when there's a problem. They listen to us, and we listen to them." Again the similarities: Sherlock's emphasis on communication at Humana Hospital University; Jaguar's quality program, which demanded face-to-face discussion directly with the work force, not through the unions; musicians serving on the San Francisco Symphony's Long Range Planning Committee.

Third, things improved at Zebco. Commitment to a cause will wane if people see that it's all rhetoric and no action. But the employees at Zebco recognized that they began to get better service from suppliers; they had evidence that quality was going up, and productivity was rising at an astonishing rate. Management asked them for their advice, then listened to it and made the necessary changes. Today, everyone still sees a direct link between his or her ideas and actions and the success of the company. Commitment has never been higher. More similarities: At Wells Fargo, Carl Reichardt told us that real commitment to cost control occurred when everyone started seeing the impact of their cost-cutting program on Wells Fargo's stock price.

Since Zebco began its quality assurance and productivity programs in 1981, the number of reels assembled per person per day has almost tripled. The company cut costs four years straight. Charvat is like a proud father: "When a line meets its quota, everyone yells. Everyone wants to do better and better, mostly because of the sheer pride that comes from it."

On the surface, the renewal we found in the municipal offices of Scottsdale, Arizona, seems at best a distant cousin to Zebco's. But both hinge on their leaders' success in articulating a cause and then creating lots of opportunities for everyone to get behind it. Six years ago the Scottsdale City Council brought in city manager Roy Pederson from California to heal some deep wounds. We/they barriers existed between managers and employees, who were a step away from unionization. The Fraternal Order of Police was becoming such a militant organization that it had taken the city to court. Interdepartmental conflict pulled people's attention away from their work. According to Pederson: "Some departments were being run like Prussian regiments and some were totally loose—country clubs."

Pederson inherited an organization that had been drifting for years without a sense of purpose. His challenge was to revitalize a demoralized, uncommitted staff, overhaul outmoded management practices, and develop organization-wide commitment to the cause of providing the best possible service for the community. Rather than hiding behind all the reasons something *couldn't* be changed, Pederson assumed that most things *could* be significantly improved.

After spending six months just talking to people all over the city offices, Pederson knew that the place to start was with the management team. They had a history of working at cross-purposes, and, with a few notable exceptions, they seemed adamantly resistant to change. Pederson saw an immediate, overriding need to refocus their attention on the organization's fundamental purpose of community service. Beyond that, he wanted to articulate new shared values that every manager would be expected to commit to. He had to smoke out the members of the top management team who couldn't or wouldn't get on board with the cause and values that he wanted to establish organization-wide.

To accomplish this, Pederson scheduled what he now calls a "Come to Jesus" meeting for all the department and division heads, where he stated the cause—serve the people in Scottsdale—and its supporting values: Be the best source of information, be cost-conscious, support city policy, plan, and treat people decently. What was the group's response? Pederson remembers: "There were no comments or questions afterwards. On the negative side, people could see I had decided it was time to get tough. On the positive side, I had made some moves toward a main thrust for the organization. About twenty-five percent of the managers were taking me seriously, fifty percent had decided to wait me out [they had seen other city managers come and go], and another twenty-five percent said, 'To hell with this.' They began to polish up their résumés."

Pederson had plenty of reason to believe that a number of managers would not at the outset be willing to get behind a broad-based renewal effort. Once he was ready to establish the new cause and set the necessary course to get there, his top priority was to give everyone on the management team an opportunity to sign up. But he also wanted to let them know that it would be tough for them to stay on the team if they chose not to support him.

Choice is crucial to commitment. So every leader must face the possibility that some managers will choose not to support the cause he or she has in mind. What should the leader do in that case? If the most competent and trusted people won't commit, the leader should take another look at the cause itself. It may be ill-conceived or stated in a misleading way. If the cause still seems worthy of pursuing, then he or she has to make it very hard for people who don't go along with it to stick around.

The leader must decide on the cause and the values. He or she should be open to question and challenge, but then be ready to commit. Once the leader commits to the cause, the top management team divides into three camps: strong supporters; no problem there. Strong opponents; they have to go. And the "mugwumps," the fence-sitters with their "mug" on one side and their "wump" on the other; they seem committed, yet they fight the program. One executive advises: "Invent tests that force them to commit or to leave."*

A manager's responsibility is to get things done. He simply can't carry people who choose not to support a major mission. The members of the team may disagree on occasion about how to reach the goal. That's inevitable in a group of committed, yet free, thinkers. But if there's dissent at the outset over the cause itself, it's unlikely the team will ever be able to join together in reaching it. One weak link on the team—one uncommitted person—can create an enormous energy leak that's both distracting and debilitating. All the key players must choose to be on board from the beginning. Pederson understood that.

But so far, all Pederson had in Scottsdale was a management team that knew they'd better buy in or move out. He still had the problem of how to gain commitment from the eight hundred people who worked within the departments. Given their old habits, the

---

* This sounds antithetical to my earlier statements that you can't order people to be committed. The difference is subtle. Here I'm talking about the leadership team. They do have a choice, though not a pleasant one: Get committed or get out.

past friction, the lingering hostility in some cases, and downright sloth in others, Pederson sensed that more might be needed than an inspiring cause and a gospel meeting.

He made the shift from cause to widespread commitment in two ways. First, he enlisted the help of two people who have turned out to be key lieutenants, Tom Davis and Dick Bowers, to spend seemingly endless hours talking with everyone. This step is a direct parallel to the process for gaining commitment we saw at Zebco, Jaguar, and a host of others.

But as powerful a force as it is, communication intensity alone may not have been enough to move this tar pit of lost causes. The second approach was inspired. Pederson, Davis, and Bowers, along with the department heads, found, invented, borrowed, and supported a cornucopia of small things that people in every nook and cranny of the organization could do. Taken one at a time, each seems too small, too gimmicky, too corny, or too insignificant to make a difference. But looking at them this way would miss the point on two counts. First, from an organizational perspective they aren't taken one at a time; hundreds of things are going on that are directionally right. Second, it is precisely the smallness of the step that leads to commitment.

Here's what is going on: People use their own actions as a way of discovering what they believe in the first place. "Did I do that? There must have been a reason. Oh yes, here's why...." If people act slightly differently from the way they have in the past, what psychologists call "cognitive dissonance" sets in. People are uncomfortable with dissonance. They can't undo the act, so they modify their beliefs a little to make them more consistent with what they just did. Dissonance reduction is one of the prime reasons that the most avid readers of automobile advertising are people who have just bought the car. They are looking for support for their decision.

Now, let's look at this process at work in Scottsdale. Community Development is the department that reviews and approves all building construction. Their typical turnaround time on any project was two months. They were so accustomed to working at cross-purposes, their automatic attitude toward anything new was to stonewall it. Tom Davis, who spearheaded the transformation of this department, told us, "When developers called to check on how far along their application had gotten in the approval process, there was no record of where it was." Davis tried a number of different ways to get them moving; nothing worked. He finally got the staff off the dime with a suggestion program for cleaning up red tape that encouraged employees to challenge outmoded or unnecessary procedures. People were asked to complete, in writing, the sentence "This seems stupid to me," whenever they came across "a dumb thing we'd been doing for a long time." People liked that idea and started writing about dumb things. A tiny action, almost trivial, yet the very act of doing it started a change in mind-set.

In the same department Davis also set up a One Stop Shop. Developers used to have to go to multiple locations to nurse their applications through the process. Now they get everything processed at one location. The service-driven values for the One Stop Shop: It is unforgivable not to make a decision; unless written policy says no, say yes; if written policy says no, ask yourself if that makes sense [and presumably, if it doesn't, fill out a "this seems stupid" letter]; each employee is allowed only two no's a week. Community Development now turns around developers' plans in five days.

When Deputy City Manager Dick Bowers said that he had collected some "artifacts" of the change process from the different departments, he didn't turn up with just T-shirts and some award certificates. Instead, there were turtle-adorned note pads and pins (WE STICK OUR NECK OUT FOR YOU) and lunch bags emblazoned with the maintenance department's slogan: WHERE WE DO COMMON THINGS UNCOMMONLY WELL. The formerly recalcitrant police department decided to affirm Scottsdale's new shared values with a KEEP THE PEACE AND SET THE PACE theme on everything from brochures to coffee mugs.

Scottsdale's motto for gaining commitment might have been "No step too small." One project that is nothing but a collection of tiny actions by everyone on the staff is called "Employees Yielding Effective Savings." The acronym is EYES; if anyone sees something anywhere in the city that needs maintenance, they're encouraged to send a notice to field operations. In stark relief to the "it's not my job" attitude that used to prevail, 5,200 two-part EYES suggestion forms were submitted last year. The bottom part of the EYES forms are collected for an annual drawing, with first prize a reconditioned city pickup truck that was scheduled to be cycled out of service. But the real incentive comes when an employee who has reported a pothole that needs to be fixed drives by a week later and sees that the job has been done. That person knows it wouldn't have happened as quickly without his or her contribution.

The seemingly cornball continues: Scottsdale has its own Emmy awards. The project behind it is serious. When a cable TV channel approached the city for approval, they were told they could have it.

But in exchange they were asked to open a channel for the city. Its use would be training and internal staff development. There was no money to produce the programs, but seventy employees volunteered their free time to be trained and then create the videos, doing the filming, editing, and voice-overs. Every year at the Emmy awards ceremony the volunteers receive the recognition they deserve, along with hats, jackets, and certificates.

This kind of thing is exactly what develops commitment. The overall causes are training, staff development, service. But Scottsdale found a way to turn the abstraction into something people can do. In producing the shows, they do something meaningful for the organization, and in turn find more meaning in their work.

Public offices don't usually budget funds for apparent "frills." But Pederson and his crew understand the mileage you can get with even a small line-item amount for awards. Dick Bowers uses $20 bills to reward people he "catches doing something right." About once a week he writes a note mentioning the "something right," tucks the note and a crisp $20 bill in an envelope, and pops it in interoffice mail. Bowers has found another small way of reinforcing the cause and a big way of paying attention.

Scottsdale is a great example of how commitment can emerge from a lackluster staff when every person is given a chance to do something that contributes to the cause. Here's an interesting case where the public sector has a thing or two to teach the private sector. Unlike many companies that—although they are in the growing service sector of the economy—still don't serve, Scottsdale has brought that intangible called "service" to life. The thousands of little things make the difference. It's similar to the earlier message on small wins. The overall impact looks big; the magic is in the minutiae. The people in the Scottsdale city offices believe they are living and serving a "world-class" city, and they are doing it in a world-class way.

These items may seem flaky at first glance—more the residue of empty-headed hoopla than meaningful activity. But that couldn't be further from the truth. Instead, they are evidence of Scottsdale's continuing effort to introduce lots of little ways for everyone in the organization to make a difference. And it all seems to increase commitment exponentially. Every time people can contribute successfully to the cause of serving the community, they become even more committed to it.

COMMITMENT TRAPS

Commitment does have its downside. In fact, research on commitment contains more reports on the uses of commitment to manipulate than on its power to motivate. The challenge for all of us is to recognize when commitment is a trap and not a source of renewal.

Scottsdale shows how lots of little actions that support a cause can increase each person's commitment to it. There's enormous incremental power in making it possible for people to succeed—to experience small wins—in ways that move directionally toward renewal. In fact, that's an almost sure-fire way to assure down-the-line support for a cause people can believe in. Both Zebco and Scottsdale are great examples of the meaning and motivation that can result from enabling everyone to act in many small, committed ways.

But there's a significant down side to this process of escalating commitment. It can be used over time to manipulate unsuspecting people into making a much bigger commitment than they really had in mind. Psychologist Irving Janis calls these "commitment traps for the unwary." He says, "Occasionally even the most vigilant decision-maker becomes trapped in a network of decisional obligations never imagined, let alone contemplated, when the commitment was made." That's how the United States became so inextricably enmeshed in the Vietnam War. The trap builds over time, piece by piece, the cumulative effect of lots of seemingly insignificant decisions.

A related trap commits the unwary when he or she takes a public stand on an issue. Visible announcements of opinion or intention greatly increase commitment to the chosen action; it's not as easy for the person to deny or forget that it occurred. As organizational theorist Jeffrey Pfeffer observes, companies make some decisions noticeably public in order to manage the amount of commitment they engender. It's a variation on Citicorp's Larry Small's theme of "selling forward." Writes Pfeffer: "When a new associate joins a law or an investment banking firm, advertisements may be taken out and announcements mailed. This publicly associates the person with the firm, thereby committing him or her more firmly to it."

Apparently, the power of commitment to influence behavior—especially if the commitment is made publicly—is a function of our nearly obsessive desire to be (and to appear) consistent with what we have already decided to do. From our commitments we create "consistency tapes" which serve as shortcuts; they keep us from having to rethink our decisions on the basis of new information.

These tapes may save us time and trouble, but they can also be quite harmful if we use them to filter out things that challenge our commitments. Robert Cialdini, in a fascinating book called *Influence*, describes ways in which we go so far as to actively reject information indicating that a commitment we made may not have been the most appropriate thing to do. We tend to discredit feedback that tells us a commitment we've made may have been misguided.

Cialdini describes some remarkable research on commitment done by psychologists Jonathan Freedman and Scott Fraser in the mid-1960s. They started by making an outrageous request of a group of California homeowners. Would they put a very large, poorly lettered sign that said DRIVE CAREFULLY on their front lawn? Most said no. Then they ran a second experiment with a similar sample of homeowners, only this time they asked them first to put up a small, unobtrusive sign urging safe driving. Of those who agreed to do that, 70 percent later were willing to put up the outrageous sign.

But the researchers didn't stop there. They wanted to know if making an even smaller commitment first—signing a petition that said "Keep California Beautiful"—would influence whether or not people would later be willing to put the outrageous sign in their front yard. Surprisingly, they got almost the same result. Reports Cialdini: "At first, even Freedman and Fraser were bewildered by their findings. Why should the little act of signing a petition supporting state beautification cause people to be so willing to perform a different and much larger favor? After considering and discarding other explanations, Freedman and Fraser came upon one that offered a solution to the puzzle: Signing the beautification petition changed the view these people had of themselves. They saw themselves as public-spirited citizens who acted on their civic principles. When, two weeks later, they were asked to perform another public service by displaying the outrageous DRIVE CAREFULLY sign, they complied in order to be consistent with their newly formed self-images."

Commitment traps can be as tricky as those Chinese finger traps where the harder you struggle to pull your fingers out of the woven tube, the more trapped you are. Not only do we sometimes discount information that runs counter to a commitment we've made, but that very information can act as catalyst for us to commit even further to the chosen course of action. That heightened investment of effort and resources leads us to become even *more* favorably inclined toward something that wasn't working out in the first place! As James Brian Quinn notes: "As a consequence, people doggedly prolong outmoded—but publicly committed—goals, rather than swallow losses and move on."

The best any of us can do is realize that there are two sides to the commitment coin. This awareness can help us strengthen the positive attributes of commitments that are related to worthy causes, and minimize the effects of the ones that are questionable at best.

STEPS FOR GETTING THERE

1. Once a year, at least, generate or update a list of the problems and opportunities you face. Sort through them and set priorities. Top-priority issues generally have the following characteristics: a) They are easy to solve; you might as well get on with them; b) something disastrous will happen if they aren't dealt with soon; c) they present a unique opportunity; grab it while you can; d) combinations of the above. Maybe an issue is closely related to an existing cause and can be addressed that way. Don't treat the issues list as static. The moveable part of the issues list is a powerful source of continuing renewal.

2. Decide your appropriate role in relation to the issues. Think of the management process as being issue-brokering as much as, or more than, issue-resolving. One of the most difficult things for some people to do is relinquish the reins to others who have the time and talent to tackle a problem. Delegating an issue to the people who are best equipped to handle it frees you to do what you're being paid to do: keep your finger on the pulse of what's going on inside and outside the organization. If you don't do that well, you won't know about half of the issues that are floating around, and you won't be able to recognize the important ones when you see them.

3. Find ways to turn dreary issues into interesting causes. Some—quality, service, employee involvement—are inspiring in themselves. Others, like cost cutting, may have to be related to some broader organizational purpose to build inspiration. Add a dash of adventure. Strive to be the best at something. Attack an issue in a way that's never been tried before. Some may be slightly

outrageous with just enough risk and plenty of fun. Take the time to state the cause in a moving, nonbureaucratic way. (Read Churchill for inspiration along that line.) Use metaphor: Don't break rocks; build cathedrals.

4. Take a close look at what your company stands for. Can your staff both agree on and identify with the causes that set your overall direction? Can you? If the answer is no, what's the reason? Are people getting mixed signals? Are they disillusioned with the end product of their work? Have they become apathetic because their repeated efforts to do their best have met with opposition—implicit or explicit? If you are convinced that your causes need to be redefined or revitalized, the time to start is now.

5. Check to see if the causes you can identify are good for both your company *and* the people who work there. Lopsided causes will skew the course your company is on and jeopardize its values, not to mention its future. In such cases, neither your organization nor your people benefit. Don't tread on individual dignity. That's what happened when companies sacrificed quality for volume, and it backfired. When you have to cut costs or automate, make that a cause by building safety nets for the people and by letting them know why it's necessary and how they can help.

6. Do some soul-searching about whether or not the causes you and your company are promoting reflect a winning attitude. Is there a chance that you are signaling a "we're only number two (or ten), so we *don't* try harder" approach to things? If your staff does not exhibit a winning attitude, what can you do to light a fire under them?

Sometimes all it takes to shake people out of the "loser" doldrums is a well-placed question or two. Remember Petersen's "Would you want this car parked in your driveway?" question at Ford, and Schutz's inquiry about the best car Professor Porsche had ever designed. In both cases the implied message was: "If we're not already making a first-rate product, or providing first-rate service, we can be."

7. Look for adventure in business. It's always there, even though our entrenched work ethic makes it difficult to see things that way; we all tend to assume that we can't have fun and earn money at the same time. But there *is* a definite link between adventure and renewal. The adventure should be neither so foolhardy that it introduces undue risks nor so laughably timid that it is more embarrassing than inspiring.

8. Once you've identified an overriding cause you want to introduce (or resurrect), at some point you're going to have to determine whether or not your core group of managers can get behind it one hundred percent. Those who aren't on board can create an enormous energy leak, both within the group itself and among the staff they supervise. You simply can't afford to tolerate a bunch of naysayers. If your team resists, double-check the cause. If the cause still seems right, force the issue. Expect that people will get forced out from time to time, and build safety nets for them (early retirement, assistance in finding jobs) that help keep their dignity intact. Be tough only when you have to, but keep in mind that disorder at the top means chaos below.

9. Communicate extensively to create the link between causes and the commitment individual employees make to them. You can't force people to be committed; neither can you control whether or not they stay committed. The best approach is to be the source of clear, consistent, honest information. When in doubt, tell people too much. The more they know about your cause, the more they can help in ways you wouldn't have expected. The more they find they can help, the more commitment they feel. Respect people enough to be straight with them about the down side as well as the up side; that, too, strengthens commitment.

Remember that commitment can be a trap for the wrong cause. As commitment increases, people become less willing to acknowledge that it may be inappropriate. Listen to your own "consistency tapes" and those you hear from others around you. Find different mirrors that will tell you what you or your organization is really committed to; examine the underlying moral implications. Are your de facto commitments either ignoble or the traps that will stop renewal? If so, you have a new, high priority that ought to move some of the others aside.

10. Keep reminding yourself of the fact that renewal comes about because everyone in your company—not just the managers—has had a chance to commit and contribute to it. Progress is the result of thousands of things done differently, not a few big management decisions. To build commitment, give people something they can do to act in alignment with the cause. Remember the Scottsdale story: Small individual actions add up to commitment.

11. Recognize the interrelationship of issues, causes, and commitment. Causes spearhead renewal; they identify a new vision for

the future that is both noble and attainable. But the causes must be seen to be relevant to the important business issues. And it's the commitment people make to those causes that transforms them from concept to reality. Remember, a cause without committed people gets nowhere, and committed people without a unifying cause go nowhere. The renewing companies use issues, causes, and commitment to forge a common bond among the diverse people who work for them.

12. Make sure that your causes are related to the shared values of the organization. Even more important, they must square with the dignity of the individual. Continually examine the causes and commitments that engage you, and the ones you ask of your people, to ensure their basic worth, humanity, and integrity.

NOTES
Page

175 Michael D. Cohen, James G. March, and Johan P. Olsen, "A Garbage Can Model of Organizational Choice," *Administrative Science Quarterly,* vol. 17, March 1972, pp. 1–25.

175 Karl E. Weick, *The Social Psychology of Organizing,* 2d ed. (Reading, MA: Addison-Wesley, 1979), pp. 194–204.

175 Viktor Frankl, *Man's Search for Meaning,* 3d ed. (New York: Simon & Schuster, 1984).

184 James Brian Quinn and Christopher E. Gagnon, "Will Services Follow Manufacturing into Decline?" *Harvard Business Review,* November-December 1986, pp. 95–103.

187 Erich Fromm, *Man for Himself: An Inquiry into the Psychology of Ethics* (Greenwich, CT: Fawcett Publications, 1947), p. 58.

191 Robert N. Bellah *et al., Habits of the Heart: Individualism and Commitment in American Life* (New York: Harper & Row, 1985), pp. 150–151.

192 *Ibid.,* p. 145.

192 James Brian Quinn, "Strategic Goals: Process and Politics," *Sloan Management Review,* Fall 1977, p. 26.

192 Barry M. Staw and Gerald R. Salancik, *New Directions in Organizational Behavior* (Chicago: St. Clair Press, 1977), p. 69.

200 Irving L. Janis and Leon Mann, *Decision Making* (New York: Free Press, 1977), p. 287.

200 Jeffrey Pfeffer, *Power in Organizations* (Boston: Pitman, 1981), p. 292.

201 Robert B. Cialdini, *Influence: The New Psychology of Modern Persuasion* (New York: Morrow Quill, 1984), pp. 66–114.

201 *Ibid.,* p. 80.

202 James Brian Quinn, *loc. cit.,* p. 23.

Testing Skyhook 4

MEANINGFUL WORK AND MOTIVATION

*Achieving grand visions despite the obstacles always requires
satisfying very basic human needs: for achievement,
belonging, recognition, self-esteem, a sense of control over
one's life, and living up to one's ideals. . . . When this is done,
the work itself seems intrinsically rewarding.*

—JOHN P. KOTTER,
A FORCE FOR CHANGE

Money is good—we won't work without it. But a paycheck,
benefit package, and all the other "extrinsic" rewards can't buy our
commitment to a dream. Sure, we'll show up every day and do
what we're supposed to do, but our performance won't be inspired.
Only when work is intrinsically, psychologically rewarding are we
likely to give the energy and ingenuity it takes to make a dream
come true.

A simple self test will begin to help you see how well you are
performing. Asking your coworkers "How am I doing?" will
complete the picture.

ASK YOURSELF

Test out how you help make work meaningful for your
coworkers by rating the accuracy of the following statements. Use a
1–5 scale ranging from "a little" to "a great extent."

• I know each person's job interests and goals.	1 2 3 4 5
• I help each person gain self-confidence.	1 2 3 4 5
• I look for ways to make work more interesting and challenging.	1 2 3 4 5
• I recognize and praise outstanding performance.	1 2 3 4 5
• I help each person to grow and test his or her potential.	1 2 3 4 5

ASK YOUR COWORKERS

If you gave yourself a "4" or "5" rating on each statement, you probably are trying hard to make work meaningful. However, you can verify your self-assessment by having a two-part discussion with your coworkers. First, ask them to talk about the importance of meaningful work so that you understand it in the same way. Second, ask them for feedback on your performance.

You'll know you're developing a common understanding about the importance of meaningful work when you hear comments like these:

> - "Understanding us as individuals is critical. Meaningful work is in the eye of the beholder."
> - "Praising the way we do our jobs is as important as the results we get. Doing it right really counts."
> - "Doing a value-added analysis for each job makes sure the work we do is meaningful. If we can't figure out how it contributes, we shouldn't do it."
> - "Daily recognition of our small wins is more important than big-time, once-a-year events."
> - "Helping people see that what they do matters to customers or coworkers gives them a real boost."

After discussing the importance of meaningful work, check out your coworkers' view of your performance by asking them to consider the five items in your self-assessment. You may find it more productive for them to answer the following questions than to give you numerical ratings on each item:

> - What am I doing right now that supports each statement?
> - What else can I do—either more or less—to show greater support for each statement?

As you listen, try to clarify your coworkers' answers and ideas. Express your appreciation for their feedback without becoming defensive. After you've listened, ask yourself, "What am I ready to do to make work more meaningful?" Develop an action plan to build on your strengths and continue to improve.

Skyhook 5

EMPOWERMENT AND SELF-DETERMINATION

*Leadership requires self-confidence to the extent that the leader
is willing to surrender authority and empower others.
A true leader gains power by surrendering and sharing power,
by bringing forth the best talents of every person and
by simultaneously inspiring them to realize that vision.*
—MARSHALL E. LOEB,
MANAGING EDITOR OF *FORTUNE*

*One of the most important ways to empower people is to help them
build their self-esteem. You do this by seeking their counsel
and getting their recommendations on how to do the job better.
This builds their feeling that they are appreciated and wanted.*
—SANFORD McDONNELL
CHAIRMAN EMERITUS OF McDONNELL DOUGLAS

Skyhook 5 Empowerment and Self-determination—Strengthen individuals and teams through education, autonomy, and accountability. Shaping the future is an all-hands effort. All people must be prepared to seize the initiative and act in their own ways in pursuit of a shared vision. Human resources are the best resources for change.

David C. McClelland and David H. Burnham put a new face on power in their classic article "Power Is the Great Motivator" when it first appeared in *Harvard Business Review* in 1976. Previously, power was usually presented in negative terms with plenty of examples of abuse by autocrats to reinforce the notion that power corrupts. The authors contend that true leaders seek power rather than avoid it and then use it to empower others. In fact, their research suggests that if you do not want power and influence, you should try a different line of work—leadership is not for you.

On the basis of their research, McClelland and Burnham report findings like these:

- A strong "need for achievement," a do-it-yourself desire for efficiency, makes entrepreneurs successful, but not leaders.
- Leaders must have a "need for power," a desire to influence others, rather than to try to do it all themselves.
- If the need for achievement is higher than the need for power, a manager will fail because he or she simply cannot do everything.
- A strong "affiliation motive," a need to be liked above all else, will cause a manager to make exceptions rather than consistently apply legitimate rules.
- The affiliation motive backfires because others see the person as inconsistent and unfair and, consequently, they become unsure of relationships or tasks.
- "Socialized power" means that the leader tries to serve the needs of the people and the organization but is not self-serving.
- "Personalized power" is a self-serving approach to influence that is aimed at "self-aggrandizement," a me-first motivation.
- Maturity is key to socialized power—when a leader is less concerned about himself or herself, he or she can be more concerned about change and empowering others to build a better organization.
- A coaching style driven by a socialized power motive makes subordinates feel strong, responsible and proud. Consequently, they become more productive.
- Managers can change their style and become effective leaders with self-knowledge and support, but some are better suited for jobs where power and influence are not core requirements.

James M. Kouzes and Barry Z. Posner build on McClelland and Burnham's research in "Strengthen Others: Sharing Power and Information," from their book *The Leadership Challenge* (1987)

Their own findings are based on studies of several thousand leaders in private and public organizations. They fully agree that the prerequisites for empowering others are a socialized power motive and a coaching style. They describe the strategies and practices that leaders can use to help people grow in any setting. When this is done well, followers are strengthened to the point where they become leaders in their own right.

Kouzes and Posner offer perspectives and suggestions like these:

- Empowerment means helping people feel strong, making them feel that they can make a difference and that they want to be responsible.
- It involves building skills, providing information, developing relationships, sharing decision making, and giving credit.
- Leaders help people grow and use their power to transform others into leaders.
- Power is expandable—you gain power and influence when you empower others.
- Power doesn't corrupt—powerlessness corrupts because it drives people to become petty, irresponsible, and political.
- Leaders know that power, influence, and respect are essential to their own effectiveness.
- People who use power impulsively, without self-control, to serve their own purposes are not leaders.
- Power tends to accumulate around "critical tasks" that are important to the organization's immediate needs. It also clusters around jobs with ample "discretion and visibility," those that allow plenty of latitude and gain plenty of attention.
- Four principles for strengthening others include giving people important work, autonomy, recognition, and connections with significant others.
- Seven immediate steps to greater empowerment range from getting to know people as individuals, to enlarging their sphere of influence, to making heroes of them.

Both sets of authors have helped take power out of the closet and put it in a positive light. Wanting power does not call for an apology as long as power is used with respect and restraint. Leaders who use their influence to empower others develop people who are strong, able, and adaptive and ensure that their organizations share the same attributes.

POWER IS THE
GREAT MOTIVATOR

DAVID C. McCLELLAND and DAVID H. BURNHAM

This article was originally published in March–April 1976. It won the McKinsey Award for excellence and has consistently been one of the best-selling HBR reprints. For its republication as an HBR Classic David C. McClelland has written a retrospective commentary.

What makes or motivates a good manager? The question is so enormous in scope that anyone trying to answer it has difficulty knowing where to begin. Some people might say that a good manager is one who is successful; and by now most business researchers and businessmen themselves know what motivates people who successfully run their own small businesses. The key to their success has turned out to be what psychologists call "the need for achievement," the desire to do something better or more efficiently than it has been done before. Any number of books and articles summarize research studies explaining how the achievement motive is necessary for a person to attain success on his own.[1]

But what has achievement motivation got to do with good management? There is no reason on theoretical grounds why a person who has a strong need to be more efficient should make a good manager. While it sounds as if everyone ought to have the need to achieve, in fact, as psychologists define and measure achievement motivation, it leads people to behave in very special ways that do not necessarily lead to good management.

For one thing, because they focus on personal improvement, on doing things better by themselves, achievement-motivated people want to do things themselves. For another, they want concrete short-term feedback on their performance so that they can tell how well they are doing. Yet a manager, particularly one of or in a large complex organization, cannot perform all the tasks necessary for success by himself or herself. He must manage others so that they will do things for the organization. Also, feedback on his subordinate's performance may be a lot vaguer and more delayed than it would be if he were doing everything himself.

The manager's job seems to call more for someone who can influence people than for someone who does things better on his own. In motivational terms, then, we might expect the successful manager to have a greater "need for power" than need to achieve. But there must be other qualities beside the need for power that go into the makeup of a good manager. Just what these qualities are and how they interrelate is the subject of this article.

To measure the motivations of managers, good and bad, we studied a number of individual managers from different large U.S. corporations who were participating in management workshops designed to improve their managerial effectiveness.

The general conclusion of these studies is that the top manager of a company must possess a high need for power, that is, a concern for influencing people. However, this need must be disciplined and controlled so that it is directed toward the benefit of the institution as a whole and not toward the manager's personal aggrandizement. Moreover, the top manager's need for power ought to be greater than his need for being liked by people.

Now let us look at what these ideas mean in the context of real individuals in real situations and see what comprises the profile of the good manager. Finally, we will look at the workshops themselves to determine how they go about changing behavior.

MEASURING MANAGERIAL EFFECTIVENESS

First off, what does it mean when we say that a good manager has a greater need for "power" than for "achievement"? To get a more concrete idea, let us consider the case of Ken Briggs, a sales manager in a large U.S. corporation who joined one of our managerial workshops. Some six or seven years ago, Ken Briggs was promoted to a managerial position at corporate headquarters, where he had responsibility for salesmen who service his company's largest accounts.

In filling out his questionnaire at the workshop, Ken showed that he correctly perceived what his job required of him, namely, that he should influence others' success more than achieve new goals himself or socialize with his subordinates. However, when asked with other members of the workshop to write a story depicting a managerial situation, Ken unwittingly revealed through his fiction that he did not share those concerns. Indeed, he discovered that his need for achievement was very high—in fact over the 90th percentile—and his need for power was very low, in about the 15th percentile. Ken's high need to achieve was no surprise—after all, he had been a very successful salesman but obviously his motivation to influence others was much less than his job required. Ken was a little disturbed but thought that perhaps the measuring instruments were not too accurate and that the gap between the ideal and his score was not as great as it seemed.

Then came the real shocker. Ken's subordinates confirmed what his stories revealed: he was a poor manager, having little positive impact on those who worked for him. Ken's subordinates felt that they had little responsibility delegated to them, that he never rewarded but only criticized them, and that the office was not well organized, but confused and chaotic. On all three of these scales, his office rated in the 10th to 15th percentile relative to national norms.

As Ken talked the results over privately with a workshop leader, he became more and more upset. He finally agreed, however, that the results of the survey confirmed feelings he had been afraid to admit to himself or others. For years, he had been miserable in his managerial role. He now knew the reason: he simply did not want to nor had he been able to influence or manage others. As he thought back, he realized that he had failed every time he had tried to influence his staff, and he felt worse than ever.

Ken had responded to failure by setting very high standards—his office scored in the 98th percentile on this scale—and by trying to do most things himself, which was close to impossible; his own activity and lack of delegation consequently left his staff demoralized. Ken's experience is typical of those who have a strong need to achieve but low power motivation. They may become very successful salesmen and, as a consequence, may be promoted into managerial jobs for which they, ironically, are unsuited. If achievement motivation does not make a good manager, what motive does? It is not enough to suspect that power motivation may be important; one needs hard evidence that people who are better managers than Ken Briggs do in fact possess stronger power motivation and perhaps score higher in other characteristics as well. But how does one decide who is the better manager?

Real-world performance measures are hard to come by if one is trying to rate managerial effectiveness in production, marketing, finance, or research and development. In trying to determine who the better managers were in Ken Briggs's company, we did not want to rely only on the opinions of their superiors. For a variety of reasons, superiors' judgments of their subordinates' real-world performance may be inaccurate. In the absence of some standard measure of performance, we decided that the next best index of a manager's effectiveness would be the climate he or she creates in the office, reflected in the morale of subordinates.

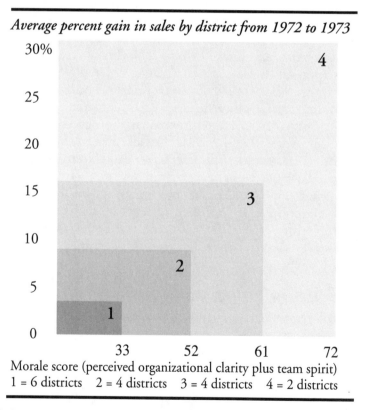

Average percent gain in sales by district from 1972 to 1973

Morale score (perceived organizational clarity plus team spirit)
1 = 6 districts   2 = 4 districts   3 = 4 districts   4 = 2 districts

Exhibit 1. Correlation between morale scores and sales performance for a large U.S. corporation.

Almost by definition, a good manager is one who, among other things, helps subordinates feel strong and responsible, who rewards them properly for good performance, and who sees that things are organized in such a way that subordinates feel they know what they should be doing. Above all, managers should foster among subordinates a strong sense of team spirit, of pride in working as part of a particular team. If a manager creates and encourages this spirit, his subordinates certainly should perform better.

In the company Ken Briggs works for, we have direct evidence of a connection between morale and performance in the one area where performance measures are easy to come by—namely sales. In April 1973, at least three employees from this company's 16 sales districts filled out questionnaires that rated their office for organizational clarity and team spirit. Their scores were averaged and totaled to give an overall morale score for each office. The percentage gains or losses in sales for each district in 1973 were compared with those for 1972. The difference in sales figures by district ranged from a gain of nearly 30% to a loss of 8%, with a median gain of around 14%. *Exhibit 1* shows the average gain in sales performance plotted against the increasing averages in morale scores.

In *Exhibit 1* we can see that the relationship between sales and morale is surprisingly close. The six districts with the lowest morale early in the year showed an average sales gain of only around 7% by year's end (although there was wide variation within this group), whereas the two districts with the highest morale showed an average gain of 28%. When morale scores rise above the 50th percentile in terms of national norms, they seem to lead to better sales performance. In Ken Briggs's company, at least, high morale at the beginning is a good index of how well the sales division will actually perform in the coming year.

And it seems very likely that the manager who can create high morale among salesmen can also do the same for employees in other areas (production, design, and so on), leading to better performance. Given that high morale in an office indicates that there is a good manager present, what general characteristics does he possess?

A NEED FOR POWER

In examining the motive scores of over 50 managers of both high and low morale units in all sections of the same large company, we found that most of the managers—over 70%—were high in power motivation compared with men in general. This finding confirms the fact that power motivation is important for management. (Remember that as we use the term "power motivation," it refers not to dictatorial behavior, but to a desire to have impact, to be strong and influential.) The better managers, as judged by the morale of those working for them, tended to score even higher in power motivation. But the most important determining factor of high morale turned out not to be how their power motivation compared to their need to achieve but whether it was higher than their need to be liked. This relationship existed for 80% of the better sales managers as compared with only 10% of the poorer managers. And the same held true for other managers in nearly all parts of the company.

In the research, product development, and operations divisions, 73% of the better managers had a stronger need for power than a need to be liked (or what we term "affiliation motive") as compared with only 22% of the poorer managers. Why should this be so? Sociologists have long argued that, for a bureaucracy to function effectively, those who manage it must be universalistic in applying rules. That is, if they make exceptions for the particular needs of individuals, the whole system will break down.

The manager with a high need for being liked is precisely the one who wants to stay on good terms with everybody, and, therefore, is the one most likely to make exceptions in terms of particular needs. If a male employee asks for time off to stay home with his sick wife to help look after her and the kids, the affiliative manager agrees almost without thinking, because he feels sorry for the man and agrees that his family needs him.

When President Ford remarked in pardoning ex-President Nixon that he had "suffered enough," he was responding as an affiliative manager would, because he was empathizing primarily with Nixon's needs and feelings. Sociological theory and our data both argue, however, that the person whose need for affiliation is high does not make a good manager. This kind of person creates poor morale because he or she does not understand that other people in the office will tend to regard exceptions to the rules as unfair to themselves, just as many U.S. citizens felt it was unfair to let Richard Nixon off and punish others less involved than he was in the Watergate scandal.

SOCIALIZED POWER

But so far our findings are a little alarming. Do they suggest that the good manager is one who cares for power and is not at all concerned about the needs of other people? Not quite, for the good manager has other characteristics which must still be taken into account.

Above all, the good manager's power motivation is not oriented toward personal aggrandizement but toward the institution which he or she serves. In another major research study, we found that the signs of controlled action or inhibition that appear when a person exercises his or her imagination in writing stories tell a great deal about the kind of power that person needs.[2] We discovered that, if a high power motive score is balanced by high inhibition, stories about power tend to be altruistic. That is, the heroes in the story exercise power on behalf of someone else. This is the "socialized" face of power as distinguished from the concern for personal power, which is characteristic of individuals whose stories are loaded with power imagery but which show no sign of inhibition or self-control. In our earlier study, we found ample evidence that these latter individuals exercise their power impulsively. They are more rude to other people, they drink too much, they try to exploit others sexually, and they collect symbols of personal prestige such as fancy cars or big offices.

Individuals high in power and in control, on the other hand, are more institution minded; they tend to get elected to more offices, to control their drinking, and to want to serve others. Not surprisingly, we found in the workshops that the better managers in the corporation also tend to score high on both power and inhibition.

PROFILE OF A GOOD MANAGER

Let us recapitulate what we have discussed so far and have illustrated with data from one company. The better managers we studied are high in power motivation, low in affiliation motivation, and high in inhibition. They care about institutional power and use it to stimulate their employees to be more productive. Now let us compare them with affiliative managers—those in whom the need for affiliation is higher than the need for power—and with the personal power managers—those in whom the need for power is higher than for affiliation but whose inhibition score is low.

In the sales division of our illustrative company, there were managers who matched the three types fairly closely. *Exhibit 2* shows how their subordinates rated the offices they worked in on responsibility, organizational clarity, and team spirit. There are scores from at least three subordinates for each manager, and several managers are represented for each type, so that the averages shown in the exhibit are quite stable. Note that the manager who is concerned about being liked by people tends to have subordinates who feel that they have very little personal responsibility, that organizational procedures are not clear, and that they have little pride in their work group.

In short, as we expected, affiliative managers make so many ad hominem and ad hoc decisions that they almost totally abandon orderly procedures. Their disregard for procedure leaves employees feeling weak, irresponsible, and without a sense of what might happen next, of where they stand in relation to their manager, or even of what they ought to be doing. In this company, the group of affiliative managers portrayed in *Exhibit 2* were below the 30th percentile in morale scores.

The managers who are motivated by a need for personal power are somewhat more effective. They are able to create a greater sense of responsibility in their divisions and, above all, a greater team spirit. They can be thought of as managerial equivalents of successful tank commanders such as General Patton, whose own daring inspired admiration in his troops. But notice how in *Exhibit 2* these men are still only in the 40th percentile in the amount of organizational clarity they create, as compared to the high power, low affiliation, high inhibition managers, whom we shall term "institutional."

Managers motivated by personal power are not disciplined enough to be good institution builders, and often their subordinates are loyal to them as individuals rather than to the institution they both serve. When a personal power manager leaves, disorganization often follows. His subordinates' strong group spirit, which the manager has personally inspired, deflates. The subordinates do not know what to do for themselves.

Of the managerial types, the "institutional" manager is the most successful in creating an effective work climate. *Exhibit 2* shows that his subordinates feel that they have more responsibility. Also, this kind of manager creates high morale because he produces the greatest sense of organizational clarity and team spirit. If such a manager leaves, he or she can be more readily replaced by another manager, because the employees have been encouraged to be loyal to the institution rather than to a particular person.

MANAGERIAL STYLES

Since it seems undeniable from *Exhibit 2* that either kind of power orientation creates better morale in subordinates than a "people" orientation, we must consider that a concern for power is essential to good management. Our findings seem to fly in the face of a long and influential tradition of organizational psychology, which insists that authoritarian management is what is wrong with most businesses in this country. Let us say frankly that we think the bogeyman of authoritarianism has in fact been wrongly used to downplay the importance of power in management. After all, management is an influence game. Some proponents of democratic management seem to have forgotten this fact, urging managers to be primarily concerned with people's human needs rather than with helping them to get things done.

But a good deal of the apparent conflict between our findings and those of other behavioral scientists in this area arises from the fact that we are talking about *motives*, and behaviorists are often talking about *actions*. What we are saying is that managers must be

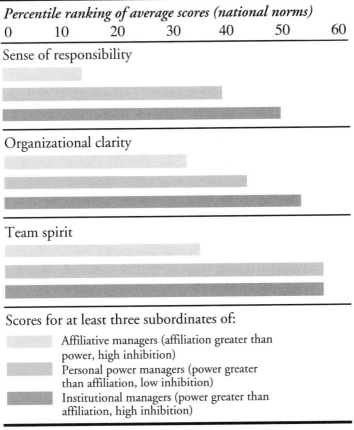

Exhibit 2. Average scores on selected climate dimensions by subordinates of managers with different motive profiles.

interested in playing the influence game in a controlled way. That does not necessarily mean that they are or should be authoritarian in action. On the contrary, it appears that power motivated managers make their subordinates feel strong rather than weak. The true authoritarian in action would have the reverse effect, making people feel weak and powerless.

Thus another important ingredient in the profile of a manager is his or her managerial style. In the illustrative company, 63% of the better managers (those whose subordinates had higher morale) scored higher on the democratic or coaching styles of management as compared with only 22% of the poorer managers, a statistically significant difference. By contrast, the latter scored higher on authoritarian or coercive management styles. Since the better managers were also higher in power motivation, it seems that, in action, they express their power motivation in a democratic way, which is more likely to be effective.

To see how motivation and style interact, let us consider the case of George Prentice, a manager in the sales division of another company. George had exactly the right motive combination to be an institutional manager. He was high in the need for power, low in the need for affiliation, and high in inhibition. He exercised his power in a controlled, organized way. His stories reflected this fact. In one, for instance, he wrote, "The men sitting around the table were feeling pretty good; they had just finished plans for reorganizing the company; the company has been beset with a number of organizational problems. This group, headed by a hard-driving, brilliant young executive, has completely reorganized the company structurally with new jobs and responsibilities. . . ."

This described how George himself was perceived by the company, and shortly after the workshop he was promoted to vice president in charge of all sales. But George was also known to his colleagues as a monster, a tough guy who would "walk over his grandmother" if she stood in the way of his advancement. He had the right motive combination and, in fact, was more interested in institutional growth than in personal power, but his managerial style was all wrong. Taking his cue from some of the top executives in the corporation, he told people what they had to do and threatened them with dire consequences if they didn't do it.

When George was confronted with his authoritarianism in a workshop, he recognized that this style was counterproductive—in fact, in another part of the study we found that it was associated with low morale—and he subsequently changed to acting more like a coach, which was the scale on which he scored the lowest initially. George saw more clearly that his job was not to force other people to do things but to help them to figure out ways of getting their job done better for the company.

THE INSTITUTIONAL MANAGER

One reason it was easy for George Prentice to change his managerial style was that in his imaginative stories he was already having thoughts about helping others, characteristic of men with the institution-building motivational pattern. In further examining institution builders' thoughts and actions, we found they have four major characteristics:

1. They are more organization-minded; that is, they tend to join more organizations and to feel responsible for building up these organizations. Furthermore, they believe strongly in the importance of centralized authority.

2. They report that they like to work. This finding is particularly interesting, because our research on achievement motivation has led many commentators to argue that achievement motivation promotes the "Protestant work ethic." Almost the precise opposite is true. People who have a high need to achieve like to get out of work by becoming more efficient. They would like to see the same result obtained in less time or with less effort. But managers who have a need for institutional power actually seem to like the discipline of work. It satisfies their need for getting things done in an orderly way.

3. They seem quite willing to sacrifice some of their own self-interest for the welfare of the organization they serve. For example, they are more willing to make contributions to charities.

4. They have a keen sense of justice. It is almost as if they feel that if a person works hard and sacrifices for the good of the organization, he should and will get a just reward for his effort.

It is easy to see how each of these four concerns helps a person become a good manager, concerned about what the institution can achieve.

MATURITY

Before we go on to look at how the workshops can help managers to improve their managerial style and recognize their own motivations, let us consider one more fact we discovered in studying the better managers at George Prentice's company. They were more mature. Mature people can be most simply described as less egotistic. Somehow their positive self-image is not at stake in what they are doing. They are less defensive, more willing to seek advice from experts, and have a longer range view. They accumulate fewer personal possessions and seem older and wiser. It is as if they have awakened to the fact that they are not going to live forever and have lost some of the feeling that their own personal future is all that important.

Many U.S. businessmen fear this kind of maturity. They suspect that it will make them less hard driving, less expansion-minded, and less committed to organizational effectiveness. Our data do not support their fears. These fears are exactly the ones George Prentice had before he went to the workshop. Afterward he was a more effective manager, not despite his loss of some of the sense of his own importance, but because of it. The reason is simple: his subordinates believed afterward that he genuinely was more concerned about the company than about himself. Where once they respected his confidence but feared him, they now trust him. Once he supported their image of him as a "big man" by talking about the new Porsche and the new Honda he had bought; when we saw him recently he said, almost as an aside, "I don't buy things anymore."

CHANGING MANAGERIAL STYLE

George Prentice was able to change his managerial style after learning more about himself in a workshop. But does self-knowledge generally improve managerial behavior?

Some people might ask, "What good does it do to know, if I am a manager, that I should have a strong power motive, not too great a concern about being liked, a sense of discipline, a high level of maturity, and a coaching managerial style? What can I do about it?" The answer is that workshops for managers that give information to them in a supportive setting enable them to change.

Consider the results shown in *Exhibit 3*, where "before" and "after" scores are compared. Once again we use the responses of subordinates to give some measure of the effectiveness of managers. To judge by their subordinates' responses, the managers were clearly more effective afterward. The subordinates felt that they were given more responsibility, that they received more rewards, that the organizational procedures were clearer, and that morale was higher. These differences are all statistically significant.

But what do these differences mean in human terms? How did the managers change? Sometimes they decided they should get into another line of work. This happened to Ken Briggs, for example, who found that the reason he was doing so poorly as a manager was because he had almost no interest in influencing others. He understood how he would have to change if he were to do well in his present job, but in the end decided, with the help of management, that he would prefer to work back into his first love, sales.

Ken Briggs moved into "remaindering," to help retail outlets for his company's products get rid of last year's stock so that they could take on each year's new styles. He is very successful in this new role; he has cut costs, increased dollar volume, and in time has worked himself into an independent role selling some of the old stock on his own in a way that is quite satisfactory to the business. And he does not have to manage anybody anymore.

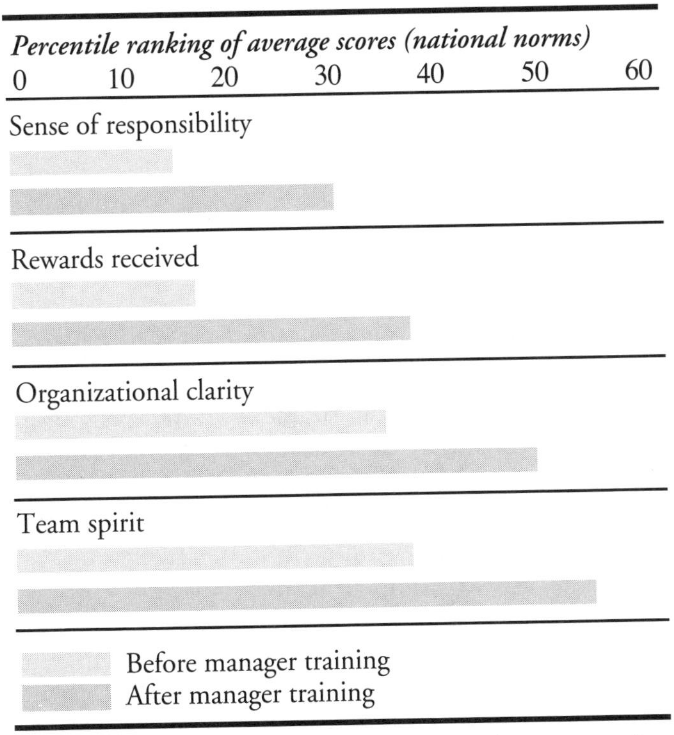

Percentile ranking of average scores (national norms)

| 0 | 10 | 20 | 30 | 40 | 50 | 60 |

Sense of responsibility

Rewards received

Organizational clarity

Team spirit

Before manager training
After manager training

Exhibit 3. Average scores on selected climate dimensions by over 50 salesmen before and after their managers were trained.

In George Prentice's case, less change was needed. He was obviously a very competent person with the right motive profile for a top managerial position. When he was promoted, he performed even more successfully than before because he realized the need to become more positive in his approach and less coercive in his managerial style.

But what about a person who does not want to change his job and discovers that he does not have the right motive profile to be a manager?

The case of Charlie Blake is instructive. Charlie was as low in power motivation as Ken Briggs, his need to achieve was about average, and his affiliation motivation was above average. Thus he had the affiliative manager profile, and, as expected, the morale among his subordinates was very low. When Charlie learned that his subordinates' sense of responsibility and perception of a reward system were in the 10th percentile and that team spirit was in the 30th, he was shocked. When shown a film depicting three managerial climates, Charlie said he preferred what turned out to be the authoritarian climate. He became angry when the workshop trainer and other members in the group pointed out the limitations of this managerial style. He became obstructive in the group process and objected strenuously to what was being taught.

In an interview conducted much later, Charlie said, "I blew my cool. When I started yelling at you for being all wrong, I got even madder when you pointed out that, according to my style questionnaire, you bet that that was just what I did to my salesmen. Down underneath I knew something must be wrong. The sales performance for my division wasn't so good. Most of it was due to me anyway and not to my salesmen. Obviously their reports that they felt very little responsibility was delegated to them and that I didn't reward them at all had to mean something. So I finally decided to sit down and try to figure what I could do about it. I knew I had to start being a manager instead of trying to do everything myself and blowing my cool at others because they didn't do what I thought they should. In the end, after I calmed down on the way back from the workshop, I realized that it is not so bad to make a mistake; it's bad not to learn from it."

After the course, Charlie put his plans into effect. Six months later, his subordinates were asked to rate him again. He attended a second workshop to study these results and reported, "On the way home I was very nervous. I knew I had been working with those guys and not selling so much myself, but I was very much afraid of what they were going to say about how things were going in the office. When I found out that the team spirit and some of those other low scores had jumped from around 30th to the 55th percentile, I was so delighted and relieved that I couldn't say anything all day long."

When he was asked how he acted differently from before, he said, "In previous years when the corporate headquarters said we had to make 110% of our original goal, I had called the salesmen in and said, in effect, 'This is ridiculous; we are not going to make it, but you know perfectly well what will happen if we don't. So get out there and work your tail off.' The result was that I worked 20 hours a day and they did nothing.

"This time I approached it differently. I told them three things. First, they were going to have to do some sacrificing for the company. Second, working harder is not going to do much good because we are already working about as hard as we can. What will be required are special deals and promotions. You are going to have to figure out some new angles if we are to make it. Third, I'm going to back you up. I'm going to set a realistic goal with each of you. If you make that goal but don't make the company goal, I'll see to it that you are not punished. But if you do make the company goal, I'll see to it that you will get some kind of special rewards."

When the salesmen challenged Charlie saying he did not have enough influence to give them rewards, rather than becoming angry Charlie promised rewards that were in his power to give—such as longer vacations.

Note that Charlie has now begun to behave in a number of ways that we found to be characteristic of the good institutional manager. He is, above all, higher in power motivation, the desire to influence his salesmen, and lower in his tendency to try to do everything himself. He asks the men to sacrifice for the company. He does not defensively chew them out when they challenge him but tries to figure out what their needs are so that he can influence them. He realizes that his job is more one of strengthening and supporting his subordinates than of criticizing them. And he is keenly interested in giving them just rewards for their efforts.

The changes in his approach to his job have certainly paid off. The sales figures for his office in 1973 were up more than 16% over 1972 and up still further in 1974 over 1973. In 1973 his gain over the previous year ranked seventh in the nation; in 1974 it ranked third. And he wasn't the only one in his company to change managerial styles. Overall sales at his company were up substantially in

1973 as compared with 1972, an increase which played a large part in turning the overall company performance around from a $15 million loss in 1972 to a $3 million profit in 1973. The company continued to improve its performance in 1974 with an 11% further gain in sales and a 38% increase in profits.

Of course not everyone can be reached by a workshop. Henry Carter managed a sales office for a company which had very low morale (around the 20th percentile) before he went for training. When morale was checked some six months later, it had not improved. Overall sales gain subsequently reflected this fact since it was only 2% above the previous year's figures.

Oddly enough, Henry's problem was that he was so well liked by everybody that he felt little pressure to change. Always the life of the party, he is particularly popular because he supplies other managers with special hard-to-get brands of cigars and wines at a discount. He uses his close ties with everyone to bolster his position in the company, even though it is known that his office does not perform well compared with others.

His great interpersonal skills became evident at the workshop when he did very poorly at one of the business games. When the discussion turned to why he had done so badly and whether he acted that way on the job, two prestigious participants immediately sprang to his defense, explaining away Henry's failure by arguing that the way he did things was often a real help to others and the company. As a result, Henry did not have to cope with such questions at all. He had so successfully developed his role as a likeable, helpful friend to everyone in management that, even though his salesmen performed badly, he did not feel under any pressure to change.

CHECKS AND BALANCES

What have we learned from Ken Briggs, George Prentice, Charlie Blake, and Henry Carter? Principally, we have discovered what motive combination makes an effective manager. We have also seen that change is possible if a person has the right combination of qualities.

Oddly enough, the good manager in a large company does not have a high need for achievement, as we define and measure that motive, although there must be plenty of that motive somewhere in his organization. The top managers shown here have a high need for power and an interest in influencing others, both greater than their interest in being liked by people. The manager's concern for power should be socialized—controlled so that the institution as a whole, not only the individual, benefits. Men and nations with this motive profile are empire builders; they tend to create high morale and to expand the organizations they head.

But there is also danger in this motive profile; empire building can lead to imperialism and authoritarianism in companies and in countries.

The same motive pattern which produces good power management can also lead a company or a country to try to dominate others, ostensibly in the interests of organizational expansion. Thus it is not surprising that big business has had to be regulated from time to time by federal agencies. And it is most likely that international agencies will perform the same regulative function for empire-building countries.

For an individual, the regulative function is performed by two characteristics that are part of the profile of the very best managers—a greater emotional maturity, where there is little egotism, and a democratic, coaching managerial style. If an institutional power motivation is checked by maturity, it does not lead to an aggressive, egotistic expansiveness.

For countries, this checking means that they can control their destinies beyond their borders without being aggressive and hostile. For individuals, it means they can control their subordinates and influence others around them without resorting to coercion or to an authoritarian management style. Real disinterested statesmanship has a vital role to play at the top of both countries and companies.

Summarized in this way, what we have found out through empirical and statistical investigations may just sound like good common sense. But the improvement over common sense is that now the characteristics of the good manager are objectively known. Managers of corporations can select those who are likely to be good managers and train those already in managerial positions to be more effective with more confidence.

Whatever else organizations may be (problem-solving instruments, socio-technical systems, reward systems, and so on), they are political structures. This means that organizations operate by distributing authority and setting a stage for the exercise of power. It is no wonder, therefore, that individuals who are highly motivated to secure and use power find a familiar and hospitable environment in business.[3]

WORKSHOP TECHNIQUES

We derived the case studies and data used in this article from a number of workshops we conducted, during which executives learned about their managerial styles and abilities as well as how to change them. The workshops also provided an opportunity for us to study which motivation patterns in people make for the best managers.

At the workshops and in this article, we use the techinical terms *need for achievement, need for affiliation,* and *need for power.* The terms refer to measurable factors indicating motivation in groups and individuals. Briefly, those characteristics are measured by coding managers' spontaneous thoughts according to how often they think about doing something better or more efficiently than before (need for achievement), about establishing or maintaining friendly relations with others (need for affiliation), or about having an impact on others (need for power). When we talk about power, we are not talking about dictatorial power but about the need to be strong and influential.

When the managers first arrived at the workshops, they were asked to fill out a questionnaire about their jobs. Each participant analyzed his or her job explaining what he or she thought it required. The managers were asked to write a number of stories about pictures of various work situations we showed them. The stories were coded according to how concerned an individual was with achievement, affiliation, or power, as well as for the amount of inhibition or self-control they revealed. We then compared the results against national norms. The differences between a person's job requirements and his or her motivational patterns can often help assess whether the person is in the right job, is a candidate for promotion to another job, or is likely to be able to adjust to fit the present position.

To find out what kind of managerial style the participants had, we then gave them a questionnaire in which they had to choose how they would handle various realistic work situations in office settings. We divided their answers into six management styles or ways of dealing with work situations. The style were democratic, affiliative, pacesetting, coaching, coercive, and authoritarian. The managers were asked to comment on the effectiveness of each style and to name the style they preferred.

One way to determine how effective managers are is to ask the people who work for them. Thus, to isolate the characteristics that good managers have, we asked at least three subordinates of each manager at the workshop questions about their work situations that revealed characteristics of their supervisors according to six criteria: (1) the amount of conformity to rules the supervisor requires, (2) the amount of responsibility they feel they are given, (3) the emphasis the department places on standards of performance, (4) the degree to which rewards are given for good work compared with punishment when something goes wrong, (5) the degree of organizational clarity in the office, and (6) its team spirit.[4] The managers who received the highest morale scores (organizational clarity plus team spirit) from their subordinates were determined to be the best managers, possessing the most desirable motive patterns.

We also surveyed the subordinates six months later to see if morale scores rose after managers completed the workshop.

We measured participants on one other characteristic deemed important for good management: maturity. By coding the stories that the managers wrote, which revealed their attitude toward authority and the kinds of emotions displayed over specific issues, we were able to pinpoint managers at one of four stages in the progress toward maturity. People in Stage I are dependent on others for guidance and strength. Those in Stage II are interested primarily in autonomy. In Stage III, people want to manipulate others. In Stage IV, they lose their egotistic desires and wish to serve others selflessly.[5]

The conclusions we present in this article are based on workshops attended by more than 500 managers from some 25 U.S. corporations. We drew the examples in the charts from one of the companies.

RETROSPECTIVE COMMENTARY

Two important changes have occurred in the workplace since David H. Burnham and I wrote "Power Is the Great Motivator" in 1976. The big, old-fashioned hierarchical organizations we studied have flattened out. And female managers have entered the workplace in full force.

Yet our findings about management style still hold true, regardless of a manager's gender, for the type of hierarchical organization we observed in the article. Successful managers—what we called institutional managers—have a strong need for power (that is, for influencing others) that is greater than their need to be liked, and they exhibit self-control.

That finding was confirmed through subsequent research, including a study of people who were promoted up the managerial ranks at AT&T. Of people who joined AT&T between 1958 and 1960, the institutional managers had been promoted 16 years later to a higher level much more often than other types of managers, we found. We also discovered that the same managerial characteristics predicted future success for both men and women who entered the AT&T system between 1976 and 1980.

However, in a recent study of PepsiCo, a large, decentralized company, we found that having a high need for achievement contributes more to success than does a high interest in influencing other people. In fact, the need for power was often a handicap in that company. That confirms earlier convincing evidence that a constant concern for improvement, for growing the business in a cost-efficient way, characterizes successful managers of small companies, which is what many subsidiaries of PepsiCo essentially function as.

To show conclusively how women manage, we still need much more information. But the AT&T follow-up research did provide an opportunity to observe the subtleties in style differences between the best female and male managers. Using an objective coding system to analyze the stories managers wrote about hypothetical situations, Ruth Jacobs, a principal at McBer and Company, and I found the women much more consensus oriented than the men. In particular, the women seemed to think about power as a resource that can be used to influence outcomes on the job and to focus the competencies of the people who work for them. Men in the study, on the other hand, tended to think of power more as an end in itself, as something they can use to react against or take power away from others in authority. Men saw power as a way to supersede others in power; women rarely did.

Since 1976, my work focus has returned to a lifelong interest in competencies in management. That has meant taking a close look at people who are outstanding managers and trying to break down exactly how they go about work vis-à-vis the way less effective managers do. The work developed as a reaction to studies that seem to resurface every 25 years or so (as they have done again recently) asserting a link between intelligence and overall competence. Intelligence, those studies claim, is a hereditary factor that cannot be altered and is therefore the only relevant measure of a person's "competence."

My work has shown the opposite to be true. In fact, results of the Scholastic Aptitude Test given to college-bound students, among others, relate little to how competently those people manage in the workplace later in life. People who scored exceptionally well on SATs often later functioned poorly as managers, and people with only average scores often made the best managers. It is not intelligence that separates the best people from the worst when it comes to job performance. To measure competency levels, I coded interviews with managers about everyday work situations for specific behaviors, including self-control, self-confidence, an ability to get a consensus from people, and strong motivations for achievement, power, or both.

Indeed such motivational characteristics (as illustrated by the institutional managers in our article) continually emerge as what separates world class managers from mediocre ones. That is as true today as when we wrote the article, and it applies to women as well as to men. What has happened in the meantime is that we have a better idea of what combination of motives and other competencies that we can measure in interviews create managerial success in the new decentralized organizations.

NOTES

1. For instance, see David C. McClelland and David H. Burnham, *The Achieving Society* (New York: Van Nostrand, 1961) and David C. McClelland, David H. Burnham, and David Winter, *Motivating Economic Achievement* (New York: Free Press, 1969).

2. David C. McClelland, William N. Davis, Rudolf Kalin, and Eric Warner, *The Drinking Man* (New York: Free Press, 1972).

3. From "Power and Politics in Organizational Life," by Abraham Zaleznik, *HBR* May-June 1970, p. 47.

4. Based on G. H. Litwin and R. A. Stringer's *Motivation and Organizational Climate* (Boston: Division of Research, Harvard Business School, 1966).

5. Based on work by Abigail Stewart, as reported in David C. McClelland's *Power: The Inner Experience* (New York: Irvington Publishers, 1975).

10

STRENGTHEN OTHERS:
Sharing Information and Power

JAMES M. KOUZES and BARRY Z. POSNER

If you want one year of prosperity, grow grain.
If you want ten years of prosperity, grow trees.
If you want one hundred years of prosperity, grow people.

—CHINESE PROVERB

"Everyone had to feel that they could make a contribution, otherwise they wouldn't come," is how Janice Halper, corporate psychologist and seminar chairperson for the Professional Women's Network in San Francisco, started out describing how she empowered the people responsible for the Network's gala "Women of Wisdom" celebration. Halper found ways to strengthen the people involved, who, like herself, were all volunteers. She had lots of meetings—they met every other week over a nine-month period. She listened a lot: "I'd ask questions, then let others talk, record their ideas, and then play them back." She facilitated interaction by creating small two-to-three-person project teams within the larger committee and then shifted members so that everyone had the chance to work with each other on an individual basis. She made others visible by having them make the committee's report to the Network's board of directors. Most rewarding for Halper was "seeing everyone take responsibility and not having to ask for it."

Empowering the citizenry to take responsibility for governing has long been the conceptual framework upon which Sunne McPeak has created political coalitions and alliances. Now in her third term on the Contra Costa County (California) Board of Supervisors, McPeak takes great pride in the large number of people and groups she's worked with on various issues who are continuing their activities in local government affairs. Having served as co-chair of the statewide Coalition to Stop the Peripheral Canal—the first successful referendum in California over the past three decades—and chair of the California Council on Partnerships (between government and business), McPeak explains that the key factor in developing and sustaining teams involving people with diverse interests (such as growers and environmentalists on the canal issue or public- and private-sector decision makers on community renewal efforts) is in providing people with the power necessary to make a difference. This entails making certain that people have the skills and knowledge needed to make good judgments, keeping people informed, developing personal relationships among the players, involving people in important decisions, and acknowledging and giving credit for people's contributions.

In our studies we found that leaders, like Halper and McPeak, made people feel strong and in so doing enabled them to take responsibility for their team's success. If people don't know what the team's score is, don't know how to tell the score, or don't know what they can do to get on the scoreboard, then they not only can't determine whether they are winning or losing the game but are unable to figure out what needs to be done to keep their team moving ahead. Leaders don't just give lip service to the common business refrain "people are our most important resource." They really believe in their human resources and utilize them to the fullest extent possible; in the process they "grow people" and use their own power to transform their followers into leaders.

POWER IS AN EXPANDABLE PIE

Traditional management thinking promotes the idea that power is a fixed sum: if I have more, then you have less. Naturally, people who hold this view are reluctant to share power. They hold tightly onto what little power they may perceive themselves to have. But this view is archaic, and it seriously retards getting extraordinary things done. Moreover, Rosabeth Moss Kanter has observed that "powerlessness corrupts, and absolute powerlessness corrupts absolutely."[1] People who feel powerless, be they managers or subordinates, tend to hoard whatever shreds of power they have. Powerless managers also tend to adopt petty and dictatorial management styles. Powerlessness creates organizational systems where political skills become essential and "covering" yourself and "passing the buck" become the preferred styles for handling interdepartmental differences.

When subordinates have very little power, managers are in a position to make these people do what they want. Under these circumstances, managers can attribute people's behavior, no matter how good it is, to their orders rather than to people's abilities and motivations. This phenomenon was cleverly documented in one experiment involving small work groups. Employees in some work groups were allowed to influence decisions about their work (were made powerful), while those in other work groups were not (were made powerless). The study revealed that the managers of the powerless groups routinely complained that their employees were not motivated to work hard. These managers saw their workers as unsuitable for promotion and downplayed their skills and talents; they evaluated the work output of their employees less favorably than did the managers of powerful work groups, although the actual output of both groups was roughly equivalent.[2]

The most extensive and systematic program of research on organizational power and influence is that of Arnold Tannenbaum and his colleagues at the University of Michigan's Institute for Social Research. Their research has been carried out in a variety of public and private organizations in the United States and abroad and has included hospitals, banks, unions, factories, and insurance companies. They have learned one vital lesson that all leaders should take to heart: the more people believe that they can influence and control the organization, the greater organizational effectiveness and member satisfaction will be.[3] In other words, shared power results in higher job satisfaction and performance throughout the organization.

We used Tannenbaum's methodology to investigate why some branch offices of a nationwide insurance company were more effective than others.[4] Senior home office management familiar with the performance of the branches, identified ten of these branch offices as high performers and another ten as low performers. These designations were highly correlated with various financial variables (for example, profit, growth, expense control) and with self-ratings by people within the branch offices. While each of the branch offices was ostensibly involved in the same business, confronted with similar policies and procedures, some did better than others. Why was that? There are many factors that might account for this difference. However, after careful consideration of financial, environmental (for example, location), and managerial factors, we found that employee power—the sense of being able to influence what was going on in their own offices—was the most significant factor in explaining differences between high- and low-performing branch offices.

Figure 1. Distribution of Power in Effective and Ineffective Branches

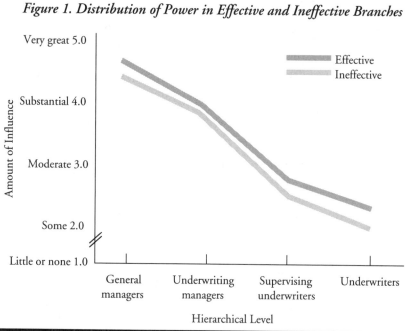

Source: Butterfield, D. A., and Posner, B. Z. "Task-Relevant Control in Organizations." *Personnel Psychology*, 1979, *32*, 773.

Figure 1 shows that power in the various branch offices was distributed across hierarchical levels in a traditional fashion: people at every level of the organization had more total power than did the people at the level below them. Figure 1 also shows that the total amount of perceived power in the high-performing branch offices was greater at every level in the hierarchy than it was in the low-performing offices. The total amount of power (computed as the total area under the curve in calculus) was greater in high-performing branches than it was in low-performing branch offices. What the leaders in the more successful branch offices understood, and acted on, was that "power is an expandable pie"—that power is not a zero-sum commodity, requiring that for others to have more, the leader must have less. The more everyone in the organization feels a sense of power and influence, the greater the ownership and investment they feel in the success of the organization.

The expandable-power-pie concept leads to greater reciprocity of influence—the leader and the follower are willing to be mutually influenced by one another. For the leader, there is the paradox expressed by Jack Telnack, chief design executive for the Ford Motor Company: "I had to give power to gain power."[5] Telnack has been involved in shortening the new car design-production process at Ford by two years and saving over $1 billion. These results give testimony to the fact that when the leader shares power with other people, those people in turn feel more strongly attached to the leader and more committed to effectively carrying out their duties and responsibilities: they feel that a failure to carry out tasks lets themselves down, as well as the boss.

When you strengthen others, your level of influence with them is increased. When you go out of your way on behalf of others, you build up credit with them—credit that may be drawn upon when extraordinary efforts are required. Leaders create a sense of covenant when they help others to grow and develop. When the leader is viewed as helpful, other people will more likely be committed to the leader and the organization's goals.

By strengthening others, you place yourself on the subordinate's side. Consequently, when you make requests and demands of others, they are likely to perceive you as saying, "we are going to do this" rather than "you are going to do this." Furthermore, when you know what other people want and are sensitive to their needs, you can make assignments that effectively match people's talents with job demands. Under these circumstances, others are less likely to challenge your requests and are more likely to go along with and accept them.[6] A synergistic and cyclical process is created as you extend power and responsibility to others, and those people respond successfully. This increases their competencies so that you can extend even further amounts of power and responsibility. This in turn has the effect of allowing you to expend more energy in other areas, which enhances your sphere of influence and brings additional resources back to your unit to be distributed among the group members.

Strengthening others by enabling them to share in influencing the decisions about their daily life also has the effect of enhancing their abilities to perform as well as their sense of personal well-being. This result was well documented in a Connecticut state-run nursing home where social psychologists studied the impact of giving people power. Residents were given the responsibility for making seemingly trivial environmental choices, such as when to see a movie or how to arrange their room. Not only did general health and psychological well-being improve, but death rates were 50 percent lower than for a comparison group who was informed that it was management's responsibility to keep them well.[7] The energy that can be unleashed as a result of giving people power is awesome. How is it that leaders manage and create power and then use power to strengthen others?

MAKING PEOPLE FEEL STRONG

When Steve Tritto took over as general manager of the Serial Printer Division of Dataproducts, a significant management crisis existed. There were a lot of talented people in disarray. They had no vision, and they had no camaraderie. The company had suffered five years of losses; in the preceding year, the loss had been $1.5 million. Turnover was 33 percent annually. Within one year, the division turned their losses into a $3.6 million profit. This marked the first time that the division had ever recorded a profit or exceeded corporate performance goals. Turnover was under 10 percent. These results are testimony to the attention that Tritto paid to strengthening everyone's abilities to contribute to the success of the organization. What Tritto did was to introduce a goal and ask everyone to buy into it. Then, he stressed the importance of *team* effort where before there had been divisiveness. Finally, he used the personal best theme to encourage everyone to excel.

Tritto's methods were straightforward and effective. For example, he made effective use of meetings. Every two weeks, he had "fireside chats" of an hour and a half with 25 people selected alphabetically, crossing over department and rank. Once he had met with all 310 people in the division, he started over again. "People talked. The agenda was open. Folks had a chance to influence decisions about everything from where we were as a company to the inadequacy of the lighting over the benches," Tritto recalled. Quarterly reviews were held in the company's cafeteria to give people an appreciation of how the company was doing, to give them the sense that they were part of a team, to build confidence, and to make them feel that they were in command of what was going on in their organization. Then there were the semiannual meetings. These events were more dramatic. Photographs of all the employees lined the walls of a local auditorium so that people could see pictures of themselves as they walked in. Music played in the background. The performance of the division was graphically displayed with a light and sound show. Achievement awards were given to employees who had made extraordinary contributions.

Steve Tritto understood that it was necessary to strengthen others before he could turn the division around. This ability to make people feel strong, claims Russ Barnett, managing director of MetroBrick in Western Australia, is the single most important contribution of leaders. And empowering others requires working side by side with them. Barnett echoes this observation: "Most leaders fail or succeed on their ability to know and understand the people they work with. You get the results of your efforts through other people, so you have to be very sensitive to each person and to their particular needs." Researchers from the Center for Creative Leadership substantiate Barnett's observation. "Insensitivity to others" was cited in their studies as the primary reason why successful executives tumbled off the track to the executive suite.[8] These researchers noted that the ability to understand other people's perspective was the most glaring difference between the arrivers and those executives who got derailed along the path. Other "fatal flaws" included aloofness and arrogance, betrayal of trust, and overmanaging (or failing to delegate and build a team).

Studies of executives who have been fired from their jobs portray them as loners—people who prefer to work independently of others, who are highly critical of their staffs, and who are unwilling to share control over projects and problem solutions. Fired executives viewed team participation and discussion as a waste of time and had poor interpersonal skills: they were ill at ease with others, frequently making insensitive and undiplomatic remarks, and looked on other people with a great deal of mistrust.[9]

Managers who focus on themselves and are insensitive to others fail. They fail because there is a limit to what they can do by themselves. Leaders succeed when they realize that the limits to what can be accomplished are minimal if people feel strong and capable. In fact, what leaders do, as paradoxical as it may seem, is make followers into leaders. They do this by using their own power in service of others rather than in service of self.

POWER IN SERVICE OF OTHERS

People in leadership positions have a healthy share of power motivation. After all, leaders must get other people to want to do something, to influence what others say and do. Over the past two decades, social psychologists have documented that the motivation for power (that is, the need to have an impact on others) is highly desirable for people with managerial responsibilities.[10] Power needs provide the assertiveness and self-confidence necessary to organize and direct group activities effectively.

Stimulating a group of people to achieve a goal is vastly different from individually achieving a goal yourself. Power motivation, or concern for having an impact on others, requires an outlook and actions considerably different from those needed for making an individual contribution. This explains why so often the best salespeople, most brilliant design engineers, or most outstanding clinical physicians fail to succeed as managers of their groups. These high achievers prefer doing things their own way and working independently. They fail to delegate or to be influenced by others. Their subordinates fail to develop a strong sense of responsibility or commitment.

People with strong power needs are concerned with gaining the respect of others. They are willing to make unpopular decisions when those decisions are necessary for effective group performance. Such people are comfortable in setting standards and in letting people know where they stand. However, having an impact on others does not mean that you have to weaken them and make them feel small while you exercise your influence. In fact, there are two different ways that people experience and express their power needs.[11] One is with the negative face of power—a "personalized power concern," or power in service of self. The positive face of power, on the other hand, is a "socialized power concern," or power in service of others.

People with a personalized power concern have little inhibition or self-control, and they exercise power impulsively. Researchers describe them as rude to other people and suggest that they drink too much, try to exploit others sexually, and collect symbols of personal prestige, such as fancy cars or big offices. While the charisma and force of some such managers can sometimes inspire loyalty and team spirit, the subordinates' loyalties in such cases are to the individual manager rather than to the organization. When the manager departs, there is likely to be disorder and a breakdown in team spirit. Additionally, the subordinates are so conditioned to obey orders that they are immobilized when they have to act independently. In sharp contrast to the personalized power manager is the person with a socialized power concern, who exercises power for the benefit of others. Such a person is more emotionally mature, is more hesitant about using power in a manipulative manner, is less egotistical and defensive, accumulates fewer material possessions, has a longer-range view, and is more willing to take advice from others. The strong need for power is expressed by exercising influence to build up the organization and make it successful. This person is more willing to sacrifice self-interests for the benefit of the organization. Because of this orientation toward building organizational commitment, this kind of person is more likely to use a participative, coaching style of managerial behavior. Social psychologist David McClelland summarizes these two faces of power and their implications for enabling others to act:

> The negative or personal face of power is characterized by the dominance-submission mode: If I win, you lose. . . . It leads to simple and direct means of feeling powerful (such as being aggressive). It does not often lead to effective social leadership for the reason that such a person tends to treat other people as pawns. People who feel they are pawns tend to be passive and useless to the leader who gets his satisfaction from dominating them. Slaves are the most inefficient form of labor ever devised by man.
>
> If a leader wants to have far-reaching influence, he must make his followers feel powerful and able to accomplish things on their own. . . . Even the most dictatorial leader does not succeed if he has not instilled in at least some of his followers a sense of power and the strength to pursue the goals he has set.[12]

The personal best experience of Ken Kenitzer provides a good case study of using power in service of others. Kenitzer was brought into Compression Labs, Inc., as vice-president of operations. His challenge was to revamp the manufacturing organization and production systems. In reflecting on that experience, Kenitzer described the following as the key leadership practices he employed:

1. Involving peers and subordinates in planning.
2. Getting the team to enroll in the project completely.

3. Delegating responsibility to others with full trust and confidence it would be done.
4. Developing team attitude and spirit.
5. Letting people know he had confidence in them, even to the point that they could do more than they themselves believe they could.
6. Finding ways to reward accomplishment.

When asked how he would most like to be remembered as a leader, Kenitzer's reply was: "As a *team leader*—one who can get team members enthusiastically involved and committed." Kenitzer was quite successful in these efforts because he used his power to enable others to act. He believed so strongly in his team's competency that his belief was contagious. With his support, the team members felt that there was no reason to accept roadblocks—there was no way that they could fail. Kenitzer's motto, "A team that works is a working team," could be rephrased as "A team with power is a powerful team."

To better understand how to use power in service of others, let us examine where power comes from. We will also examine ways to increase the amount of power that you have.

SOURCES OF POWER

Within an organization, we generally think of power as control over valued resources.[13] Everyone has resources—personal and situational—but the key to unleashing the potential of these resources lies in creating value for them in the minds of others. Leaders are seen by others as powerful. It is, paradoxically, followers who make leaders powerful. They do this by placing value on the resources controlled by the leader. Two implications flow out of this view of power as the creation of value for resources that you control. The amount of power that individuals or units (departments) possess is derived from (1) the ability to perform important tasks and (2) the degree of discretion and visibility associated with the job.

Critical Tasks. Power flows to those who have resources that others need. The more that people want or need what you have, the more influence you will have with them. Those people who are most central to solving the organization's crucial problems and ensuring the company's long-term viability have the most power. For example, if a company is going through a merger or acquisition, then power will flow to the financial and legal specialists. If the central concern of a company is improving quality, then power will flow to the operations and manufacturing systems people. Engineering will be most dominant in technology-driven companies.

Changes in the social and political environment affect the relative importance of a leader's tasks or abilities. Faced with increasing worldwide competition, people with manufacturing experience are becoming more highly prized and rising to senior executive ranks. Just a few years ago, it was people with legal experience who were breaking into the executive ranks because of their ability to handle increasing governmental interference and litigious public interest groups. So a leader's power can ebb and flow with changing conditions.

Consequently, leaders must keep in step with the times. Our case studies of personal bests are all examples of people confronting critical organizational issues, be they improving quality, reducing manufacturing start-up times, changing customer perceptions, inventing turnkey systems, or mobilizing legislative initiatives. This requires that leaders must be attuned to the particular set of tasks and abilities needed by the organization and seek to develop or acquire the appropriate necessary skills.

Power flows to people whose tasks are helpful to the organization in dealing with critical problems. This is true not only when their resources are critical but when their resources are in short supply. Leaders have more organizational power precisely because they are not easy to replace. Power remains untapped potential, however, unless you are capable of effectively executing critical tasks. Kanter has found that a leader's ability to execute important tasks depends upon three factors.[14] The first is being able to supply the resources that a unit needs, whether money, materials, staff, or time. The second is having information, being "in the know." When you understand the premises on which decisions are based, you can exercise greater influence on the organizational system. Understanding what alternatives are available increases your maneuverability. Support is the third factor affecting your ability to perform effectively and garner power. Support from subordinates, peers, superiors, and outsiders ensures that important tasks are accomplished. Support enables you to take actions and exercise judgment generally outside of your formal scope of responsibility and authority. Superiors may act as sponsors to provide the needed backing. Peers with broad access to the corporate grapevine may offer timely information and warnings about shifting political forces. Subordinates may be counted on to pick up the slack, and outsiders can confer status and provide key external alliances. All these various forms of support are necessary for leaders to carry through with their important tasks.

Discretion and Visibility. The way that your job is designed and located in the organization also influences both the perception and reality of organizational power. Frustration, panic, and a sense of helplessness—all demotivating experiences—are what Lisa Mainiero's studies of people in powerless jobs revealed.[15] Some of the major ways in which various factors contribute to power and powerlessness are summarized in Table 1. Two key dimensions for enhancing power are by designing jobs that have discretion and visibility.

Table 1.
Ways That Organizational Factors Contribute to Power or Powerlessness

Factors	Generates Power When Factor Is	Generates Powerlessness When Factor Is
Rules inherent in the job	Few	Many
Predecessors in the job	Few	Many
Established routines	Few	Many
Task variety	High	Low
Rewards for reliability/predictability	Few	Many
Rewards for unusual performance/innovation	Many	Few
Flexibility around use of people	High	Low
Approvals needed for nonroutine decisions	Few	Many
Physical location	Central	Distant
Publicity about job activities	High	Low
Relation of tasks to current problem areas	Central	Peripheral
Focus of tasks	Outside Work Unit	Inside Work Unit
Interpersonal contact in the job	High	Low
Contact with senior officials	High	Low
Participation in programs, conferences, meetings	High	Low
Participation in problem-solving task forces	High	Low
Advancement prospects of subordinates	High	Low

Source: Kanter, R. M. "Power Failures in Management Circuits." *Harvard Business Review,* July-Aug. 1979, p. 67. Reprinted by permission of the *Harvard Business Review.* Copyright © 1979 by the President and Fellows of Harvard College; all rights reserved.

Discretion is the ability to take nonroutinized actions, exercise independent judgment, and make decisions that affect how you do your job without having to check with the boss. It means not being tied down to a standard set of rules, procedures, or schedules. The opportunity to be flexible, creative, and adaptive is what gives you the ability to make the fullest use of your skills and abilities. It also makes you feel more personally powerful and in control of your own life. If you hold a broadly defined job, you will have opportunities to use discretion, because you will have more choice about *how* to accomplish the objectives. With discretion, however, generally comes greater responsibility and obligation to do what is needed.

The New United Motor Manufacturing, Inc. (NUMMI), plant in Fremont, California (a joint venture between General Motors and Toyota), uses "pulling the rope" as a way to give people discretion and make them feel powerful. Workers have fifty-four seconds to do their job, whether it's installing steering wheels, attaching bumpers, or bolting down car seats. However, if workers fall behind or notice a quality problem, they can pull a cord overhead to stop the line. A GM internal audit showed that the NUMMI-produced car, the Chevrolet Nova, was among the best in the American auto industry. "I used to write up five or ten items on every car," says Richard Aguilar, a NUMMI inspector who worked for GM for nineteen years. "Now, only one out of ten cars has a problem."[16]

Power does not flow to unknown people. Unfortunately, as many new hires discover, simply doing a good job is not enough to get on the company's fast track. Presumably everyone is doing a good job—or they wouldn't have been hired or retained. The key is getting others to notice your achievements and their importance. *Visibility* is the means to enhancing power by calling attention to your accomplishments. Visibility is important also because being noticed is the precursor to developing key strategic alliances with others. If other people don't know about the central importance of your tasks and abilities, they will (1) take them for granted or (2) be uninterested in forming connections and relationships. Finally, unless your contributions gain visibility, you are unlikely to receive formal recognition from your organizational superiors. This reduces access to higher-level sponsors as well as to the increased resources that generally flow to successful people.

GIVING POWER AWAY TO STRENGTHEN OTHERS

Your capacity to strengthen and empower others begins with the degree of power that you hold—your connection to lines of supply, information, and support. We are talking not about power for the sake of the leader (yourself) but about power for the sake of others. Only leaders who feel powerful will delegate, reward talent, and build a team composed of people powerful in their own right. Leaders can use the power that flows to them in service of others. They can give their own power away to others in the same way that they acquired it themselves. These four principles, articulated by Rosabeth Moss Kanter, strategically strengthen others:

1. Give people important work to do on critical issues.
2. Give people discretion and autonomy over their tasks and resources.
3. Give visibility to others and provide recognition for their efforts.
4. Build relationships for others, connecting them with powerful people and finding them sponsors and mentors.[17]

Assigning Important Tasks. Assigning people to work on critical issues is a way to help them to become central and relevant to the organization's concerns and thus acquire power and influence. At Sunset Publications, for example, making sure that the recipes in their cookbooks taste right is a responsibility that is taken very seriously. Everyone, from the most senior to the most junior people, signs up to be taste tester in the company's kitchens. Recipes don't go into the cookbooks until the taste tester gives his or her okay. This empowering process creates a sense of ownership by integrating responsibility and pride. More and more companies, especially those in manufacturing, have begun turning over to the hourly workers the job of calling on customers. In some instances, they even visit foreign competitors to determine firsthand how their own products stack up.

Leaders strengthen others by keeping people up to date on the latest developments affecting their business. They keep people informed about crucial issues, demonstrating and reminding their team about how their job (or unit) addresses these issues. For example, Chaparral Steel Company, a minimill operation thirty miles outside of Dallas, has tried to bring research right into the factory. "We make the people who are producing the steel responsible for keeping their process on the leading edge of technology worldwide," explains Gordon Forward, president and CEO. "If they have to travel, they travel. If they have to figure out what the next step is, they go out and find the places where people are doing interesting things. They visit other companies. They work with universities."[18] Staying relevant also means understanding what skills the organization values and offering opportunities for people to use those competencies. When necessary, leaders are prepared to build and develop or acquire the skills that they or others lack. In this way, leaders build for the future.

Providing Autonomy and Discretion. Leaders seek out projects that will increase the discretionary range of their team and provide greater decision-making authority and responsibility. Doug Schumer was managing a small research group at the Ohaus Scale Corporation when he was put in charge of a "crash development" program. The team had nine months to design and deliver a new product, with technical issues outside of his own area of expertise (applied physics). "A key to my success," explained Schumer, "was that I allowed the experts and leaders in the parallel activities to obtain their results their way and to tell me what had to be done to satisfy their requirements. There was no formal reporting, but I maintained very close personal contact with all the key players." Schumer also found it necessary to negotiate broadly defined objectives for his team's activities. By doing this, he enlarged the team's degree of freedom in taking action and maximized their opportunities for flexibility and creativity.

Leaders delegate important tasks and thus maximize the discretion that their team can exercise in their jobs. Gordon Forward explains how this has been done with the security guards at Chaparral Steel: "Normally, when you think of security guards at four o'clock in the morning, they're doing everything they can just to stay awake. Well, ours also enter data into our computer—order entry, things like that. They put the day's quality results into the computer system each night. We upgraded the job and made a very clear decision not to hire some sleepy old guy to sit and stare at the factory gate all night. Our guards are paramedics; they run the ambulance; they fill up the fire extinguishers; they do the checks in the plant; now they're even considering some accounting functions."[19]

Giving Visibility and Recognition. Leaders ensure that their team members are highly visible, that individual and team efforts are noticed and recognized. Telling people, both inside and outside the department, about what people are doing and publicizing their work are just two ways leaders use to increase visibility. Pictures of employees of the month on the wall, stories about people and their achievements in newsletters and advertisements, bouquets of flowers on the desks, references to interpersonal conversations in company speeches, and unsolicited letters of appreciation to the boss are other ways that leaders make the contributions of people on their team visible to others.

Major General John Stanford demonstrated his dedication to increasing the visibility of his people when he spoke at one of our workshops. He wore his full dress uniform that day, but over his own name tag he placed that of his aide-de-camp. We thought that there had been some mix-up and wondered how to tactfully tell him about it. But before we had the chance, Stanford told the group: "My aide-de-camp Albert A. A. Cartenuto III couldn't be here today. I hope I represented him well." Stanford wanted to give visibility to Cartenuto and to acknowledge the lieutenant's contributions. When Doug Schumer's project team reached milestones, he advertised their success and made the responsible individuals at all levels visible to the others. And Herman Miller's 1985 annual report, entitled *Say Hello to the Owners*, presents side-by-side, full-figured pictures of all 3,265 people who work in the company.

Helping to Build Strong Relationships. Building strong relationships is empowering in two ways. First, it helps people to more easily get in contact with others who can help them accomplish their task. This networking is the grease that often smoothes the way through interdepartmental boundaries and territorial disputes. Second, relationships that are durable and require frequent interactions provide incentives for people to assist and support one another. At Herman Miller, this empowering process is referred to as "theory fastball." As Max De Pree, chairperson and CEO, explains: "In the process of work many of us are outstanding pitchers, able to throw the telling fastball, but it is also true that those pitchers can only be effective if there are many of us who are outstanding catchers."[20]

Russ Barnett describes exceptional "battery mates" as another outcome of building relationships: "You know, if you put a production fellow and a sales fellow together, you're going to find out rather quickly whether something has a chance of getting off the ground. And if it does, having them there at the start talking with one another means that you have a pretty good chance of making things work—and fast." Providing entry to senior executives, fostering outside contacts, and developing and promoting promising subordinates are some of the other ways that leaders build relational networks. Visibility is also enhanced when leaders keep their team members in contact with people outside of their department—for example, by placing people on task forces and committees whose members come from across the organization or by encouraging active participation in professional and community groups. Supervisor McPeak takes pride in the number of people she has worked with who have gone on to higher administrative and elected political offices. Good press is much of what contributes to people moving up in their organizations.

The following case study provides an excellent example of how a leader strengthens the team and what results in the process:

> An otherwise successful chemical company found that it had a stubborn problem. About 10 percent of all its orders were sent from its loading dock with one sort of defect or another: wrong material, wrong size containers, too much or too little merchandise. A crackdown would bring only a month or two of improvement.
>
> Finally, one enterprising executive decided on a new approach. He knew that in most companies the loading dock team is, at best, lightly regarded. He bet that if the low status of the loading dock worker was turned around, greater productivity would follow. Each member of his team, he decided, would no longer be a worker. He would be a manager. Each would be assigned an account list and would be held responsible for any orders going out to any of his customers.
>
> Suddenly, every shipment that went out had a sponsor, *on* the dock. It wasn't just the company's shipment anymore. It was a manager's shipment. And each manager cared very much that his order went out without flaw. Within 90 days, the error rate dropped to two percent. And it has stayed there—or lower—ever since.[21]

By empowering the loading dock personnel, this chemical company executive *enabled others to act.* The loading dock area became a critical issue for the company. The employees were given discretion in their tasks and provided with visibility and recognition for their accomplishments. Their relationships with one another were enhanced, and connections were made between their efforts and those of other departments in the company.

COMMITMENT . . .
Strengthen People by Sharing Information and Power and Increasing Their Discretion and Visibility

Putting gasoline into your car engine is like strengthening other people—without power, the capabilities of the finest-tuned, highest-performance automobile will be useless. Leaders are motivated to use their power in service of others because empowered people perform better. When others are strengthened and enabled to accomplish extraordinary things on their own, the leader's own sphere of influence is enhanced.

Empowering others is essentially the process of turning followers into leaders themselves. The process of building and enhancing power is facilitated when people work on tasks that are critical to the organization's success, when they exercise discretion and autonomy in their efforts, when their accomplishments are visible and recognized by others, and when they are well connected to other people of influence and support. There are several strategies that you can use to build more power for yourself and create more power for others:

1. *Get to know people.* As we have learned in this chapter, sensitivity to others is a prerequisite for success in leadership. Insensitive leaders are eventually derailed. Sensitivity to others begins with the disclosure of facts and feelings about yourself and with the willingness to actively listen to what others have to say about themselves.

The most genuine way to demonstrate that you really care and are concerned about other people as human beings is to spend time with them. So schedule some time daily just to get acquainted with others. And we do not mean schedule time to have yet another business meeting; instead, make it unstructured time to joke and kid and learn more about each other as parents, or athletes, or musicians, or artists, or volunteers, and so on. It does not have to be hours at a time. Often five or ten minutes is sufficient, if done regularly. Walk the halls at least thirty minutes each day, stopping to talk with people who are not on your daily calendar. Go around the chain of command by chatting with subordinates' subordinates, a boss's boss, receptionists, customers, suppliers, and so on. Eat in the employee cafeteria, if there is one, or go out to lunch with folks from other functional areas. Leave your office door open, move your desk onto the factory floor, grab a cup of coffee in the employees' favorite gathering place. We know a CEO who even takes people on rides in his car, often for two or three hours, solely for the purpose of getting acquainted. Just take some kind of daily action that forces you to interact with people you know and want to know better and with people you do not know and need to.

Never take another person for granted. You demonstrate respect for other people by never taking them for granted, even when you know that you can count on them for support. To assume that you needn't talk with them, listen to their ideas, or consider their suggestions runs the risk of being seen by others as insensitive, aloof, and arrogant.

2. Develop your interpersonal competence. Becoming sensitive to the needs of others requires a great degree of interpersonal competence. Some people learn these skills early in life, others do not. If you feel your interpersonal abilities have room for improvement, sign up for the first available training opportunity. There is strong evidence that you can dramatically improve face-to-face communication skills through effective training. Every leader ought to know how to paraphrase, summarize, express feelings, disclose personal information, admit mistakes, respond nondefensively, ask for clarification, solicit different views, and so on. Also, by participating in interpersonal skills training programs you demonstrate to others that you are sincere and serious about building a climate of trust and respect.

The team-building retreat is another useful way to improve relationships among members of your staff. Cross-functional retreats can help people from different functional areas learn what their colleagues do as well as learn how their functions are seen by others. We strongly suggest, however, that retreats always be led by competent and sensitive facilitators. The local chapter of Certified Consultants International can help you locate qualified group facilitators in your area.

Flexibility is another important demonstration of a leader's understanding of others. There is no one best style of leadership. You should be able to use all the practices and behaviors we discuss in this book, but you ought to be versatile enough to adapt a style that is appropriate to each different situation you face. Versatility also expands your capacity to function in a wide range of cultures and environments. If you get feedback that you are too one-dimensional in your approach to situations, you ought to look into a development program designed to expand your flexibility. Ask your organization's training director for guidance.

3. Use your power in service of others. There should never be any need for a leader to tell other people how powerful and influential he or she is. There is never a need for a leader to show off prestigious supplies. The thickness of the carpet, the size of the desk, and the price tag on the art are simply unnecessary displays of importance. Visible ways of drawing attention to one's power are puffery and demonstrate insecurity.

People prefer to work for managers who are upwardly and outwardly influential. Successful leaders know that it is necessary and important to let others know that you can and will use your power to help them get their jobs done. Ask the people who work for you what they need to do their jobs most effectively, then go get it for them. Watch how much your esteem goes up in the eyes of others.

Yes, leaders are power brokers. But they are power brokers on behalf of those they lead. Consider this analogy: you continue to give funds to your stockbroker only if that person is able to increase their value (make money for you). The more successful the stockbroker is, the more resources you are willing to entrust with him or her and the more willing you become to follow his or her investment advice. Since the stock market is unpredictable, the key to whether you stick with that stockbroker during turbulent and difficult times is whether he or she has developed a personal relationship with you—not that you are necessarily friends, but that you have become better informed about the stock market because of your broker and believe that, given the same information, you would have made the same decisions yourself. It is this type of interaction that sustains the personal relationship between broker and investor or leader and follower over time so that investors and followers aren't continually shopping around for some mythical guru or wizard.

As a power broker, however, you have to manage dependencies. When you create value for others' resources and, hence, power, they can become dependent on your skill, information, or support. But no one really likes to feel dependent on another person. Your challenge is to give your power away. If you get power and then hold and covet it, you will eventually be corrupted by it. The intriguing paradox of power is that the more you give away to others the more you get for yourself.

4. Enlarge people's sphere of influence. One way to give some of your power away is to increase the amount of autonomy and discretion others have. Delegate. Form quality circles and other problem-solving groups. Put the authority to make key decisions in the hands of others. Enable people to make decisions without checking with you. Use whatever means fits in your organization, but give people a button to push, a rope to pull, a movie to select, so that individuals have a strong sense of personal autonomy and control.

The increased sphere of influence also ought to be over something relevant to the pressing concerns and core technology of the business. Choosing the color of the paint may be a place to start, but you had better give people influence over more substantive issues. If quality is top priority, then find ways to expand people's influence and discretion over issues of quality control. If innovation is a priority, then increase people's influence over the development of new products, processes, or services. The same applies for all the critical issues of the business.

One caution: provide people with the training to make use of their decision-making power and discretionary tasks. Successful quality programs, for example, all have in common the fact that the group members receive training in basic statistical measurement methods, group communication skills, and problem-solving techniques. Without training and coaching, people will be reluctant to exercise their authority because they do not know how to perform the critical tasks or they fear being punished for making mistakes when they do.

And don't stop with training. Provide all the other necessary resources to perform autonomously. That means materials, money, time, people, and information. There is nothing more disempowering than to have lots of authority to do something, but nothing to do it with.

5. Keep people informed. Everett T. Suters was CEO of a small but rapidly growing Southwestern company. Everyone was putting in long hours and giving enormous effort but Suters began to pick up innuendoes that seemed to say: "We're doing the work but you're getting most of the credit and all of the money." He was irritated by these comments because he didn't believe they were true, and so he called together the management team. He asked them to write down what the company profits were and how much money they thought he was personally making. When he gathered their papers he was amazed: everyone had guessed much too high. So, he passed out copies of the company's financial statement, went over it line by line, and indicated how much money was going to be needed to finance future growth. Everyone started asking questions and requesting more information. Suters says he could see them becoming "as interested in all facets of the company as I was." One manager told Suters some time later: "If I had to tell you in one sentence why I am motivated by my job, it is because when I know what is going on, and how I fit into the overall picture, it makes me feel important."[22]

The more that people know about what is going on in the organization, the better off you will be. Without information, you can be certain that people will not extend themselves to take responsibility; armed with information, people's creative energies can be harnessed to achieve extraordinary results. In our study of effective insurance branch offices, we found information and access to decision makers were significant predictors of why people felt they had influence in their organizations.[23] Information empowers people, strengthening their resolve and providing them the resources they need to be successful.

6. Make connections. It is not only what you know but also who you know that counts. Being connected to people who can open doors, offer support and backing, provide information, mentor and teach, and add to one's reputation are all ways power is increased. You can increase your own power by forming strategic relationships, and you can empower others in the same way. Take the time to introduce the staff in your organization to the people they need to know. Get them access to influential others. Take members of your staff to important meetings, business lunches, and customer organizations. Find ways to connect them to sources of information.

7. Make heroes of other people. The late Wilbert L. Gore, chairperson of W. L. Gore & Associates, once said that one of his skills was "making heroes of other people." If there is one phrase that best expresses the philosophy of strengthening others, that would have to be it. Leaders find ways to shine the spotlight on the achievements of others rather than on their own accomplishments. They make other people the visible heroes and heroines of their organizations. Gore once did this by issuing Sarah Clifton, a line worker, a business card that read: "Sarah Clifton, Supreme Commander." We reported earlier how Major General John Stanford did it by wearing Albert A. A. Cartenuto III's name tag.

There are hundreds of ways you can incorporate similar actions into your daily routine. Just think about how they do it at the movies. At the end of every film there is a long list of credits. Everyone who worked on the film is mentioned, from star to grip, from director to gaffer. Borrowing a page from the movies, John Couch took out a full-page newspaper advertisement naming and thanking all the people who worked on the Lisa project at Apple Computer. For the national conference of the Organization Development Network, the steering committee produced a poster that listed all the names of the more than two hundred people who helped to plan the conference. The poster was mailed to all the members of that professional association.

At North American Tool and Die the names of all the winners of Super Person of the Month are affixed to plaques that hang very visibly over the wash basin on the plant floor. At Stew Leonard's Dairy the pictures of all employees of the month for the last several years, not just the current month, line the walls of the store. At General Electric's corporate training facility at Crotonville, glass cases are filled with hundreds of plaques listing the names of people who attended classes there. Public speeches and newsletters are other available media for making people's accomplishments visible. And isn't it always empowering to receive a letter from someone who tells you how they heard other people talking about what a good job you have done?

We urge you to shine the spotlight on at least one person each day. Let others know how someone has contributed to getting extraordinary things done in your organization.

NOTES

1. Kanter, R. M. Presentation on *The Change Masters,* Santa Clara University, March 13, 1984.

2. Kipnis, D., Schmidt, S., Price, K., and Stitt, C. "Why Do I Like Thee: Is It Your Performance or My Orders?" *Journal of Applied Psychology,* 1981, *66* (3), 324–328.

3. See, for example: Tannenbaum, A. *Control in Organizations.* New York: McGraw-Hill, 1968; Tannenbaum, A., and others. *Hierarchy in Organizations: An International Comparison.* San Francisco: Jossey-Bass, 1974; Tannenbaum, A., and Cooke, R. A. "Organizational Control: A Review of Studies Employing the Control Graph Method." In D. J. Hickson and C. J. Lammers (eds.), *Organizations Alike and Unlike.* London: Routledge & Kegan Paul, 1979.

4. Butterfield, D. A., and Posner, B. Z. "Task-Relevant Control in Organizations." *Personnel Psychology,* 1979, *32,* 725–740.

5. Telnack, J. J. "How To Improve Product Design Processes." Presentation to the Executive Seminar in Corporate Excellence, Santa Clara University, Feb. 11, 1987.

6. Bradford, D. L., and Cohen, A. R. *Managing for Excellence.* New York: Wiley, 1984.

7. Langer, E. J., and Rodin, J. "The Effects of Choice and Enhanced Personal Responsibility for the Aged: A Field Experiment in an Institutional Setting." *Journal of Personality and Social Psychology,* 1976, *34* (2), 191–198; Rodin, J., and Langer, E. J. "Long-Term Efforts of a Control-Relevant Intervention with the Institutionalized Aged." *Journal of Personality and Social Psychology,* 1977, *35* (12), 897–902.

8. McCall, M. W., Jr., and Lombardo, M. M. *Off The Track: Why and How Successful Executives Get Derailed.* Technical Report no. 21. Greensboro, N.C.: Center for Creative Leadership, 1983.

9. Hagberg, R. A., Jr., Conti, I., and Mirabile, R. J. *Profile of the Terminated Executive.* Menlo Park, Calif.: Ward, Hagberg, 1985.

10. See, for example: McClelland, D. C. *Power: The Inner Experience.* New York: Irvington, 1975; Winter, D. G. *The Power Motive.* New York: Free Press, 1973.

11. McClelland, *Power.*

12. McClelland, *Power, p.* 263.

13. See, for example: Pfeffer, J. *Power in Organizations.* Marshfield, Mass.: Pitman, 1981; Pfeffer, J., and Salancik, G. *The External Control of Organizations: A Resource Dependence Perspective.* New York: Harper & Row, 1978; Hickson, D. J., and others. "A Strategic Contingencies Theory of Intraorganizational Power." *Administrative Science Quarterly,* 1971, *16* (2), 216–229.

14. Kanter, R. M. *The Change Masters: Innovation for Productivity in the American Corporation.* New York: Simon & Schuster, 1983; Kanter, R. M. *Men and Women of the Corporation.* New York: Basic Books, 1977.

15. Mainiero, L. A. "Coping with Powerlessness: The Relationship of Gender and Job Dependency to Empowerment-Strategy Usage." *Administrative Science Quarterly,* 1986, *31 (4),* 633–653.

16. Chethik, N. "After a Year, There's Still Enthusiasm at NUMMI Plant." *San Jose Mercury News,* Jan. 19, 1986, pp. 1 ff.

17. Kanter, *The Change Masters;* also see: Pfeffer, *Power in Organizations.*

18. Reprinted by permission of the *Harvard Business Review.* Excerpts from "Wide-Open Management" by Alan M. Kantrow (May/June 1986, p. 99). Copyright © 1986 by the President and Fellows of Harvard College; all rights reserved.

19. Kantrow, "Wide-Open Management," p. 102.

20. De Pree, M. "Theory Fastball." *New Management,* 1983, *1* (4), 29–36.

21. Peters, T. J. "Let the Crew Sail the Ship." *Success,* 1985, *32,* 12.

22. Suters, E. T. "Show and Tell." *Inc.,* 1987, *9 (4),* 111–112.

23. Posner, B. Z., and Butterfield, D. A. "Personal Correlates of Organization Control." *The Journal of Psychology,* 1979, *102,* 299–306.

EMPOWERMENT

Powerlessness corrupts.
Absolute powerlessness corrupts absolutely.
—ROSABETH MOSS KANTER,
HARVARD BUSINESS SCHOOL

Letting go of authority can be scary for managers who were taught that control is good and micromanagement is the way to run the business. However, the real danger is in hoarding authority because, as Rosabeth Moss Kanter points out, feelings of powerlessness bring out the worst in people—hostility, apathy, selfishness. Leaders who help people to feel competent and confident in their roles promote very different attitudes—cooperation, commitment and community. Empowered people welcome the challenge of bringing their vision into reality.

A simple self test will begin to help you see how well you are performing. Asking your coworkers "How am I doing?" will complete the picture.

ASK YOURSELF

Test out how well you empower your coworkers by rating the accuracy of the following statements. Use a 1–5 scale ranging from "a little" to "a great extent."

• I am comfortable sharing power and authority with my coworkers in important matters.	1 2 3 4 5
• I let everyone know what is going on throughout the organization.	1 2 3 4 5
• I encourage each person to do his or her job as he or she sees fit.	1 2 3 4 5
• I look for ways to give my coworkers visibility and get the credit they deserve.	1 2 3 4 5
• I try to link up my coworkers with people who are influential in the organization.	1 2 3 4 5

ASK YOUR COWORKERS

If you gave yourself a "4" or "5" rating on each statement, you probably are working hard at empowering others. However, you can verify your self-assessment by having a two-part discussion with your coworkers. First, ask them to talk about the importance of empowerment so that you understand it in the same way. Second, ask them for feedback on your performance.

You'll know you're developing a common understanding about the importance of empowerment when you hear comments like these:

- "Allowing people to try out ideas that you clearly disagree with shows you really believe in empowerment."
- "Information really is power. The more we know about what's really going on, the better we'll act."
- "Setting boundaries and priorities actually increases our sense of freedom. Nobody wants to find out what the limits are the hard way."
- "Empowerment and accountability go together. You get the job done and then you celebrate or you learn from your mistakes."
- "Empowering people is more than delegating authority and responsibility. It takes training, tools, budget, and connections to act independently."

After discussing the importance of empowerment, check out your coworkers' view of your performance by asking them to consider the five items in your self-assessment. You may find it more productive for them to answer the following questions than to give you numerical ratings on each item:

- What am I doing right now that supports each statement?
- What else can I do—either more or less—to show greater support for each statement?

As you listen, try to clarify your coworkers' answers and ideas. Express your appreciation for their feedback without becoming defensive. After you've listened, ask yourself, "What am I ready to do to empower my coworkers more than ever?" Develop an action plan to build on your strengths and continue to improve.

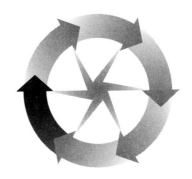

Skyhook 6

TEAMWORK AND INVOLVEMENT

Everyone's dignity is raised by having a say in where the enterprise is going. Empowerment is really about involvement. Empowerment starts with truly believing that everyone counts.
—JACK WELCH,
CHAIRMAN OF GENERAL ELECTRIC

Empowering leadership means bringing out the energy and capabilities that people have, and getting them to work together in a way they wouldn't do otherwise.
—BILL GATES,
CHAIRMAN OF MICROSOFT

Skyhook 6 Teamwork and Involvement—Make people partners by giving them a significant role in core business activities. Change can be paralyzing because people feel they have lost control. Things are being done to them, not with them. Involving people in meaningful decisions and acting in concert with others gives them a renewed sense of potency and fate control.

Teamwork and employee involvement have almost become mantras for running a business in the 1990s. If you have problems with productivity, quality, or innovation, just pull a team together and let them have at it. If it were only that simple.

Fifty years ago the potential benefits and inherent problems of teamwork were becoming clear. Robert Tannenbaum and Fred Massarik outlined the dynamics of involving employees in areas usually reserved for management in "Participation by Subordinates in the Managerial Decision-Making Process" (1950). Even then much was known about participation, but they acknowledged there was much more to be learned.

Tannenbaum and Massarik describe the advantages, requirements, and limitations of teamwork with points like these:

- The primary reason for developing opportunities for employee participation is to achieve organizational goals, not for ethical or democratic reasons.

- Participation usually occurs at the first two steps in the decision-making process: identifying alternatives and predicting consequences. But the final step of actually selecting or accepting an alternative remains a management responsibility.

- Participation can take place in one-on-one discussions or in a larger team setting, which tends to be more effective when it comes to implementation.

- Participation has many potential advantages, such as increased productivity, quality, and responsibility. It is especially important for developing a greater readiness to accept change.

- To make team contributions, people need certain prerequisites, such as knowledge and communication skills. They should also share common ground with other team members to minimize social tensions and breakdowns.

- Other conditions outside the individual are also needed for effective participation such as adequate time, a positive cost-benefit ratio, and open communication channels.

- Participation is not a stand-alone device—it must be part of a comprehensive leadership process to sustain its benefits.

Rosabeth Moss Kanter strongly advocates that leaders use teamwork and involvement to facilitate change in "Dilemmas of Participation," from *The Change Masters* (1983). As the chapter title implies, bringing people together to bring about change is no easy feat. Earlier, Tannenbaum and Massarik had predicted that more experience with participation would strengthen their conceptual framework. The lessons learned and reported by Kanter reinforce the benefits of participation, but they also emphasize and expand on the barriers and liabilities.

Kanter provides encouragement to leaders and admonitions as well with points like these:

- Masters of change are masters of participation who know how to deal effectively with the perils, problems, and dilemmas involved.

- Participation may not be the best way to run the day-to-day business, but it is the best way to stay ahead of change.

- To live up to its claims, participation needs to be managed because it creates new problems while solving others.

- Dilemmas of Beginning include the irony that participation usually starts with a high-level directive, not grassroots activism.

- Dilemmas of Structure and Management reflect the need for specific tasks, boundaries, and managers who stay involved.

- Dilemmas of Choice limit participation to issues that people can deal with effectively.

- Dilemmas of Teamwork recognize that inequalities can drive wedges between members.

- Dilemmas of Linking Teams to Their Environment deal with turnover, ownership, and too much team spirit.

- Dilemmas of Evaluation caution against having expectations that are too high for the benefits of participation—it will not produce Utopia.

- Participation works best when there is balance in control, timing, and team spirit.

Teamwork and involvement are powerful leadership tools, as the authors describe. However, participatory practices should be clearly labeled "Use as needed—handle with care." Involve people when there is a high need for ownership and creative thinking on issues related to a shared vision. Take a more unilateral approach when the issues are of little consequence or relevance. Teamwork is too important to allow it to become just another meeting, task force, or committee.

11

PARTICIPATION BY SUBORDINATES IN THE MANAGERIAL DECISION-MAKING PROCESS

ROBERT TANNENBAUM and FRED MASSARIK

I. INTRODUCTION

The role of "participation" by individuals or groups in American culture in general and in industrial organizations specifically has been treated by many writers. Its implications for political theory as well as for a theory of human relations in formal organizations are numerous. However, in spite of this academic and extra-academic interest, a clear-cut, operational definition of the concept, or a precise set of hypotheses regarding its dynamics, has not been developed. While to do so will be the object of this paper, the treatment will not be completely operational. The development of appropriate methods of measurement is conceived as a next step that should follow the preliminary one of conceptual clarification undertaken in this paper.

A review of the literature indicates that three major approaches have been taken in dealing with "participation":

1. *The experiential approach.* This approach is exemplified by writers who in the course of their experience in enterprise work have obtained a "feel" for the role of participation in the decision-making

From the *Canadian Journal of Economics and Political Science*, 1950, pp. 408–418. Reprinted by permission of the authors.

process and have put down their experiences in article or book form.[1] Writings such as these provide a set of insights and hunches whose verification in any systematic fashion has not been attempted. The actual referents from which these formulations are derived often are single sets of observations in a single or in a few enterprises—observations generally made in an uncontrolled fashion.

The experiential approach, operating outside the bounds of scientific method, nonetheless adds to scientific knowledge indirectly by providing the raw material from which hypotheses may be molded. The precise structure of these hypotheses is not stated neatly by the experiential writers, but rather remains to be formulated.

2. *The conceptual, non-experimental approach.* This approach characterizes the writings of authors who are, essentially, academicians with strong theoretical backgrounds. It is typified by writings that deal with "conditions," "functions," and other abstractions, generally of a socio-psychological nature, that attempt to explain the dynamics of participation.[2] The conceptual, non-experimental approach at its best is the process of theory or hypothesis formulation. Ideally it lays the groundwork for actual testing and experimental work, but much of this type of technical literature so far published on participation lacks the clarity of conceptual definition necessary to make it useful as a basis for experimental work.

3. *The experimental approach.* This approach is found in the writings of authors who have seen fit to apply experimental techniques either to especially constructed social situations involving participation, or else in natural settings in which participational activities prevail.[3] With adequate controls and with a meaningful theoretical structure within which individual findings may be placed, this approach is doubtless the most fruitful. Ideally it indi-

---

[1] For example: H. H. Carey, "Consultative Supervision and Management" (*Personnel*, Mar., 1942); Alexander R. Heron, *Why Men Work* (Palo Alto, 1948); Eric A. Nicol, "Management through Consultative Supervision" (*Personnel Journal*, Nov., 1948); James C. Worthy, "Changing Concepts of the Personnel Function" (*Personnel*, Nov., 1948).

[2] For example: Douglas McGregor, "Conditions for Effective Leadership in the Industrial Situation" (*Journal of Consulting Psychology*, vol. VIII, Mar.–Apr., 1944); Gordon W. Allport, "The Psychology of Participation" (*Psychological Review*, May, 1945).

[3] For the concept of the "natural experiment," see F. Stuart Chapin, *Experimental Designs in Sociological Research* (New York, 1947), and Ernest Greenwood, *Experimental Sociology* (New York, 1945).

cates what will happen under specified sets of conditions and with what degree of probability. Unfortunately, up to now experimental work on the dynamics of participation in the decision-making process has been sporadic.[4]

The present paper is of the conceptual, non-experimental type. Participation in the decision-making process is conceived here as an instrument that may be used by the formal leadership of an enterprise in the pursuit of its goals. No attempt will be made to examine it from an ethical standpoint or in terms of its consistency within the frame of a democratic society, although it is by no means assumed that such considerations are less important than the ones set forward here.

II. DEFINITION OF PARTICIPATION

It is essential, in dealing with participation, to make clear the meaning which is to be attached to the concept. One must specify both who the participators are and in what they are participating. Too frequently in the available literature on the subject the reader must determine these matters for himself since no explicit statements bearing on them are made by the writers.

As already indicated, this paper is primarily concerned with participation as a managerial device. Attention is therefore focused on the subordinates of managers in enterprises as the participators. It is important to note that these subordinates may be either non-managers or managers.[5] If they are managers, they are subordinates of superior managers in the formal organization of the enterprise in addition to having subordinates who are responsible to them.

Because of space limitations, consideration of the participation of individuals as union members in specific activities of an enterprise is excluded from the scope of this paper. Suffice it to say here that in those cases where the participation of union members is direct and personal, the benefits to be derived by the enterprise are similar to those derived from participation within the superior-subordinate relationship. However, in those cases (which are the greatest in number) where the participation of the union member is indirect and impersonal, it is doubtful if such is the result. It is our

---

4   For a good summary of relevant experimental work, see Ronald Lippitt, "A Program of Experimentation on Group Functioning and Productivity" (in *Current Trends in Social Psychology*, Pittsburgh, 1948).

5   For definitions of these terms as used here, see Robert Tannenbaum, "The Manager Concept: A Rational Synthesis" (*Journal of Business*, Oct., 1949).

conclusion that most of the statements which follow are relevant to the former cases.[6]

What then is the meaning of participation, and with what type of participation by subordinates are we here concerned? An individual participates in something when he takes a part or share in that thing. Since taking a part or sharing is always involved, participation takes place in a social context. Managerial subordinates in formal enterprises are responsible to their superiors for the performance of designated tasks. In such performance, they are participating in the production of the good or service of the enterprise. They also participate (share), through the receipt of wages or salaries, in the distribution of the total revenue received by the enterprise. These types of participation are common to all enterprises. But there is another type of participation which is much less frequently encountered, although its use as a managerial device has, of recent years, grown rapidly in importance. This type involves participation by subordinates with their superiors in the managerial decision-making process.

Decisions are made by managers in order to organize, direct, or control responsible subordinates to the end that all service contributions be coordinated in the attainment of an enterprise purpose.[7] Since managers are those who accomplish results through subordinates, the latter are always directly and intimately affected by managerial decisions and therefore may have a considerable interest in them. Because of this possible interest, subordinates may have a strong desire, particularly in a nation with deeply ingrained democratic traditions, to participate in the determination of matters affecting them. It is of importance, therefore, to consider the form which such participation might assume.

Decision-making involves a conscious choice or selection of one behavior alternative from among a group of two or more behavior alternatives.[8] Three steps are involved in the decision-making process. First, an individual must become aware of as many as

---

[6] In connection with this discussion, it should be noted that when participation takes place within the superior-subordinate relationship, managers have primary control over the nature of the activity; when it takes place as part of the manager-union relationship, they may or may not, depending upon the relative power of the two parties.

[7] See Tannenbaum, "The Manager Concept: A Rational Synthesis."

[8] This discussion of the decision-making process is based upon Robert Tannenbaum, "Managerial Decision-Making" (*Journal of Business,* Jan., 1950).

possible of those behavior alternatives which are relevant to the decision to be made. Secondly, he must define each of these alternatives, a definition which involves a determination of as many as possible of the consequences related to each alternative under consideration. Thirdly, the individual must exercise a choice between the alternatives, that is, make a decision.

In enterprises, managerial subordinates, as subordinates, can participate in the first two steps of the managerial decision-making process. They cannot participate in the third step. The actual choice between relevant alternatives must be made or accepted by the manager who is responsible to his superior for the decision.[9] However, subordinates can provide and discuss with their manager information with respect both to relevant alternatives and to the consequences attendant upon specific alternatives. In so doing they are participating in the managerial decision-making process.[10]

---

[9] In a democratic group, the choice can be made through a vote participated in by the rank and file. But, in such a case, the leader is organizationally responsible to the rank and file, and the members of the rank and file are not properly, in so far as the decision is concerned, subordinates of the leader.

Members of a democratic group, making the final choice in matters directly affecting them, may be more highly motivated as a result thereof than managerial subordinates who are granted the right to participate only in the first two steps of the managerial decision-making process. For evidence of the motivational effects of group decision, see Kurt Lewin, "Group Decision and Social Change" (in T. M. Newcomb and E. L. Hartley (eds.), *Readings in Social Psychology*, New York, 1947).

[10] It is this type of participation that most writers, who deal with human relations in enterprises, have in mind when they use the concept. The following examples illustrate this contention: "One of the most important conditions of the subordinate's growth and development centers around his opportunities to express his ideas and to contribute his suggestions before his superiors take action on matters which involve him. Through participation of this kind he becomes more and more aware of his superiors' problems, and he obtains genuine satisfaction in knowing that his opinions and ideas are given consideration in the search for solutions" (D. McGregor, "Conditions for Effective Leadership in the Industrial Situation," p. 60); "I am not suggesting that we take over intact the apparatus of the democratic state. Business cannot be run by the ballot box. . . . We must develop other inventions, adapted to the special circumstances of business, which will give employees at all levels of our organizations a greater sense of personal participation and 'belonging'" (J. Worthy, "Changing Concepts of the Personnel Function," p. 175); "Action initiated by the responsible head to bring his subordinates into the picture on matters of mutual concern is not a sharing of prerogatives of authority. Rather, it is an extension of the opportunity of participation in the development of points of view and the assembly of facts upon which decisions are made" (H. Carey, "Consultative Supervision and Management," p. 288).

The participation with which we are here concerned may take place in two different ways. First, it may involve interaction solely between a subordinate and his manager.[11] This would be the case where a worker originates a suggestion which he transmits to his boss. Secondly, it may involve interaction between a group of subordinates and their manager. This would be the case where a manager calls his subordinates together to discuss a common problem or to formulate a recommendation.[12]

III. POSSIBLE ADVANTAGES OF PARTICIPATION AS A MANAGERIAL DEVICE

It becomes useful to inquire why managers might find it advantageous to use this device. In other words, what are the possible benefits which might accrue to an enterprise whose managers made it possible for subordinates to participate in the decision-making process? In providing an answer to this question, it is first necessary to indicate the criterion which would guide the managerial choice relating to the use of participation.

A manager of an enterprise (profit or nonprofit) who behaves rationally will attempt to make a selection from among alternatives related to any problem which will maximize results (the degree of attainment of a given end) at a given cost or which will attain given results at the lowest cost.[13] This is the criterion of rationality. Guided by this criterion, rational managers will find it advantageous to use participation whenever such use will lead to increased

---

[11]   The concept of interaction as used here is not restricted to direct person-to-person, two-way communication (as in the process of superior-subordinate discussion), but encompasses more indirect forms (such as, for example, written communication) as well.

[12]   It may be observed that participation in the latter way, where there is communication between participators and where the act of participation is carried out through the medium of the group (as in cases of "group decision"), may often yield the more useful results. The level of derivable benefits may be higher than if participation had proceeded through channels in which there had been no inter-participator communication. Some factors important in this context are the following: *(a)* the feeling of "group belongingness" obtained by means of "action together" and *(b)* the role of norms, set as a result of group discussion, toward which behavior will tend to gravitate.

[13]   The term *cost* is here used in its highly precise form to refer to whatever must be given or sacrificed to attain an end. See "Price," *Webster's Dictionary of Synonyms.* The term *end* is broadly conceived to embrace whatever factors (monetary or nonmonetary) the managers themselves define as the formal ends of the enterprise.

results at a given cost or to the attainment of given results at a lower cost.

There are many advantages which *may* stem from the use of participation as a managerial device. The following are the principal ones:

1. A higher rate of output and increased quality of product (including reduced spoilage and wastage) as a result of greater personal effort and attention on the part of subordinates.[14]

2. A reduction in turnover, absenteeism, and tardiness.

3. A reduction in the number of grievances and more peaceful manager-subordinate and manager-union relations.

4. A greater readiness to accept change.[15] When changes are arbitrarily introduced from above without explanation, subordinates tend to feel insecure and to take countermeasures aimed at a sabotage of the innovations. But when they have participated in the process leading to the decision, they have had an opportunity to be heard. They know what to expect and why, and they may desire the change. Blind resistance tends to become intelligent adaptation as insecurity is replaced by security.

5. Greater ease in the management of subordinates.[16] Fewer managers may be necessary, the need for close supervision may be reduced, and less disciplinary action may be called for. Subordinates who have participated in the process leading toward a determination of matters directly affecting them may have a greater sense of responsibility with respect to the performance of their assigned tasks and may be more willing to accept the authority of their superiors. All managers possess a given amount of formal authority delegated to them by their superiors. But formal author-

---

[14] For examples, see Lippitt, "A Program of Experimentation on Group Functioning and Productivity"; John R. P. French, Jr., Arthur Kornhauser, and Alfred Marrow, "Conflict and Co-operation in Industry" (*Journal of Social Issues,* Feb., 1946); *Productivity, Supervision and Morale* (Survey Research Center Study no. 6, Ann Arbor, 1948).

[15] See, for example, Alex Bavelas, "Some Problems of Organizational Change" (*Journal of Social Issues,* Summer, 1948); Elliott Jacques, "Interpretive Group Discussion as a Method of Facilitating Social Change" (*Human Relations,* Aug., 1948); Lewin, "Group Decision and Social Change."

[16] See, for example, L. P. Bradford and R. Lippitt, "Building a Democratic Work Group" (*Personnel,* Nov., 1945); O. H. Mowrer, "Authoritarianism vs. 'Self-Government' in the Management of Children's Aggressive (Anti-Social) Reactions as a Preparation for Citizenship in a Democracy" (*Journal of Social Psychology,* Feb., 1939, pp. 121–126).

ity is not necessarily the equivalent of effective authority. The real source of the authority possessed by an individual lies in the acceptance of its exercise by those who are subject to it. It is the subordinates of an individual who determine the authority which he may wield. Formal authority is, in effect, nominal authority. It becomes real only when it is accepted. Thus, to be effective, formal authority must coincide with authority determined by its acceptance. The latter defines the useful limits of the former.[17] The use of participation as a managerial device may result in a widening of these limits, reducing the amount of resistance to the exercise of formal authority and increasing the positive responses of subordinates to managerial directives.

6. The improved quality of managerial decisions. It is seldom if ever possible for managers to have knowledge of *all* alternatives and *all* consequences related to the decisions which they must make. Because of the existence of barriers to the upward flow of information in most enterprises, much valuable information possessed by subordinates never reaches their managers. Participation tends to break down the barriers, making the information available to managers. To the extent that such information alters the decisions which managers make, the quality of their decisions may thereby be improved.

These, then, are the principal advantages which *may* stem from the use of participation as a managerial device.[18] The conditions under which it *will* accomplish them—under which participation will lead to motivation—is the concern of the section which follows.

IV. THE PSYCHOLOGICAL CONDITIONS OF EFFECTIVE PARTICIPATION

All managers of an enterprise are faced with the problem of eliciting service contributions from their subordinates at a high level of quality and intensity. These service contributions are essential if the formal goals of the enterprise are to be attained. What induces subordinates to contribute their services? What motivates them?

A motivated individual is one who is striving to achieve a goal; his activity is goal-oriented.[19] But it should be stressed that moti-

---

[17] This concept of effective authority is expanded upon in Tannenbaum, "Managerial Decision-Making."

[18] These advantages will henceforth be referred to as enterprise advantages.

[19] A goal is defined as a result which, when achieved, has the power to reduce the tension of the organism that has caused the organism to seek it.

vation is only *potential* motion towards a goal. Whether or not the goal is reached depends not only upon the strength of the force in the direction of the goal, but also upon all other forces (both driving and restraining) in the given situation.[20] To illustrate, a person may be motivated to produce 200 units of an item per day, but the restraining force in the form of machine failure or a quarrel with the foreman may lead him to attain an output of only 150 units.

In enterprises, the goals toward which individuals strive may be of two kinds. They may be the formal goals of the enterprise, or they may be other goals which are complementary to the formal goals. The latter is the typical case. Individuals may strive for monetary reward, prestige, power, security, and the like; or they may strive for certain psychological gratifications through the very act of doing the job (that is, they work because they like their work). The primary reason why they contribute their services is to attain these latter goals. In attaining these desired goals, they make possible the attainment of the formal goals of the enterprise which to them are simply means to their own ends. In this sense, the desired goals and the formal goals are complementary.

In the former case, the goals desired by the individual and the formal goals are the same. The individual contributes his services primarily because such contribution makes possible the attainment of the formal goals of the enterprise which coincide with his own personal goals. To the extent that this coincidence of goals exists, the necessity for managers to provide complementary goals for subordinates is thereby lessened, and related costs are reduced. It is suggested that participation tends to bring about a coincidence of formal and personal goals.[21] It may be that through participation,

---

[20] Thus, motion in the direction of goals may be achieved not only by adding forces in the goal-direction, but also by reducing forces impeding such motion. See K. Lewin, "Frontiers in Group Dynamics" (*Human Relations,* vol. I, no. l, 1947, pp. 26–27).

[21] It must be noted that participation as used in this context is only one device which may lead to additional motivation by bringing about a coincidence of formal and personal goals. For example, some other devices that under certain conditions may result in motivational increases and their derivative benefits to the enterprise are permitting personal discretion to the person to be motivated and stimulation of a sense of pride of workmanship. In the former context, managers in all enterprises must always decide the amount of discretion to permit to subordinates. Many considerations naturally underlie this decision. For present purposes, it is important to emphasize that in many circumstances, the granting of considerable discretion may lead to substantial increases in

the subordinate who formerly was moved to contribute his services only because he sought, for example, security and financial rewards, now comes to be moved additionally because he recognizes that the success of the enterprise in turn will enhance his own ability to satisfy his needs.[22]

Whether one conceives of participation as involving separate subordinates with their superiors or subordinates-in-groups with their superiors, in the final analysis one must not lose sight of the fact that the subordinate is a unique human being with a given personality. This implies that whether or not participation will bring forth the restructuring of his goal pattern (incorporating the formal goals within the scope of the personal goals) will depend upon a set of dynamic psychological conditions, the primary ones of which are outlined below:

1. The subordinate must be capable of becoming psychologically involved in the participational activities. He must be free from "blockages" which may prevent him from rearranging his particular goal pattern in the light of new experience. He must possess some minimum amount of intelligence so that he may grasp the meaning and implications of the thing being considered. He must be in touch with reality. If he responds to a dream world, any "real" developments, such as opportunities to take part in certain decision-making processes, may not penetrate without gross distortion and as a result miss their point.

2. The subordinate must favor participational activity. In other words, the person who believes that "the boss knows best" and that the decision-making process is none of his business is not likely to become strongly motivated if given an opportunity to participate. It is apparent that for personality types shaped intensely by an authoritarian system, opportunities for participation may be regarded as signs of weakness and leadership incompetence and on that basis may be rejected unequivocally.[23]

---

motivation. Several devices may be used concurrently, and the dynamics of the devices themselves are interrelated. For example, use of discretion may bring about an enhanced pride-of-workmanship feeling.

[22] It must be recognized that typically goal configurations, rather than single goals, act as motivating agents.

[23] For example, see A. H. Maslow, "The Authoritarian Character Structure" (in P. L. Harriman (ed.), *Twentieth Century Psychology,* New York, 1946). For more detailed treatments see the major works of Erich Fromm and Abram Kardiner.

3. The subordinate must see the relevance to his personal life pattern of the thing being considered. When he realizes that through participation he may affect the course of his future in such a fashion as to increase its positive goal elements and to diminish the negative ones, he will become motivated. For example, a person who can see the relationship between "putting his two bits" into a discussion of a new way of using a stitching machine and the fact that this may mean greater job security and increased pay for himself may be motivated.

4. The subordinate must be able to express himself to his own satisfaction with respect to the thing being considered. He must be psychologically able to communicate; and, further, he must feel that he is making some sort of contribution. Of course, if he cannot communicate (owing to mental blocks, fear of being conspicuous, etc.), by definition he is not participating. If he does not feel that he is contributing, he may, instead of becoming motivated, come to feel inadequate and frustrated. This presupposes that not only is he articulate, but that he has a certain fund of knowledge on which to draw. Participation may fail if it involves considering matters that are quite outside the scope of experience of the participators.

All of the above conditions must be satisfied to some minimum extent. Beyond this requirement, however, the conditions may be mutually compensating, and a relatively low degree of one (although necessarily above the minimum) may be offset somewhat by an extremely high degree of another. For example, if a subordinate is unusually anxious to take part in participational activity (perhaps for reasons of prestige desires), he may come to be quite involved in the process of restructuring his goal pattern so that it will include some of the formal goals, even though he is not always certain as to whether or not he is really contributing anything worthwhile. Further, the relationships specified by the conditions are essentially dynamic. Opportunities for participation, reluctantly used at first, ultimately may lead to a change of mind and to their enthusiastic acceptance.[24]

---

24 It should be stressed that "life spaces" of individuals (that is, their conceptions of themselves in relation to the totality of a physical and psychological environment) and their readiness for action in the light of these conceptions are never static. Constant change and "restructuring" take place, making for an essentially dynamic patterning of behavior. For alternative definitions of the concept "life space" see Robert W. Leeper, *Lewin's Topological and Vector Psychology* (Eugene, 1943), p. 210.

It is apparent that individual differences are highly important in considering the effectiveness of participation as a motivational device; however, the "amount of participation opportunities" made possible by the managers is also a variable quantity. Thus, it is necessary to inquire what the limits to opportunities to participate are in terms of maximum results.

Common sense experience indicates that when some subordinates are given too many opportunities for participation, or too much leeway in participating, they may tend to flounder; they may find themselves unable to assimilate effectively the range of "thinking opportunities" with which they are faced.[25] On the other hand, if they are given little or no opportunity to take part in the decision-making process, by definition they will not come to be motivated by participational activity. For each individual, an amount of participation opportunities lying somewhere between these two extremes will result in a maximum amount of motivation. A hypothesis stemming from this formulation is that for effective operation of participation as a motivational device in a group situation, the members of the group must respond similarly to given amounts of participation, for wide divergences of response may bring forth social tensions and lack of team work within the group.

Of course, many factors act together to motivate an individual. Therefore, the usefulness of the conceptualization advanced depends upon the possibility of breaking down the total of motivational forces into those owing to participation and those owing to other factors. Experimental control methods, matching of cases, and similar devices may have to be utilized to make such an analysis possible. Whether or not the increment of motivation owing to participation is worthwhile depends to an important extent upon the level of intensity of motivation that prevailed previous to introduction of the device of participation. No doubt, there are upper limits to intensity of motivation, and, if motivation has been strong all along, the effect of participation may not be very great.

---

[25] For the belief that "thinking" as a solution for the industrial problem of motivation is usable more effectively on the supervisory level, but less applicable on the "lower levels" of the organizational hierarchy, see Willard Tomlison, "Review of A. R. Heron, *Why Men Work*" (*Personnel Journal,* July–Aug., 1948, p. 122).

V. EXTRA-PARTICIPATIONAL CONDITIONS FOR EFFECTIVE PARTICIPATION

Beyond the factors governing the relationship between participation and possible resultant motivation, certain conditions "outside" the individual must be considered by the managers in deciding whether or not this particular device is applicable.[26] It would be possible to distinguish a great number of such outside conditions that may determine whether or not the use of participation is feasible in a given situation. Those here indicated are suggestive rather than fully definitive. All are viewed with this question in mind: "Granting that participation may have certain beneficial effects, is it useful in a given instance if the ends of the enterprise are to be achieved?"

To answer this question affirmatively, the following conditions must be met:

1. *Time availability.* The final decision must not be of a too urgent nature.[27] If it is necessary to arrive at some sort of emergency decision rapidly, it is obvious that even though participation in the decision-making process may have a beneficial effect in some areas, slowness of decision may result in thwarting other goals of the enterprise or even may threaten the existence of the enterprise. Military decisions frequently are of this type.

2. *Rational economics.* The cost of participation in the decision-making process must not be so high that it will outweigh any positive values directly brought about by it. If it should require outlays which could be used more fruitfully in alternative activities (for example, buying more productive though expensive equipment), then investment in it would be ill-advised.

3. *Intra-plant strategy.*

a. *Subordinate security.* Giving the subordinates an opportunity to participate in the decision-making process must not bring with it any awareness on their part of unavoidable catastrophic events. For example, a subordinate who is made aware in the participation process that he will lose his job *regardless* of any decisions toward which he might contribute may experience a drop in motivation.

---

26 For analytical purposes, this article differentiates between conditions regarding the dynamics of participation as a psychological process and all conditions outside this psychological participation-to-motivation link. The latter category of conditions is treated under the present heading.

27 See Chester I. Barnard, *Organization and Management* (Cambridge, 1948), p. 48.

Furthermore, to make it possible for the subordinate to be willing to participate, he must be given the feeling that no matter what he says or thinks his status or role in the plant setting will not be affected adversely. This point has been made effectively in the available literature.[28]

b. Manager-subordinate stability. Giving subordinates an opportunity to participate in the decision-making process must not threaten seriously to undermine the formal authority of the managers of the enterprise. For example, in some cases managers may have good reasons to assume that participation may lead nonmanagers to doubt the competence of the formal leadership, or that serious crises would result were it to develop that the subordinates were right while the final managerial decision turned out to be in disagreement with them and incorrect.

4. *Inter-plant strategy.* Providing opportunities for participation must not open channels of communication to competing enterprises. "Leaks" of information to a competitor from subordinates who have participated in a given decision-making process must be avoided if participation is to be applicable.

5. *Provision for communication channels.* For participation to be effective, channels must be provided through which the employee may take part in the decision-making process. These channels must be available continuously and their use must be convenient and practical.[29]

6. *Education for participation.* For participation to be effective, efforts must be made to educate subordinates regarding its function and purpose in the over-all functioning of the enterprise.[30] It must be stressed that the conditions stipulated in this section are dynamic in their own right and may be affected by the very process of participation as well as by other factors.

VI. EFFECTS OF PARTICIPATION AS A FUNCTION OF TIME

An area of research that still remains relatively unexplored is that relating to the variation of the effects of participation with

---

[28] See McGregor, "Conditions for Effective Leadership in the Industrial Situation," *passim.*

[29] For a rigorous mathematical treatment of channels of communication within groups see Alex Bavelas, "A Mathematical Model for Group Structures" (*Applied Anthropology,* Summer, 1948, pp. 16 ff.).

[30] See French, Kornhauser, and Marrow, "Conflict and Co-operation in Industry," p. 30.

time. Some experimental studies have examined these effects in terms of increased productivity over a period of several weeks or months and found no appreciable reductions in productivity with time; while other evidence indicates that in some cases participation may have a sort of "shock" effect, leading to a surge of interest and increased motivation, with a subsequent decline. Inadequate attention seems to have been given to this rather crucial question, and the present writers know of no studies that have traced the effects of participation (or other motivational devices) over periods as long as a year. However, on a priori grounds, and on the basis of experimental evidence, it would seem that, after an initial spurt, a plateau of beneficial effects will be attained, which finally will dissolve into a decline, unless additional managerial devices are skillfully employed.

12

DILEMMAS OF PARTICIPATION

ROSABETH MOSS KANTER

"It's a quagmire."

"That's not a very attractive image."

"Well . . . it's a lobster trap. Once you're in it, it's hard to get out. I'm saying, it's worth it, but look at the risks realistically."

—INTERVIEW WITH A MANUFACTURING MANAGER
AT HEWLETT-PACKARD

One way or another, the innovating organization accomplishes a high proportion of its productive changes through participation.

Corporate entrepreneurs—single-minded individuals that they are—still get their projects done by crafting coalitions and building teams of devoted employees who feel a heightened sense of joint involvement and contribution to decisions. The integrative, participative vehicles surrounding innovators—open communication, interdependent responsibilities, frequent team efforts—keep them close to the power sources they need to operate, ensuring access to information, resources, and the support needed for implementation. Involving grass-roots employees on participative teams with control over their own outcomes helps the organization to get and use more ideas to improve performance and increase future skills. Whether called "task forces," "quality circles," "problem-solving groups," or "shared-responsibility teams," such vehicles for greater participation at all levels are an important part of an innovating company.

Masters of change are also masters of the use of participation.

But some of the claims for the effects of greater team participation make it sound like Ms. Lydia Pinkham's Organizational Elixir: millions of dollars in cost savings at a bank! production time cut in half at an instrumentation factory! labor grievances reduced by a factor of nine! "deadwood" transformed into live wires! work-force contentment! energy! productivity!

Many of these claims have solid evidence behind them. Energizing the rank-and-file through participation in team problem solving has indeed produced significant results for many companies. And the effect on the employees themselves does resemble that of a "tonic": the excitement of getting involved and making an impact,[1] especially for those who have never experienced it, for those for whom it is a departure from organizational routine.

But mention "participation" to others, and it may seem like just one more staff or committee meeting. One innovating company's initial definition of participation was "task forces"; getting something done meant working through a task force. So at the drop of an issue, a task force would be formed. There were task forces for major events, and task forces for trivia. There were meetings upon meetings upon meetings, until conference rooms overflowed, and offices seemed empty. And there were also loud groans, after a year or two of this, if anyone dared to suggest that a task force should be convened. Not only were people using task forces where it made more sense to do something else, but they had also neglected to devise any ways to get rid of many of them when they finished their initial work. Some groups were good at finding more things to do, and they were rapidly turning into standing committees, with more and more task forces piling up on top of them. Zealous managers, eager to show that they were in tune with the CEO's push for participative management, started counting their task forces rather than thinking about the substance of what was, or was not, being accomplished. No wonder people at that company were beginning to question the value of participation.[2]

Participation, it is clear, needs to be managed just as carefully as any other organization system, and it creates new problems demanding attention in the course of solving others.

Participation in a team with responsibility for a joint output is not always a preferable process for carrying out tasks; there are circumstances under which authoritative, unilateral decisions or delegation to a single individual makes more sense. Several decades of social-psychological research[3] and the accumulated wisdom of the companies struggling with participation make clear that the use of teams is most appropriate for purposes closely related to staying ahead of change: to gain new sources of expertise and experience; to get collaboration that multiplies a person's effort by providing assistance, backup, or stimulation of better performance; to allow all of those who feel they know something about the subject to get involved; to build consensus on a controversial issue; to allow representatives of those affected by an issue to influence decisions and build commitment to them; to tackle a problem which no one "owns" by virtue of organizational assignment; to allow more wide-ranging or creative discussions/solutions than available by normal means (e.g., to get an unusual group together); to balance or confront vested interests in the face of the need to change; to address conflicting approaches or views; to avoid precipitate action and explore a variety of effects; to create an opportunity and enough time to study a problem in depth; to develop and educate people through their participation: new skills, new information, new contacts.

In short, a great deal of innovation seems to demand participation, especially at the action or implementation stage.

Simply reverse these conditions, and it is clear that there are also times when participation or employee involvement is *not* appropriate: when one person clearly has greater expertise on the subject than all others; when those affected by the decision acknowledge and accept that expertise; when there is a "hip-pocket solution"—the manager or company already knows the "right answer"; when someone has the subject as part of his/her regular job assignment, and it was not *his/her* idea to form the team; when no one really cares all that much about the issue; when no development or learning important to others would be served by their involvement; when there is no time for discussion; when people work more happily and productively alone.[4]

Participation is a way to involve and energize the rank-and-file; it is not a single mechanism or a particular program. And it is certainly not the latest new appliance that can be purchased from a consultant or in a do-it-yourself kit, assembled, plugged in, and expected to run by itself. There are a large number of perils and problems, dilemmas, and decisions that have to be addressed in managing participation so that it produces the best results for everyone. These revolve around how teamwork is initiated; how it is structured and issues chosen—both the inner workings of teams and their relationship to the rest of the organization; and how both members and onlookers evaluate the whole process.

It is striking that many of the problems of participation arise less sharply and are easier to resolve in integrative environments than in segmentalist ones. A foundation of mutual respect, cooperation, open communication, and crosscutting ties—the empowering conditions described in an earlier chapter—can make it easier to add still more teamwork, extending it to lower levels of the organization, providing an important multiplier.

DILEMMAS OF BEGINNING

Participation-by-command: the paradox of initiation. Several years ago I coined an informal definition of participation, to poke fun at the contradictions involved in the launching of most corporate participation programs: *Participation is something the top orders the middle to do for the bottom.*

I found that this definition was true enough to get applause regularly from managers listening to me talk about participation: they were commanded to stop commanding. More often than not, participative activities are initiated because someone at a high level directs others to get involved in task forces, to set up teams, or to treat their subordinates differently—and sometimes tells them, in addition, that they will be measured on how well they do this. In short, lower-level employees are to be given a greater voice, but their managers—who will be rewarded or punished for doing it—have little say. It certainly appears that leaders are not modeling the behavior they want others to adopt.

But how else can participation get launched? Even in situations in which leaders carefully work out all details with the managers below them first, or give employees a say in when and how participation will begin, someone somewhere still has to be the initiator and pusher. In business organizations, grass-roots activism or revolution is neither likely nor desirable as an impetus for participation. *Someone* has to start the ball rolling, and it is hard to prevent at least some others from feeling that participation has been imposed.

This paradox can block action. The "democrats" among us may avoid beginning participative activities until they have complete consensus and voluntary involvement—which at best slows everything down and at worst forestalls any action. After all, people find it difficult to vote in favor of a system they have never experienced, so it may be necessary to push the first experiment in order to get enthusiastic consensus about the second.

Sometimes there are concerns about the contradiction between the command style of top management and the participative activities it is pushing, a concern that arises particularly in segmented companies emphasizing vertical command. This was the case in one major industrial corporation, in which the chief executive foisted the idea of participation on his staff in what some considered an authoritarian manner, and then directed the rest of the organization to set up a variety of participatory structures. The corporate organization-development consultant was bothered by the contradiction and spent most of his time trying to confront the chief executive about his personal style in the hope of changing him. Meanwhile, the organization was indeed gearing up for a number of participative activities that could have used the consultant's help. In a sense, the chief executive's personal style did not matter; the important thing was that he was enabling—or forcing—a number of vehicles for greater employee involvement throughout the rest of the organization. Making those work would eventually have greater impact on the organization than teaching its leader to say "please."

There is an ideal middle ground, of course, that involves key managers and employees in making the decision to go forward by exposing them to the same information the initiator has, by making the initiator's thought processes transparent, and by engaging them in a pilot project for which they help set the ground rules and standards. The first step in many successful employee-involvement efforts, like the one at "Chestnut Ridge," is extensive education and formation of a steering committee. But still, someone pushes, and some others may at first feel forced to go along.

The irony of participation-by-command will eventually fade into historical memory as participation becomes seized and owned by those engaged in it—as long as a second dilemma of initiation is handled well.

"Why aren't they grateful?": the paternalism trap. Participation sometimes appears to be imposed on employees by an organization's leadership in "the employees' own interest," in a liberal "Father knows best" style of organizational change, or what has been called "liberating the masses by beneficent dictate": "Like it or not, you're free."[5] The management expects gratitude for the gift it has given, even though workers may not have sought it and have other concerns. So the thank-you note to management contains resentment and a pouring out of other accumulated complaints, rather than praise for management's enlightenment. Management,

in turn, concludes that its employees are ungrateful, and tries to take back its gift.

Even when participation is undertaken in response to perceived interest by employees, leaders can easily fall into the paternalism trap by treating participation as a gift rather than a *right* and as a luxury rather than a results-oriented, task-related organizational tool. Imagine employees' reactions to these two different ways of announcing the start of a participation program:

> *Announcement A:* "Because we at Widgets International care about our people and want all our people to feel included, we are spending some of our 1980 profit to develop a series of employee task forces and work teams that will give employees a chance to express their views to management."

> *Announcement B:* "Our business at Widgets International has been changing over the last few years, and we are increasingly concerned about improving productivity and quality and developing new production methods in order to stay competitive. We need to use the talents of all our employees more fully in order to do this. We are creating a series of employee problem-solving teams to help us work on these issues."

Announcement A is likely to be greeted with amusement, skepticism, and passive indifference, although a few employees might indeed feel grateful for their company's paternalism. Announcement B, on the other hand, is a more straightforward, businesslike statement of what management hopes to gain by tapping its people's talent.

Employees resent being treated like children for whom managers decide what they *really* need, and this can cast a negative shadow over early participative activities—even though, ironically, participation may give workers their first chance to *tell* management what they really need. Furthermore, treating participation as a management gift makes it vulnerable to removal: "Management giveth, management taketh away." Rights are protected, and people do not have to grovel for them. But gifts keep the giver in control and carry obligations of reciprocity—leaders expecting something in return. A "Petrocorp" Marketing Services Department director warned his managers, "You don't give someone opportunity as though it were a gift. You present them with a *chance* and hope like hell they grab it."

Furthermore, treating participation as a luxury is insulting to employees; they do not want to waste their time at something that management hardly takes seriously and does not consider relevant to business objectives. Rather than making employees feel that "we're doing this for them," management should be clear about, and acknowledge, its own gains from participation, and make sure it is choosing and designing participative activities to get them: e.g., more creative solutions to problems, more worker responsibility for quality and production, programs better tailored to employee concerns, better "early-warning systems" for communication about problems, and more ownership of new systems so that they get implemented faster. Instead of hoping for gratitude for how enlightened and giving they are, leaders would instead be engaging employees' talents in getting something beneficial to the organization.

"Participate or else": the question of voluntariness. Another issue in launching participation is which people get involved, and how. Must participation be obligatory, if not mandatory, in order to deserve the label? That is, must everyone be included? Or does participation by definition require volunteers? Can people choose not to participate or to abdicate their decision-making rights to others—representatives, leaders, or managers? Or should participation be a matter of interest in the issue and willingness to volunteer? There is a clear dilemma here: if participation relies on volunteers, it may not be representative; if it does not, it may be coercive.

A variety of evidence suggests that people differ in their interest in participation,[6] although, as we see later, this often has much to do with the nature of the job. But certainly people care more about some issues than about others, and it is unreasonable to assume that all employees will contribute or involve themselves in the same way. It is also unreasonable to hold off making decisions or taking action unless everyone is involved, just as the search for consensus can often hang up a group. And some kinds of participation, such as problem-solving teams, require the right skill mix. Thus, it is important to establish criteria for action, representation, and membership on teams.

The question of voluntariness of participation is always tricky. On one hand, it is important to handpick people for teams or task forces who have the skills and enthusiasm for carrying out the activities. On the other hand, it is equally important to avoid making participation simply another "job" that people are assigned to without any say in the decision, in true segmentalist, authoritarian fashion. In the Petrocorp Marketing Services Department project, the first members of the Communications Council were appointed by the directors. One appointee, questioning his involvement, said, "*I don't see any problems with communication in this department,*" and the appointed chair missed the council's second meeting.

Even if the official "rule" for participative activities is volunteers-only, informal pressures can arise that make participation mandatory *de facto* if not *de jure*. For example, quality circles in U.S. companies generally consist of volunteers from each work unit who want to put in the time and effort. But what happens if those involved get differentially rewarded because of greater visibility or access to information? What if nonparticipants in task forces are labeled "non-team players" because they turn down the opportunity? Thus, it is also important to avoid the kind of peer and management pressure that makes it difficult for workers to say no even if they are asked formally whether they want to get involved. What is important here is balance.

DILEMMAS OF STRUCTURE AND MANAGEMENT

"Escape from freedom": the need for structure. This reflects the importance of clear limits in making an empowering, freedom-generating process like participation work. Erich Fromm's classic book title was intended to convey the ways that people slide into neurotic behavior when given freedoms they cannot handle. True "freedom" is not the absence of structure—letting the employees go off and do whatever they want—but rather a clear structure which enables people to work within established boundaries in an autonomous and creative way. It is important to establish for people, from the beginning, the ground rules and boundary conditions under which they are working: what can they decide, what can't they decide? Without structure, groups often flounder unproductively, and the members then conclude they are merely wasting their time. The fewer the constraints given a team, the more time will be spent defining its structure rather than carrying out its task.

Total freedom, with no limits set, will not occur in a business organization anyway. But the limits can be vague, unclear, contradictory, hidden and subject to guesswork. So the group might make a large number of false starts before it finally learns what is permissible and what is not. It might spend most of its time discussing *how* to decide rather than deciding. Too many choices, too much up for grabs can be frustrating. Anchors are necessary, something to bounce off of, some constraints or criteria or goals.

Thus, turning over a task or an issue to a group of organization members with no guidelines, objectives, constraints, or limits can be extremely ineffective; yet some people (both advocates and detractors) think that this is what participation must mean. Responsible parties (managers or leaders) do not give up all their control or responsibility for results just because they are involving a wider circle of people; nor ought they to leave the participating members to flounder without help. Honeywell's DMSG developed its steering committee for innovative problem-solving "task teams" to deal with just that need. A large number of task forces had been established in the group to create new policies and programs, but until the top-management steering committee was formed, they reported nowhere, had no standards to meet, and received no guidance. The steering committee, which included the vice-president/general manager, quickly brought order and direction, and the task teams went on to produce impressive products.

It is significant in this respect that participation works better where the parties involved in it are strong, and there is clear leadership in the organization. It is a common statement by those experienced in union-management committees that these do not work where either the union or management is weak. The benefits of participation do not seem to occur in stalemate situations where no one has enough power to generate action, or in situations where power is equalized but low. In a comparison of twelve plants, more participation was associated with better communication, better performance, interunit cooperation, top-management support, lower costs, and less work pressure—a better-organized system with better management; but flatter and thus theoretically more equal power distributions alone were not associated with such positive results. However, when participation was coupled with everyone having *more* power (more total influence in the system to get things done), the benefits were even greater.[7] In short, *leadership*—the existence of people with power to mobilize others and to set constraints—is an important ingredient in making participation work.

But structure means giving people full information about the ground rules; it does not imply the imposition of mindless formulas for action—giving people a set of rote motions to go through that have worked somewhere else or have been specified in minute detail. This is the problem with many packaged programs that have been sold to U.S. companies under the "participation-and-" label. (The "and-" generally refers to productivity improvement or quality improvement or morale improvement.) Many American companies are fond of using what Barry Stein has called the "appliance model of organizational change": buy a complete program, like a "quality-circle package," from a dealer, plug it in, and hope that it runs by itself. The opposite extreme from no-structure is overstructuring participative activities with no thought to the appropriateness of the structure for the place where it is being used, and with the elimination of one of the values of participation to employees: the chance to exert more control over work situations.

Quality circles are especially prone to being introduced by overly specific structuring of actions rather than by education in the principles and skills to make this kind of involvement work. The most effective set of work teams handling quality issues at a Hewlett-Packard facility were a natural outgrowth of existing practices, and they were called "quality teams" rather than quality circles. The initial structure consisted of forty hours of training for supervisors, who then devised their own methods. In six months, efficiency was improved by 50 percent by the leading teams, and space was cut by 25 percent. A manufacturing head concluded, "It was not a rote process." In contrast, a neighboring plant that adopted the formula method, complete with one-two-three do-this/do-that structuring, ran into problems with its quality circles. Treated by employees as "a typical fad, a typical campaign," this program was "running out of gas."

Delegation ≠ abdication. Thus, related to the structure issue is a key lesson for managers: delegating responsibility to other people does not mean abdicating managerial responsibilities for monitoring and supporting the process. Some managers assume an either/or world where either they are in complete control or they have given up all control. But delegation—whether by a management team to a set of employee teams or by a single manager to his or her subordinates—means that the manager not only sets the basic conditions but also stays involved, available to support employees, reviewing results, redirecting or reorienting the team as necessary. Leaders can also help to coordinate activities, centralize record keeping, and serve as points of contact with other departments. Of course, sometimes a manager who simply wants to prove that participation does not work will throw a task at an unprepared team and abdicate all responsibility—thereby setting up the whole thing for failure.

People frequently want leadership and guidance. The problem of authority in organizations in which employees are given a greater chance to contribute and participate is not resolved by its elimination. In one company's experience with autonomous (no-supervisor) work teams which all "evaporated" within two years, a skilled worker involved in one observed:

> Looking at the . . . work project, basically it's a [no-supervisor] structure in order to give the individual more incentive. What I want to say is that it is a waste of time logically and theoretically. . . . I was wondering if QWL couldn't restructure the project; define an ideal lead, and train a person to be that ideal lead. The more I think about it, the structure of manufacturing is authority and supervision; and without it, it would be chaos.[8]

A senior manager agreed that there were problems, but associated them with the failure of higher-level management to provide the right amount of structure and not with the problems of team responsibility:

> The girls out there . . . are really down. . . . They're dissatisfied, because they don't feel they've been getting the things to do the job properly. That's partly our fault. I think we've gone through a bit of a learning process in that we've kind of turned them out on their own. A brand-new product, a different concept of working, and it's floundering. I think, given enough time, we could make it successful, even without authority. There's some natural leadership coming out of this.[9]

"Who cares?": reporting and accountability. One of the reasons for managers to stay involved, even when delegating responsibility in a participative fashion, is that—ironic though it may seem—the personal concern of the manager for results is the sign to employees of caring. If the manager or the initiator of a team simply walks away from the process once having launched it and never asks for reports, or monitors and measures output, then employees begin to wonder whether this is indeed a high-priority use of their time. They wonder whether anybody really cares about this. Was it simply an empty activity to give them the illusion of participation? But clear accountabilities and reporting relationships are a way of indicating to employees exactly who *does* care and exactly what the value of their activities is.

The twenty-five-hour-day problem. The last issue in launching participation is to find and manage time. Participation in teams and involvement in decisions are time-consuming, or they take time in addition to core jobs, and time is a finite resource. So where will the

time come from? Will participation be on company time, or employee time? If it is on company time, is it off the budget of the
particular manager, or is it compensated in another way? Members
or workers may not always feel that the extra time they must invest
in meetings and in informing themselves is justified, particularly
where they feel inadequately paid for it. Worker apathy can be a
problem; teams can shirk responsibility because they do not feel like
putting in the time. So corporations must legitimate participative
activities and entitle participants to take time for them as long as
they can still do their core jobs effectively.

When time use is not legitimized, inequities can result. People
have different amounts of control over their time, and thus greater
or lesser opportunities to participate. In Norway, for example,
women are less able than men to take advantage of widespread
industrial and civic democracy because they must rush home to
shop or take care of the children, while the men in this traditional
family system are free to put in time after work hours in employee
and community councils. In American companies, professionals are
likely to control their own time or get easy management approval
for task-force involvement, while clerical workers are not, making it
harder for them to put in the effort or play as important a role in
participative problem solving.

Time negotiation involves more people than simply those
directly authorizing or involved in participative activities that extend beyond the immediate job: managers who need to "release"
their subordinates' time, peers who wonder if they will have to pick
up the slack for a colleague with other commitments. A segmentalist tradition is likely to produce resistance to releasing employees,
who are hoarded . . . just like any other commodity not easily
"lent" to another area. For the first "volunteer"-task-force head in
the Petrocorp Marketing Services Department, this created a
number of uneasy situations. There was no clear negotiation with
her managers, and she had to promise the people *on* the task force
that they would not have to spend much time. She described the
rewards and punishments she found in trying to get the task force
moving to department managers who were trying to learn how to
manage participation more effectively:

> This project grew on its own. . . . There was commitment to
> the idea, but the reality of spending time and the money has
> not been borne out. I was not really given the blocked-out
> time. . . . I got people to join the Central Resources Task

Force by telling them they wouldn't have to do any work—
advise only. I've been stuck with all the work. I didn't realize
I'd be spending this much time on this work.

The rewards are sort of nebulous. There's an ego thing
involved. The punishments are quite specific: my boss im-
plying that I wasn't doing my regular work. This caused a
lot of personal pain; what am I supposed to be doing? I took
my task-force work home to do. My secretary paid the price
for helping me. She always had to go back to a loaded desk.

Her boss replied:

Before, this project of Jennifer's came out of the blue. I
didn't think too much about it at first. After a while I began
to see more and more of it. Maybe too much?

Everyone listening agreed that top management would need to
legitimize task-force and project involvement, letting managers
know that employees were entitled to take the time if they could
show that their core job would be done just as effectively.

DILEMMAS OF ISSUE CHOICE

The "big decision" trap. People are generally paid in corporations
to do their jobs. The more time and energy participation appears to
take away from this, with no compensating rewards, the more it will
be resisted. But the closer the arena for participation is to the job
territory, the more it will be embraced. Local, task-related issues
seem to work best. Concrete agendas and clear technologies also
make it easier for groups to find the stability to proceed. John
Witte's quantitative pre- and postparticipation survey measures at
"Sound, Incorporated" showed that participation on company-
wide, joint planning committees may have *increased* alienation, but
participation on work teams with control over the immediate job
situation *reduced* it.[10] Other observations confirm this. The more
distant, broad, and open-ended the territory over which participation extends, the less likely is it to have the desired results without
considerable difficulty. This is what I call the "big decision" trap.

A common assumption by managers in debates about participation is that people want to be involved in the "big decisions" about
the overall management of their organization or other sweeping
concerns. But my observations and a wide variety of evidence indicate that at least initially, employees would rather be involved in
local issues reflecting daily annoyances, and that they see some

issues as quite appropriately belonging to management. In surveys at two companies about to launch participation programs, workers expressed clear preferences for more involvement in issues such as work procedures and work rates (78/83 percent wanting "some say" or "a lot of say"); quality standards and wages were next in line. But questions of management salaries, hiring and firing, and job assignments held low interest, and the setting of production levels was of interest to only slightly more than half the workers.[11]

It is important not to make assumptions about issues of greatest concern to employees; they should be asked. But secondly, it is striking how often people are most concerned about the "little things" (at least in the eyes of managers) that make a great deal of difference to them in their daily working environment. Involvement in these immediate and local issues is often what they care about most, and they may be content to leave the "bigger" issues to experts and managers.

There is an instructive joke about how a husband and wife divide up their decision territories. He takes all the "big" ones: U.S. foreign policy, the energy crisis, the stock market. . . . And she takes all the "small" ones: which house to buy, school for the children, purchasing decisions. . . . Unfortunately, some organizations approach participation in just this way, surveying employees about their reactions to distant aspects of corporate policy but giving them no say in the "small," local matters that may concern them most. It can be frustrating to be just one of many people voicing an opinion about large decisions (the anonymity of the vote) while having no control over local ones (such as the arrangement of equipment or the timing of coffee breaks) that could make a significant difference in work-life quality.

Furthermore, as a place to begin moving toward more participatory systems, local issues for specific, smaller groups make the most sense. People might feel uninformed about macro-issues and thus threatened by having their opinions solicited. Or they might feel that one more voice does not matter anyway. But when it comes to local issues, people can talk from their own experience, respond from their own needs. People are always experts on themselves and on what touches them personally. There is no knowledge gap between workers and managers here.

The "agenda" trap: the need for visible results. These are more likely to be produced by local work teams than by broad, open-ended policy groups anyway. People need to feel that their scarce time is well spent on things that produce something tangible and visible. Therefore it is important, in assigning the tasks for participation, that they be clear, concrete, and likely to produce a solid result.

In the beginning, of course, there may be a certain number of teams or activities that I call "agenda-setting": simply generating issues that will be discussed later. At one leading high-participation company, efforts to increase involvement seemed to be faltering because of disaffection on the part of members of several high-visibility task forces chartered by top management, and the same kind of disaffection was occurring in work-team meetings. It turned out that the method of participation the company had hit upon was to pull together teams to make recommendations about general approaches to a subject. Then each of the recommendations of the first wave of teams would be handed over to a second round for refinement and further specification. Then the second-wave recommendations might go to still a third team or individual to consider implementation issues. In short, each team was setting an agenda for another team rather than engaging in action that would have organizational impact.

At a certain point, then, people become impatient with simply setting agendas and want to be in a position to take action and bring in results.[12] It is better to involve people in teams at the work site or task forces with a specific action mandate than simply to have a number of committees engaging in loose discussion that seems to go nowhere. "Too much talk, too little action" is a common complaint about participative vehicles that do not have concrete tasks to carry out. For this reason, a Hewlett-Packard facility uses its MBO process to prioritize a team's activities; they are encouraged to work on a succession of easy problems before tackling tough ones.

People are skeptical about participation just for show, without any impact on substance: for example, endless surveys of employee opinion without change in the underlying conditions giving rise to that opinion. One company with repeated survey results showing negative attitudes decided that this proved it needed more surveys; several cynical managers said they would "lie" on the next round to give the company the findings it wanted, in the hopes that the time-consuming surveys would end.

Participatory mechanisms that simply set agendas rather than produce action, such as representative councils or advisory bodies, can come to be regarded as part of the control system of the organization, rather than an empowering device, if those mechanisms have no real impact on at least some activities—an attempt to manipulate people by giving them the illusion of a voice.[13] In short, if people are given a chance to talk, other people have to listen—and perhaps modify something as a result. Tangible signs of both the listening and the new outcome are important.

"Is participation its own reward?" There is also another kind of visible result beyond impact on the organization: rewards to participants, compensation, and recognition.

For a while, participation is indeed rewarding in and of itself, especially if it is novel and exciting and provides access to higher-level management as well as the fun of working in a spirited team. But once participation leaves the experimental stage, compensation and recognition have to be more formal. Without this, people can quickly lose enthusiasm, or their efforts will go where the money and the recognition are. There is research evidence that extrinsic rewards for participation are important,[14] that people need to feel that they benefit from contributing more to an organization's effective functioning. In a trucking company, employee stock ownership coupled with participation was associated with more commitment, involvement, and satisfaction than participation alone,[15] indicating the payoff for people who see that they will be personally and individually rewarded for the effort involved in participation. Similarly, workers who participate in productivity-improvement projects need to feel that eventually, they as well as the organization will benefit. At "Chipco's" Chestnut Ridge plant, the solution was to add parallel-organization participation to job descriptions and performance-appraisal forms.

The issue of credit and recognition is important to resolve at the beginning, or there can be problems later. The experience of a major manufacturer with task forces on a variety of employee concerns is instructive. One task force worked particularly well, turning in early its highly professional recommendations for a new communication program, based on extensive hearings with rank-and-file employees. All the recommendations were accepted by the steering committee, and task-force members felt proud of their achievement. So proud, in fact, that the task-force chair carried around with him a diagram of the program, which he showed to anyone he encountered, clearly presenting it as "his" program. He even told a colleague that out of his thirty years of company service, *this* was what he would be remembered for. He was leaving his mark on the company via the task-force project.

All well and good so far. The company was hoping that participation would stimulate just such responses, the moments of energy and excitement punctuating what some employees felt were otherwise grim or routine existences. But the chair was not alone in feeling that he had produced something of value—so did the other team members, especially a professional who was an expert on the program area and felt that he had been particularly influential in the results. For him, it was twenty years of service, but the feeling was the same: *This* is my first above-and-beyond creative contribution. He wanted recognition and credit too. But since the company had not thought about how to recognize task-force members, and since the chair seemed to be monopolizing attention out of his own previous deprivation, it was unclear whether the rest of the task force would ever have any reward beyond their own private knowledge that they contributed.

DILEMMAS OF TEAMWORK

One of the things that help a team work well is the feeling on the part of members that they are an integral, connected part of the group. In a task-oriented team, this means that their contributions are welcome and valued, that they are as important as any other member of the team to the final product. After all, why waste scarce organizational time to feel irrelevant? "Participation" must mean much more than observation and tacit approval of others as *they* do all the important work.

But four kinds of "inequalities" can drive a wedge between individuals and the team.

The seductiveness of the hierarchy. Segmentation cannot be overcome just by sudden definition of "teams." Teams that are pulled together from different external statuses, with the awareness that they will be returning to them, may slip into deference patterns which give those with higher status more air time, give their opinions more weight, and generally provide them with a privileged position in the group. There is a great deal of experimental social-psychological evidence that external status strongly influences the reactions of others in a group discussion. Similarly, stories from marooned military units indicate that people fall into positions determined by their place in the military hierarchy even though external constraints are removed, and the survivors constitute a "community" more than a hierarchy.

So teams, especially in segmentalist environments unaccustomed to the mixing and matching of an integrative culture, may end up duplicating the organizational hierarchy in miniature inside themselves: higher-status people dominating, lower-status people dropping out. Members of one task force in the Petrocorp Marketing Services Department felt that the most important factor inhibiting their participation was the presence of the boss. At two different high-technology companies where I observed cross-hierarchical task forces in operation, the same pattern was repeated: I could guess the relative levels of participants in meetings just by noting who "took over" and whose comments were treated most attentively—regardless of who was officially the chair. In another sense, the chair *was* the highest-status member of the group, and meetings were run as though the rest of the participants were staff that had been assigned to him, instead of partners in a joint task.

The seductiveness of the hierarchy has emotional roots. The emotions that make it easier to reproduce the hierarchy than to operate as partners are principally fear and comfort. The basis for fear is obvious: "crossing" a powerful figure in a group, even if the purpose of the group is to get diversity of opinions, can make people afraid of external retribution later. So the lower-status people hold back, or feel very daring if they contribute. But there is also a comfort factor: it is easier to maintain familiar patterns of relationships and interaction than to experiment with the unfamiliar. Over time, with appropriate support from the higher-status figures, people are more likely to try to act in ways that place them outside the hierarchy. This is what we mean when we say that a group "loosens up."

"Participators are made, not born": the knowledge gap. There are also task-related reasons that hierarchies magically reproduce themselves inside teams designed to "level" status and improve cross-hierarchical communication and cooperation to solve a problem, or that other forms of "inequality" develop. Effective participators are, to an extent, "made, not born." It takes knowledge and information to contribute effectively to task teams, and this has to come from somewhere. Those people with more information about the matters at hand have an advantage over the others, and those in communication-rich integrative companies are all more likely to have the tools for effective participation than those in companies when segmentation significantly reduces information flow.

Often organizational position, with resulting differentials in information access, can create this difference in the team. Wherever there is a knowledge gap that is not closed with information before the team meets, inequalities develop that are often frustrating to the less well-informed group members, who respond by dropping out or failing to appear at meetings.

Participation *per se* does not always equalize power and may even increase discrepancies. If more poorly informed members sit with the more knowledgeable and skilled in meetings where all of them are theoretically making joint decisions, the less knowledgeable not only may be "shown up" for their lack of knowledge, thus losing power, but may also be forced to endorse, *de facto*, the decisions they supposedly helped make. Their right to complain later is lost.[16] This is one reason that worker participation on boards of directors was found to have mixed, rather than positive, benefits in Europe. People of managerial or equivalent status had an automatic information advantage. (Of course, the same thing is true of inside versus outside directors, leading to the common observation that management's viewpoint dominates board discussions.)

The secretaries in the commercial section of the Petrocorp Marketing Services Department eventually decided *not* to continue their rotating participation in section meetings because of the knowledge gap, which in turn stemmed from the segmentalist culture. Far from making them feel included and giving them a voice, sitting in on section meetings made one of them feel "dumb," since she could not follow the content of all the discussions. A few others felt they had to keep quiet, since they clearly knew less than anyone else. Some were bored and felt it was a waste of time. Special briefings by one of the managers before the meetings were a help, but not enough to compensate for the inequality caused by differential organizational status. This is not a "woman's" problem, either; I have observed the same hesitation and frustration on the part of male production workers in noninnovating companies suddenly thrust into management meetings unprepared.

Differential personal resources. There are also related problems from unequal distribution of skill and personal resources. People bring to groups different levels of personal attractiveness, verbal skill, access to information-bearing networks, and interest in the task.[17] Victor Vroom and other psychologists have argued that there are personality differences among people that make some "fit" better than others in participatory groups requiring responsibility and active involvement, although the evidence for these differences is mixed.[18] It is easy to see, however, that personal characteristics and mutual attraction can play a role in helping people become connected to social networks outside the team that give them an advantage inside it: more informal status, better reputation, earlier gossip. Furthermore, interpersonal attractions among team members can lead to subgroups engaged in "natural" patterns of friendly communication which give people an advantage in team discussions. It is not simply that people may support one another on the basis of friendship, but also that the opportunity for people to discuss issues in smaller units outside the group may mean that they come to the meetings with their thoughts better formulated and their arguments rehearsed.

There are also specific skills involved in articulating opinions, developing arguments, and reaching decisions that are differentially distributed across organizational populations—and not just because individuals are intrinsically different. Hierarchy, or at least the structure of the line organization, intrudes on the participative team again. Development of the kind of skills necessary for effective participation—ability to push a point of view, ability to see issues in context and so on—is closely associated with job characteristics. The effectiveness of participation in local department committees at British Rail, for example, was a function of the job; jobs with high autonomy (which required working alone and unchecked, as well as initiating action) predisposed people to learn the requirements of decision making. Thus, the conditions described in *The Change Masters,* Chapter 5 that stimulate innovation, which include broad assignments and the ability to initiate, also help make people more effective team participants. Then, on top of that, actual involvement in a decision-making process on the job (obtaining and processing information, evaluating outcomes, defining action strategies) tends to teach people to articulate corporate goals. Finally, jobs with more information passing through about local and corporate issues also give their occupants an advantage in effective participation.[19]

The seniority/activity gap. A final source of inequality comes from relative seniority or activity in the team itself. Outsiders or newcomers or those not attending meetings regularly often feel uncomfortable about speaking up, especially if the group has developed its own language, abbreviations, or understandings. Sometimes the group will deliberately close ranks in the presence of a newcomer as an occasion to reinforce its own solidarity. And in what has been termed a "competence multiplier," the most active members may gain a monopoly on the skills required for effective decision making and therefore become even *more* active, beginning an exclusionary cycle.[20]

Thus, in general, the "best" participators who come to dominate team discussions may again turn out to be those already best placed in the hierarchy and in the networks spawned by it. "What kinds of things inhibit your participation?" members of a functional area were asked in an anonymous survey, in reference to their quality-circle-like, problem-solving meetings. Among the replies: "Know-it-all centers"; "Owl and Pussy-Cat group glances"—meaning side-long looks exchanged by just a few members; "lack of information on subject under discussion"; "things outside my responsibility and interest"; "fear of being attacked by group"; "older members who make newer members feel insecure."

Overwhelmingly, the element of the meetings that everyone liked best was the presentations by the group's boss—relying on the familiar hierarchy and reducing any feelings of peer competition, because during *his* presentation no one had to feel unequal to a peer. There were also feelings that individual participation would be improved if people did not feel they had to perform and if they all got the same information in advance.

The internal politics of teams. Of course, declaring people a "team" does not automatically make them one, nor does seeking decisions in which many people have a voice ensure that democratic procedures will prevail. A philosophy of participation in no way eliminates jockeying for status or internal competition if people bring self-serving interests into a group, or if they have differential stakes in the outcome, or if they come from segmented organizations whose structure and culture encourages divisiveness and non-cooperation across areas. There may be differential advantages to individual members to be gained by pushing particular decisions over others; there may be differential benefits to be reaped outside the group by appearing to be a dominant force in it—like the ambitious young manager who wants to impress his boss with his "leadership" skills. People bring different needs and interests into any kind of group from their location outside it, and these can serve as the origins of team politics.

How much differential needs and interests politicize a team is in large measure a function of how the team is set up in the first place. Group dynamics becomes more competition-centered when re-wards or recognition outside the team are scarce, and members are direct competitors for them. There is also more internal politicking when some functions, represented by team members, think they stand to lose by certain decisions of the team, and the representing member is under pressure from colleagues as well as personally con-cerned. It is a simple psychic-economic calculation: do the gains from dropping certain interests/goals in the name of cooperation outweigh the losses? Cooperation and reduced politicking are more likely to occur when team members are participating in the group as individuals rather than as representatives, because they can make individual deals free of the pressure of a "shadow group" symbolically looking over their shoulders. (Indeed, when teams begin to jell as cooperative entities, even representatives sometimes forget their external group affiliation in favor of team identification—sometimes to the detriment of the constituency supposedly being served by the participation of its representative.)

Beyond the politics of interest maximization, teams are also arenas for the flexing of power muscles in and of themselves. There is often nothing inherently more "democratic" about certain decisions because they were made by teams rather than individual managers. Teams can turn into oligarchies, with a few dominant people taking over and forcing the others to fall into line. There are many examples in history of supposedly representative mechanisms sliding into oligarchies—e.g., the reputed takeover of some unions by small groups with shady ties. The benign "tyranny" of peers can substitute for the benign "tyranny" of managers, with conformity pressures as strong and sanctions for deviance as impelling. In one highly participative factory, workers complained that they felt too dependent on their teams for evaluation and job security and feared being ostracized by a clique.[21] Members of autonomous work teams in a Cummins Engine plant were likely to be harder on absent members, according to a former plant manager, than management would have dared to be; they would often appear at the doorstep to drag a person in to work if the claimed illness did not satisfy team members. (Of course, they relied on each other's contributions more than in a conventional work situation.) Indeed, management often *counts* on this peer pressure to stay in line as a side benefit of participation.

Finally, teams become politicized when there are historic tensions between members that have not been resolved before the "team" is formed, tensions that are more likely in category-conscious, segmentalist cultures than in integrative ones, where ties cut across levels, functions, and social categories.

These tensions can rise to greater importance when hostile parties are thrown together and forced to interact, especially if they have to rely on each other for reasonable outcomes. This statement challenges a classic social-psychological cliché, based on a famous experiment by Muzafer and Carolyn Sherif, that groups in conflict who suddenly find themselves dependent on each other for survival develop "superordinate goals" which relieve the tensions; they discovered this by fostering group rivalry and then imposing a crisis at a summer camp.[22] But that was summer camp, not a corporation. Experience from joint labor-management participation in problem solving suggests that there are circumstances in which hostility may increase, rather than decrease. If no attempt has been made to create a more integrative system, to resolve tensions and improve communication before the meeting, and if the situation is frustrating—as meetings can easily be—the emotions may rise to the surface, and members of the opposing camps may start blaming each other for team problems. At British Rail, participation by worker representatives in management meetings resulted in increased tension between managers and workers, especially because worker representatives tended to include those more critical of management.[23]

Successful labor-management committees that seem to belie this do so not because participation automatically created a "team" out of adversaries but because careful groundwork was laid before the parties ever came together to begin joint problem solving. The Sherifs' hypothesis seems to be borne out by the cooperative relationship of the automobile manufacturers and the United Auto Workers, making mutual concessions in a time of crisis, where the "superordinate goal" is survival of the U.S. auto industry. But the two groups got to the point at which joint participation was possible only because of preceding efforts to improve communication, demonstrate good faith, and remove irritants.

Thus, "power" and "community" can run at cross-purposes. The more forces there are that fan the political flames within a participative "team," the more likely it is that members will feel uncommitted to the team and unwilling to invest scarce organizational time to make it work. "Political" conflicts and tensions need not be conscious or overt to be disruptive; there may simply be subtle discomforts that members can barely articulate which tell them that this is a place to withhold commitment.

The myth of "team." "Inequality" and "politics" in team discussions are not generically so bad. After all, the people we are talking about have learned to live with both in the rest of their service in the corporate hierarchy. Dominance of the "best"—most skilled, most informed—participators seems likely to produce better decisions. "Political" discussions may mean that a variety of interests are more accurately reflected in ultimate decisions. So the solution to the problems of lowered commitment that these phenomena create should not lie in expecting the skilled and informed to stay out of discussions or those with special needs or interests to forget them. But that "solution"—holding back—is in fact what is fostered by the next dilemma of participation: "team" mythology.

The mythology that surrounds the idea of "team" in many organizations holds that differences among members do not exist— because they are now a "team"—and therefore it is not legitimate to acknowledge them or talk about them. Everyone has to act as if they were all sharing equally in the operations of the group. While inside the team, they have to pretend that they do not see that some are more able than others, or that the highest-level people are dominating, or that the chair is railroading another decision through. Where "team" mythology is strong, only an outsider— a consultant or facilitator or naive visitor—can open it for examination.

In some organizations (or perhaps it is an American phenomenon), the idea of participation is imbued with a mystique that makes legitimate differentiation among participants difficult. Falling back on the external hierarchy is easier for a group than developing internal rankings, because the hierarchy was created by someone else and does not force the group members to confront their own differences or inadequacies. Even though implicit "rankings" are manifest in practice, as the group carries out its deliberations, it is threatening to the fragile solidarity of a newborn team to acknowledge them. This is a good example of "pluralistic ignorance": everyone knows individually but assumes that no one else does. And as long as no one says it aloud, it might not even be true.

Thus, the members who feel out of the group cannot bring up their concerns because of the myth that everyone is in. People with less to contribute because they are less informed do not feel comfortable seeking help in getting more information to contribute more because of the myth that everyone has an equal chance to contribute. At the same time, the dominant participators might feel slightly guilty or uneasy about their absorption of a major share of the air time, so they decide to keep quiet for a meeting or two, thereby depriving the group of speedier motion toward solutions.

I have heard variants of all of these feelings expressed by members of participative groups. The more task-driven the group, the more they are muted in the urgency of the task, but they still exist where "participation" is assumed to mean rote equality, nondifferentiation. The task may get accomplished, but people harbor secret feelings that participation is not worth the emotional drain, or they may decide that involvement makes them feel *worse* rather than better. Or they simply stop coming to meetings.

Differentiation within a participative team is difficult, of course, in segmentalist corporate cultures that have not found a way to make people feel important or valued for their contributions unless they are in charge. Teams of peers, for example, might thus prefer to pretend that no one is any different from anyone else rather than have it appear that some are admitting to being less important on some issue. But again, where groups are task-driven they may manage to create some kinds of differentiation without too much trouble: individual assignments, choice of a leader or chair, nods to specialized competencies.

However, there are some kinds of distinctions among members that it is difficult for *any* team to make—some decisions that might be better handled by a hierarchy rather than by participation, as we see in the next dilemma.

"It is hard to fire your friend." If a team works, it often develops close bonds which mean that people cannot always be open and honest with one another for fear of hurting or because of norms developed in the group. Groups develop a variety of social and emotional pressures resulting from friendship that make it difficult sometimes for people to confront one another, rate one another accurately, or discipline one another. Thus, there are some issues for which managers need to step in and take responsibility. For example, if teams are asked to evaluate the performance of their members, they often resist singling out individuals either positively or negatively and want to give everybody the same rating. There are some issues on which it is a relief to have a higher-status authority figure who simply takes over and decides; it would be too difficult, or too emotionally pressuring, for the group itself.

DILEMMAS OF LINKING TEAMS TO THEIR ENVIRONMENT

"You had to be there": problems of turnover. Team spirit is ineffable; it does not reduce to a set of events that can easily be described to someone who did not share the experience—as anyone knows who has ever tried to tell a husband or wife about the "high" of everyone in the office up against a deadline, pulling together after hours to rush out a major report. Somehow, it cannot mean the same thing in the retelling. Newcomers, latecomers, and outsiders have not shared the group's experiences, cannot see what all the fuss is about, and may even be put off by the enthusiasm of

team members. They are less likely to understand the previous problems that current practices were designed to solve, and therefore the practices.

For example, this dialogue took place in a work-unit team discussing its operations; two newcomers had just joined:

NEWCOMER 1: I feel we're supposed to be confessing something, and I don't know what I'm supposed to be confessing. . . .

NEWCOMER 2: I feel you're all dealing in abstracts all the time. I hope something comes out of this that makes us more efficient. I see you've got a "machine," but I don't know what it's supposed to make.

OLD-TIMER: Getting together like this is very helpful if everyone's desirous of improving. It's different in here in our attitudes, even our vocabulary. Inviting a newcomer does impose a problem for them. We have a responsibility to help them.

The newcomer situation is clearly less of a problem where the team is a clearly bounded work unit and new people simply do not enter. It is also less of a problem at innovating companies operating in integrative modes, like Chipco and Hewlett-Packard, where there is a shared culture in the organization, where newcomers are likely to understand "teams" because of having had similar experiences in another part of the system, or where there is an explicit educational socialization process for newcomers or late arrivals. But it is more of a problem for committees, task forces or "forums" that have looser boundaries and greater turnover of the population of attendees. At the Salem bearing plant, even production work teams suffered from too much turnover. The churning of team members because of movement between shifts to permit seven-day operation hindered the formation of strong relationships and the transfer of information. Supervisors, too, rotated every six months; just as they became familiar with the team, they were rendered "lame ducks."[24]

At the least, some team momentum is dissipated in the need to form new relationships and bring newcomers up to speed. Just as when there are long delays between meetings, the group may start spending more time catching up than advancing on the task. Moreover, the new people may all have new suggestions. There was so much variance in attendance for one fifteen-person task force at a high-tech company that five meetings all began by repeating the information provided at the first one. Regular attendees were so frustrated that soon *they* stopped coming, too.

Even more damaging situations can arise when the newcomer has managerial power and can undercut the group's work or take the team in new directions. By not understanding the team's history or the importance of what seem to a stranger like intangible and even "silly" aspects of team spirit, even a favorably disposed manager may unknowingly eliminate some factors responsible for the team's results: "Why do we need a conference room when space is so scarce?" One of the major reasons for the erosion of participation and autonomous work teams at the General Foods Topeka plant was a leadership vacuum after the managers involved in initiating the system left; later managers had too little understanding of it or vision of what it could be.[25]

Thus, turnover is a problem for teams not only because experienced people leave, but because new people enter. So that a team does not have to constantly repeat itself, revise early decisions, or find its work suddenly changed, continuity of people is clearly required, or at least the kind of socialization to a common culture more characteristic of innovating organizations.

The fixed-decision problem is another important continuity/ stability issue. The process of "participation" implies the ability to be involved in a wider, and sometimes open-ended, set of decisions. But the requirements of efficient tasks make progress toward the group's goals dependent on "fixing" some decisions so that they are effectively removed from constant negotiation in the participation arena. Furthermore, it is frustrating both to team members and to those setting their own expectations based on team outputs to constantly have the ground shifted, to review and re-argue what appeared to have been settled. This angry dialogue occurred at a worker-management planning-council meeting at "Sound, Incorporated," discussing whether to reopen the question of a four-day week, which was low on the original priority list:

WORKER REP I [*Angrily*]: We keep going over the same thing.

WORKER REP II: Yeah, we've been going over the same thing, whether to issue something like this—

MANAGER I: I haven't attended all the meetings, but I thought we agreed this was down the list—

PROFESSIONAL: To me this is evidence of something we discussed before. If we made a decision, were we willing to stick by it? Now, we set up a list of priorities . . . we voted . . . okay, those three top priorities have been set up, and we have to stick to them.

REP I: You already—

PROFESSIONAL: Wait a minute—

REP I: You already changed the list.

WORKER REP III [*Sarcastically*]: No, we didn't.

REP I: How many times? My point is that those people want us to work on the four-day week, and no one seems to be willing to do anything about that.

MANAGER II [*Loudly*]: That is why we set priorities—so we could work at these things in order.

REP I: I thought we also decided that we could change anything we decided on at any time.[26]

Participation need not mean that everything needs to be created from scratch again as soon as new people are involved to give them a sense of "full" participation. This would be ridiculous and wasteful, as well as extremely frustrating for all the people who have already put in time. For example, once a team has invented a new performance-appraisal system, this issue has to be removed from the participation arena long enough for costs of the new system to be recovered. So some decisions are always fixed and operate as constraints, whether they are constraints from managers or simply past decisions or commitments to be honored. This needs to be made clear to each new team or each new participant.

But the fixed-decision requirement creates a paradox: participatory processes are established to involve organization members in decisions at one point, but then some things (parameters) get set, which later members have to live with, setting constraints on action. Thus, more "participation" is theoretically possible toward the beginning or in newer situations, when the ground rules are being established, or in situations where dramatic change is desired, than later in a system's life. This may be why standing committees on long-ago-decided subjects seem so boring and unappealing, while task forces inventing or creating a new system are so exciting: there is more participation and more power in the second instance. Thus, except in early stages or in revolutionary situations, participation will always be constrained by previous and, therefore, fixed decisions which place limits on debate and action possibilities. It is also likely that whoever the constraint setters are—managers or employee representatives or longer-term team members or simply the weight of organizational tradition—they will be the targets of some resentment from those who did not participate *then* and want to open an issue *now*.

At the same time, the reasons for participation include broader involvement and organizational renewal (i.e., better problem solving). Thus, continuity and fixed-decision requirements, which help the *team* do its work, need to be balanced by other organizational considerations: giving new people a chance, replacing older team members who have too much ownership of their points of view to consider new options in the light of external changes, broadening the team's perspective, suggesting revisions made possible by new technology, questioning what was "fixed" in order to search for the next generation of systems or programs. Especially in "entrepreneurial" and growing organizations, teams may never experience the degree of continuity and stability that they desire, and an air of constant negotiation will surround team deliberations.

The more that participation is localized and deals with issues under the team's control, the easier it is for the team to find enough stability to make progress on its tasks while permitting the organization to seek renewal by creating new problem-solving teams.

"Suboptimization": too much team spirit. What if the team works together so well that it closes itself off from the rest of the organization, creating its own segmentation? A group can become *too much* involved in its own goals and activities and lose sight of the larger context in which it is operating. For example, the kinds of things that can help a group pull together—a retreat offsite to communicate better, a sense of specialness and unique purpose, private language and working arrangements—can also wall it off from everyone else. At one innovative factory designed around self-regulated work teams with a great deal of power over their own activities, engaged in completing whole subassemblies of engine parts, the only serious problems the plant encountered involved cross-team competition and lack of interest in collaboration on issues affecting the whole plant.

This is what management theorists call "suboptimization": a group optimizing its own subgoals but losing sight of the larger goals to which they are supposedly contributing. This occurred in one major company that had established a series of employee-manager task forces to develop recommendations for new personnel-related programs. One of them was so carried away by its own momentum and enthusiasm for the task that it began to communicate directly with employees as though its recommended program were a *fait accompli*. None of them bothered to communicate with the others, even though the proposals they were developing had implications for the other groups' plans and, occasionally, overlapped them.

So while team spirit is a good thing for the team's operations, the group has to remember its relationship to the larger organization and has to be encouraged to remain open to the outside rather than closing itself off. The cultural-island problem that killed the Petrocorp Marketing Service Department's project can be generated by the group itself, especially if the next dilemma is not handled.

Stepping on toes and territories: the problem of power. The team-spirit dilemma leads us to the larger question of the link between a participative group and the rest of the organization: the power problems that arise because there are other constituencies who also feel that they have a stake in the problem with which the participative team is dealing. The team needs to be linked appropriately to these other parties, ideally from the beginning. Indeed, those whose legitimate territory involves the issues around which the participation is occurring should themselves be included in planning for it or carrying it out. An early task is to identify all the parties with a legitimate stake in the issue and decide how they will be involved and informed as the activities are carried out.

Power is a particular problem: managers do not want to give it up.[27] And why should they? In many segmentalist corporations, supervisors and middle managers, as I have shown elsewhere, feel sufficiently powerless anyway so that they may be even more resistant to schemes that take away what limited authority they feel they have and do not also give them something else to do to feel important and useful.[28] Sometimes they have reason to be fearful, as companies discover how participation in the form of team "self-management" cuts down the number of supervisors required. But more often they merely feel they are losing control (as in concerns by managers about flextime) without getting a meaningful new role to play, or that they are giving up rights to make decisions and will now be forced to bow to the will of the group.

Unions may also resist participatory programs out of concern about encroachments into their prerogatives if they cooperate with management. American unions are gradually coming to support various modes of worker involvement in planning, problem solving, or decision making, but there may still be skepticism about the potential for "co-optation": reducing union power by getting workers to identify with management.

"NIH" (not invented here): the problems of ownership and transfer. It is a familiar organizational phenomenon, especially in segmentalist cultures, that organization units want to do things their own way and are reluctant to adopt somebody else's solution. But the do-it-yourself mentality can conflict with building on the results of a participating team's efforts. This is less of a problem, of course, if the participants simply constitute a work unit that is solving its own problems with no implication that anyone else will need to do the same thing, and more of a problem if the team is set up to devise programs and procedures that could be potentially useful elsewhere: a task force, a model team, or a pilot project.

The NIH problem highlights another apparent contradiction of participation in large organizations: participation appears to suggest that by definition, everyone will have a voice in new systems and developments that fall within the arena for participation; but the realities of the division of labor and constraints of time mean that some people are going to be the recipients of programs designed by others. Some people are inevitably left out. The same ideas that some arrived at by high participation and that seem so intelligent and useful to them may be rejected by other parts of the organization simply because these creative team ideas are now imposed givens which they played no role in shaping. One division of a leading manufacturing organization, for example, set up a task force to review its pay program, within the limits of corporate policy. The new program was met with great success inside the division, and it received universal praise from top corporate executives. But taskforce members seemed certain that no other division would adopt the same system, despite the team's willingness to turn over all its records and to make presentations about the program.

Simple jealousy may play a role. The fact that power goes to pioneers or plan developers rather than to administrators of someone else's plan can apply to teams or work units as well as individuals. Furthermore, a work unit may feel that it needs its *own* identity and flavor—and how can that program which works so well over there in that foreign territory possibly fit *us*?

There are always some NIH problems around diffusion of any organizational innovation, but somehow the problems seem worse when a participative process was involved in developing the innovation. Maybe managers and employees resent their peers' successes more than they resent having new systems pushed down as a result of top-management deliberations. Maybe the existence of participation has to imply decentralization: local units' putting their own stamp on things, coming to their own decisions, shaping their own programs—a diversity of expression within a common culture. But this latter assumption, which sounds reasonable on its face, has to be balanced against the need for an organization to learn from its own experience—meaning, in this case, the experience of its parts. Aside from those programs or systems which have to be organization-wide, for legal or efficiency reasons, there would be duplication and waste if each area invented everything from scratch—similar to the problems we saw earlier around the fixed-decision dilemma.

So transfer of results is important. In some kinds of organizations it would seem almost impossible if left voluntary. At one extreme, companies like "Southern Insurance" and "Meridian Telephone" operate in an atmosphere of enough scarcity and peer resentment that programs pushed down from the top have almost a better chance of being adopted. At the other extreme, companies like Chipco that reward people for having an entrepreneurial spirit and inventing their own jobs encourage managers to devise their own program rather than accepting someone else's—even if it conflicts with someone else's or reduces efficiency.

But there are also ways to set up problem-solving teams that are more likely to have their results and solutions diffused throughout the organization or repeated elsewhere. For example, representatives of other areas can routinely meet with the participating team. Or team membership can include some people from nonlocal areas, who will be the carriers of the idea back to their home territories (if *they* remember to keep their back-home constituents informed and involved).

"A time to live and a time to die." While it is easy for teams to take on a life of their own, participation needs constant renewal, for the sake of both team members and the organization. Even local work-unit teams seem to experience burnout after about eighteen months of intense activity; this is a common report from companies experienced with large numbers of quality teams or semiautonomous work teams. Periods of intensity need to alternate with periods of distance in order to give people the energy to continue, and so new teams form or rev up just as old teams begin to drop out.

In other forms of participation, such as task forces or councils, the question of life cycle is different. Bodies that are intended to be permanent may simply need to change their membership periodically to get new representatives and new ideas. But task forces or other ad hoc problem-solving devices may appropriately dissolve as their work is completed—even though some of them may want to continue the euphoria of organizational centrality and turn themselves into standing committees.

Organizations often do not think of how they will ensure the continuity of generations when they launch participation. But planning for the birth and death of teams is important for the organization's ability to reap the full benefits of participation. Those who are left out of one round of participative activity can know that they will be included in the future; those among the "elite" of participators know that they will be re-merging with the organizational masses in their regular jobs. What former participants can leave behind is a legacy of their learning to be used to train and involve new participants, to smooth the passing for the dying and the birth for the neophyte. As these cycles become institutionalized, other linking issues become easier; participating teams and the ability to be effective team members are spread throughout the organization, cutting through it in many ways.

DILEMMAS OF EVALUATION

The "great expectations" trap: hoping for an organizational Utopia. It is important to remember that regardless of how well participation works, it will not solve *all* organizational problems. We have never created the perfect organization yet, and it is unlikely that we will in the future—if perfect means problem-free. However, by the use of participative techniques we can at least come closer to organizations that can involve their employees in staying ahead of change. Participatory systems are often painted by their proponents as organizational Utopias that will automatically improve everything. But it is not participation *per se* that has benefits for the company as much as other things associated with it.

With respect to productivity, experience shows that results can be mixed and can vary even in the same organization from department to department. Furthermore, the extent to which the organization allows for or facilitates participation may not be as large a contributor to productivity as formerly thought. Other factors, such as improved goal setting or training, account for increases in productivity in studies where participation has been offered as the major contributor. This was certainly true at both the Chestnut Ridge plant and the Petrocorp Marketing Services Department. Participation provided the *occasion* for broadening the skill base of employees and taking advantage of their talents to solve problems and invent needed programs.

If a system of participation does not automatically improve productivity, it also does not automatically counter the "alienation" and withdrawal of people in closely supervised, low-skill, repetitive jobs. The nature of the job itself—technology and job content— needs to be tackled first, and then interest in and favorable response to participation might follow.[29]

Increased *satisfaction* is more often a "guaranteed" result of participatory processes than increased *performance*, and satisfaction and performance are not always related. In one study, people with an "internal locus of control" (those who see outcomes as determined by themselves) performed better when they could plan their own assembly procedures, while those with an "external locus of control" (who see others controlling outcomes) performed better when a manager planned for them. (However, both groups were most *satisfied* in the self-planning condition.) But for some people, already "saturated" by involvement in *too many* decisions, even satisfaction may not result from participation; they would rather be *less* involved in meetings.[30]

Participation can have a few positive effects and no negative effects and still disappoint people. Disappointment with the results of participation, for both leaders and employees, is likely to be proportional to the amount that was initially promised. There is a tendency to try to sell participation by allowing expectations to float upward and hiding the problems in fine print. But organizations that appear to promise a great deal—that make it easy for "great expectations" to develop—can also disappoint people more. There is more frustration and cynicism if expectations that are aroused are not fulfilled. We can see some of this cynicism interwoven with the favorable reports in accounts of employee-owned-and-run companies like IGP (International Group Plans) in Washington.[31]

Part of the potential for disappointment in participative systems lies in the way in which most of us judge any new, change-oriented system. It is very easy for all of us to forget what the alternatives are when we evaluate our current situation. So new systems are often judged not in terms of how much better they are than others, but in terms of how far short of their promises they fall.[32]

It is just this problem of expectations that managers often mention as a reason (or an excuse) not to try new programs which could expand opportunity and power: "Let's not arouse expectations we can't meet and end up with employees who are more troubled than before." But this is a good excuse for inaction. It is possible to manage expectations by setting realistic and attainable goals. If people are given realistic information at the outset about exactly what they can expect, and are not promised everything, then they can calibrate their own personal goals accordingly. This means communicating clearly exactly what will and will not come out of this process for management and employees, exactly what benefits might or might not occur for employees' careers, and exactly how results will be measured.

Dashed hopes will not be totally eliminated just because there is better communication when expectations are set; the imagination/reality gap may be narrowed rather than closed. Some people may be initial skeptics about participation—e.g., managers doubting that there will be any results at all worth the time, workers doubting that management really means it—but others may be incurable romantics, imagining a more perfect end state than is realistic, and a less bumpy path to get there. And there are still others who may know better but still want a "quick fix"—the one-time program that can keep the employees happy and producing for all time so that managers will not have to worry about employee performance anymore.

Richard Walton, the Harvard Business School professor involved in many new-plant start-ups using participative teams, has pointed to two equally important errors in these situations: *management pessimism* and *management optimism*. Undervaluing the potential of employees and hemming them in with too many rules and restrictions can lead to as many problems as overestimating what employees will be able to do without guidance and periodic redirection. These two types of errors correspond to a paradox inherent in evolutionary processes: In the beginning of a new team system or organization being managed by participation, there is a "human-resource gap," in that people may have less skill or experience with a problem than the amount of opportunity for dealing with it. Later in an organization's or team's life, when many decisions have been made, there may be a "human-resource surplus," in that people now have more skill and experience than they can apply. People become more skilled just as the system becomes more routinized. Thus, managers have to be careful to let the reality of what the system lets people do correspond to their developmental stage: more attention to helping people get skills in the beginning, and not expecting too much of them; more attention to giving people a chance to use their skills once they have experience, and not suddenly reverting to lower expectations as the period of pioneering and invention dies down.[33]

I should mention another sense in which more participative arrangements do not constitute organizational Utopias: they may guarantee more involvement *in general* without ensuring that all groups get equal access to the vehicles. A greater degree of organizational participation by itself is no guarantee that more equal treatment of women and minorities, for example, will automatically follow. "Participation" alone will not wipe out sexism and racism.[34] Although the more highly innovating organizations I examined also seemed to be more integrative in every sense, including equal opportunity, this is not necessarily an automatic result of greater employee participation; teams, as I showed earlier, can be exclusionary and politicized too. Finally, we know practically nothing about the effects of increased participation at work on relationships outside of work, such as family life. While past evidence would suggest positive "spillovers,"[35] several company human-resource managers are concerned that the increased absorption in work which accompanies intense participative problem solving might show up in family tensions.

"A little taste whets the appetite": what next? Let's assume that all goes well. The teams do their work effectively; the participative vehicles produce useful solutions and a satisfied sense of involvement. There is then one further dilemma of participation, but one that is still largely hypothetical rather than arising from experience: the question of whether participation is appetite-stimulating rather than appetite-satisfying. Once employees get a taste of decision making on a small scale, do they inevitably want to go on to decision making on a larger scale? Do changes in participation on the job lead to more political activities off it? Once more employees have a chance to develop their own work systems or personnel programs, do they want to go beyond this to play a role in other business activities? After tasting some participation, do they get hungrier for more—dissatisfied with the amount they now have, forgetting that they had even less before? Will "gain sharing," for example—a scheme for giving workers a piece of the action when productivity goes up, a system now being considered at places like Honeywell—have to become the standard practice?

There are no real answers to these questions yet, though they are being asked with increasing frequency. Some experiences with worker participation, such as the ones John Witte reported at "Sound, Incorporated," or my observations at Honeywell, Hewlett-Packard, and Chestnut Ridge, indicate, first, that there are sufficient problems with participation that no one wants to go whole hog very quickly; second, that there is a preference on everyone's part to keep some issues out of the participation arena; and third, that it is possible to keep participation bounded without negative effects on morale.

THE NEED FOR BALANCE

Participation would appear to work best when it is well managed. "Well-managed" systems have these elements: a clearly designed management structure and involvement of the appropriate line people; assignment of meaningful and manageable tasks with clear boundaries and parameters; a time frame, a set of accountability and reporting relationships, and standards that groups must meet; information and training for participants to help them make participation work effectively; a mechanism for involving all of those with a stake in the issue to avoid the problems of power and to ensure for those who have input or interest a chance to get involved; a mechanism for providing visibility, recognition, and rewards for teams' efforts; and clearly understood processes for the formation of participative groups, their ending, and the transfer of the learning from them.

Note, of course, that most, if not all, of the means to resolve the dilemmas of participation are somewhat more readily attainable in integrative, as opposed to segmentalist, systems. At Honeywell's largest division, the management steering committee for the division's innovative projects has set up guidelines for handling each of those issues and a format for communicating them as part of the training for new team members.

Innovators needing to build teams to carry out innovative projects do better when they manage expectations from the start, neither promising nor expecting too much and allowing people to define for themselves the level of involvement they desire, opting out of participation in areas they do not care about. Political sensitivity is also important, finding a way to involve parties whose power might be at stake and giving them a reason to support the changes. When "more participation" *is* the change, this becomes even more critical.

But while encouraging participation, innovators still maintain leadership. "Leadership" consists in part of keeping everyone's mind on the shared vision, being explicit about "fixed" areas not up for discussion and the constraints on decisions, watching for uneven participation or group pressure, and keeping time bounded and managed. Then, as events move toward accomplishments, leaders can provide rewards and feedback, tangible signs that the participation mattered.

It is clear that managing participation is a balancing act: between management control and team opportunity; between getting the work done quickly and giving people a chance to learn; between seeking volunteers and pushing people into it; between too little team spirit and too much.

There are no rules or formulas for making participation work that substitute for the sensitive judgment of leaders about how to make the right trade-offs in a particular situation. A Chipco manufacturing manager, excited by the results from his team, cautioned his colleagues to use their own judgment when they heard about problems in a particular team: "Don't believe everything or every gripe you hear. A survey you run tomorrow may look radically different from the one you run today. People don't say what they mean when they're feeling down or frustrated. Subordinates may push you to 'act more like a boss,' but their interest is usually more in seeing someone else brought to heel than in getting bossed themselves."

Managing participation is a matter of balance—and patience. "Hang in there, baby, and don't give it up," an innovative manager encouraging the use of teams advised his reports. "Try not to 'revert' just because everything seems to go sour on a particular day." A vice-president of a progressive Midwestern communications company wrote me that she was discovering that her company's QWL programs were teaching her patience, a virtue that little in her previous career had taught her how to cultivate. But this is central to making participation work, to netting the greater gains that can come with team involvement. It takes longer to weld people into a team than to order them around; it takes longer to teach people a variety of jobs than to give them one simplified task. And it will take time for either the positive results of the participative system or any negative results of the authoritarian kind to reveal themselves. So wherever there is pressure for *quick* results, people will be unlikely to support participation.

But the long-term impact of well-managed participatory vehicles for energizing the grass roots and involving them in innovation should be a more adaptive organization, one that can more easily live with, and even stay ahead of, change. It is not so much that employee motivation will be improved as that the organization may be better able to tap and take advantage of employee ideas. Employees, in turn, may be more adaptable—more skilled and thus more flexible, more able to move with changes, and more favorably disposed toward management initiatives for change in which they know they can play a role.

The role of organization members in adaptive change, then, comes about through periodic integrative opportunities to step beyond their roles in the hierarchy of core jobs and get involved in team problem-solving efforts. These constitute episodes of drama and excitement, of almost communal solidarity, that punctuate an otherwise more routinized set of task activities which occur by necessity in the line structure.[36] These participative opportunities constitute the transition mechanisms by which the organization and its people see the need for changes and exercise control over the change process.

In short, participation is not a "program" or a "formula," and it may not necessarily be a permanent way of doing everything. Like the transition rituals of traditional societies that alternate with the more routine everyday structure, participatory processes should be seen as task oriented, integrative rituals of high involvement and transformation—a way to engage many talents in the mastery of change.

NOTES

1. This has sometimes been labeled a "Hawthorne Effect," after the classic studies at the Western Electric Hawthorne Works in the 1930s. In one of the Hawthorne experiments, a team of women workers were given a separate work area where their production would be measured while a variety of environmental conditions such as lighting and rest breaks were varied. Productivity tended to go up regardless of the changes in physical conditions. One conclusion was that being singled out to be in a high-visibility experiment was highly motivating in and of itself; calling this the "Hawthorne Effect" was in part a way of dismissing the claims made by new "human relations" programs, arguing instead that any change involving increased management attention and special treatment would have positive effects for a little while. But of course, as I have pointed out elsewhere, there was more going on at Hawthorne than just

the effects of an experiment. The women had their own separate territory. They were freed from supervision and instead had a research coach, so they became a team (an early example of a self-managed team inside a conventional factory?) helping one another do the work. A few who did not get along were replaced, helping the team coalesce. There was constant feedback on performance. An ambitious young woman saw this as her chance to catch the eye of top management and advance—and indeed, these workers *were* more visible to the top. There were special celebrations, such as ice cream parties after regular medical exams. Hawthorne, then, was one of our early experiments in increasing opportunity and power through participation and attention to "quality of work life." (One of the original reports of Hawthorne is F. J. Roethlisberger and William J. Dickson, *Management and the Worker*, Cambridge, Mass.: Harvard University Press, 1939.)

2. I am using the term participation to mean involvement in a team with joint responsibility for a product—which might be a set of recommendations, a plan, a decision, a solution to a work-area problem, or the output of the work area itself. For the purposes of this analysis, I am equating participation with teamwork, and participative management with the building and nurturing of a collaborative team that is more fully consulted, is more fully informed, and shares responsibility for planning and reaching outcomes. But it is important to note that a wide range of policies and practices not involving teamwork are currently in use in companies under the *label* of participation, including employee-opinion surveys, suggestion systems, and job enrichment. See Rosabeth Moss Kanter, "Participation," *National Forum*, Spring 1982.

3. Victor H. Vroom and Philip W. Yetton, *Leadership and Decision-Making*, Pittsburgh: University of Pittsburgh Press, 1973.

4. Thus, there are times when autonomy and individual responsibility are more important than participation and team responsibility. Invention and innovation are often not "democratic" processes, and they may sometimes be best pursued by individuals who care passionately about an issue and build their *own* team of supporters and workers. . . . Participation and autonomy are two different—and occasionally contradictory—forms of empowerment. In two book-publishing firms, one a "collective" and the other a conventional hierarchy, the distinction was clear. Some employees were happier in the low-participation hierarchy than in the high-participation collective, because while those in the collective had a greater voice in decisions and a greater involvement in tasks outside their job, they also had more intrusion from others who had some right to a say in these same activities—and in their jobs. (Frederic Engelstad, Norwegian sociologist, personal communication on work in progress.)

5. Daniel Zwerdling, "At IGP, It's Not Business as Usual," in R. M. Kanter and B. A. Stein, eds., *Life in Organizations*, New York: Basic Books, 1979, pp. 349–63.

6. Victor H. Vroom, *Some Personality Determinants of the Effects of Participation*, Englewood Cliffs, N.J.: Prentice-Hall, 1960.

7. J. Timothy McMahon, "Participative and Power-Equalized Organizational Systems," *Human Relations*, 29 (1976): 203–14.

8. John F. Witte, *Democracy, Authority, and Alienation in Work,* Chicago: University of Chicago Press, 1980, pp. 122–23.

9. *Ibid.*

10. *Ibid.,* p. 146.

11. *Ibid.,* p. 32.

12. Richard Hackman's research on job design supports this. The ideal design involves: experienced meaningfulness (task significance); task identity or responsibility for a defined chunk; and knowledge of results. Hackman and Greg R. Oldham, *Job Design,* Reading, Mass.: Addison-Wesley, 1980.

13. Bertil Gardell, "Autonomy and Participation at Work," *Human Relations,* 30 (1977): 513–33.

14. R. M. Powell and J. L. Schlacter, "Participative Management: A Panacea?" *Academy of Management Journal,* 14 (1971): 165–173.

15. Richard J. Long, "The Relative Effects of Share Ownership vs. Control on Job Attitudes in an Employee-Owned Company," *Human Relations,* 31 (1978): 753–63.

16. Mauk Mulder, "Power Equalization through Participation?" *Administrative Science Quarterly,* 16 (1971): 31–40.

17. Jane Mansbridge, "Time, Emotion, and Inequality: Three Problems of Participative Groups," *Journal of Applied Behavioral Science,* 9 (1973): 351–77.

18. Vroom, *Personality Determinants,* Thomas L. Ruble; "Effects of One's Locus of Control and the Opportunity to Participate in Planning," *Organizational Behavior and Human Performance,* 16 (June 1976): 63–73.

19. E. Linden Hilgendorf and Barrie L. Irving, "Workers' Experience of Participation: The Case of British Rail," *Human Relations,* 29 (1976): 471–505. Furthermore, it has also been found that the greater the autonomy and skill level in the job, the greater the interest in and demand for participation; see Gardell, "Autonomy and Participation."

20. On "outsiders" or people who are "different" in a work group: Rosabeth Moss Kanter, *Men and Women of the Corporation,* New York: Basic Books, 1977, Chapter 8. On the "competence multiplier": S. S. Weiner, "Participation, Deadlines, and Choice," in J. G. March and J. P. Olsen, *Ambiguity and Choice in Organizations,* Bergen, Norway: Universitetsforlaget, 1976, pp. 225–50.

21. Richard Walton, "Establishing and Maintaining High Commitment Work Systems," in J. R. Kimberly and R. H. Miles, *The Organizational Life Cycle,* San Francisco: Jossey-Bass, 1980, p. 227.

22. Muzafer Sherif *et al., Intergroup Conflict and Cooperation: The Robbers Cave Experiment,* Norman, Okla.: University Book Exchange, 1961.

23. Hilgendorf and Irving, "Workers' Experience of Participation."

24. Walton, "High Commitment Work Systems," p. 237.

25. *Ibid.,* p. 287.

26. Witte, *Democracy, Authority,* p. 65.

27. Some critics argue that most participation is a subtle extension of management control anyway, but in a sophisticated new form.

28. Kanter, *Men and Women of the Corporation*, Chapter 7; "Power Failure in Management Circuits," *Harvard Business Review*, 56 (July-August 1979): 65–75.

29. Gardell, "Autonomy and Participation."

30. On productivity and satisfaction: A. C. Filley and R. J. House, *Managerial Process and Organizational Behavior*, Glenview, Ill.: Scott, Foresman, 1969; Suresh Srivastva *et al., Job Satisfaction and Productivity*, Cleveland: Case Western Reserve School of Management, 1975. On the experiment: Ruble, "Locus of Control." On saturation effects for those already involved in many decisions: Joseph A. Alutto and James A. Belasco, "A Typology for Participation in Organizational Decision Making," *Administrative Science Quarterly*, 17 (1972): 117–25.

31. Zwerdling, "IGP."

32. Rosabeth Moss Kanter and Louis A. Zurcher, "Evaluating Alternatives and Alternative Valuing," *Journal of Applied Behavioral Science*, 9 (1973): 381–97.

33. Walton, "High Commitment Work Systems."

34. Michele Hoyman, "Leadership Responsiveness in Local Unions and Title VII Compliance: Does More Democracy Mean More Representation for Blacks and Women?" *Proceedings of the Industrial Relations Research Association*, December 1979, pp. 29–42.

35. Rosabeth Moss Kanter, *Work and Family in the United States*, New York: Russell Sage Foundation, 1977.

36. Victor Turner, *The Ritual Process*, Chicago: Aldine, 1969.

Testing Skyhook 6

TEAMWORK AND INVOLVEMENT

In an environment of trust and open communication, people working interdependently are able to generate creativity, improvement, and innovation beyond the total of their individual but separate capacities.

—STEPHEN COVEY, *PRINCIPLE-CENTERED LEADERSHIP*

Two heads or more really are better than one when people trust each other and speak freely. More often than not, the results prove that teamwork is more productive than any individual effort. Moreover, the psychological aspects of involvement ensure not only that good ideas are produced but that they have the support they need to work. The involvement process generates a heightened sense of individual commitment, responsibility and ownership for the end product.

A simple self test will begin to help you see how well you are performing. Asking your coworkers "How am I doing?" will complete the picture.

ASK YOURSELF

Test out how well you promote involvement and teamwork by rating the accuracy of the following statements. Use a 1–5 scale ranging from "a little" to "a great extent."

• I believe teamwork can often produce better results than a single person can do on his or her own.	1 2 3 4 5
• I structure work so it can be done by teams as much as possible.	1 2 3 4 5
• I ask for everyone's ideas on decisions that affect our work.	1 2 3 4 5
• I encourage team members to be actively concerned about each other's personal and professional well-being.	1 2 3 4 5
• I encourage my coworkers to discuss ways to improve our team's effectiveness.	1 2 3 4 5

ASK YOUR COWORKERS

If you gave yourself a "4" or "5" rating on each statement, you probably are emphasizing involvement and teamwork. However, you can verify your self-assessment by having a two-part discussion with your coworkers. First, ask them to talk about the importance of teamwork so that you understand it in the same way. Second, ask them for feedback on your performance.

You'll know you're developing a common understanding about the importance of teamwork when you hear comments like these:

> • "Teamwork is absolutely necessary, but it's not for every minute of every day. Sometimes one person can 'just do it' and the rest of us can get on with life."
> • "Setting group goals with joint accountability sets up teamwork from the start. If you have the same goals, you'll have more teamwork."
> • "Protecting diversity is everyone's job, especially the leader's. Different personalities, thinking styles, and viewpoints have to be valued."
> • "Training is required for high-performing teams. There is a lot to learn about facilitating meetings, dealing with differences, and giving helpful feedback."
> • "Teams can get better if they work at it, but teamwork takes time and effort."

After discussing the importance of involvement and teamwork, check out your coworkers' view of your performance by asking them to consider the five items in your self-assessment. You may find it more productive for them to answer the following questions than to give you numerical ratings on each item:

> • What am I doing right now that supports each statement?
> • What else can I do—either more or less—to show greater support for each statement?

As you listen, try to clarify your coworkers' answers and ideas. Express your appreciation for their feedback without becoming defensive. After you've listened, ask yourself, "What am I ready to do to increase involvement and teamwork?" Develop an action plan to build on your strengths and continue to improve.

Skyhook 7

TRANSFORMATIONAL STYLE

What it takes to be a leader in the 1990s and beyond is really handling change.

—ROBERT GOIZUETA,
FORMER CHAIRMAN OF COCA-COLA

As business leaders we have to find out how to make change a satisfier rather than a dissatisfier.

—DAVID T. KEARNS,
FORMER CHAIRMAN OF XEROX

Skyhook 7 Transformational Style—Face change with optimism and a conviction that apparent differences can be reconciled in mutually satisfying ways. Find win-win solutions to traditional conflicts between organization and individual needs, profit and community service, work and play. Old "either-or" thinking needs to shift to an integrative "and-also" mindset. Lead by example and help everyone develop a can-do attitude and a culture of transformation. Move forward with a sense of urgency and patience.

Transformational style, the final skyhook, is both a summation and an extension of the other components of the Skyhooks Leadership Model. It is an approach to leading change that incorporates the other components from vision through teamwork. However, it is more than just technique. Transformational style conveys a philosophy and attitude. It accepts the challenge of change with optimism and enthusiasm and makes change "a satisfier rather than a dissatisfier." At its best, it sees opportunities and possibilities for growth where others see only threats and probabilities of loss.

Robert R. Blake and Jane S. Mouton forecast a dramatic shift in management style in "The Developing Revolution in Management Practices" (1962). Their Managerial Grid provides a framework to compare and contrast a transformational style with other less developmental approaches. The model presents different styles as a function of the concern for the two primary components of any work situation—people and production. If you see an inherent conflict between what needs to be done and those who need to do it, your style likely will be reactionary rather than transformational.

Blake and Mouton based their Managerial Grid on a behavioral sciences foundation rather than on "rule of thumb" or "seat of the pants" efforts. They make points like these:

- Behavioral sciences research shows that there are predictable consequences for human interaction, and, therefore, management and leadership can be learned.

- The Managerial Grid describes nine styles based on the mix of concern for people and production requirements.

- All but one style is based on the "either-or" assumption that conflict between people and production is inevitable—pick one or the other because you can't have them both.

- Task, Country Club, and Impoverished Management styles appear to be very different but are all rooted in the conviction that people and production, the needs of the individual and of the organization, are irreconcilable.

- Only the Team Management style proceeds from a mindset that sees a natural integration of people and production concerns.

- The word "team" emphasizes unity of effort, interdependence, and "moving together."

- Sound and mature interpersonal relations based on trust and mutual support are essential for creativity and innovation.

- The Team Management position on the Managerial Grid is the only one that is transformational because it is the only one that does not see change as a threat to relationships or production.

James O'Toole brings transformational style to life in "The Corporate Rushmoreans," in *Leading Change: the Argument for Values-Based Leadership* (1996). He names current leaders who have done such outstanding jobs of transforming their organizations that they are worthy of having their images chiseled in stone. Like those who take Blake and Mouton's Team Management approach, they are masters of paradox who avoid falling into "either-or" traps. They are able to effectively integrate disparate elements that others are convinced are mutually exclusive.

As O'Toole presents his Rushmorean leaders, he emphasizes that leaders succeed more by virtue of attitude and philosophy than by using how-to techniques. For example:

- Rushmorean leaders are those who can lead change both morally and effectively.

- They practice values-based leadership that is both principled and pragmatic—tactics may change but vision and values are never compromised.

- Failure to lead change has to do with an attitude about followers—without respect and trust for followers, you can't lead them.

- Four Corporate Rushmoreans are Max DePree, Herman Miller; James Houghton, Corning; Robert Galvin, Motorola; and Jan Carlzon, SAS.

- Each Rushmorean leader is dedicated to vision, continuous change and renewal, and common values—trust, integrity, empowerment, involvement, and, especially, respect for people and their potential.

- Rushmorean leaders manage paradox effectively—they strive for continuity *and* change, short- *and* long-term goals, accountability *and* freedom, planning *and* flexibility.

- They use a similar change strategy based on top management support, building on strengths, full participation, and an understanding that change is constant.

- Continuous renewal requires that leaders create conditions for everyone to challenge everything about the status quo, where nothing is sacred except the future and the fundamental values which guide their actions.

Transformational style must be appreciated on two levels. At the most discernible level, it draws on all of the skyhook components previously described. Leaders transform their organizations through vision, trust, open communication, meaningful work, empowerment, and teamwork.

At a more basic level, transformational style rests on a philosophy about the nature of change. Unlike the approaches that strive to minimize change to preserve current performance or relationships, transformational style does not view change in negative or even neutral terms. Change defines our existence: It is life itself. When the change process comes to an end, so does life for biological, social, or economic systems. It is fair to say that when leaders embrace change and engage in transformation, they affirm and celebrate our most vital process.

13

THE DEVELOPING REVOLUTION IN MANAGEMENT PRACTICES

ROBERT R. BLAKE and JANE S. MOUTON

A searching inquiry regarding conventional practices of management is underway. Traditional ways of deploying people to achieve production are being challenged. This examination of many so-called tested and true, yet antiquated, assumptions about managerial behavior which have evolved from "rule of thumb" and "seat of pants" efforts of the past has been impelled by the impact of developments in the behavioral sciences.

The significance of advances made in behavioral sciences during the past decade parallels important strides over the past fifty years in the physical sciences. In the latter, creation of new products, development of new processes, and design of new procedures has resulted in a dramatic transformation of technical aspects of work. The implications of the advent of the behavioral sciences for improvement in the management of people engaged in work are no less than have been and will continue to be as great as the implications of physical sciences regarding new approaches to the technical side of work and productivity.

A SCIENCE OF MANAGEMENT

A most striking consequence of these developments is that a science of management is replacing what only a short time span ago was referred to as the "art of managing." The art of managing people of the immediate past era was something that people either had or did not have. Whether an individual did or did not have it, one basic assumption prevailed. It was that the man who *was* skillful in the art of management couldn't teach it to others, and the person who was not, probably could not learn it no matter how he tried.

The science of management now taking shape is based on two related considerations. On the one hand, research in the behavioral sciences has produced a body of systematic knowledge regarding the consequences of various conditions of human interaction during the performance of both mental and physical work. On the other, new training techniques developed over the past fifteen years now make it practical to teach individuals to use this body of systematic behavioral science knowledge regarding the nature of human conduct in the practice of management. In other words, an applied science of management, founded on systematic techniques, is now at hand.

Over the past decade, particularly in the last five years, a number of America's major corporations have been investigating intensively the implications and consequences for organization improvement that are contained in these concepts and teaching methods. Now is the time for description of theory and technique and for initial evaluation.

Results to date are most encouraging.

In some situations union-management conflict has been relieved and restored to conditions of cooperation and problem-solving.[1] Mutual suspicion and distrust between operating departments and the staff groups intended to serve them has been reduced in others. Disturbed relationships between headquarters and the plants reporting to them also have been corrected through experimental applications of behavioral science concepts.[2] The theory and training methods to be described have been successfully employed to perfect team effectiveness by bringing about more effective decision-making among the management of large industrial organizations.[3] Most interesting is the fact that with only small adaptation, the same concepts of management and techniques of training have been used at operating levels to aid people, who for a decade had been classified as untrainable, to learn how to handle complicated chemical units and electronic equipment.[4] Best judgment available indicates positive profit improvement results from these behavioral science application ventures.

What is being said, then, is this. A revolution in the behavioral sciences is producing a science of management. Simultaneously a revolution in training technology is producing the techniques by which managerial personnel can learn principles of human behavior in such a concrete way as to permit their application in a manner consistent with theoretical specifications in the context of work.

OVERVIEW

I would like to delve more deeply into these important matters in three separate sections of this presentation. The first deals with the basic theory of modern management practices which underlies the remarks made above. I refer to the *Managerial Grid®*, which is a systematic statement describing nine theories of how production through people is accomplished. The most satisfactory theory of production-people integration, entitled team management, is presented here. Each and all of these theories are found in application in management situations today. The *Grid* theory is basic for appreciating the shift from any one management *style* to the application of management *science*. Having completed this presentation, attention then is turned to an examination of the training techniques by which a sound applied science of team management can be taught. Then, I want to indicate what I believe to be the broader implications for the future of this developing revolution in management practices.

I–THE MANAGERIAL GRID: CONDITIONS OF INTERACTION BETWEEN PRODUCTION AND HUMAN RELATIONSHIPS

The Managerial Grid, shown in Figure 1, offers a schematic behavioral science framework for comparing nine theories of interaction between production and human relationships.

The horizontal axis represents *concern for production*. The vertical axis indicates *concern for relationships* among those engaged in production. Each is expressed as a nine-point scale with the one end representing minimum concern and the nine end representing maximum interest. Before going on, however, a word needs to be said about *concerns for* as variables reflecting attitudes underlying the organization of people into production units. The variables do not necessarily reflect *how much* production is obtained or the degree to which human relationship needs are *actually* met. Rather, emphasis here is placed on the degree of *concern for,* because action is based on underlying attitudes which dictate what those actions should or will be.

By orienting these two variables at right angles to one another, nine theories regarding possible relationships between concern for production and concern for relationships can be evaluated. Emphasis is placed on the corners and the midpoint of the grid to bring out the various ways in which production and human relationships interact. While these extreme positions are to be found in pure form only rarely in the production settings of today, nonetheless, many situations are rather close approximations of one or the other of the pure conditions.

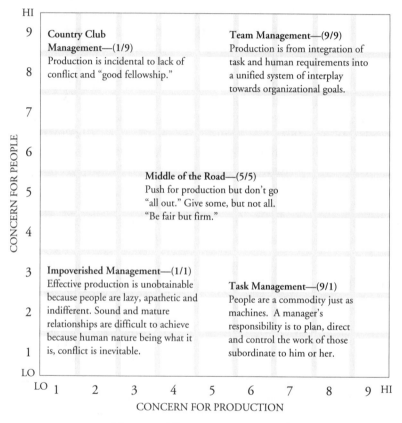

Figure 1. The Managerial Grid

Theories in Which Concern for Production and Concern for Relationships Are Seen to Be in Conflict

Three theories rest on the notion that production requirements and human relations needs essentially are in basic opposition. The logic of the argument rests on two assumptions. One is that the way to achieve production is to push in such a way as to violate people and treat them with suspicion. The other is that if people are treated "nicely," that is in a friendly sociable manner in the work situation, there will be soldiering, dragging of feet and shirking. In other words, it is impossible to obtain high production on the easy notion that people will respond to trust with trust. This is the kind of attitude that says that *concerns for production and concerns for relationships* are in essential conflict with one another; attainment of either one means the other must be sacrificed.

Task Management: The 9/1 Approach to the Production–Human Relations Interaction. The lower right hand corner where 9, high concern for production, intersects 1, low concern for people, represents an approach referred to as *Task Management.* Here the primary concern is for output of the enterprise with people being viewed in terms of their contribution to production. This theory is based on the notion that a manager's central responsibilities are to plan, direct and control the actions of subordinates in such a manner as to achieve the production objectives of the enterprise. Subordinates are expected to react with compliance to various plans, directions and controls placed upon them. The situation is one of authority and obedience with respect to production. Need for understanding and agreement among those engaged in production is not given serious consideration. According to 9/1, a job is a job and someone has to do it. Like machines, people are seen as production tools. They are obligated to comply and execute what they have been told to do.

A 9/1 supervisor questioned by a subordinate reflected his managerial attitude in the following manner.

"These are your instructions. Do it, and don't give me any lip. If there's anything I detest, it's insubordination."

At lower levels, concern for production may be easily thought of in terms of actual *output.* The results of concern for production at the managerial levels, in terms of decision-making and policy formulation, are just as critical as units of output are among operators. The following kind of advice which was given to managers in the middle levels is characteristic of a 9/1 orientation.

"For an executive to challenge orders, directions and instructions, policy and procedures, rules and regulations, etc., smacks of insubordination or lack of cooperation. It shows his failure to understand the need for decisions at higher levels and for direction and control of operations."

Under the 9/1 theory, people should comply with job procedures, specifications, rules and policies which are demanded of them by the more rational organization. Therefore, heavy emphasis is placed on quantifying the efforts and procedures concerned with output. One focus is on measuring the requirements of a job, simplifying it to the maximum degree possible and then training individuals one-by-one to perform the operations according to "scientific" standards. An additional consideration involves intensively evaluating the "fit" between the individual's capacity and requirements for doing the job. The basis of concern for people is that of designing the operations and the work place to minimize effort and fatigue, while obtaining maximum output.

Another important assumption of 9/1 is the sharp and definite division drawn between the planning and the execution of work. Planners plan and doers do. The relationships between those who plan and those who do is on the strictest concepts of authority and obedience. Management exercises authority, in the extreme, over the slightest motions of the doer. The person who performs the operations is obligated to oblige, in the sense of doing what and how he is told.

Management effort can be so perfect as to anticipate an individual's physical needs under a condition of obedience and to prescribe the best conditions of his work in such a way as his participation can only be in the compliant doing. As a result of this authority and obedience basis for cooperation much resistance is generated. Rather than increasing productivity, which clearly is possible under this managerial approach, it may actually be reduced by those who execute the operations in order to avoid being taken advantage of.

The managerial thinking of 9/1 management focuses mostly on the production side. Even here, because of the separation of planning and doing, very little provision for the psychological needs of meaningfulness in work are provided. Meaningfulness for those who plan stems from the challenging mental effort remaining. For those who are planned for, however, the job becomes one of mechanical obedience to another's format. Thus, 9/1 fails to regard needs for meaningfulness of effort. In addition, through the exercise of power via the authority and obedience model, mutual trust, which leads to a sense of personal worth, has been essentially eliminated as a consideration.

An assumption concerning relationships which is basic to 9/1 management, is that the productive unit is the man, and that the dominant relationship in work is the supervisor-subordinate pairs.

The effort is to isolate individuals for working arrangements in order to prevent social relationships or human interaction from interfering with work. The assembly line and the concept of the one-man gang are two familiar procedures for accomplishing this aim. The effectiveness of the informal work group in slowing down production under 9/1 management has been amply documented.

Under these circumstances of a 9/1 orientation tensions among people who are with one another arise in the course of production. When people with ideas seek a way to express them and needs for personal worth and mature human interactions are denied, resistance and conflicts arise. Conflict itself implies a faulty relationship between production needs and human relationships requirements.

As tension erupts, it is necessary to make an effort to deal with it in some manner. The basis of conflict management in 9/1 is mostly in terms of suppression. The phrases "If you don't like it, lump it" or "yours is not to question why, yours is but to do or die" are indicative of a 9/1 approach. Conflict is suppressed by the person in the position of authority. Most systems based on 9/1 provide a rich assortment of *disciplinary* arrangements which can be taken against the individual who fails to obey. If people fail to comply with the obedience requirement, they are seen as troublemakers or weaklings or resistant people. Unfortunately, however, disciplinary action all too frequently fails to correct the cause of the conflict. The sources of the conflict therefore remain essentially unrelieved.

Another symptom of difficulty associated with 9/1 management, particularly on the production axis, is seen in the richness of creative techniques employed by people who are related around the production activity in order to slow production down to a low and sometimes to a disturbing unacceptable level. When this happens, it is clear that the creativity of which people are capable is not being used to enhance production. Rather, the capacity for creative and innovative thinking is being used in ways which are detrimental to work. The 9/1 theory tends, then, to be associated with unsound human relationships among those within the production setting who should be operating in an integrated manner.

The 1/9 Orientation to the Production-Relationship Interaction. The country club approach to production, 1/9, is in many respects the reverse of the 9/1 style. The 1/9 appears contradictory to the very purpose for which an industrial situation is organized, since it places key emphasis on relationships and offers little concern for production.

The approach starts from the opposite end in the sense that relationships among people are seen to be all important, and direct concern for production is minimal. The goal of 1/9 in other words, is to achieve harmonious relationships, without particular regard for the effect on production results. A comfortable or slack work tempo can be maintained within the framework of a happy, secure, social atmosphere.

It is necessary to understand two circumstances in order to appreciate how 1/9 can become an organizational way of life. The first has to do with the history of competitive economics within the plant. Many settings, where profit is on a fixed contract cost plus basis or where there is an acute market shortage and quasi monopolistic conditions exist, constitute situations favorable to the appearance of a 1/9 managerial approach. Under any of these circumstances, the manufacturer can return a profit without being truly effective because there is little or no pressure from competition. As a result, it becomes unattractive to make efficiency moves that spread anxiety and that lead to conflict. It is simpler to take the easy way out and to let things go as they are. Such a decision is negative from the standpoint of genuine production, but it favors the development or maintenance of good relationships. Such relationships, however, are not sound in a basic sense. The point being made here, in other words, is that there are situations where competition pressures are so weak that a profit can be returned without genuinely using or creating the conditions under which people can make an effective contribution to it. As a result, the term "country club" has been used to refer to this approach.

Where results didn't turn out so well as they might, a 1/9 supervisor is likely to express his lack of concern for production in the following manner.

"Don't take it too hard, we all make mistakes. Maybe we'll have better luck next time."

Rather than focusing on the job itself, or the way in which it was done, he assumes that contented people will produce as well as contented cows, if they are given the chance.

Executives also are aware of the need to "be nice" under the 1/9 approach to management. A 1/9 manager whose decision was not looked upon favorably describes his way of proceeding:

"I withdrew my decision to keep harmony, but followed-up on a 'soft sell' basis. You've got to keep making peace with people at all levels by winning allies for your cause."

Not only is the 1/9 managerial theory ineffective in the sense of achieving high output but it is also unlikely to achieve any meaningful human relations gains.

With respect to actual planning and work direction, the 1/9 manager frequently adopts one of two modes of dealing with subordinates, who, of necessity, are looking to him to establish conditions of work. One procedure commonly is described as "I try to lead, rather than push." The assumption is that people should be shown, rather than commanded. They should be supported and aided in their work efforts, in the sense of doing for them those difficult parts of the job for which the supervisor has more technical knowledge rather than allowed or expected to struggle for themselves. Under these conditions people should be willing followers. Other techniques are those of the "soft sell" or pseudo-participation approaches in which the order becomes either a request or the subordinate is led to see the error in his own thinking through gentle persuasion by the supervisor. These and other approaches can be typified by the "be nice" school of thought.

Although work is likely to be planned in an undivided manner, as is true in 9/1, the use of the "group" as a basis for social interaction is frequent in 1/9. Here, members of the work unit get together with the primary goal that of providing good relations among people. Sharing of information, discussing issues that arise for recommended action, family dinners and parties, and so on are all used as means to achieving harmony and happiness by letting people know that management is interested in them as people. However, the best way of understanding the 1/9 approach is to return to the concept of conflict. For some individuals, conflict between themselves and others or even conflicts in which they are not directly involved, except as observers, are experienced as intolerable—something which must be avoided at all costs. The result is that a 1/9 individual tends to operate in such a way as to take whatever actions he can to maintain harmony and to prevent the eruption of conflict in relationships. The actions that he takes as a consequence of this orientation are frequently detrimental to production and seen as "soft" by more production-minded people.

There are many subtle ways in which surface harmony can be maintained and the open appearance of disruptive conflict avoided. One way is to separate those who argue and disagree so that they don't have the opportunity to come into contact with one another. In this way conflict is avoided, even though the advantages that come from the clash of ideas may be thrown out by such a gesture.

Another way is to pour oil on troubled waters. In this way, conflict is smoothed over even though the problem remains underneath the surface. A third is to act in such a way that the conditions of inter-action among people are summarized through generalizations and abstractions that are of such a high level that everyone can agree with them, even though the abstraction or conclusion or summary fails to come to grips with the basic problem. Finally, it frequently is possible to table a decision until tensions reduce, or other issues become more pressing.

The quotations below are ones typical of country club manage-ment. The "be nice" approach, which smothers conflict or which seeks to avoid the conditions that will produce it, can lead to a situ-ation of harmony on the relationship side, but a result is that production requirements can simultaneously suffer severely. While the 1/9 manager is seen as a likeable fellow, a good Joe, and a big brother, who is prepared to make his subordinates happy and satis-fied regardless of production costs, nonetheless 1/9 fails to achieve an integration of relationships among people around the require-ments of production. Therefore, it also fails to marshal the creative and innovative thinking needed regarding how production can best be accomplished. Not only is the 1/9 approach ineffective in the sense of achieving high output, but it is also unlikely to achieve any lasting human relation gains since conflict and frustration are not in any realistic manner dealt with and relieved, but rather they are smoothed over or avoided.

The point wants reemphasis here that the production/human relations interaction in which little or no emphasis is placed on get-ting production through people but rather emphasis is placed on achieving good relationships by not upsetting the apple cart and creating the conditions under which needed changes actually are effected is no way to get a job done. Nonetheless, the 1/9 approach is far more common than would be expected on casual examination of how people are integrated in the context of production.

The 1/1 Position. The lower left hand corner of Figure 1 is entitled "impoverished management." The reason is that neither the attainment of production nor of sound relationships are positive values. 1/1 deemphasizes both. It is an "ostrich" situation where the goal is that of "staying out of trouble" by avoiding involvement in thinking or in feelings. In terms of production requirements, the individual does enough to keep an appearance of effort, but his actual contribution is little.

Under the 1/1 orientation the following remarks are typical of a person in the lower levels of an organization.

"My goal is to keep my nose clean. The best way to do it is to shoot for minimum output. I do enough to get by and to keep people off my back."

Within the executive level, a 1/1 orientation can be found under the circumstances where a person has been repeatedly passed by or has reached the highest level possible in the company. Rather than looking elsewhere, he adjusts in the work setting by minimal performance, seeking satisfaction elsewhere.

"The work isn't too bad. We like the town; we have a comfortable house. You might say that I'm *marking time* until my retirement."

With respect to the problem of conflict, rather than suppressing conflict as in the 9/1 situation, or smothering it as in 1/9, the goal of a 1/1 manager is to *avoid* conflict by avoiding involvement. When actually faced with conflict, though, the 1/1 approach is to withdraw by such means as ignoring it, postponing confrontation or ultimately leaving the situation.

The 1/1 managerial style is certainly not prevalent. A factory operated under 1/1 circumstances would be unable to stay in business very long. On the other hand, numerous *individuals* relate to the organization in a 1/1 manner and are able to survive for long periods of time. This is particularly so in production situations that have become bureaucratic in nature and where "no one is ever fired."

In some respects 1/1 is an unnatural condition. It is a situation of personal defeat that an individual "comes to," rather than "beginning with." 1/1 as a way of relating to an organization represents a system of failure for the individual and for the organization. It is failure of the organization to integrate individual production efforts with sound relationships and failure for the individual who has accepted defeat and withdrawn his involvement to the degree that even criticism carries no prick.

Five "Mixed" Theories

Five additional approaches represent combinations or "mixes" of the 9/1 and 1/9 positions already discussed. All in one way or another stem from the notion that concern for production and concern for human relationship are in irreconcilable conflict and therefore are not subject to any true integration. Yet, the two concerns must, in some manner or other, be combined within a single organizational setting.

The 5/5 Position. In the center of the *Managerial Grid* is the "middle-of-the-road" theory. The same underlying assumptions regarding the impossibility of achieving high production under conditions of high concern for human relationships exists. The 9/1 theory of work planning and control is maintained. Nonetheless, the necessity for avoiding disruptive effects of poor relationships also is recognized in action consequences. The 5/5 theory is middle of the road in that the managerial organization is "push enough to get acceptable production, but yield to the degree necessary to develop or to maintain morale." As a 5/5 supervisor would say,

> "Look, all we want is a fair day's work for a fair day's pay. We know a fellow gets tired. Put out as much as you can, but don't kill yourself. Try to maintain a steady pace that's fair to the company, but that treats you right, too."

Balancing getting the job done with some concern for what people basically "want," also applies higher up the managerial ladder. For example, a 5/5 manager does not *command* as does the 9/1 manager.

> "I don't just *tell* my people what to do. I always try to remember to give the reason why. Of course, it takes a little longer to do it this way, but people basically resent being told what to do."

When the happy medium is achieved, too much production is not expected as people recognize that one must be flexible and "give." Under 5/5 it is believed that by clever string pulling, management can prevent either of the two *concerns* from blocking the satisfactory attainment of the other.

In a number of respects it would appear that the majority of present day organizations have abandoned the severe 9/1 separation between "planning" on the one hand and "doing" on the other and have tended over time to gravitate toward the 5/5 position. Restoration or maintenance of "good" relations among people engaged in work have been obtained through a 1/9 approach. The shift is not a healthy one since 5/5 retains important elements of the theory of work direction contained in 9/1 with the theory of human relations, or 1/9 added to it. It does not "solve" the problem. Rather, a "live and let live" situation is created under which the real problem is muted. In a 5/5 organization the "balance" between output and morale is sought for in connection with work. As a 5/5 manager said, "Maintenance of man is just as important as maintenance of machines."

Paternalism. Paternalism is another more or less stable "mix" of two anchor positions. Paternalistic organizations also tend to push for output in a 9/1 way. In time, the feelings of arbitrariness and alienation take on disturbing proportions. Additional steps are taken to "satisfy" or to correct negative human relations resulting from it. While 9/1 production controls are retained, concern for people is expressed through "taking care of them" in a 1/9 fashion. Organizational members are "given" many fine things—good pay, excellent benefits programs, recreational facilities, retirement programs and even low cost housing. These are not made available however, to acknowledge contribution to output but rather, at best, to gain respect and, at worst, to get subservience.

The mood of paternalism is caught in the following quotation. A supervisor, 20 minutes before the break of work, called one of his men over and said,

> "Joe, you've put in a good day's work and finished all your assignments. Go over to the smoking shack and have yourself a butt."

A paternalistic executive tends to retain tight control in work matters, but to be benevolent and kindly in a personal way. In other words, he treats his junior executives as part of his managerial "family." On the one hand, he encourages them to take initiative and to be responsible. On the other, he is unable to truly delegate and frequently is heard to characterize a succession of subordinates in this way.

> "My assistant won't accept responsibility. He's a bright, capable fellow with plenty of knowhow, but he checks and double checks everything he does with me. He will not take the ball and run. It's difficult to see how he'll ever get to the top of the ladder."

The work situation approaches 9/1 conditions in terms of direction and control, but it is coupled with the 1/9 style of concern for the well being of people. The reward for subordinates' complying with direction, control and push in work is security, happiness and "being taken care of" in terms of financial and social security.

Although paternalism has failed repeatedly to solve problems of getting production through the involvement of people, it is still a rather widespread attitude underlying much organizational thinking.

Wide-Arc Pendulum Theory. The wide-arc pendulum theory is one way of combining the 9/1 and the 1/9 positions in a temporal manner. When tightening up for increased output occurs, as often happens under thin profit margins or recession conditions, production pressure is applied in a manner consistent with 9/1 attitudes. At this point in time the organization would truly be described as 9/1. As a result, relationships can become so disturbed that production suffers. The organization feels forced to ease off and increase its concern for the thoughts, feelings and attitudes of people in a 1/9 manner. The negative results from 9/1 then start a pendulum swing. For a subsequent period of time the organization could validly be described as 1/9. When a degree of confidence has been restored, a tightening up occurs to regain losses in production suffered during the previous pendulum swing towards 1/9.

One of the best times for viewing wide-arc pendulum dynamics is before and after a certification election in companies that want to preserve an independent union which is challenged by an international union. Supervisors say,

> "The signal is out. Management wants to insure that the present union will win the forthcoming representation election. For the next few months, let up on the tough stuff. Ease up on washup time and the coveralls and gloves policy. Show an interest in people. Find out what's griping them. Take whatever actions are required to help the wage man recognize that management is interested in him."

Cracking down to get efficiency and then easing off to restore confidence and then pushing for increased production again is the pendulum swing from hard to soft to hard, etc.

Counterbalancing. Counterbalancing is another way of applying 9/1 and 1/9 simultaneously. Again, the line organization is operated in the direction of 9/1 principles of getting production. However, an antidote is supplied within the structure of the organization for 9/1 attitudes which result in suppressing negative feelings of the kind that can fester and smoulder and that eventually can erupt with devastating effects on production. The antidote or safety valve is the *personnel* function, which is designed as a 1/9 counterforce to relieve the conflict and tension generated from the line organization's pressures for production. A strong 1/9 personnel department is intended as a balancing weight where gripes and grievances can be aired and where corrective action can be obtained. Thus, both 9/1 and 1/9 attitudes are present in a "cold war" state of co-existence between two parts of the organization, with the line seeing personnel as hopelessly "soft" and personnel's viewing the line as hopelessly "hard-nosed."

The Two-Hat Theory. The two-hat theory of management occurs when considerations of production are viewed independently from concerns for people, but both are deemed of significance. Under this arrangement, rather than a split occurring within branches of the organization, the separation is maintained in the thinking of those responsible for overall policy and planning. For example, in a two-hat organization it is likely that one day a week, say on Monday, the top group gets together to consider issues concerned with efficient company operation. Then on another day, say Wednesday, the same group meets again, this time to review problems of people. The actions relative to production taken on Monday, though they may have deep implications for the problems that appear on Wednesday, [are] not considered in the context of their possible impact on relationships. The same is true when difficulties on the human side of the enterprise are encountered. Production aspects are held or tabled until the appointed time. Again, the basic assumption is that it is impossible to achieve an integration between production and relationships so that high production is obtained under conditions of satisfying relationships.

Review

All the styles above accept conflict between concerns for production and concern for people as more or less inevitable. Each deals with the assumed basic contradiction in a different way. The 9/1 and 1/9 two-hat and pendulum theories are "either or" in that the emphasis at any one point in time is *either* on production *or* on people. 5/5 paternalism and counterbalancing are efforts to achieve some sort of reconciliation between the two by using some of each simultaneously. The "ostrich" dynamic of 1/1, where involvement in the situation has been withdrawn can, under certain conditions, aid an individual to escape conflict by "hiding" from it. Under the 1/1 approach, the manager does the minimum.

The ways for bringing about some kind of connectedness between concerns for production and concerns for relationships above can be regarded as indications of what more or less skillful practitioners of the "art of management" achieve. None can be accepted as healthy, in the sense of representing a sound basis of operational life. The critical question now is, what is the managerial theory based on the application of behavioral science concepts in the context of work? This question can now be dealt with.

Integrating Production and Human Relationships: The 9/9 Position

The final position in Figure 1 is "team management." The team concept is based on the interdependence of people engaged in work activities. The productive unit is not viewed as an individual working in isolation of others whose output is added to the overall total of the unit. Rather, the building block of a 9/9 situation is the team. The word *team* emphasizes the concept of unity of effort of individuals in the work group, of interdependence between members, of "team play," and of "moving together." Team leadership avoids the blunder of person-centeredness. Individuals are seen, not one-by-one as separate entities, but team management recognizes relationships of members with one another since all are embedded and interconnected with one another in the context of production. As a result, attitudes toward achieving production in the 9/9 situation are vastly different than under any of the other theories mentioned above.

Certain distinctions for gaining an appreciation of 9/9 team effort can be made by drawing comparisons between 9/1 concepts and 9/9 on the one hand and 1/9 concepts and 9/9 on the other. Planning of work is one way in which contrasts can be drawn. In the 9/1 situation responsibility for planning tends to be centralized, with the responsibility of those who execute the work being that of following the instructions they receive. The goal of 9/9 management is to arouse participation and to get involvement in planning, so that all who share concerns for production can find the opportunity to think through and to develop a basis of effort which reflects the best thinking of all.

Team participation is not for social purposes or to "maintain morale" as an end in itself, nor does the team concept provide a cloak of anonymity within which inadequate performance can be buried or hidden. Rather, sound interpersonal relations are seen as the *best* way to achieve or to maintain production at peak levels. It is accepted as a given fact that people interact with one another in a context of production, and that feelings and emotions arise. As production problems are thought through, interpersonal feelings affect thinking and vice versa. Conflict is one result. The reason is that when a number of people interact around problems of production, it is likely that different points of view regarding how to solve production problems will develop. People have intense feelings about their own points of view. Conflict, in other words, is bound to appear. An important problem of 9/9 is concerned with how conflict around conditions of production is to be dealt with.

The sound way of conflict management as viewed from the 9/9 position is an approach which offers an opportunity for conflict to be relieved or "worked through" rather than to be suppressed, smothered, denied or avoided. As a result, one of the critical managerial skills present under 9/9 circumstances is the skill of bringing protagonists into relation with one another such that they can work through their differences and points of view rather than separating them as might be true in 1/9 or punishing them as might be true in 9/1.

9/1 managers are likely, under superficial examination, to see 9/9 as soft because it makes strenuous efforts to arouse participation of people and involve their creative and innovative thinking in the solutions of problems. The involvement and participation are what a 9/1 manager may see as weak. On the other hand, a 1/9 manager is likely to see a 9/9 operation as hard, for the reason that it places key emphasis on production. That is, the basis of interrelationships among people is that of achieving the goal of the organization, namely that of production. Furthermore, conflict is not avoided or played down as a 1/9 manager might do, but is actively dealt with.

Finally, it may be possible to give further clarification to the concept of 9/9 management by considering the psychological needs of people for the opportunity to apply mental effort in the attainment of production. This basic psychological need must also be considered in the context of the other and equally important need, namely that of establishing sound and mature relationships among people, which can be characterized as ones of mutual trust, mutual support, pleasure and satisfaction. The position stated here is that thinking through problems of production is most possible when individuals are related in such a manner that there is trust and mutual support, rather than distrust, suspicion, and tension. The interaction of production and people under 9/9 is one which takes advantage of the capacities of individuals to think creatively and innovatively by creating the conditions under which the relationships among people are centered on and conditioned by the need for solving problems of production. . . .

In our view, the implications are no less than are the similar implications which can be drawn from present day applications of the physical, biological and earth sciences. A general trend is under way in which the operation of society, at an ever increasing pace, is being transformed and brought into line with basic and systematic understanding of the appropriate conditions of human behavior. These include the conditions of commitment and involvement, the conditions that produce creative thinking, and the conditions of introducing meaningful direction and acceptable control into human activities: in a word, 9/9. As a result, action is based on understanding and agreement, rather than on compliance or subservience. The implications for a more mature production-oriented society are obvious.

Where the trend may end is not easy to say. The implications are great, and the significance over the long term is difficult to fully comprehend at this time.

NOTES

1. Blake, R.R., & Mouton, J. S. "Union-Management Relations: From Conflict to Collaboration." *Personnel*, Vol. 38, 1961.

2. Blake, R.R., & Mouton, J. S. "Headquarters-Field Training for Organizational Improvement." *Journal of the ASTD*, March, 1962.

3. Blake, R.R., & Mouton, J. S. "How Executive Team Training Can Help You and Your Organization." *Journal of the ASTD*, Jan. 1962.

4. Bidwell, A.C., Farrell, J. J., & Blake, R. R. "Team Job Training—A New Strategy for Industry." *Journal of the ASTD*, Oct. 1961.

14

The Corporate Rushmoreans

How to Lead Change Effectively and Morally

JAMES O'TOOLE

What can business leaders learn from the Rushmoreans? Can they discover a surefire process or blueprint for leading change? No. Success does not hinge on which of the many available change methods, programs, and processes is employed. Why? Because leadership effectiveness has little to do with matters of what to do or how to do it.

Contrary to received wisdom, when leaders fail to bring about change, the fault seldom lies in a mistaken choice of how-to manuals. Our review of the Rushmorean approach to leadership prepares us for a different conclusion: leaders fail when they have an inappropriate attitude and philosophy about the relationship between themselves and their followers. Those who do not respect and trust their followers cannot lead them. Conversely, those who succeed at bringing about effective and moral change believe in and act on the inherent dignity of those they lead—in particular, in their natural, human capacity to reason. In bringing about change, these leaders of leaders always include the people affected in the change process. Hence wherever successful leaders may start the process, whatever particular program they may adopt, and however they may choose to proceed along the way, they always practice the art of inclusion.

That *always* may still stick in the craw of people attracted to the moral relativism of contingency thinking. Indeed, there are exceptions to the rule: Rushmorean leadership does not exist in traditional (often called primitive) societies. And even in advanced, modern societies, the paternalist, the authoritarian, the strong man or woman may for a time get away with exclusionary leadership. In fact, for a period of time such individuals may be praised for their boldness, their brilliance, their strength, and their capacity to enforce their will on others. But in the final analysis, most such leaders will join the ranks of yesterday's heroes.

Consider the case of American Airlines's CEO, Robert Crandall. As the 1980s drew to a close, Crandall was widely acclaimed as America's toughest boss, the paradigm of the successful, forceful, no-nonsense leader. There were two reasons for his high standing in the media and academia: his company was a financial winner in an industry characterized by losers, and he was unashamedly as tough as they came. On the latter score, *The New York Times* called Crandall "the bully of the skies." Reporter Stephen Solomon wrote that "Crandall retains a volcanic temper and frequently erupts with a range of expletives that would stand out on the docks of New York." By admirers and critics alike, Crandall was called autocratic, hard on people, even abusive. Then, in 1993, after a spell of steadily declining profits, American was hit by one of the costliest strikes in airline history. That's when the employees whom Crandall had been bullying for a decade got their revenge: they refused to compromise on the terms of a new contract. Not only was the strike settled on the employees' terms, but the bully of the skies was forced to eat crow on prime-time news. Crandall, who had not shown great interest in the welfare of those who worked for him, thus found the attitude returned at the first opportunity. But he didn't get the connection. After the settlement, he told Solomon, "I work like hell all year and at the end of the year we have a big loss. That makes me a loser." Note carefully his choice of pronouns: *I* work, but *we* have a big loss.

FRANCES HESSELBEIN

Unlike Crandall, Frances Hesselbein doesn't use the pronoun *I* in the organizational context; she makes change a matter of *we*. On July 4, 1976, Hesselbein assumed the leadership of the Girl Scouts of the United States of America. The organization was a big one, with some three million members, a largely volunteer workforce of 650,000, a headquarters budget of $26 million, and cookie sales grossing a third of a billion dollars annually. But the Girl Scouts had lost its way. Because of enormous social changes that had occurred over the previous decades, the world's largest and most venerable organization of girls and women no longer knew what business it was in. Before Hesselbein acted, she met with her board and management team for six months to study and debate the purpose and mission of the scouts. She encouraged everyone in the organization with whom she consulted to "question everything—every assumption, policy, practice, detail."

Eventually they distilled the purpose of the organization into nine words: "To help each girl reach her own highest potential." Probably unconsciously, the Girl Scouts had thus restated the most basic natural right of each human being, in effect dedicating itself to making good on Jefferson's promise of the pursuit of happiness for all girls in America. It was immediately clear to the leaders of the scouts that this promise included nonwhites as well as whites. But the facts belied the promise: the Girl Scouts was largely a white club. The leaders then dedicated themselves to tripling their minority membership. But how to achieve this enormous change? "We could sit in New York and say, 'Let there be diversity,' " Hesselbein now explains, "but the neighborhood leaders in Altoona had to really believe in this [new] vision of why we were in business, and in our passionate belief in equal access."

She could not command the change because her position had little inherent power. But she had a clear philosophy of leadership: "The more power you give away, the more you have." She started by throwing out the organization chart ("Boxes make you feel boxed in") and introduced a "bubble chart" with sets of concentric rings to represent "participatory leadership, sharing leadership, to the outermost edges of the circles." Following that philosophy, her authority grew as she practiced the art of including dissenters and resisters in the process of change. Two examples will make this clear. First, when the national organization voted to replace the traditional 1912 Girl Scout eagle pin with one that contained multiracial profiles of three girls "facing the future," the reaction on many fronts was, "You can't take my eagle away from me." So Hesselbein didn't. Treating the dissenters with respect, she promised them that "as long as one person in this organization wants to wear the traditional pin, we will manufacture it." The upshot? Resistance melted.

Second, the national leadership sought to include in membership children as young as five, little girls from single-parent households who had come out of the Head Start program. The initiative met with predictable resistance from some mothers in the field who balked at becoming "baby-sitters" for five-year-olds. In fact, the vast majority of the organization's 335 national councils did not favor the plan. Instead of forcing the issue, Hesselbein began work immediately with the seventy-eight councils that were "ready to move." A year later, 225 councils were on board. Why? Hesselbein explains: "Paradoxically, I think the respect for differing opinions helped build cohesion within the organization rather than splinter it."

When she retired in 1990, not only had the Girl Scouts been reinvigorated and its diversity goals been met, but the organization was united in a way that it never had been in its seventy-eight-year history. Hesselbein says that the key was values-based leadership: "This could not have happened if we had not begun with the mission and had not emphasized the values undergirding everything we did to achieve it." The values she practiced—service, community, self-worth, friendship, fair and equitable treatment—became an umbrella broad enough for members from a variety of backgrounds to cluster under comfortably. She says that such "leadership is basically a matter of how to be, not how to do it. Leaders need to lead by example, with clear, consistent messages, with values that are 'moral compasses,' and a sense of ethics that works full time."

In a 1990 *Business Week* cover story, Peter Drucker concluded, "If I had to put somebody in to take Roger Smith's place in General Motors, I would pick Frances Hesselbein . . . because the basic problem is in turning around a huge bureaucracy, and that is her specialty." To skeptics, Drucker's conclusion may seem naive: the challenge of leading change in the Girl Scouts is surely different from leading a for-profit corporation. But is it? The facts speak otherwise. With just a little searching, we can find corporate examples of values-based leaders of leaders in the mold of Frances Hesselbein.

CORPORATE RUSHMOREANS

If I were a sculptor, I'd chisel a Mount Rushmore frieze of corporate leaders. Choosing the quartet to portray would be harder than choosing America's four greatest presidents, so I'd make the task easier for myself by arbitrarily limiting the candidates to living CEOs of large, publicly held corporations. That would free me from having to choose among such legendary entrepreneurs, managers, and financiers as Andrew Carnegie, Henry Ford, Alfred Sloan, J. C. Penney, Pierre Du Pont, Lincoln Electric's James Lincoln, Polaroid's Edwin Land, Wal-Mart's Sam Walton, AT&T's Theodore Vail, Johnson & Johnson's Robert Wood Johnson, Atlantic Richfield's Thornton Bradshaw, and Sears's Robert Wood. And if I had more than four votes to cast among the living, I'd want to include profiles of John Deere's William Hewitt, Levi Strauss's Robert Haas, Sony's Akio Morita, Avis's Robert Townsend, Ford's Donald Petersen, Dayton Hudson's Kenneth Macke, Cummins's J. Irwin Miller, Chapparal's Gordon Forward, Saturn's Skip Le Fauve, Phillips-Van Heusen's Larry Phillips, Ben & Jerry's Ben Cohen, Body Shop's Anita Roddick . . . and how could I leave out Disney's Michael Eisner if transformation were a main criterion of inclusion? Hey, who set the rules for this silly game anyway?

I'll discuss some of those leaders later, but here I'll play my own game and carve out brief portraits for my personal Mount Rushmore as exemplified by just four well-known CEOs: Herman Miller's Max De Pree, Corning's James Houghton, Motorola's Robert Galvin, and Scandinavian Airlines's Jan Carlzon.

Like the four famous U.S. presidents, these corporate Rushmoreans are more unlike each other than they are similar; they are imperfect human beings who have made mistakes (some of them serious) during their careers, and they all have suffered the slings and arrows of outrageous criticism from rivals, the press, the financial community, and cloistered academics. Moreover, they are not comfortable on white horses and hence will never be mistaken for the leaders at the heart of my next project: a military Rushmore of Alexander the Great, Napoleon, General Patton, and Charles de Gaulle! In fact, I have chosen my Corporate Rushmoreans not because they are exemplary leaders in the military sense but because they are exemplars of outstanding leadership in the moral sense. This is a significant distinction. These four corporate CEOs have in common the practice of inclusionary leadership. In their respective companies, they created conditions under which many others also led. They created systems in which the talents of the many more than compensated for whatever strengths they themselves may have lacked. The famed ad man David Ogilvy almost had it right when he described the benefits of such leadership in the following way: "It does an organization no good when its leader refuses to share his leadership function with his lieutenants. The more centers of leadership you find in a company, the stronger it will become."

That would be it in a nutshell, except at Herman Miller, Corning, Motorola, and SAS, people do not think of themselves as anybody's "lieutenant." All the employees of these companies act "as if they own the place," in the words of Max De Pree. In Max's marvelous little book *Leadership Is an Art* he describes in loving detail the policies, programs, and practices at Herman Miller that caused employees at all levels to feel that the company was every bit as much theirs as it was Max's. When Max retired a few years back, he left behind a system under which all employees could be leaders, were encouraged to be leaders, and were rewarded for exerting leadership, but were free not to be leaders if, for whatever reason, leadership was not what they wanted to (or could) contribute to the firm. Yet most significant about the environment at Herman Miller, Corning, Motorola, and SAS is that when given the opportunity, the vast majority of employees at all levels opt to exert leadership. Let us see how De Pree, Houghton, Galvin, and Carlzon became leaders of leaders.

MAX DE PREE

The first person I'd portray on my corporate Mount Rushmore would be De Pree, former CEO of Herman Miller, one of the country's largest producers of office furniture. The company was founded in 1923 by D. J. De Pree, Max's dad, and it has generated ripples of distinction—and waves of innovation—since the 1930s. For years, Herman Miller has been respected internationally for the quality of its products and especially for its contribution to design (its Eames chair is in the permanent collection of both New York's Museum of Modern Art and the Louvre's Musee des Arts Decoratifs). The open office, the wall-attached desk, stackable chairs—these are among the many Herman Miller innovations.

How, you might ask, could such radical design ideas come from a company headquartered in Zeeland, Michigan, a frosty town with no trendy watering holes and no theaters? Don't all top designers live in New York, Paris, or Rome? They came to Zeeland, Max says, because D. J. "had the strength to abandon himself to the wild ideas of others." D. J. talked some of the greatest designers of the century—Gilbert Rhode, Charles Eames, and Robert Propst— into visiting Zeeland, where he promised them a free hand in designing what Eames called "good goods." D. J. had decided that there was a market for good design and that great designers needed freedom to try out their wild ideas. In short, D. J. concluded a long time ago that Herman Miller would be a leader, not a follower. His son followed suit.

Max De Pree, like his dad, believed in the rule of "abandoning oneself to the strengths of others." Not just expert others—that is, not just world-class designers and people with university degrees— but trusting the strengths of all Herman Miller employees. For example, through the company's Scanlon plan, workers make suggestions to management for ways to improve such things as customer service, quality, and productivity. The Scanlon plan has been the modus operandi at Herman Miller since the early 1950s. The Scanlon idea is simple: when workers suggest ways to improve productivity, they are cut into the financial gains that result from their contributions. One day a month, top managers report to workers on the company's productivity and profits—the kind of information that is normally hoarded in most big U.S. firms—and the managers also report on the status of all employee suggestions. This wasn't unbridled fun for Max and his top management team. Imagine being the CEO of a Fortune 500 firm facing a monthly interrogation on your performance by shop floor workers: "Max, why didn't you do what we told you last month?" "Why hasn't top management purchased that new equipment we told you about?" "Why does it take so long to change procedures that keep us from responding directly to customers?" "Our profits would be higher if you guys would respond faster to what we tell you to do."

Why did Max put up with this? Wasn't it hard work? Wasn't it threatening for a boss to be grilled by subordinates? Didn't Max abandon power by abandoning himself to the ideas of others? Listen to what Max says about leadership, and remember that he practiced what he preached:

- The first responsibility of the leader is to define reality. The last is to say thank you. In between, the leader is a servant.

- The signs of leadership are among the followers. Are they reaching their potential? Are they learning? Are they achieving the desired results? Are they serving? Do they manage change gracefully, and do they manage conflict?

- Leaders don't inflict pain, they bear it.

- Leaders respect people. Leadership is about relationships. Relationships count more than structure.

- Good communication means a respect for individuals. Good communication is an ethical question.

- The best communication forces you to listen. Information is power, but it is pointless if hoarded. Power must be shared for an organization or a relationship to work.

The problem in most organizations, according to Max, is that CEOs limit the capacity of their firms to their own level of competence. That is, they surround themselves with loyal "lieutenants" who are nonthreatening. Unlike many of his peers, Max was willing to admit that he couldn't do most of the jobs in the company nearly as well as the people who held them. He wanted people who were more qualified than himself to do every job in the organization. He also knew that he couldn't be everywhere in the company at all times, nor could he invent rules to ensure that everyone always did the "right thing." All he could do was to make it possible for all Herman Miller employees to take responsibility for meeting whatever situation might arise—that is, to act as Max or his top management team would have done had they been there themselves. Again, as Max always said, "around here the employees act as if they own the place." And isn't that the goal of organizational leadership? Isn't that the employee attitude that every CEO would nurture if it weren't so threatening "to abandon oneself to the strengths of others"? What Max did was institutionalize responsibility and continuing change. How could there be resistance to change if the source of innovation was the followers themselves?

I have often been asked to describe Max's leadership "style," and after many unsatisfactory attempts to do so, I came to realize that my difficulties stemmed from a false premise inherent in the question. Indeed, most of us wrongly assume that leadership has something to do with style. The error is perpetuated in management books in which leaders are portrayed, variously, as charismatic personalities, showmen, cheerleaders, con artists, visionaries, autocrats, and circus stuntmen. They bark orders and run around doing everybody else's work for them. How preposterous that this could work in a company of a thousand (let alone a hundred thousand) employees!

Max's idea of leadership is different. He knows from experience that it is not a leader's strong voice, the snap of a whip, or a trendy TV persona that motivates employees. The art of leadership, as Max says, is "liberating people to do what is required of them in the most effective and humane way possible." Thus the leader is the "servant" of the followers in that the leader removes the obstacles that prevent them from doing their jobs. In short, the true leader enables followers to realize their full potential. That is not a matter of style.

To lead effectively is a matter of clear thinking on the part of the leader. Leaders must be clear about their own beliefs: they must have thought through their assumptions about human nature, the role of the organization, the measurement of performance, and so on. Max De Pree leads by asking questions. Because he has carefully considered his questions in advance, he has the self-confidence "to encourage contrary opinions" and "to abandon himself to the strengths of others." In short, Max is a listener. He listens to the needs, ideas, and aspirations of his followers; then, within the context of his own well-developed systems of belief, he responds to these in an appropriate fashion. That is why leaders must know their own minds. That is why leadership requires ideas.

And that is why leadership requires integrity. Integrity has at least two meanings relevant to a discussion of leadership. It is synonymous with truth-telling, honesty, and moral behavior. It goes without saying that a true leader must behave with integrity in this sense by being an honest and ethical individual, someone whose every word and deed is consistent. That describes Max to a T. But such morality, though necessary, is insufficient. In addition, the leader needs that related type of integrity that has to do with "selfness," with the integration of one's personality (to use the language of psychologists). Integrity in this sense refers to the much-admired trait of wholeness or completeness that is achieved by people who are said to have healthy self-confidence and self-esteem. People with integrity "know who they are." Their self-esteem allows them to esteem and respect others. Such leaders' ease with themselves allows others to esteem and respect them. Max De Pree is one of those people who is so comfortable with himself that he makes other people comfortable with themselves. Without Max's trying, people follow him.

But they wouldn't follow him willingly if he were so wishy-washy as to agree with the last person to visit his office or so rigid that he couldn't listen and respond to ideas different from his own. Both of those familiar types lack integrity. According to Warren Bennis, all successful leaders must know "what they want, why they want it, how to communicate that to others to gain their support to get it." You don't have to become someone else to be a leader, Bennis says; "you have to become yourself." *That's* integrity.

But how does one know what one wants? The key, as the poet writes, is to "know thyself." That requires listening carefully to Ralph Waldo Emerson's "inner voice" and heeding that voice "all others to the contrary." In short, the only way one can be a leader is to be true to oneself, and that is hard to do. The world may say that it prizes originality and individuality—but then it goes and punishes their expression. That is where moral courage comes in. We all know what is right. But it is the leaders among us who behave in the right way no matter what others may say. Thus Bennis observes that "conformity is the enemy of leadership. We let others define ourselves." But aren't leaders also supposed to listen to their followers? Leadership requires listening to followers but not becoming prisoners to their low expectations. Fortunately, as Bennis writes, "we can have unity without conformity." And in that seeming paradox is the escape from the terrible organizational dilemma that bedevils would-be leaders of change: a "paradox of values" in which leaders must create a culture with strong strategic unity while at the same time fostering sufficient internal openness to encourage freedom of action and entrepreneurial initiative.

The resolution of that paradox does not rest on a technique, a skill, or a style of leadership. Such leadership is an attitude, as Frances Hesselbein puts it, an attitude that rests on the most important value practiced by Max De Pree: respect for people. Above all else, Max created an organization in which the different abilities and contributions of all people were respected and rewarded. Everything the company did, all its goals and objectives, were subsumed under that master value.

Respect for people leads to the right of all employees to participate in the decisions that affect their own work and the right to share in the fruits of their labor (through the Scanlon plan and through stock ownership). Among employees with over a year of service, 100 percent are stockholders by way of a profit-sharing plan. While executives in other companies were busy "taking care of number one" by arranging golden parachutes for themselves, in 1986 Herman Miller introduced "silver parachutes" for all its employees with more than two years of service. In case of an unfriendly takeover of Herman Miller that led to termination of employment, the silver parachute plan would offer a soft landing for the people in the ranks of the organization whose welfare is ignored in most acquisitions. But then, Herman Miller wasn't like most other business organizations. For example, company policy limited the CEO's salary and bonus to no more than twenty times the average paycheck (in 1991, when most CEOs of *Fortune* 500 firms were drawing seven figures, Herman Miller's highest-paid executive made $490,000 and the company's average employee made $28,000). That's respect for people.

Yet some executives have told me that Max cannot stand as a practical model of leadership because he is "too good," that is, because his character is almost saintly. It is true that Max is an extremely moral man in his *private* life, but I do not believe that goodness is what made him a successful leader. He inspired followers because he was trustworthy in his *public* leadership role. He showed his respect for employees in sound, practical business ways, such as involving them in decision making and profit sharing. Had Max been a saint off the job, yet failed to respect his associates at Herman Miller, he would not have attracted followers.

One question remains: Does it work? Is such moral leadership effective? During Max's eight-year term as CEO, the company was seventh on the *Fortune* 500 in total return to investors. A hundred dollars invested in Herman Miller stock in 1975 had grown in value to about $5,000 in 1986. Was the success of Herman Miller related to Max's leadership? The answer is an unqualified yes. Bear in mind that the affirmative comes from a skeptic who has learned (painfully) that there is almost always a gap between what a CEO *claims* his philosophy to be and what he actually does on the job. For a time I had treated what Max De Pree said about leadership as mere theory, until I could put it to the ultimate test of asking his followers what *they* thought of Herman Miller's top management.

Then I got my first chance to visit a Herman Miller factory. I was given carte blanche to go anywhere and talk to anyone, managers and workers alike. The only problem was that I couldn't tell one from the other. People who seemed to be production workers were engaged in solving the "managerial" problems of improving productivity and quality. People who seemed to be managers had their sleeves rolled up and were working side by side with everybody else in an all-out effort to produce the best products in the most effective way. As Max says, "The signs of outstanding leadership are found among the followers." I found that Max was a leader of leaders.

And I found that Max's excellence as a leader was manifested in the spirit of *self-management* that I found in every Herman Miller employee with whom I spoke. Among the dozens of corporations I had previously visited, I'd never seen anything like it. I discovered that not only did Max practice what he preached, but so did the people who worked for him, the people Max *served*. These people were dedicated to the beliefs and ideas that Max espoused; they even sounded like Max when talking about the company's values, but were all rugged individualists with their own ideas about how to realize those values and how to live their own lives. As Warren Bennis says, "We can have unity without conformity."

Having sketched this glowing portrait, I hasten to add that there is no such thing as the perfect company or the ideal leader. Max lost his deft touch while establishing a process for choosing his successor, who lasted in the CEO's job just long enough to discover that he did not want to be a CEO. As he came to this realization, the competitive environment in the furniture industry changed, and customer responsiveness became as important for success as product quality. Recognizing that the CEO was not coping with this change, the board resolved to look for a new change-oriented leader who, at the same time, was committed to preserving the company's values.

With Max's active participation, the board identified an individual from outside the company who appeared to have the requisite qualities. However, after a couple of years during which it became clear he too was unable to bring about needed transformation of the company's strategy and product line, the new CEO did what many leaders do when faced with a crisis: he got tough. He resorted to classic situational leadership. Failing to understand that, while leadership requires constant changes of strategy and tactics, it equally requires steadfast adherence to basic principles, he fired nearly the entire top management of a company in which firing had occurred only in rare instances of misconduct. Worse was the abusive manner in which the deed was done: a stranger to the Herman Miller community assembled those who had been chosen for termination—most of whom had no inkling of what was about to transpire—and summarily announced that they had been dismissed.

In one blow, five decades of goodwill that had been accumulated under three De Prees—D. J., Hugh (Max's brother, who had been CEO for seventeen years), and Max himself—was squandered in one gratuitous act of "get tough" leadership. The essential glue of trust that had held the company together was suddenly dissolved. Max had just retired from the board, but the shocked directors immediately understood what had happened and removed the CEO before he could do more damage.

There is a chance that Herman Miller might still recover but, for now, the company stands as a cautionary tale of how easily the trust that undergirds values-based leadership can be lost. And Max, for all his skill, reminds us that the most difficult of all leadership tasks is, perhaps, developing worthy successors. Yet, because he so brilliantly fulfilled the other tasks of leadership, I unhesitatingly put him on my Mount Rushmore. As we shall see, no mortal is a perfect leader.

JAMES HOUGHTON

The second leader I would profile on my Corporate Rushmore is Corning's James R. Houghton, who in the 1980s revitalized the $3 billion glassworks that had been founded by his great-great-grandfather in upstate New York over a century and a quarter before "Jamie" became CEO. In 1983, facing the prospect of his family's legacy gradually withering as the result of new technologies and global competition, Houghton called together his top management team to discuss how to resuscitate the firm. They decided that the key was quality. Among the first American executives to hear W. Edwards Deming's message, Houghton's team committed the company to the earliest of the "total quality" programs that would soon take American industry by storm.

But Corning differed from most of these companies that would follow in that Houghton recognized almost immediately that the issue wasn't just quality but the total transformation of the culture of the old-line firm. Just prior to his assuming the CEO role, the company had been characterized publicly as a "dictatorship," and relations with its employees, unions, and local community had deteriorated to the breaking point. This challenge was not one to which Jamie Houghton was born. Scion of the American aristocracy, he was not naturally given to the Rushmorean traits needed to turn the company around. But he committed himself not only to changing the company but also to starting that process of change with himself. People at Corning now talk of him respectfully as the "CTO" (chief transformation officer), and that transformation began the day he asked a soon-to-retire executive, Forrest Behm, to direct the quality program. Behm gave Houghton just one piece of advice: "*You* have to lead the program, not me." And lead it he did (with Behm as his coach).

Houghton began by committing a third of his time to the quality effort. He started with a series of meetings with Behm and "the Six-Pack," the group of officers who reported directly to him. Their first task was to agree on what their values were and what those values meant for the change process. The values they identified—quality, integrity, performance, industry leadership, and technology—were not unusual in and of themselves, but they were built on the foundation of another value: the individual. They decided that this meant that "each employee must have the opportunity to participate fully, to grow professionally, and to develop his or her highest potential." (Again, we find Rushmorean leaders coming back to Jefferson's promise of the pursuit of happiness.)

To realize this value, it was obviously necessary that Jamie Houghton would have to eliminate the "management by fear" that had caused Corning to be branded a dictatorship. He did this in part by pledging to introduce self-management among the company's largely unionized workforce, and to make Herculean efforts to attract, retain, and promote women, minorities, and others who had been leaving the company in droves in pursuit of more open and accepting work environments.

But it isn't what you say that counts, it's what you do. Jamie Houghton soon learned that if he were to transform the company, he must lead by example—and that would take more than the third of his time that he had planned to devote to the process. According to Behm, one critical event signaled a fundamental change in Jamie Houghton. Early in the quality program, it became clear that someone had made a very costly mistake. On hearing this bad news, Jamie blurted out, "Who did it?" Then he caught himself. His face reddened with embarrassment, and he rephrased his line of questioning: "Why did it happen?" "How can we fix it?" "What is our responsibility as leaders to make sure that it doesn't happen again?" From that defining moment of leadership, the successful transformation of Corning was assured.

Houghton and the Six-Pack then worked outward in ever-broadening circles, bringing more and more people into the process of leading change. Jamie himself visited fifty worksites a year, explaining his vision and the values of the company and calling on employees to spend 5 percent of their time annually in training to prepare them to lead the quality effort and to become the industry pacesetters in technology. No "benchmarking" for Corning; let others follow Corning's lead! Year in and year out, through patience and repetition, Houghton went back to the same groups with the same message, demonstrating that this commitment to their enablement was not merely a fad of the month. Gradually, they learned to trust him and began to accept responsibility for making change come about.

Significantly, Houghton says that he leads as he does not because it is expedient but because treating employees with respect is the right thing to do. Thus Houghton has cited the need for "redefining leadership":

- We have traditionally viewed leaders as heroes who come forward at a time of crisis to resolve a problem. But this view stresses the short term and assumes the powerlessness of those being led. . . .

- The true spirit of leadership is the spirit that is not sure it is always right. Leaders who are not too sure they are right are leaders who listen. Leadership is about performance over time, not charisma—about responsibility, not privilege. It is about personal integrity and a strong belief in team play. . . .

- Which points to one more element of leadership: developing strong subordinates and potential successors and staying out of their way. Companies can no longer afford leadership by the few. If organizations are to move ahead and not just play catch-up, every employee must become a responsible leader.

- Employees must have responsibility and the power that goes with it; anything less leads to cynicism and skepticism—and nothing is more demoralizing for employees than to find their skepticism justified.

Does Houghton's new definition of leadership work? Is it effective? It does and it is, as the following example illustrates. At the company's Erwin Ceramics Plant, workers responded to Houghton's quality initiative by taking on the process of change as their own responsibility. They prepared a "vision statement," "a set of beliefs and rights that we value and are fundamental to our future," among which were the rights to "be treated with dignity and respect" and to "participate in decisions that affect our work-life." The vision was, in effect, a description of the kind of place where they wanted to work. To implement the vision, they created a joint management-labor team to plan the changes needed in the existing system. This plan called for the elimination of eighty jobs through attrition and changes in work rules and processes that in the first year led to a 38 percent reduction in defects. Here's the Corning lesson: where there is Rushmorean leadership, rights and responsibilities become complementary rather than antithetical, just as labor and management become, in the words of Horace Mann, "fraternal rather than antagonistic."

ROBERT GALVIN

The third corporate leader I would immortalize in granite is Motorola's Robert Galvin. Thanks to Galvin's understated leadership, Motorola has probably done the best job of any large U.S. corporation at institutionalizing change. When Galvin assumed the CEO role in the late 1950s (on the death of his father, Paul, Motorola's founder), he worked with the top management team to lay out a ten-year plan for transforming the company. Galvin quickly saw that the plan could not be realized without the support of all Motorola employees. In fact, he saw that he would have to involve them immediately in creating the plan. To do this, operations were radically decentralized, and employees were formed into teams, each responsible for such things as quality, productivity, cost and inventory control, and customer service.

Because these teams were truly self-managing—and because all employees were rewarded with healthy bonuses when they met the goals they had set for themselves in consultation with management—Motorola created a system in which workers had a greater say and stake than competing Japanese workers had in their firms. Motorola workers also had a high degree of autonomy: in the 1970s, one Motorola worker proudly explained to me that "like Japanese, we play softball on excellent company facilities; unlike Japanese, we play when we want to, not on cue!"

Motorola became the first large company in America to enable its workers to be leaders themselves. Through a system of constant communication and feedback, Motorola employees came to understand what their individual and group piece of the business was, and how that contributed to the grand corporate scheme, and were thus able to make rational decisions without the need for constant managerial coercion. The system grew out of a no-holds-barred analysis of the company's basic assumptions about workers and work, an analysis that led to the conclusion that employees are intelligent, curious, and responsible and hence it was incumbent on management to create a system in which they could exercise their ability to reason.

Motorola ended up with an industrial system under which people are treated with dignity without losing discipline, and power is widely shared without degenerating into anarchy. The means are simple and sensible: all employees participate in the decisions that affect their own work, and all participate in the financial rewards that come about as the result of their efforts. This dual approach works because participation in decision making without participation in financial gains would be viewed as illegitimate by workers who saw the fruits of their efforts reaped by others. And participation in financial gains without participation in decision making would be seen as illegitimate by workers who were powerless to influence the things that determine the size of their paychecks. The results of Motorola's system are well known: perhaps the highest-quality products in American industry; regular introduction of innovations in semiconductors, pagers, and handheld communications; and, of course, high profits.

What did Bob Galvin do to accomplish this? Very little himself. I have heard of few instances where he ever gave a direct order to anyone (with the exception, perhaps, of his son, Christopher, a top Motorola executive—again, nobody's perfect). Basically, Galvin removed the obstacles that might have prevented his employees from being fully effective. He encouraged them to take initiative and to be as fully productive as possible without violating Galvin's strong moral values, the foremost of which is trust. Galvin trusted everyone at Motorola—the people who reported to him and the people who reported to them—to create a system of unusually high productivity: "One's creativity depends on interaction with others—others one trusts, others who feel trusted. For one to be unfettered in risking creative interaction with another, that other must know the trust of openness, objectivity, and a complementary creative spirit. . . . Trust is power. The power to trust and be trusted is an essential and inherent prerequisite quality to the optimum development and employment of a creative culture."

Galvin was a leader of leaders, a leader of such admired executives as William Weisz, George Fisher, Gary Tooker, Christopher Galvin, and others, who in fact ran the company. Moreover, the spoils at Motorola went to employees who successfully challenged inappropriate premises advanced by those at the top. As one manager explained to me, "The expectation is that you will challenge any idea. The top guys disagree with each other in front of their managers. The upshot is a healthy disrespect for the idea that those at the top are necessarily the wisest."

Bob Galvin explains where this comes from:

Our challenge is to continually evidence a willingness to reach and risk, a willingness to *renew*. I saw at a young age that my father had to change to survive. . . . My father was a "natural" at changing his mind. He would pound on the table telling you he was right. Then you would tell him the consequences of his decision, and he'd change his mind right there. There is no master plan that can anticipate change. That is why my father counseled, "Be in motion." He didn't believe in milking things to the end, until they became failures. We saw what happened to our former competitors Philco, Zenith, and Admiral and swore that we wouldn't let it happen to us. We looked at the companies that didn't survive, and we learned from them. As a management team we read John Gardner's *Renewal,* and we've lived by its precepts ever since.

The attitude of constant renewal pervades the entire Motorola corporation, not just the executive suite. There is a healthy sense of dissatisfaction with the status quo, which manifested itself when Motorola was on top of the world, having just won the first Malcolm Baldrige Award for quality. Instead of resting on its laurels, the company committed itself to the creation of American industry's most ambitious training effort. At Motorola University, every employee now partakes in at least five days of classwork annually. In fact, at Motorola, everyone has a "right" to training—a Jeffersonian right to make all that they can of themselves in order to participate in the continuing renewal of the company.

JAN CARLZON

The choice of a fourth Corporate Rushmorean was the hardest. With one strong reservation, my candidate would be Jan Carlzon, CEO of Scandinavian Airlines (SAS) and author of one of the few books on leadership by a corporate executive that is worth reading (along with Max De Pree's). His *Moments of Truth* offers a quintessential overview of how to lead change. There is no need to repeat here what he does so well in that book. Instead, we focus on one of the clearest examples of the peculiar kind of resistance to change that is the unique focus of our inquiry. In late 1985, just before his book was published, Carlzon visited Los Angeles, where, at the invitation of Warren Bennis, he addressed some two dozen of the most powerful executives in California, most of them unfamiliar with the story of SAS's transformation, which has since become legendary. On that memorable occasion, I was a fly on the wall.

Carlzon began his talk with an explanation of the conditions he inherited at SAS, a description of the process of change he employed, and a review of the consequent results. He also described his philosophy of leadership, with specific reference to his now-famous notion of "turning the organizational pyramid upside down" so that leaders may serve followers. He explained why and how every SAS employee had been empowered—without the requirement of prior approval from supervisors—to do whatever was necessary to satisfy customers: "You can get people to develop their specific goals not by steering them with fixed rules but by giving them total responsibility to achieve a specific result." To get that result—namely, customer satisfaction—the key resource that employees needed was information: "An individual without information cannot take responsibility; an individual who is given information cannot help but take responsibility."

Carlzon then recounted examples of the exercise of such responsibility from the fifty million "moments of truth" that occurred annually when SAS employees had direct, one-on-one contact with customers. He argued that the sum total of these moments added up to the general level of satisfaction that had made the airline number one in Europe among business travelers.

At this point in the discussion, the American executives started to grow fidgety. After much nervous coughing and paper shuffling, one CEO could take no more. Clearly enraged, he slammed his palm down hard on the table in front of him and with the other hand pointed an accusatory finger at the Swedish guest speaker: "OK, Carlzon, now own up. How many of those fifty million moments went sour? How many times did your employees abuse the responsibility you gave them? How many times did somebody do something dumb that ended up costing your shareholders money?"

Carlzon, soft-spoken and low-key, took no offense at the interruption. Instead, he weighed his words carefully in reply: "Do you want the data from the first year or for the entire six years since we introduced the change?"

"The whole works. Come on, 'fess up!"

"I believe we have had about a half dozen serious instances of the type you mention. Those were times when employees went far beyond what was a reasonable effort on behalf of customers and, in so doing, caused costly errors."

Satisfied that he had made his point, the American turned to his peers and said, "There, I thought so. That's what you get when you let the lunatics run the asylum—anarchy!"

Politely, Carlzon mentioned that at SAS they thought that six errors in three hundred million positive experiences was a pretty good ratio (and I wanted to add that professors fall victim to the same fallacy of the exception when they argue against adopting the honor system on the grounds that "someone might cheat"—but I had sworn a vow of silence during the session).

Tasting blood, and ignoring Carlzon's explanation, the American interlocutor went back for more. "Now that you are shooting straight, tell us what you did about the employees who were ripping off your shareholders."

Either Carlzon didn't understand the CEO's vernacular, or he understood but couldn't believe his ears. "I'm sorry, what do you mean?"

"In plain English, how did you punish them?"

Carlzon got the drift. "Punish them? Why should we have punished them when it was *our* fault? We believe the task of leaders in a large company is to articulate the values of the organization, to create a system in which people can be productive, and to explain the goals that the system was established to achieve. We also believe that people don't act maliciously. If we in top management had done those jobs properly—if we had explained adequately the purpose behind employee empowerment—those few errors would not have occurred. That is why we went back to evaluate our own communication skills."

Carlzon's view, in brief, was that the challenge of change requires more than a leader; it requires leadership. American executives at that time could not see the difference between those two related concepts. I suspect that by now most of them have come to understand the difference, but too few of them are acting on it. The thoughts that the angry CEO expressed a few short years ago may have become "managerially incorrect," but there is little evidence that managers who now know better are as yet willing to entrust others in the manner Carlzon demonstrated.

Earlier I mentioned that I cite Jan Carlzon with reservation. The postscript to this story is inconsistent both with my argument and with what Carlzon practiced and preached at SAS. Shortly after having achieved Rushmorean status, Carlzon threw away much of his credibility in one fell swoop. Competition in the airline industry suddenly heated up, and small airlines like SAS found their existence threatened. In what can only be called a panic move, SAS formed an alliance of convenience with Continental, then headed by Frank Lorenzo, a CEO whose leadership philosophy was the antithesis of everything Carlzon stood for. Thus I end up feeling about Carlzon being on my Mount Rushmore the way I do about Thomas Jefferson being on the real thing: though no leader is perfect, it is the failings of the good ones, not the sins of bad ones, that break your heart. . . .

COMMONALITIES

Certain themes run through these examples of Rushmorean leadership. Each of the individuals cited is an inclusive leader of leaders. That inclusion is a big tent, extending over all affected parties, constituencies, and stakeholders. Inclusive leaders enable others to lead by sharing information, by fostering a sense of community, and by creating a consistent system of rewards, structure, process, and communication. They are committed to the principle of opportunity, giving all followers the chance to make a contribution to the organization. The values-based leadership they all practice is based on an inspiring vision. And each is dedicated to institutionalizing continuous change, renewal, innovation, and learning. And the bottom line in what they do is adherence to the moral principle of respect for people.

Importantly, that respect is not contingent on anything. On all of the factors just mentioned, the Corporate Rushmoreans are consistent and persistent—which is different from being rigid and inflexible, in that the former attitude accommodates and even encourages disagreement and divergent viewpoints, whereas the latter is deaf to dissent. If this distinction seems somewhat paradoxical, in fact, Rushmorean leadership is often about the management of paradox. Simultaneously, these leaders are concerned with both continuity and change, with the short and the long term, with accountability and freedom, with planning and flexibility, with, in fact, the intrinsic contradiction between leadership and participation. In a practical, business sense, values-based leadership provides for internal, strategic unity while at the same time encouraging independent entrepreneurial initiative.

Let us now analyze the relevant examples of leading change among the organizations described above—specifically, the Girl Scouts, Herman Miller, Corning, Motorola, SAS, Phillips-Van Heusen, Polaroid, Schering-Plough, MasterCard, Ford, and

ARCO—to see what commonalities they might share. Though the leaders of these organizations shared the philosophical commonalities just cited, they each changed their organizations—indeed, remade those cultures, and themselves, radically—by using *different methods*. To repeat a central theme: Rushmorean leadership is *not* a function of technique; rather, it is a function of attitudes and ideas. There was no one formula that enabled these leaders to alter the outmoded ways of their organizations. Instead, they each institutionalized a variety of change processes—processes that in some cases took as long as ten years to show clear results. Though the mechanisms by which change was achieved vary in detail, all entailed one form or another of decentralization of decision making, monitoring of stakeholder needs, challenging of assumptions, and providing appropriate rewards and incentives for all of these activities.

In each case, the process began with a sine qua non of change: a clear, long-term, top-management commitment to the hard work of altering corporate culture, beginning with themselves as leaders. Let me clarify what such change really means, as it is not like changing furniture or changing channels on TV. As the Ford example illustrates, it is just as absurd to talk of changing the culture of a firm into something radically different as it is to talk about manipulating your personality to become someone you aren't. In the 1980s, the usefulness of the concept of corporate culture was nearly lost when management gurus defined culture in terms of symbols, slogans, heroes, rites, and rituals. These may be *manifestations* of culture—although any graduate student in anthropology could come up with more sophisticated examples—but they are *not* culture. A culture is a system of beliefs and actions that characterize a particular group. Culture is the unique whole—the shared ideas, customs, assumptions, expectations, philosophy, traditions, mores, and values—that determines how a group of people will behave. When we talk of a corporation's culture, we mean the complex, interrelated whole of standardized, institutionalized, habitual behavior that characterizes that firm and that firm only. Thus to talk about a culture as "it" is absurd: culture is "us." To talk about top management's role in changing corporate culture is to talk about people changing *themselves,* not changing some "it" or "them" outside the door to the executive suite.

To think in terms of "it" is to fall into the trap that ensnared the deceased shah, Mohammed Reza Pahlavi. He tried to change Iranian culture by bringing the country up-to-date a bit: giving women a few rights, taking away some of the power of the clergy, introducing Western education and material goods. In fact, the erstwhile shah was a champ at manipulating symbols, slogans, heroes, rites, and rituals (just think of the big party he threw in the desert to commemorate the founding of Persepolis—a ritual that set him back a few million smackers, what with the elephants and the helicopter shuttle service and all).

Significantly, it is *exactly* the shah's approach to change that was advocated by the 1980s culture vultures. A favorite story used by consultants at the time to illustrate "how to do a successful culture change" concerned a Silicon Valley company in which the CEO decided to "shake up his troops." He called an off-site meeting at a nearby motel and started into the usual, boring routine with over-heads and flip charts when, suddenly, out on the lawn landed several helicopters manned by "guards" who took the executives "captive" and whisked them off to a remote beach. There the exec-utives found the elements of the new "culture" that the CEO had cooked up for them. There were belly dancers with the new com-pany logo on their tummies and elephants sporting banners with the new company slogan, omnipresent during two days of rituals designed to demonstrate a complete break with the past. It was a great story. I have only one trouble with the whole idea: I don't believe it worked—or if it did, it didn't last. For all the shah's fun and games, bread and circuses, rites and rituals, he failed *completely* to alter Iran's underlying fundamentalist Islamic values. Why should we believe that the Silicon Valley CEO would have had any more success than the shah? (That the shah was also corrupt and authoritarian didn't help, either; but even if he had been an honest and decent guy, he was still going about change in the wrong way.)

Effective change builds on the existing culture. A group will reject a foreign system of values the way a healthy body rejects a virus. Anthropologists know that culture change occurs in one of two basic ways. The first is revolutionary. This is always the course of disaster. Whether it is a planned, Maoist-like cultural revolution or the unplanned collapse of a primitive culture that results from contact with the powerful technology, organization, and religions of the West, revolutionary culture change is always shocking, painful, disruptive, and undesirable. The second form is evolutionary. For example, over time, American culture has evolved from a rural European, Protestant, and traditionalist past to an urban, heteroge-neous, secular, and modernist present. The agents of change— politicians, business leaders, inventors, union organizers, artists, writers, scholars—moved the country forward by reference to the "things that have made this country great." Can you name a Democratic candidate for president who didn't remind the citizenry that his was the party of Jefferson and Jackson or a Republican candidate who didn't evoke Lincoln, much as Lincoln himself evoked the Founders? Every one of these agents of change has known that success depends on the active support of the people, and for the people to become involved in change, they must see some familiar elements of continuity. Franklin Roosevelt could succeed in changing America because he put the radical reforms he sought in the context of traditions, systems, and beliefs with which the people were familiar; in contrast, American Communist leaders of the same era failed to make converts because they tried to *impose* a system that was foreign to the traditions and values of the citizenry.

If you are starting to get the idea that altering the culture of a corporation is slow, hard work, you're getting the picture. But when the leaders of a company understand that change must be based on the current culture of the company (Lee Iacocca's "new Chrysler" was still Chrysler at heart—he couldn't have turned it into a cultural clone of IBM no matter what), and when they have the patience to involve the entire organization in the process of change, it is possible to turn a company around—given the better part of a decade to do it.

In general, the successful processes of change initiated at the companies cited in this chapter had the following things in common:

- *Change had top-management support.* Because the process of changing the entire culture of a large organization is a slow one, the leaders of the corporation must make a commitment to the long, hard work involved—including the commitment to change their own behavior.

- *Change built on the unique strengths and values of the corporation.* Organizations don't start with a coherent philosophy or set of values. These evolve over time, pragmatically, and grow out of experience. New values can't be created by fiat.

- *The specifics of change were not imposed from the top.* Instead, all levels of the corporation participated broadly and openly in all stages of the process. Those at the top seldom "do" anything. Rather, leaders create the conditions in which followers may take productive action.

- *Change was holistic.* Because the parts of a culture are all complexly interrelated, changing one part requires changing them all to achieve consistency among objectives, strategies, rewards, structure, training, management style, and control systems.

- *Change was planned.* The long-term process was mapped out in advance, and there was a period of education in which every employee was informed about the what and the why of the effort. The process was broken down into small, doable tasks.

- *Changes were made in the guts of the organization.* Power relationships, information access, and reward systems all must be altered in meaningful ways.

- *Change was approached from a stakeholder viewpoint.* Because the goal of change must be to meet the needs of all corporate stakeholders as efficiently as possible, the primary source of impetus and direction for change usually comes from the external environment, often from customers.

- *Change became ongoing.* Because the environment doesn't stand still and the needs of stakeholders aren't static, the idea is to institutionalize a process of continuing change.

All of this—especially the final point—requires Rushmorean leadership. Indeed, most Rushmorean leaders encourage the challenging of sacred cows as the source of continuing renewal. Max De Pree once explained what that process entails: "The part of our strategy that is renewing is our continuing to question what it is that has changed—the asking of ourselves, figuratively, what day it is. And then asking, if this is the new condition and the new day, what is the need and what is appropriate?"

Max may have inherited the change "gene" from his father, D.J., but how can a company institutionalize what the De Prees did naturally? Verne Morland, an executive at NCR, suggests that the same effect can be had by hiring a corporate "fool." Like King Lear's Fool, the corporate equivalent would be licensed "to challenge by jest and conundrum all that is sacred and all that the savants have proved to be true and immutable." Though not necessarily dressed in motley, spangles, and bells, the fool would be obligated to "stir up controversy, respect no authority, and resist pressures to engage in detailed analyses." In keeping with William James's observation that "genius . . . means little more than the facility of perceiving in an unhabitual way," management consultant Nancy Reeves suggests that women may be natural to this role because "they have been outside the status quo ante, and are free to marshal historic exclusion for positive ends. . . . Women have not learned, [and] therefore do not have to unlearn, principles no longer pertinent. . . . Women might be the utterers of today's imperative blasphemies." If she is correct, that much misused word *diversity* has a practical application.

No matter how they do it, Rushmorean leaders create a climate in which assumptions can be continually tested and, if proved wanting, revised. And the opportunity to do this is not reserved to one leader (or even a privileged few). Because they recognize that wisdom seldom, if ever, resides exclusively in one powerful source, the corporate Rushmoreans create organizations open to taking long, honest looks at themselves, to identifying their strengths and weaknesses, their warts as well as their beauty marks. Ironically, the least Rushmorean of presidents, Calvin Coolidge, understood the risk of failing to do this and the reward inherent in success: "Progress depends very largely on the encouragement of variety. Whatever tends to standardize the community, to establish fixed and rigid modes of thought, tends to fossilize society. . . . It is the ferment of ideas, the clash of disagreeing judgments, the privilege of the individual to develop his own thoughts and shape his own character, that makes progress possible."

Caveat: All this heady talk about change and flexibility might easily be misinterpreted as supporting contingency, or situational, leadership. In fact, it is exactly the opposite. While the Corporate Rushmoreans are masters at quickly and appropriately changing their strategies, structures, policies, and programs to meet the exigencies of the competitive environment, they almost never change their fundamental values. An even stronger distinction is this: the Rushmoreans change their pragmatics, not their moral principles. Indeed, it is by always remaining true to moral principles, such as respect for people, that Rushmoreans create a climate of trust in which their followers are willing to risk strategic and tactical change.

We conclude this review of the Corporate Rushmoreans with an unsolved mystery: if the benefits of values-based leadership are so great, why don't more executives practice it? . . . We find that the answer to that question is simple, but overcoming the resistance to the practice of values-based leadership is complex and complicated. It turns out that the source of resistance to the Rushmorean approach is so deeply rooted in our collective psyches, experiences, and assumptions that we must dig to painful depths to reveal it. We all resist committing ourselves to the practice of such leadership, and most of us deny that we hold back our commitment. We now turn to the arduous and, for some people, threatening task of revealing why, at heart, so few of us are Rushmoreans.

NOTES

Much of what I report in this chapter I learned at the source. Unless otherwise indicated, all facts, data, and quotes are derived from corporate publications and unpublished corporate documents, from interviews with the leaders cited or with employees of their organizations.

p. 348, *After the settlement, he told Solomon:* S. D. Solomon, "The Bully of the Skies Cries Uncle," *New York Times Magazine,* September 5, 1993, p. 12.

pp. 348–350, For more on the amazing Frances Hesselbein, see Laura Sharper Walters's "A Leader Redefines Management," *The Christian Science Monitor,* September 22, 1992; Patricia O'Toole's "Thrifty, Kind—and Smart as Hell," *Lear's,* October 1990, p. 26; and R. Todd Erkel's "One Tough Cookie," *Pitt Magazine,* October 1990.

p. 350, *In a 1990* Business Week *cover story:* "Profiting from the Nonprofits," *Business Week,* March 26, 1990.

pp. 352–359, All Max De Pree quotes are from De Pree's *Leadership Is an Art* (Doubleday, 1989). Much of what is here appears in different form in my Foreword to that book.

pp. 354–357, I draw heavily on Warren Bennis's *On Becoming a Leader* (Addison-Wesley, 1989).

p. 356, *Ralph Waldo Emerson's "inner voice":* W. Bennis, 1989.

pp. 359–361, I draw here on interviews with Forrest Behm. Houghton speaks articulately for himself in his speech "Leadership's Challenge: The New Agenda for the '90s," reprinted in *Planning Review,* September/October 1992, p. 8, and in "World-Class Quality," *The TQM Magazine,* 1991, 3(1), p. 27.

p. 361, The description of Erwin Ceramics is taken from Robert Levering's and Milton Moskowitz's *The 100 Best Companies to Work for in America* (Doubleday, 1993), pp. 75–77.

p. 362, *in the words of Horace Mann:* H. Mann, "The Importance of Universal, Free, Public Education," In M. Mann (ed.), *Lectures and Annual Reports on Education*, Vol. 3, 1867.

pp. 362–364, I draw here on lengthy profiles of Galvin and Motorola in my book *Vanguard Management* (Doubleday, 1985).

p. 364, *"Our challenge is to continually evidence:* R. Galvin, *The Idea of Ideas,* Motorola University Press, 1991, p. 12.

p. 364, *His* Moments of Truth *offers a quintessential overview:* J. Carlzon, *Moments of Truth,* Harper & Row, 1987.

pp. 367–373, Information—including the De Pree, Morland, and Reeves quotes—is recycled from my book *Vanguard Management.*

Testing Skyhook 7

TRANSFORMATIONAL STYLE

If you are interested in keeping your job, ask yourself at the end of the day, every day, "What exactly and precisely and explicitly is being done in my work area differently from the way it was done when I came to work this morning?"

—TOM PETERS, *THRIVING ON CHAOS*

Transformational style is possible only if your attitude about change is right—that it's a way of life and not a major threat or even a minor inconvenience. But it's not all attitude and philosophy, it's action too. You have to have good, solid answers to the kind of questions Tom Peters asks, answers about a change in a work process, another person, or your own thinking. Without a good answer about what you've changed at the end of the day, Peters says, "Then you haven't been alive."

A simple self test will begin to help you see how well you are performing. Asking your coworkers "How am I doing?" will complete the picture.

ASK YOURSELF

Test out your transformational style by rating the accuracy of the following statements. Use a 1–5 scale ranging from "a little" to "a great extent."

• I encourage everyone to challenge every policy, practice and procedure and come up with better ideas.	1 2 3 4 5
• I welcome conflict and debate because it can produce creative ideas.	1 2 3 4 5
• I enjoy coaching individuals and helping them grow professionally.	1 2 3 4 5
• I am just as concerned about my own learning and growth as I am about my coworkers'.	1 2 3 4 5
• I judge my leadership in terms of continuous improvement in our area.	1 2 3 4 5

ASK YOUR COWORKERS

If you gave yourself a "4" or "5" rating on each statement, you probably have a strong transformational style. However, you can verify your self-assessment by having a two-part discussion with your coworkers. First, ask them to talk about the importance of transformation and change so that you understand it in the same way. Second, ask them for feedback on your performance.

You'll know you're developing a common understanding about the importance of transformation and change when you hear comments like these:

> - "Putting day-to-day changes in the context of our long-term vision helps makes sense of it all. We see that it all fits, that it isn't change for change's sake."
> - "Managing conflict is everyone's job. We have to make sure we attack the problem and not each other."
> - "Individual development plans put you in the right frame of mind about change. When you're changing personally, other changes seem more natural."
> - "When the boss is first in line to try out new tools or techniques, it shows that change is for everyone."
> - "Celebrating change shifts our mindset. When we stop and celebrate our big and small wins, change becomes something we can look forward to."

After discussing the importance of transformation and change, check out your coworkers' view of your performance by asking them to consider the five items in your self-assessment. You may find it more productive for them to answer the following questions than to give you numerical ratings on each item:

> - What am I doing right now that supports each statement?
> - What else can I do—either more or less—to show greater support for each statement?

As you listen, try to clarify your coworkers' answers and ideas. Express your appreciation for their feedback without becoming defensive. After you've listened, ask yourself, "What am I ready to do to strengthen my transformational style?" Develop an action plan to build on your strengths and continue to improve.

Appendix A—
Best Manager–Worst Manager

Early in the Alpha Process Workshop, participants complete the Best Manager–Worst Manager exercise. It has three primary purposes:

1. To surface common leadership values.
2. To establish valid measurement criteria.
3. To define leadership compared to management.

You may find it useful to answer the same questions participants are asked before turning the page.

- Think about 2–3 of the best managers you've known—what characteristics or practices distinguished them from other managers?

  –

  –

  –

- Think about 2–3 of the worst managers you've known—what characteristics or practices distinguished them from other managers?

  –

  –

  –

TEAMWORK ON PROFILES

After individually noting their answers, participants form teams and develop a common profile of their best and worst managers. They are instructed to base their profiles on real people doing real work, not on theoretical or abstract concepts.

The profiles the teams produce are remarkably similar no matter what their business, organization or even nationality. Apparently, our best managers and worst managers have universal characteristics. These are typical profiles produced by the teams.

Our Worst Managers	*Our Best Managers*
• Focus on the short term.	• Share a vision of what's possible.
• Manage by intimidation.	• Lead by example.
• Manipulate and deceive others.	• Demonstrate honesty and integrity.
• Micromanage every detail.	• Trust and empower others.
• Take credit for what others do.	• Recognize and appreciate good work.
• Play favorites.	• Teach and coach everyone.
• Dictate all the rules.	• Listen with respect.
• React defensively to different opinions.	• Keep an open mind.
• Avoid personal risks—CYA.	• Create a passion for work.
• Show a "my way or the highway" attitude.	• Inspire a "we can do!" attitude.

TEAMWORK ON BEST MANAGER MATRIX

Once the profiles are completed, each team is asked to focus on its Best Manager Profile and refer to the 16 items in the matrix. After reviewing each item, they are to select the 5–6 items that are most closely associated with their Best Manager Profile. All 16 items reflect worthwhile characteristics so it's not a matter of separating "good" items from "bad" items.

Again you may find it useful to select 5–6 items that reflect the best managers you have known before turning the page.

1. Knows his or her personal strengths and areas where improvement is needed.	2. Develops plans that cover all aspects of what needs to be done.	3. Organizes work into units with clear lines of authority and responsibility.	4. Provides detailed directions on the best ways to achieve goals and objectives.
5. Shows trust in and respect for people's character and capability to shape the future.	6. Manages his or her time effectively in light of priorities.	7. Selects skilled staff members and places them where they are needed.	8. Establishes control systems to reduce costs and maximize profits.
9. Empowers others to take initiative and do what is right.	10. Demonstrates that honesty and integrity are important corporate values.	11. Seeks personal growth opportunities both on and off the job.	12. Ensures that systems and people are operating at peak efficiency.
13. Brings out the best in people by making their work more than just a job.	14. Creates a climate for teamwork and cooperation between different functions.	15. Shows high concern for both people's needs and corporate goals.	16. Strikes a balance between his or her work and family.

CONCLUSIONS

As shown, the matrix is structured around attributes that are primarily related to management or leadership, or attributes that serve us well as individuals.

Good leaders rely on their ability to develop vision and trust, integrity, inspiration, empowerment, teamwork, and continuous improvement (5, 9, 10, 13, 14, 15). ➔

Management

Individual Effectiveness

Leadership

← Good managers rely on their ability to plan, organize, give direction, staff, and control and monitor performance (2, 3, 4, 7, 8, 12).

↖

Effective individuals know their capabilities, manage their time, like to learn, and value both work and family (1, 6, 11, 16).

Teams invariably list items 5, 9, 10, 13, 14, and 15 as those most closely associated with the best managers they have known. By the end of the exercise, participants arrive at two important conclusions:

- Leadership attributes are valued most highly, even though management competence is also needed.

- The leadership attributes in the matrix are valid criteria for measuring their own performance.

During the rest of the Alpha Process Workshop, participants receive feedback to assess their performance in each leadership area. They also receive information from thousands of other leaders on best practices so that they can build on their strengths and improve their soft spots.

Appendix B—Skyhooks and Performance

The six enabling principles surrounding vision in the Skyhooks Leadership Model are closely linked to individual and organizational performance. The trail of research is long and clear, reaching back almost five decades. When the principles are put into practice, individuals and organizations are better off.

During the twenty-year period from the mid-1950s through the mid-1970s, basic behavioral science theory and research held out a number of promises to managers. If they would follow six leadership principles, they could achieve extraordinary results from ordinary people. The principles relate to trust, communication, motivation, empowerment, teamwork, and leadership style. Among the most prominent early spokespersons for these principles were Chris Argyris, Robert Blake and Jane Mouton, Fred Herzberg, Joseph Luft, David McClelland, Douglas McGregor, and Robert Tannenbaum and Fred Massarik.

PROMISES MADE

Each of the six leadership principles can be phrased as a promise:

1. If you trust people to do their best, they won't disappoint you.[1]
2. If you communicate openly and honestly, you will promote healthy relationships and excel at problem solving.[2,3]
3. If you help others find more meaning in work than making money, they will do more than put in time.[4,5]
4. If you share power with others, they will use it to renew themselves and the organization.[6]
5. If you work as a team to get the job done, you will do better than anyone can do alone.[7]
6. If your leadership style shows that purpose and people are equally important, you can transform your organization and thrive in a changing environment.[8]

These principles are sound theories. They were developed from basic research, close observation, and rigorous reasoning. However, until a theory is verified through applied research—Does it really work?—it is as much hope as fact.

PROMISES KEPT

Beginning in the mid-1970s and continuing through the 1980s and 1990s, a growing body of evidence shows that the six leadership principles are not just theory but that they hold up well in practice. Successful managers and successful companies distinguish themselves from their counterparts by the way they follow the six principles. The evidence comes from a variety of researchers including Warren Bennis, James McGregor Burns, Stephen Covey, Jay Hall, Rosabeth Moss Kanter, James Kouzes and Barry Posner, Michael Maccoby, James O'Toole, William Ouchi, Richard Pascale and Anthony Athos, Tom Peters, Robert Waterman, and Ron Zemke.

Trust: If you trust people to do their best, they won't disappoint you.

Trust is absolutely essential to any productive and satisfying relationship on or off the job. A would-be leader has to ask, "How much trust and confidence do I really have in people?" It's a tough question with heavy consequences. A sign in an American auto plant lays it out: "Without trust, any human relationship will inevitably degenerate into conflict. With trust, anything is possible."

Jay Hall looked at trust and managerial achievement in classic Theory X (distrust) and Theory Y (trust) terms. He was able to divide the 16,000 managers in his study into Low, Average, and High Achieving managers depending on how far they had progressed in their careers and how long it took them. As shown in Figure 1, lack of trust was a clear predictor of managerial derailment.[9]

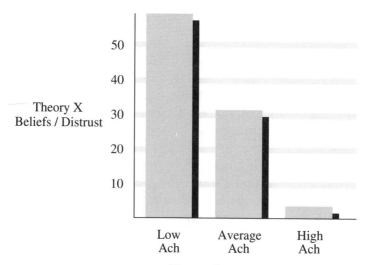

Figure 1.
Level of managerial achievement in relation to Theory X beliefs / distrust.

Trust continues to be a core issue in many recent well-known leadership studies. For example, Tom Peters and Robert Waterman looked at successful companies in *In Search of Excellence* and found that they stood firmly on a bedrock of Theory Y beliefs. They found, just as Douglas McGregor had proposed twenty years before, "one key to a people orientation: trust. . . . It all stemmed from the simple belief that people will respond well to being treated as grown-ups."[10]

Warren Bennis, one of the most prominent spokespersons for leadership excellence, addresses trust in *Leaders: The Strategies for Taking Charge*: "The ability to trust others even if the risks seem great is wiser in the long run than taking it for granted that most people are incompetent or insincere."[11] Bennis underscores the fact that once distrust taints a relationship, it is very difficult for others to forgive and forget.

Interpersonal Communication: If you communicate openly and honestly, you will promote healthy relationships and excel at problem solving.

Effective communication is more than exchanging information accurately. The way a manager communicates conveys to everyone his or her openness, honesty, and integrity. Does he or she share ideas, opinions, and concerns, ask others for improvement ideas, welcome feedback on his or her performance, openly express appreciation, and then encourage others to behave the same way? If so, relationships within the team will benefit as well as the team's ability to analyze problems and find innovative solutions.

The impact of interpersonal competence is shown in Figure 2.[12] Low-achieving managers do not communicate in other than bureaucratic ways, and they promote a depersonalized climate for everyone else. Average achievers are selective, being open on some issues but not on others or being honest with some people but not with others, either of which seriously jeopardizes their integrity. Only high-achieving managers demonstrate the kind of two-way communication that sets the standard for openness, honesty, and integrity.

Hall's research also revealed a mirroring effect between a manager's communication practices, and his or her subordinates'. Whatever the manager's practices, his or her subordinates adopted the same approach. For better or worse, the phrase "what goes around, comes around" applies to interpersonal competence.

When James Kouzes and Barry Posner studied more than 1,000 managers before they wrote *The Leadership Challenge*, they, too, saw the importance of the managers, acting as a role model for open and honest communication. Managers need to take the lead in the risky business of open communication: "Until the leader takes the risk of being open, it

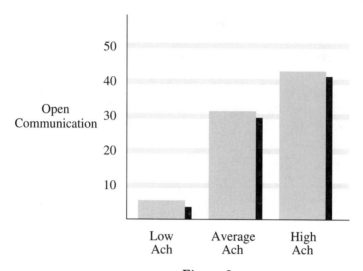

Figure 2.
Level of managerial achievement in relation to open communication.

is difficult to get others to take a similar risk — and thereby take the first steps necessary to build interpersonal trust."[13] When it comes to setting the communication standard for others to follow, "You got to walk the talk" has never been more true.

Motivation: If you help others find more meaning in work than in making money, they will do more than put in time.

In too many places, for too many managers, motivation is largely a compensation issue. People put in time, they are compensated for their loss with money and other tangible benefits, and that's that. The approach to motivation is extrinsic, external to the individual, and the rewards are economic for the most part. Most people would agree that there is nothing wrong with a plump salary and benefit package, but it alone does not move people to do their very best.

On a higher plane, motivation is intrinsic. It goes beyond economic and tangible rewards to the psychological and intangible. At that level the rewards flow from opportunities to enjoy a collegial relationship with coworkers, to savor recognition and appreciation, and to feel the excitement of personal growth and development.

Few managers move beyond the motivational basics and concentrate on creating opportunities for intrinsic rewards. As shown in Figure 3, those who do are significantly more successful, most likely because of their subordinates' performance—they put more into their work because they get so much more out of it.[14] When ordinary people produce extraordinary results, it shows up in their manager's performance review.

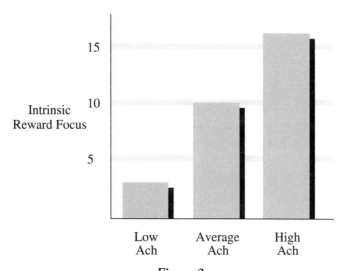

Figure 3.
Level of managerial achievement in relation to focus on intrinsic rewards.

The need to put meaning into work has been a dominant theme in many recent leadership works. The Japanese helped many people see that they were missing opportunities to move beyond the time-for-money trade-off and engage the whole person. A sample of key lines illustrates the effort:

Principle-Centered Leadership: "The first fundamental transformation of thinking required of American management is to develop new basic attitudes toward the intrinsic dignity and value of people, of their 'intrinsic motivation' to perform to their maximum capabilities."[15]

Theory Z: "Motivation in work will be maximized when each worker pursues individual goals and experiences psychological growth and independence."[16]

The Renewal Factor: "Man seeks meaning in organizations."[17]

The Art of Japanese Management: "Great companies make meaning."[18]

With all the emphasis in the literature on the need for more attention to intrinsic motivation and psychological rewards, it would be nice to think that managers in the real world are answering the call. The best of the 1,000-plus managers studied by Kouzes and Posner have responded positively: "We believe that intrinsic motivation must be present if people are to do their best."[19] However, that belief is not shared by all. Too many still ask the question: "Why, heaven forbid, would anyone find satisfaction in anything that did not pay a lot of money or provide a lot of prestige?" The question reminds us that we haven't put Henry Ford's "fair day's work, fair day's pay" dictum far enough behind us.

Empowerment: If you share power with others, they will use it to renew themselves and the organization.

At its best, the leadership function is a matter of power and influence, although it is not always easy for people to see it that way. As Harvard professor Rosabeth Moss Kanter once noted, "It is easier to talk about money—and much easier to talk about sex—than it is to talk about power." Power has been abused so often for personal gain that it is hard for many managers to pursue it with a clear conscience.

To lead, a manager needs to have power, but then he or she must be willing to share it. The value of having power is to empower others, to help them gain greater autonomy and authority over their work through education and training, delegation, information sharing, and networking. Successful managers are far more willing to share power to develop their organizations than are their counterparts who are preoccupied with career concerns or avoiding conflict. Figure 4 shows the differences.[20]

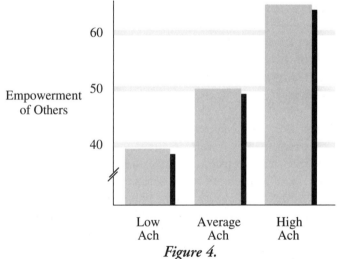

Figure 4.
Level of managerial achievement in relation to empowerment.

In *The Renewal Factor,* Robert Waterman notes companies that continue to evolve and prosper rely on empowerment: "They give up a measure of control in order to gain control over what counts: results."[21] That does not mean, however, that people are turned loose to do whatever they please. His term for empowerment is "directed autonomy." People are encouraged to do things their own way, but with a clear end in mind and well-defined boundaries to operate within.

When Ron Zemke studied the 101 best customer service companies, he found that an emphasis on empowerment was common to most of them. In his book *The Service Edge,* he stresses that employees at all levels need to act quickly to serve their customers and not be blocked or delayed by red tape or long chains of command. "Empowerment . . . It means encouraging and rewarding them for extra effort, imagination and initiative — and tolerating their missteps when well-intentioned efforts fail to work out exactly as planned. The goal is that best of all business worlds where empowered employees confidently and capably address unique problems and opportunities when and as they occur."[22] As quality and cost differences continue to diminish in the marketplace, customer service will become the prime means of differentiation, of convincing customers that you offer unique value. As that happens, empowerment will be more important than ever.

Teamwork: If you work as a team to get the job done, you will do better than anyone can do alone.

Teamwork has to be viewed in a broad context to be fully understood. It is not a stand-alone practice; it cannot exist without the support of the previously described principles. Teamwork becomes viable only when trust, open communication, intrinsic motivation, and empowerment principles are in place. When leaders believe that team members' contributions will be valuable, that collectively they will be more potent than the leader alone, that communication is free-flowing and unguarded, that people want to be part of a high-performing group— then teamwork can become an effective way to take on tough tasks.

Unless the first four principles are place, teamwork is likely to be a superficial exercise or even a manipulative way to push a particular agenda. For example, without trust, teams will be allowed to deal only with classic "no-brainers" like where to locate the water fountain or what to serve at the holiday party. Without real empowerment, team members may be coaxed to endorse a decision that management has already made but for which wants the PR value of a "team decision." Nobody is fooled for long. In no time, the word is out that teamwork is just another fad, soon to be replaced by the next bright idea from the business press.

Figure 5 shows quite clearly that the teamwork principle is put in place only by the most successful managers.[23] There is no second-place or half-way approach to teamwork—you do or you don't. The data shown in Figure 5 are from team members, not managers. They reflect the reality of teamwork as it is experienced by team members—strong feelings of responsibility, commitment, satisfaction.

Robert Waterman, in *The Renewal Factor,* also sees a gap between praising and practicing teamwork. The gap is most evident at the senior management level. Executives talk sincerely and at length about the need for teamwork at all levels. However, on a day-to-day basis they

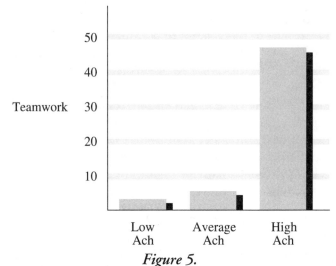

Figure 5.
Level of managerial achievement in relation to teamwork.

display a hard-nosed, authoritarian approach and rely on a few key in-dividuals to call the shots: "Less than 40 percent of the effort expended by the top-level corporate teams can accurately be described as 'team-work.' "[24] Since the top team has such a powerful influence down the line, the 40 percent figure in all likelihood decreases level by level. Waterman stresses that the trend needs to be reversed. Teamwork and trust must be the dominant characteristics at all levels for corporate renewal to take place.

Rosabeth Moss Kanter echoes Waterman's findings on teamwork and renewal. In *The Change Masters* she found: "One way or another, the innovating organization accomplishes a high proportion of its pro-ductive changes through participation."[25] She also found that team-work is easier to praise than practice, citing no less than two dozen pitfalls managers are likely to encounter when trying to utilize team-work. Nonetheless, in *Teaching Giants to Dance,* she found the compa-nies dealing most successfully with change had "flat, lean structures, multi-skilled employees, and team configurations."[26] Teamwork isn't easy, but it isn't optional, either. Teamwork is a key ingredient in the corpo-rate survival and success formula for the 21st century.

Leadership style: If your leadership style shows that purpose and people are equally important, you can transform your organization and thrive in a changing environment.

The concept of leadership style provides a way to explore an individual's personal aspirations and how he or she reconciles two es-sential components of the leadership function, purpose and people.

Four distinct styles emerge from shifts in the relative concern for the people and purpose components.

- An Authoritarian Style has High Purpose but Low People concerns.
- A Harmonizing Style has Low Purpose but High People concerns.
- A Bureaucratic Style has both Low Purpose and Low People concerns.
- An Integrative Style has both High Purpose and High People concerns.

In terms of the previously described principles, only the Integrative Style adheres to all five. The other styles are characterized by very limited trust, open communication, intrinsic motivation, empowerment, and teamwork.

The personal motivation underlying the selection of a style highlights what genuine leadership is all about. The first three styles are driven by very personal and self-serving interests:

- Personal success and self-interest drive the Authoritarian Style.
- Personal acceptance and conflict avoidance drive the Harmonizing Style.
- Personal survival and security drive the Bureaucratic Style.

The Integrative Style is decidedly altruistic and other-directed compared to the personal focus shared by the other three styles. It is driven by a need to make a difference, to build more effective systems, to develop more capable people, and to leave the organization a better place than when he or she came on the scene. In short, it strives for change.

Figure 6 not only shows the relationship between integrative practices and achievement; it shows there is poetic justice in the business world. For all the self-interest inherent in the Authoritarian, Harmonizing, and Bureaucratic styles, only the Integrative Style actually pays off.[27]

Leaders who use an Integrative Style fit what James McGregor Burns calls "transformational leadership" in his Pulitzer Prize–winning book *Leadership*. They are not satisfied with simply managing the current state of affairs; they want to transform it: "The ultimate test of practical leadership is the realization of intended, real change."[28] Constructive change is how they want to leave their mark. If kudos are gained in the process, they will be accepted and appreciated, but the real prize is in seeing their efforts lead to something that is better than before.

Transforming leaders do not achieve change by force of will or by

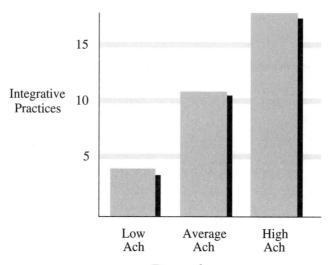

Figure 6.
Level of managerial achievement in relation to integrative practices.

some charismatic power over others. In *Leaders,* Warren Bennis found that leaders are quite nondescript: "Short and tall, articulate and inarticulate, dressed for success and dressed for failure, and there was virtually nothing in terms of personality or style that set them apart from their followers."[29]

Similarly, the diverse group of leaders Michael Maccoby studied for *The Leader* did not convey a General Patton or JFK-like aura: "They are not especially charismatic . . . all share a caring, respectful, and responsible attitude, flexibility about people and organizational structure; a participative approach to management, the willingness to share power."[30] James O'Toole agrees, in *Leading Change,* as he describes Corporate Rushmoreans, the leaders who are dedicated to "continuous change, renewal, innovation, and learning. And the bottom line in what they do is adherence to the moral principle of respect for people."[31] The style of leadership Maccoby and O'Toole describe is the kind, all things considered, that adhering to the six principles can provide.

LEADERSHIP, ADAPTIVE CULTURE, AND ORGANIZATIONAL PERFORMANCE

As noted, practicing each of the six leadership principles is rewarding for individuals. The more a leader practices each principle, the more he or she is recognized and rewarded by his or her organization. The rewards are well deserved because the organization has gained a valuable competitive advantage in the marketplace.

Figure 7 shows the one-to-one relationship between leadership as

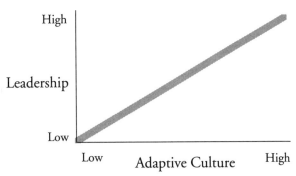

Figure 7.
Relationship of Leadership and Adaptive Culture.

defined by the six principles and an organization's adaptive culture as defined by its ability to deal proactively with internal and external changes.[32,33]

Figure 8 shows the same kind of one-to-one relationship between the strength of an organization's adaptive culture and its marketplace performance as defined by economic indicators such as net income growth, return on investment, and stock price increase.[34,35]

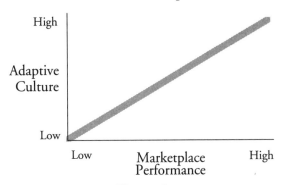

Figure 8.
Relationship between Adaptive Culture and Marketplace Performance.

The two figures suggest a kind of Darwinian truth for organizations in the next century. Only the fittest will survive and enjoy success. Being fit will depend on having the kind of leadership that enhances adaptivity.

CONCLUSION

The six leadership principles reaching back almost five decades are more than just good ideas. The evidence accumulated over the past two decades shows that the promises that were made have been kept. If the six principles are followed, individuals and organizations can flourish in the 21st century as their vision becomes their reality.

NOTES

1. Douglas McGregor, *The Human Side of Enterprise*. New York: McGraw-Hill Book Company, 1960.

2. Chris Argyris, *Interpersonal Competence and Organizational Effectiveness*. Homewood, Ill.: Richard D. Irwin, Inc., 1962.

3. Joe Luft, *Of Human Interaction*. Palo Alto, Calif.: National Press Books, 1969.

4. Abraham H. Maslow, *Motivation and Personality*. New York: Harper and Row, 1954.

5. Frederick Herzberg, *The Motivation to Work*. New York: John Wiley & Sons, 1959.

6. David C. McClelland, *Power: The Inner Experience*. New York: Irvington, 1975.

7. Robert Tannenbaum and Fred Massarik, "Participation by Subordinates in the Managerial Decision-Making Process." *Canadian Journal of Economics and Political Science*, 1950.

8. Robert R. Blake and Jane S. Mouton, *The Managerial Grid*. Houston: Gulf Publishing Company, 1964.

9. Jay Hall, "To Achieve or Not: The Manager's Choice." *California Management Review, XVIII*, 1976.

10. Thomas J. Peters and Robert H. Waterman, *In Search of Excellence*. New York: Harper and Row, 1982.

11. Warren Bennis, *Leaders: The Strategies for Taking Charge*. New York: Harper and Row, 1985.

12. Jay Hall: *op. cit.*, 1976.

13. James M. Kouzes and Barry Z. Posner, *The Leadership Challenge*. San Francisco: Jossey-Bass, 1987.

14. Jay Hall: *op. cit.*, 1976.

15. Stephen R. Covey, *Principle-Centered Leadership*. New York: Simon and Schuster, 1990.

16. William G. Ouchi, *Theory Z*. Reading, Mass.: Addison-Wesley, 1981.

17. Robert H. Waterman: *op. cit.*, 1987.

18. Richard Tanner Pascale and Anthony G. Athos, *The Art of Japanese Management*. New York: Simon and Schuster, 1981.

19. James M. Kouzes and Barry Z. Posner: *op. cit.*, 1987.

20. Jay Hall: *op. cit.*, 1976.

21. Robert H. Waterman, *The Renewal Factor*. New York: Bantam Books, 1987.

22. Ron Zemke, *The Service Edge*. New York: Plume, 1989.

23. Jay Hall: *op. cit.*, 1976.

24. Robert H. Waterman: *op. cit.*, 1987.

25. Rosabeth Moss Kanter, *The Change Masters*. New York: Simon and Schuster, 1983.

26. Rosabeth Moss Kanter, *Teaching Giants to Dance*. New York: Simon and Schuster, 1989.

27. Jay Hall: *op. cit.*, 1976.

28. James MacGregor Burns, *Leadership*. New York: Harper and Row, 1978.

29. Warren Bennis: *op. cit.*, 1985.

30. Michael Maccoby, *The Leader: A New Face for American Management*. New York: Simon and Schuster, 1981.

31. James O'Toole, *Leading Change: The Argument for Values-Based Leadership*. San Francisco: Jossey-Bass, 1996.

32. Jay Hall, *The Competence Connection*. The Woodlands, Tex.: Woodstead Press, 1988.

33. John P. Kotter and James L. Heskett, *Corporate Culture and Performance*. New York: Macmillan, 1992.

34. John P. Kotter and James L. Heskett: *op. cit.*, 1992.

35. Edgar H. Schein, *Organizational Culture and Leadership*. San Francisco: Jossey-Bass, 1992.

Appendix C — Alpha Process FAQs

Alpha Process is a leadership development workshop based on the Skyhooks Leadership Model. Managers receive a highly personalized learning experience and find out how well they are performing in each of the seven leadership areas. During the workshop, "frequently asked questions" deal with such issues as real-world importance, personal change, customer satisfaction, and situational differences. For the most part, our answers come from the ongoing research that we conduct as we help our clients develop leaders in their organizations.

Does leadership as you define it really matter to me, or is it really just another management development program?

If you care about how your performance is recognized and rewarded, the leadership issues we deal with in Alpha Process really do matter. Other studies have shown that each separate component has been linked to high performance and career success. Our research shows that the total leadership process, involving all seven components, distinguishes the best and the brightest from the rest of the crew.

In one recent study, we compared leadership scores of R&D managers in a multinational firm. Half the managers had received an "outstanding" rating on their corporate performance reviews, and half had received an "average" rating. The outstanding managers received scores from their coworkers on the seven Skyhooks components that were 35 percent higher than those of their "average" counterparts. There are obvious compensation and career implications here, but we don't want to present the leadership-reward connection as a purely self-serving relationship. Sure, the individual benefits, but only after he or she has demonstrated his or her leadership value to the organization.

Can individuals really change their leadership style, or are they pretty much locked in by personality and background?

The answer is "yes, you can change," but there are a number of caveats. First and foremost, personal change requires personal commitment. Becoming a more effective leader is certainly possible, but it isn't as simple or easy as learning a "how to" skill. It takes soul-searching and perhaps giving up some cherished notions about people and business. When the desire is there, along with a support system, individuals can achieve dramatic leadership improvements in a relatively short period of time.

One of our year-long projects demonstrated what is possible. We were asked to help develop leadership in one of today's toughest franchise systems—selling American luxury cars in import-loving California. At the beginning of the year, dealership managers were rated by their coworkers as absolutely average leaders—a kiss of death in that highly competitive environment. Eight months later, they had changed their leadership style so dramatically that their coworkers rated them in the upper quartile, alongside leaders in today's most innovative companies. Their transformation was based on two key factors. First, they were intensely committed to change because they truly believed that improved leadership would lead to more car sales and more satisfied customers. Second, a high-touch/low-tech support system helped them stay focused on their development plans. Their plans were always at risk of getting pushed aside in the rush of everyday business. The support system consisted only of quick phone calls and short on-site visits. The contacts focused on two questions: "What's working well?" and "What are you going to do next?" That may not seem like a very impressive support system in this era of satellite hook-ups and teleconferences, but it was very, very effective—low cost with high impact.

Should we try to improve our managers' leadership when the organization itself is changing, or should we wait until things settle down to launch a major effort?

While a reorganization makes a leadership development effort more complex because structures and relationships are churning, it may be the best time. Consistency in leadership values and principles across management levels adds a valuable dimension of stability in changing times. You may not know who your next boss will be, but you know pretty much how he or she will lead.

The parts and service division of a world-wide manufacturing firm had been "going global" for several years. In the first year leadership practices were benchmarked during the Alpha Process workshops. Overall, the division looked well prepared for change. Its management had scores in the upper quartile compared to others in their industry. After two years of revamping products and processes and disrupting life as they knew it, leadership practices were measured again—40 percent of the managers improved, 40 percent were able to maintain their strengths, while 20 percent lost ground. Even in quiet times the scores would be laudable. The generally shared view was that the leadership development effort running concurrently with the reorganization enhanced the change process by adding stability while in motion.

Do people in different work situations need different types of leadership?

The leadership values and principles in the Skyhooks Leadership Model apply across the board, whether your coworkers are in engineering, manufacturing, sales, or wherever or whether they are veterans on the line, new MBAs, or whomever. However, it is not exactly a one-size-fits-all approach. It varies when it comes to execution, how you actually carry out each step in the process. Principles are constant, but "best practices" vary from situation to situation.

After 500 managers in a division larger than most Fortune 500 companies attended the Alpha Process Workshop, we held focus groups with their coworkers, people who reported to them. We wanted to hear about leadership from the other side of the leader-follower relationship. The focus groups were mixed, with individuals from units like market research, quality assurance, and supply sitting next to others from engineering, administration, and field sales. We probed leadership issues like trust, empowerment, and meaningful work to find out where they fit in the everyday scheme of things.

For the most part, the responses were uniform in content and intensity. The respondents wanted leaders who looked to the future and would get to know them as individuals, inform them on important issues, and involve them as partners in planning and decision making. Only when it came to "how to" details did we hear differences. For example, "get to know me as a person" to some meant finding out what they did in their spare time and knowing their family situations, while to others it meant sitting down twice a year for lengthy career discussions.

Our number one priority is improving customer satisfaction, so why should we take time to improve our leadership?

Customer satisfaction is an inside-out proposition—you've got to get it right on the inside, with your employees, before you can get it right on the outside, with your customers. Many companies have found out the hard way that giving the front line a new set of service skills had little impact except to deplete the training budget. Only after leadership improved and employees began to feel like valued customers did they in turn improve their service to the people who paid the bills.

Earlier we mentioned working with managers in California car dealerships and the dramatic improvements they were able to make in less than nine months. At the same time, we tracked customer satisfaction ratings measured by the manufacturer. The gains in leadership within the dealerships were mirrored by gains in sales and service satisfaction from customers outside the dealership. In numerical terms, customer satisfaction scores moved up nearly a half-point on a very tight scale. In real-world terms, that meant that customer perceptions of the sales and service experience improved from "You're so-so" to "It's good to do business with you!" That is high praise in the notoriously demanding California car market.

If we're trying to improve our organization's leadership at all levels, should we bypass top management, since they're doing a pretty good job right now, and focus on middle managers and supervisors?

Top management must be full participants for organization-wide leadership development to be successful. While they may well be "pretty good leaders right now," others in the organization hold them to extremely high standards. Furthermore, they must promote a culture of continuous leadership improvement. As role models, they have to walk the talk: "Do as I do, not just as I say." Finally, they must actively support other managers' improvement efforts and hold them accountable for personal change.

The Alpha Process surveys measure current behavior as well as desired behavior. The difference between the two allows a manager to gauge the need for change. Desired scores for top management are usually higher than desired scores for those at other levels. In other words, desired scores for a typical manager indicate that coworkers want him or her to be as good as eight or nine out of ten other managers. When it comes to top management, coworkers' desired scores show they want them to be a "perfect ten," at least as good as the very best. Even as top managers improve, desired scores continue to increase—their coworkers raise the bar.

In our follow-up studies, we try to learn what helps and what hinders individual leadership improvement. We first focus on the 20 percent that improved the most and ask, "What went right?" We then turn to the 20 percent that got derailed and ask, "What went wrong?" Top management is often mentioned in both categories. "My boss was/was not involved" is often the differentiating factor. When top managers share their own action plans, ask for support and report progress, it is a powerful catalyst for other managers. The environment is much more conducive to change than when managers at the top tell the middle to make sure that lower-level supervisors shape up. Additionally, when leadership improvement plans are treated like other performance objectives, top-management's message is clear—"This is important!" Without accountability, a sorry variation on an old axiom prevails—"What doesn't get measured doesn't get done!"

How relevant are these leadership issues in different countries with different cultures?

The values and principles in the Skyhooks Leadership Model transcend territorial and cultural boundaries. Vision, trust, honesty, and the like have universal appeal, perhaps because they appeal to the human heart, not just the business head. While we must be respectful of differences between countries and cultures, leadership based on the Skyhooks Model has global relevance.

Through the Alpha Process surveys we have developed a data bank for managers from countries in Europe, North and South America, and across the Pacific Rim. Since the surveys measure "desired" as well as "current" behavior, we are able to gauge national and cultural norms. If desired ratings differed significantly from one place to another we would question the general relevance of a particular behavior. To date, however, desired ratings have been essentially the same in all locations. The only noteworthy variation is in face-to-face communication. In some European countries people prefer communication to be extremely direct, while in some Asian countries they prefer more subtlety. These slight statistical differences should not obscure the universal desire for interpersonal honesty.

Suggested Readings

Each of the twenty-one titles listed is recommended. However, they are not all recommended in the same way or to the same degree. The comments can help you decide which would be most interesting to you.

Bennis, Warren, and Nanus, Burt. *Leaders: The Strategies for Taking Charge.* **New York: Harper and Row, 1985. 244 pages.**

Although "taking charge" sounds quite authoritarian, that isn't what Bennis and Nanus have in mind. True, the "transformative" leadership they propose hinges on the effective use of power, but "leadership is not so much the exercise of power itself as the empowerment of others." Their findings are based on ninety interviews with leaders in the private and public sectors such as Ray Kroc, who launched McDonald's, and Vernon Jordan, former head of the Urban League. The authors found that these leaders used four common strategies: an attractive vision, communicating for commitment, trust through consistency, and continuous learning for themselves and their organizations. They offer numerous examples to illustrate how the strategies actually work.

Bennis, Warren. *On Becoming a Leader.* **Reading, Mass.: Addison-Wesley, 1989. 226 pages.**

In his first book, *Leaders*, Bennis cover the *whats* of leadership. In his second book, he turns to the *hows*. He focuses on how people become leaders, how they lead, and how organizations encourage or stifle potential leaders. Bennis has an academic background, but he is not an academician who prefers theory over practice. He studied thirty prominent leaders from a variety of fields except politics. They ranged from Herb Alpert and Betty Friedan to Sydney Pollack, John Scully, and Gloria Steinem. He asked questions like, "What role has failure played? How did you learn?" Bennis found that becoming a leader isn't easy, but leadership is easier to learn than most of us think. Learning to lead is an inside-out proposition. His study suggests that "know thyself" is the first indispensable step toward becoming a leader. For a leader's potential to be fully realized, he or she also has to understand the workings of contemporary organizations. "It's not just that the rules have changed—it's a different game."

Burns, James McGregor. *Leadership*. New York: Harper & Row, 1978. 531 pages.

This is the big book, the one considered to be the best general book on the nature and origins of leadership. It's a heavy, deep book, but it's not inaccessible—it won a Pulitzer Prize and a National Book Award. Burns coins the phrases "transactional" and "transformational" as he explores the nature of management and leadership. Management deals with a steady state, while leadership deals with change. A moral fervor pervades the work. True leadership not only facilitates change but emphasizes moral advancement. Tyrants may bring about change, but they fail the moral advancement test. Hitler, Mussolini, et al., therefore, are not up for consideration.

Covey, Stephen R. *Principle-Centered Leadership*. New York: Fireside, 1990. 332 pages.

Covey's first claim to fame was *The Seven Habits of Highly Effective People,* which charts a path to both spiritual and temporal improvement. This collection of thirty-one of Covey's essays takes a similar personal-professional development approach. He presents his leadership principles on four levels—personal, interpersonal, managerial, and organizational. Much of what he says is familiar, but his metaphors are certainly novel. For example, "Principle-centered leaders are men and women of character who work with competence 'on farms' with 'seeds and soil' on the basis of natural principles." Likewise, to "sharpen the saw" refers to continuous improvement, and "fishing the stream" relates to organization complexity.

De Pree, Max. *Leadership Is an Art*. New York: Dell Publishing, 1989. 148 pages.

De Pree is the chairman of Herman Miller, one of the best-run companies in the country. It has been that way since his father founded the company in the 1920s. Herman Miller is proof positive that a company can be a laboratory for human resource innovation and make a lot of money at the same time. It isn't easy to describe the content and organization of a book with this opening line—"You can start this book anywhere." In broad terms, it is about trust, grace, spirit, and intimacy, the human values that are the heart of extraordinary organizations and leadership. The book is not sentimental, it is perceptive and personal and a pleasure to read. Its only flaw is that it's too short.

Drucker Foundation. *The Leader of the Future: New Visions, Strategies and Practices for the Next Era.* **San Francisco: Jossey-Bass, 1996. 319 pages.**

This is a collection of essays by the current heavy hitters in leadership and organization development. Peter Drucker provides a short introduction, followed by essays by luminaries such as Charles Handy, Frances Hesselbein, and Marshall Goldsmith—thirty-one in all. The collection claims to present "the best ideas of an amazing array of the best authors, practitioners, consultants, academics, and philosophers." It lives up to that claim by delivering straightforward essays, which are usually less than ten pages. The Drucker Foundation also offers "Leader to Leader," a quarterly journal that presents similar high-quality "original articles from people you know are worth listening to."

Gardner, John W. *On Leadership.* **New York: The Free Press, 1990. 220 pages.**

The book is the product of a five-year field study and Gardner's unique opportunities to closely observe national leaders for more than forty years. He chaired commissions for Kennedy, Johnson, Carter, and Reagan, founded Common Cause, and served as U.S. Secretary of Health, Education, and Welfare. Not surprisingly, with those credentials he takes a broad view of leadership. His premise is that leaders can release energy lying dormant in the U.S. He analyzes the fundamental nature of leadership and related issues such as power, relationships with constituents, and leadership development. His chapters on the moral dimension and renewal are particularly important. Leadership is a moral endeavor demanding rock-solid ethics. Leaders need to renew themselves as well as their organizations because "the dry gavel of boredom does not kindle fires."

Kanter, Rosabeth Moss. *The Change Masters: Innovation for Productivity in the American Corporation.* New York: Simon and Schuster, 1983. 432 pages.

Kanter believes that everyone must become a change master "adept at the art of anticipating the need for, and leading, productive change." According to her analysis of our increasingly competitive marketplace, there will soon be only two types of companies—the quick and the dead, those that quickly adapt to change and those that are slow to seize opportunities. Using power and engaging people are key. Kanter doesn't offer a new box of silver bullets. As she says, "the problem before us is not to invent more tools, but to use the ones we have."

Kotter, John P. *A Force for Change: How Leadership Differs from Management.* New York: The Free Press, 1990. 180 pages.

Kotter makes it very clear that leadership and management are different. However, he does not subjugate management to some lesser role. Both leadership and management are important for an organization's success. The management function involves the legitimate exercise of control in areas such as planning, budgeting, and staffing to ensure a necessary level of consistency and order. The leadership function involves facilitating change by using vision, aligning people, and inspiring them. The problem has been, to use Warren Bennis's phrase, that we've been overmanaged and underled. Kotter's intent is to promote a better balance by demonstrating how leadership works and what it can achieve. He uses numerous examples of turnarounds within companies such as Arco, Digital, Kodak, and PepsiCo. The leadership-management distinctions can be very helpful as you find your role shifting in a rapidly changing environment.

Kotter, John P. *Leading Change.* Boston: Harvard Business School Press, 1996. 187 pages.

This is Kotter's most recent book on leadership, and it includes many of the concepts he presented in earlier works. For an academic, he is refreshingly free of jargon, abstract analyses, and arcane references. Instead, he is clear-headed, direct, and even inspiring. He begins by describing why change efforts fail, from allowing complacency to neglecting the culture. He goes on to provide an eight-stage process for leading change that counteracts each common fault. Establishing a sense of urgency, creating coalitions, and generating short-term wins are a few of the stages. While Kotter says that this book is the product only of his personal observations, he is overly modest. His observations are based on some of the most extensive and rigorous research on leadership in the past twenty-five years.

Kouzes, James M., and Posner, Barry Z. *The Leadership Challenge: How to Get Extraordinary Things Done in Organizations.* **San Francisco: Jossey-Bass, 1987. 362 pages.**

Kouzes and Posner did their homework before offering their ideas. The book is based on their analysis of more than 1,000 managers, using survey research and in-depth interviews. They found that good leadership varies little from industry to industry. It follows the VIP model—vision-involvement-persistence. In practical terms, they suggest ten actions ranging from searching for opportunities and taking risks to recognizing contributions and celebrating accomplishments. Their chapter on how to develop a personal vision is outstanding.

Kouzes, James M., and Posner, Barry Z. *Credibility: How Leaders Gain and Lose It, Why People Demand It.* **San Francisco: Jossey-Bass, 1993. 331 pages.**

A leader's credibility provides the glue that holds the leader-constituent relationship together. The glue is trust. Without it, things fall apart. Leaders who have credibility share six characteristics. They are self-confident, appreciative, affirmative, empowering, purposeful, and encouraging. Kouzes and Posner devote a chapter to each characteristic and provide paths for self-development. At the end of each chapter is a "First Steps/Next Steps" section to help the reader move from print to practice. Like their earlier work, *The Leadership Challenge*, they draw their ideas from research. In this case they analyzed 15,000 surveys and 400 case studies to understand credibility and its dynamics.

McGregor, Douglas. *The Human Side of Enterprise.* **New York: McGraw-Hill, 1960, 1985. 246 pages.**

If you had room for only one book on your leadership bookshelf and asked around for recommendations, this would get more votes than most. It is a seminal work in that every author writing on leadership since 1960 owes McGregor a debt in one way or another. His Theory X and Theory Y concepts raised the critical point that an individual's beliefs need to be addressed before he or she can consider new practices. You can't adopt new people-centered practices while clinging to traditional "people-dislike-work" Theory X assumptions. With Theory Y assumptions that people are basically bright, energetic, and trustworthy, there is a fit with practices like participative management, collaborative performance appraisal, and profit sharing. The success of the twenty-fifth anniversary edition is proof of the book's staying power.

Nanus, Burt. *Visionary Leadership: Creating a Compelling Sense of Direction for Your Organization*. San Francisco: Jossey-Bass, 1992. 237 pages.

Since the leadership process starts with vision, Nanus's book is a good place to start an in-depth development effort. His purpose is to "help you develop the right vision for your organization . . . to help you understand how to do it and guide you through the process." He has nine chapters in three major sections, What Vision Is and Why it Matters; Developing the Vision; and Implementing the Vision. Nanus would prefer you to think of it as a workbook rather than a text to read and shelve. By following the process he outlines, you should be able to develop a vision that is both practical and inspiring, that is rooted in the realities of your business while it raises exciting possibilities.

O'Toole, James. *Leading Change: The Argument for Values-Based Leadership*. San Francisco: Jossey-Bass, 1995. 282 pages.

O'Toole argues for leadership that is based on deep-seated convictions rather than on expediency. He takes the situational "it all depends" school of thought to task because he feels it's essentially amoral. Therefore, he doubts overnight converts like GE's Jack Welch, who suddenly switched in the mid-1980s from being one of America's most authoritarian CEOs to one who speaks eloquently about involvement and the need for employee voice—concepts he had opposed and even ridiculed. Is he real, or is it just lip service? The book is organized around three questions: What are the causes of resistance to change? How can leaders effectively and morally overcome that resistance? Why is contingency theory neither effective or moral? He illustrates his argument with numerous examples of current leaders, both those worthy of Rushmorean prominence and those who fall short.

Peters, Thomas J., and Waterman, Robert H., Jr. *In Search of Excellence.* **New York: Harper and Row, 1982. 360 pages.**

A good book with good timing makes for a great seller. At a time when everyone seemed to be idealizing Japan and criticizing the U.S., Peters and Waterman pointed out that the best-run American companies were worth emulating. Their research identified eight basic principles, including an action orientation, a focus on people, and loose controls with tight values. Don't be put off because some of their examples of the best-run companies have since faltered. Their eight principles make excellence possible, but they don't guarantee it. There are other forces loose in the marketplace that can bring you down.

Peters, Tom. *Thriving on Chaos: Handbook for A Management Revolution.* **New York: Alfred A. Knopf, 1987. 561 pages.**

"Revolution" is the key word to Peters's follow-up to *In Search of Excellence.* One of the most revolutionary aspects of the book is the speed at which he believes change must take place. Forget 50 percent quality improvements over five years—he talks about 90 percent in thirty-six months. To thrive on the chaos of change requires a new approach to customers, innovation, empowerment, leadership, and systems. He offers forty-five prescriptions for action within that framework. The books layout is quintessential Tom Peters—bold print, bullets, underlinings, and subtitles that shout, "Hey, you, pay attention!" Such theatrics can be annoying, but he really does have a lot to offer.

Rost, Joseph C. *Leadership for the Twenty-First Century.* **Westport, Conn: Praeger Publishers, 1991. 220 pages.**

Rost provides a complete review of leadership studies—past, present, and what he sees for the future. He covers leadership definitions from 1900 to 1979 and those that began to emerge in the 1980s. He goes on to describe the nature of leadership, how it compares with management and its strong ethical component. Along the way, he freely takes other authors to task over their fuzzy thinking or faulty logic. "Wholly unsatisfactory!" "Almost as bad!" "Equally bad!" are the kind of comments that pepper his observations on his colleagues. Imagine a curmudgeon in cap and gown, an intellectual Andy Rooney. He makes a scholarly work fun to read.

Senge, Peter M. *The Fifth Discipline: The Art and Practice of the Learning Organization.* New York: Doubleday, 1990. 424 pages.

Senge believes that developing learning organizations is the primary function of leadership. These organizations tap people at all levels and cultivate their capacity to learn. The faster you learn, i.e., change, the more competitive you can be. Systems thinking, the ability to see the whole, not just the parts, is the fifth discipline that unites four component disciplines—personal mastery, mental models, shared vision, and team learning. Senge provides numerous diagrams to illustrate the interrelatedness of actions in complex organizations. The leader's new work is to become a designer and steward of vision and a teacher who helps others work creatively within the bounds of reality. The book is not an easy read, probably because it pulls us out of our old ways of thinking.

Waterman, Robert H., Jr. *The Renewal Factor: How the Best Get and Keep the Competitive Edge.* New York: Bantam Books, 1987.

This is an extension of *In Search of Excellence*, but it is not a copy or rehash. Waterman continues to study successful companies and finds again that people are the main source of renewal. He goes on to celebrate a leadership style that combines direction and empowerment and can deal with the reality of politics. He provides examples from Ford, IBM, Steelcase, and others. At the end of each of the eight core chapters are "Steps for Getting There," ideas for taking action on the issue at hand. These are thought-starters rather than full-blown how-to recipes.

Wheatley, Margaret J. *Leadership and the New Science.* San Francisco: Berrett-Koehler, 1992. 166 pages.

This is not your average, or even above-average, book on leadership. You seldom find leadership issues framed by quantum physics, self-organizing systems, and chaos theory. Wheatley uses these elements of the new science for "learning about organization from an orderly universe." The new models of science can help you reconsider long-standing issues—order and change, structure and flexibility, planning and innovation. There has always been a strong relationship between business and science, but, Wheatley asserts, we need to move away from seventeenth-century science models to those more suited for the twenty-first century. All this may sound intimidating for the science challenged. However, the author makes the complex both simple and lucid in a style that has been described as "practical and poetic."

Index